JG PEOPLE IN (

D0076180

"I am extremely impressed with this book. It covers all the key areas in HRM in clear and appropriate language. It is a useful, relevant and practical book which should be a helpful guide to HRM post-graduate students, tutors and managers. It is very well researched, showing a breadth of literature and current research, including those of women at work, ageing populations, work–life balance and a refreshing update on stress."

– Angela Mansi, Senior Lecturer in Occupational
Psychology – HRM, Westminster Business School, UK

"*Managing People in Organizations* by Dr Jeremy Adams is a useful, though challenging, source book for management practitioners who wish to assess their work and experience in the light of contemporary research. Drawing primarily from psychology, the book offers frameworks for understanding many facets of management to serious students on postgraduate and final level under-graduate courses in business and occupational psychology. Particularly suited to programmes where depth of comprehension and explanation are valued concepts."

– Dr Nigel van Zwanenberg, Principal Teaching Fellow,
Durham Business School, Durham University, UK

"*Managing People in Organizations* is a wonderful global resource. Adams has done an excellent job of defining the state of today's global workplace and environment and has provided a practical, application-based resource that is perfect for classes in Human Resources and Organisational Behaviour. This text can also serve as a great reference for practitioners in human resources, strategic planning and consulting."

– Dr Christopher Leeds, Director, Graduate Business Programs,
Dominican University of California, USA

"Jeremy Adams' approach of scouring the latest academic and popular literature for pearls of wisdom has produced a fascinating review of the state of the art."

– Sebastian Bailey, Product Director, The Mind Gym

"What a pleasure to read such a well-researched AND easily accessible AND practical textbook! Dr Adams has gleaned all the gems from recent research and presented them to you as a sumptuous feast. To make material 'BrainFriendly' he has included mind-diagrams as a summary of the key points of each chapter. Further he has provided another mind-diagram at the start of each chapter to lead you to the links with other chapters. Add to that a great section of current best practice, so you can actually discover who has applied the tenets and had success and some very practical bullet points as to what to do under each topic. Well done!"

– Vanda North, Founder & CEO of The Learning Consortium

"In this book, Adams captures the dramatic changes in the world of work. This is a must-read for leaders who are serious about preparing their organizations for success in the coming decades."

– William Arruda, President, Reach Communications
(www.reachcc.com)

Managing People in Organizations

Contemporary Theory and Practice

Dr Jeremy Adams

First published 2007 by
PALGRAVE MACMILLAN
Houndmills, Basingstoke, Hampshire RG21 6XS and
175 Fifth Avenue, New York, N.Y. 10010
Companies and representatives throughout the world

PALGRAVE MACMILLAN is the global academic imprint of the Palgrave
Macmillan division of St. Martin's Press, LLC and of Palgrave Macmillan Ltd.
Macmillan® is a registered trademark in the United States, United Kingdom
and other countries. Palgrave is a registered trademark in the European
Union and other countries.

ISBN-13: 978–1–4039–9796–8
ISBN-10: 1–4039–9796–9

This book is printed on paper suitable for recycling and made from fully
managed and sustained forest sources.

A catalogue record for this book is available from the British Library.

A catalog record for this book is available from the Library of Congress.

10   9   8   7   6   5   4   3   2   1
16   15   14   13   12   11   10   09   08   07

Printed and bound in China

For Heather, thank you for your love and support

Contents

Preface

Scope and aims

This textbook has a dual purpose: first, it represents a comprehensive review of the economic, psychological, and popular literature concerned with improving organizational performance, through the amelioration of human resource management, staff satisfaction, workplace stress reduction, managerial enhancement, and company-wide learning. Second, it offers an inclusive and, to date, unique overview of the modern workplace practices that are being used by highly rated *Fortune* 500 companies and other progressive workplaces worldwide, with the goal of educating readers to help organizations to:

- enhance organizational performance and profitability
- increase employee satisfaction and accomplishment
- inspire loyalty and commitment
- generate a sense of meaning and purpose in the workplace.

Unlike many other texts, this book is not written for the complete novice, rather the author's aim is to provide an already educated reader with a state-of-the-art understanding of the written material in the fields of human management and managerial practice, published worldwide since the mid-1990s. By knowing what has been written, it is possible to understand what, how and why things are being done. Armed with this knowledge, it is hoped that readers will help themselves to determine where they should go next.

Readership

Because of the broad scope of this book, calling on research articles and opinion pieces sourced worldwide and from a large variety of academic, professional, and popular periodicals, it will be of interest to a wide range of readers. Nevertheless, the book was written with the following readers in mind:

- Graduate level students, especially in MBA, or other Masters level programs that address human resources, management, economics, or industrial/organizational (I/O) psychology.
- Given the very large range of sources (over 600) covered by this text, it will be of especial interest to students undertaking a written or research-based thesis.

- High-level undergraduate students studying management, international communications, economics, or I/O psychology.
- Practitioners, including managers, consultants, and senior executives, who wish to understand more about the changing face of business and how they can influence their organizations to make positive workplace changes for organizational success.

Introduction

A cursory glance at the popular and scientific literature concerning economics and business practice will show that workplace systems are changing. In the business arena, phrases such as "best practice", "intellectual capital", "intangible assets", "knowledge sharing", and "workplace satisfaction" have become commonplace. Nevertheless, behind the "buzz factor" of these catch-cries, many respected academic and professional authors and practitioners are reporting that traditional work practices are no longer effective or even appropriate in the 21st century.

In the opinion of the celebrated psychologist Mihaly Csikszentmihalyi (2003), modern living has changed not only the nature of work, but also its meaning. In modern times, work has become an activity performed largely to be able to take "time off" from work in order to "play". However, in earlier human history there was little distinction between the work that was done to survive and the rest of a person's life; all activities were considered a part of everyday living with no real distinctions between work and play. More recently, however, artificial temporal rhythms, modern technology, and consumer economies have resulted in a strong distinction between a person's work and his or her "life". Nevertheless, as Csikszentmihalyi has pointed out, humans are, in effect, built to work; we are at our most effective, psychologically and physiologically, when stimulated by productive activity. The quandary lies in the disparity between our needs and desires; despite figures that show that over 80 per cent of employees would continue to work, even if they had no financial need to do so, most people dislike the work that they do, and cannot wait to leave their workplace at the end of each day. This paradox has reduced the ability of organizations to continue to produce and innovate: when workers are dissatisfied, they are unlikely to be motivated. Unfortunately, modern managerial practices have, for the most part, not addressed this problem. Whilst the goal of management is to "create value through the labour of people working together for a common cause" (Csikszentmihalyi, p. 85), most managers are concerned with getting the most, rather than the best, out of employees. This distinction goes some way towards explaining the current epidemic of workplace dissatisfaction.

Why this book is written

The changing nature of work in the 21st century has highlighted the need for organizations to modify their human resources practices in order to remain innovative and profitable. Whilst this need is immediate, a lack of pertinent information on effective change can hamper this change process and, consequently, the ability of organizations to remain competitive. Likewise, the need for organizational change also emphasizes the need for effective education, so that tomorrow's leaders are informed and ready. Nevertheless, although there have been a number of popular books written to help existing practitioners understand the necessity of humanism in the workplace, there are no scholarly works of this type designed to educate and inform high-level students of human resources, management, or economics. Moreover, whilst there is a wide range of high-quality texts that provide information about Human Resources Management (HRM) theories and practices, few of these texts focus on contemporary research and strategies. In fact, to date, there have been no texts that represent a comprehensive review of contemporary (that is, over the last 10 years) humanistic literature applied to the management of people in modern organizations. Consequently, this book was written to help organizational leaders, managers, employers, employees, researchers and students understand how they can effect important, humanistic changes to the workplace: it includes a comprehensive review of over 600 contemporary papers from the psychological and economic literature pertaining to employee satisfaction, and organizational productivity and profitability, as well as recommendations for effective humanistic organizational change. Whilst other sources such as papers from managerial and HRM publications were also referenced, the decision to focus predominantly on psychological and economic sources was made in order to highlight contemporary thinking and practice in these often opposed fields. In other words, whilst psychological research typically focusses on how humans interact with each other and with their environment, economic papers remain focussed on theories pertaining to financial systems and organizational strategy. This book contrasts these opinions, in order to show that the human element is a very important aspect of organizational strategy, which is often overlooked by economists. In fact, the humanistic flavour of the majority of these papers will be evident immediately: as will be shown, in order to enhance organizational efficiency, practice, and performance, the human element is, in fact, the most important.

A reader's guide

Despite what you might have learnt at school, there are many ways to read a textbook. Although the information in this book is presented in a conceptual order, it is not really necessary for you to read it in a conventional way; it depends on what information you need, and whether you want that information to be predominately theoretical, practical, or specifically geared towards organizational productivity.

The book is laid out in 6 sections with a total of 16 chapters. The sections are themed, so that the chapters within each section are related. Likewise, the sections (and chapters) progress in a related manner that provides increasingly focussed information. For instance, the first section looks at recent changes to workplace practices, and leads into ideas on enhancing organizational practice (Section 2), which in turn progresses to the enhancement of individual performance at work (Section 3), and so on. Because the text is divided into distinct informational themes, you will be able to find the information that you need, rather than having to read material unrelated to your interests; but as the sections lead into one another, you will find that there is often a lot more to a given area than you might have thought.

Consequently, because this book covers a lot of information, it has been written with a flexible reading approach in mind, so that you can find the information you need rapidly (even if you are new to human resources or management) using several complimentary methods. Apart from the usual index and table of contents, the section-by-section summary at the beginning of the book offers a synopsis of each section's contents, as well as a list of the most important things you should know after reading that chapter. You will also find a summary, a "Mind-Diagram" summary, case studies, best practice recommendations, and review questions in each chapter to help you acquire, digest, and consolidate the information from that section.

Moreover, at the beginning of each chapter, you will find a simple iconic "rating", designed to help you determine just how relevant that section is to you, based on what you need to know. The icon representing a book indicates that the information in that chapter is predominantly theoretical, so by reading chapters marked with the book icon you will get a good understanding of the background of a given topic. The icon representing balance scales indicates that the chapter combines a relatively even mix of theoretical and practical studies; by reading chapters marked with this icon you will learn about both the background to a topic and practical advice on making change. The final icon, showing a person interacting with machine cogs, indicates that this chapter is focussed predominantly on practical recommendations regarding the topic. By reading chapters marked with this icon, you will learn practical skills for approaching that particular topic.

Also at the beginning of each chapter there is a "mind-diagram" of the keywords for that chapter that represents how each keyword relates to other chapters and sections. Use these mind-diagrams to get a grasp of how each chapter is related to other parts of the book, and to get ideas for researching a particular area. For example, when reading Section 1, Chapter 1, you might want to know what other parts of the book deal with downsizing. By referring to the keyword relationships mind-diagram, you can see that "downsizing" is related to the chapter on transformational leadership – in Section 5, Chapter 13. Think of these mind-diagrams as a form of visual index, to help you navigate relationships within the text.

Finally, at the end of each chapter you will also find a mind-diagram summary. Each of these "maps" is a visual summary of the contents of that chapter, allowing you to get a comprehensive overview of the contents of that chapter before, during, or after your reading. These maps make an ideal revision tool: by studying the mind-diagram before and after your reading, you are substantially more likely to remember what you have read, and see the connections between different topics. When reading a mind-diagram, remember that they start with main headings (at the centre) and branch out on each subheading to include more and more detail. Each subheading uses pictures to help you remember the content more effectively. For some excellent information on mind-diagrams, and how to use them to enhance your learning and work, I recommend that you read *Use Your Head* by Tony Buzan (1989).

Remember, this book exists to help you understand how modern human resource management can allow organizations to thrive in the changing marketplace of the 21st century. Consequently, make sure that you get the most from your reading experience (and your valuable time), by getting to the information that you need, how and when you need it.

The five most important things to learn by reading this book

This book contains a lot of information. If you want, you can drill down to find very specific recommendations on a wide variety of topics. However, whilst reading, keep in mind the following five most important themes. By reading with these themes in mind you will remain aware of the overall purpose of the book, and better integrate the various parts into the overall message.

1. Economic rationalistic practices, such as downsizing, in the 1980s and 1990s were only successful in the short term: recent evidence has shown that in the longer term, companies and employees suffered. By removing a large proportion of their intellectual assets and firing the people who did and knew how to do the actual work, companies stripped themselves of their ability to be competitive and innovative, and destroyed any sense of organizational community, trust, and well-being. The consequence to employees has been work intensification, increased pressure and stress, and more illnesses, which, in turn, has resulted in ongoing, increasing costs for employers.

2. It is not necessary for workplaces to be stressful, humourless, and overly demanding. In fact, when employees are able to satisfactorily balance their work and home lives, reduce stress, exercise regularly, have fun at work, and take regular breaks, they will be more productive, more loyal, less likely to quit, and physically and psychologically healthier; they will perform better and miss fewer work days. Moreover, when employees feel supported at work by their employer, their supervisors, and their colleagues, they will also be happier and more productive.

3. Managers do not need to be excessively domineering in the workplace. In fact, when employees are encouraged to work autonomously, and are given greater control over their tasks, resources, time, interactions, and goals, they will perform substantially better, resulting in greater organizational performance. Consequently, managers need to learn how to encourage employee development by acting in a supportive, coaching or mentoring role, rather than as an overseer or administrator.

4. The recognition that employees are valuable intellectual assets allows firms to realize that an organization's real value is inherent in its intangible assets. Because they are difficult to quantify, intangible assets are confusing for senior executives who base their business decisions on accounting-based

recommendations. Nevertheless, the modern knowledge-based economy, in which people and their abilities, skills, and knowledge are the most important factors, has outgrown traditional accounting methods. Management must now see their highly skilled employees as innovators rather than machinery.

5. Modern firms require leaders who are able to look towards, envision, and plan for a sustainable future. Transformational leadership, in which a leader subsumes his or her personal needs for those of the organization and, in order to achieve the organization's goals, encourages employees to do likewise, represents an ethical solution to the problems of many modern corporations. Rather than being concerned only with shareholders and short-term profit, long-term organizational success comes when leaders are concerned with the well-being of all of the organization's stakeholders, making sure that conditions are put in place, and factors accounted for (such as changing socio-economic conditions and environmental pressures) that will allow the firm to continue successfully into the future.

At a glance: A Section-by-Section guide

Changing workplace practices have resulted in widespread employee dissatisfaction, increased work stress, consequent rise in stress-related illnesses, psychological withdrawal, and burnout and, financially, substantial increases in the costs associated with ill health. Consequently, in many organizations, workers are unmotivated and disenfranchised through a lack of meaning and personal investment in their work. Because of the causal relationship between employee satisfaction, well-being and meaning in the workplace, and corporate performance, those organizations that wish to remain viable in the 21st century need to pay close attention to the variables that motivate their employees. By modifying the workplace to address workers' abilities to personally control their time, resources, work hours, goal setting and management, and work-role flexibility, organizations can substantially increase their productivity. Likewise, by taking pains to make the workplace healthier and reducing environmental stress; by increasing the availability of useful, relevant training; by allowing workers to develop existing skills and to learn new ones; by providing alternative advancement pathways; by addressing managerial deficiencies and encouraging adaptive leadership; by encouraging organizational and individual learning; and by making the workplace more fun, organizations can become places that stimulate meaning and provide purpose for their employees, and can realize long-term financial success through consistently enhanced performance.

Section 1: The changing face of work practice and the new costs and challenges for employers

Economically driven changes to corporate practice over the last 20 years have substantially changed the face of modern business. Corporate streamlining and downsizing has resulted in an increasingly temporary workforce, and a corresponding increase in workplace stress, employee dissatisfaction, and worker turnover. In fact, typically, in the modern workplace, employees remain with a given firm for less than three years at a time. Simultaneously, there has been a substantial rise in organizational costs associated with the psychological and physiological illnesses consequent to workplace stress. Often, these expenses, coupled with the costs associated with reduced organizational commitment and its consequence – lowered performance – are considerably higher than the financial savings that resulted from the original organizational changes.

Moreover, societal changes have modified the workplace demographic: in the last 20 years, there have been substantial increases in the number of women, minority, and elderly workers. Unfortunately, traditional managerial practice has failed these new workplace entrants, because of the use of systems designed for a workforce dominated by long-term, male, white, middle-class, middle-aged workers. Nevertheless, several organizational practices recognize these shortcomings, and changes that incorporate an increasing recognition of the individual needs of employees, such as health, fitness, stress reduction, and increased personal control, are being implemented.

What you should look for:

- understanding of how workplaces have changed
- a better comprehension of potentially negative economic practices, such as downsizing
- knowing why traditional managerial practices are increasingly inappropriate in the modern workplace
- what some companies are doing to adapt to a changing workforce with changing needs.

Section 2: Enhancing corporate performance

Recent corporate changes have resulted in a loss of individual performance, because of conditions that have reduced employee satisfaction and increased workplace stress. Nevertheless, a few organizations have realized that individual performance is linked causally to organizational performance; that is, in corporations that are comprised of motivated, creative, and interested workers, communication, productivity, and innovation increase, along with financial performance.

In the 21st century, increases in corporate performance require attention to HRM practices, a commitment to a consistent view of the future inherent in a strong mission, viable strategic principles, and corporate vision. Likewise, by maintaining a workforce that is committed to these goals, comprised of employees who are recognized for their intellectual assets (that is, knowledge, abilities, and skills), these organizations remain consistently more innovative and, consequently, more economically viable. Moreover, the recognition of the financial worth of an organization's intangible assets, such as the intellectual resources, organizational knowledge, and irreplaceable skills inherent to a given workforce, is vital to its future success. In many corporations the ratio of intangible to tangible assets has grown to the point where it is solely the value (inherent in the intellectual resources) of employees that defines an organization's economic worth. Consequently, those organizations that value the importance of their employees and communicate this worth are rewarded through greater financial performance.

What you should look for:

- understanding of the link between the performance of an employee and the organization for which he or she works
- better comprehension of why creativity and innovation are important to a company
- knowing why a strong mission, strategic principles and effective vision are necessary corporate tools
- understanding of intangible assets and why they are an increasingly dominant market force in a knowledge economy.

Section 3: Developing individual and team performance in the workplace

Because corporate performance is strongly linked to individual workplace performance, a competent organization is comprised of highly functioning individuals. One way to enhance the way in which an individual operates is to increase his or her perception of control over the immediate environment; by allowing an employee to have more say in the way in which he or she spends his or her time at work, as well as his or her implementation and management of goals, incentive types, and temporal rhythms, a person will view himself or herself as more valuable and more effective to the organization. These employees will, in turn, be less stressed, more motivated to perform and, consequently, more productive. As well, when workers better understand the causes of their stress, and the best ways to manage it, they are less likely to suffer from stress-related illnesses, or a loss of motivation. Training programs that effectively increase stress coping in the workplace are, therefore, of substantial value to an organization. Another way to increase individual workplace functioning is through the effective application of rewards. When rewards (either formal or informal) are given contingent to high performance or creativity, the resultant increase in perceived control can increase intrinsic motivation. That is, they can help a person to become motivated to work for its own sake: when work represents a process of freedom and fulfilment it is rewarding in its own right. Moreover, rewards that are customized to a given person's needs, personality, and preferences are more likely to motivate.

What you should look for:

- comprehension of the organization as the sum of many individuals, each with unique needs
- understanding of perceived control, why it is necessary in the workplace, and the organizational benefits that come from a high level of individual perceived control

- Awareness of how to increase the perception of control in the workplace
- Knowledge of motivation in the workplace and of the most effective rewards for increasing intrinsic motivation.

Section 4: Increasing workplace satisfaction and productivity

Burnout is a common consequence of workplace stress. Because modern workplaces are often stressful, it is often only a matter of time before a person experiences psychological withdrawal from his or her work role. Organizations that understand that the psychological withdrawal of their employees is undesirable, both because of the direct and indirect financial costs of employee turnover and as a result of the loss of morale and the consequent likelihood of the spread of withdrawal within the organization, can take pains to prevent it. The two most effective mechanisms for reducing psychological withdrawal in the workplace involve the employee's perception of organizational support, and whether he or she discerns a sense of meaning in his or her job role. Organizational support involves the belief, by an employee, that the establishment has his or her best interests at heart, manifest in timely, appropriate feedback from supervisors, clear communication of goals, an understanding, combined with underlying flexibility, of the job role, and a strong sense of meaningful relations at work. Moreover, when these conditions are met, so that an employee feels that he or she is able to make a difference to the organization as a whole and is encouraged and able to align his or her beliefs, interests, and ambitions with the organization's goals, the resulting sense of meaning can substantially increase enjoyment at work and, consequently, loyalty, productivity, and performance.

What you should look for:

- Understanding of the causes and effects of workplace stress and burnout
- Knowledge of the negative organizational consequences of workplace stress and burnout
- Comprehension of the most effective methods for reducing the likelihood of workplace stress and burnout
- Awareness of the benefits of organizational support to an individual and an organization, and the most effective method for a firm to demonstrate support for its employees.

Section 5: Improving managerial and leadership practices, and motivating employees

Too often, modern managerial practice is overly concerned with administration at the expense of leadership. Management represents, simply, the ability to motivate others to work together to produce value, even when the work is potentially aversive. Nevertheless, managers seldom pay attention to the motivation or stimulation of employees, unless this motivation is extrinsic (for example, financial reward, potential advancement, or threats).

When managers take pains to develop their leadership skills, their abilities to motivate others to perform also increase. Moreover, as leadership involves an interest in the well-being and performance of subordinates, the employees of effective leaders are often more motivated to work productively. Thus, on the one hand, leaders are concerned with getting the best from their charges, a process that requires attention to workers' needs, desires, and ambitions; whilst on the other hand, administrators are more interested in getting the most out of employees, and are less likely to inspire loyalty or performance.

One particular leadership style, adaptive or transformational leadership, is particularly effective for motivating others and for increasing their performance. Adaptive leaders are able to readily assess the organizational culture and are sensitive to the varying requirements necessary for dealing with different situations, people and problems. Further, transformational leaders respond flexibly to challenge, being able to modify a given approach to better deal with each new trial. Consequently, they are able to both motivate performance in employees and command loyalty from their followers.

An important aspect of organizational leadership is the ethical actions of both the leader and the organization. Ethics, the application of morals, can be interpreted in many ways. Nevertheless, whilst transformational leaders place the needs of the organization and its members above their own personal wants and desires, pseudo-transformational and transactional leaders often use an organization's resources for their personal or financial betterment, frequently at the expense of their employees, the community, and the environment. Despite the various ethical philosophies, many authors agree that virtuous actions, in which the organization and its leader work to enhance the lives of both the organization's direct members and those with which it interacts, represent the pinnacle of ethical achievement.

Workplace motivation represents the key to organizational performance. Employees who are motivated to work do so, and produce work that is more consistent, more creative, and of a higher quality than their unmotivated colleagues. Enhanced employee motivation means workers must feel a sense of control and freedom over their work role, their time constraints, work content, and learning and skills development. Moreover, a workplace environment that is stimulating, but not stressful, and that embodies ergonomic principles (for example, the effective use of lighting, colour and temperature to increase cognitive functioning and physical health) is more likely to be both motivating and enjoyable.

When employees feel that their job role is stimulating, challenging, and worthwhile, they are often intrinsically motivated to perform. In these cases, the work is its own reward; workers feel a sense of meaning and purpose inherent in their daily activities, and enjoy what they do. This is particularly evident in employees who also have meaningful relationships in the workplace, especially with a supportive supervisor who understands the value of a mentoring role. At work, the presence of someone who is both supportive and understanding, and who can act as a coach when learning new or challenging skills, is both comforting and empowering.

What you should look for:

- Comprehension of the difference between administration and leadership
- Understanding of the importance of leadership for organizational effectiveness
- Awareness of the motivational abilities and other qualities of effective leaders
- Knowledge of different leadership styles, including transformational leadership, and the benefits of a transformational leadership style for organizational performance
- Understanding of the various ethical perspectives, and how they align to transformational leadership practices ·
- Awareness of the importance of individual motivation on employee productivity and creativity
- Increased understanding of the most effective methods and workplace environmental changes for enhancing employee motivation
- Understanding of why a sense of meaning and purpose in the workplace increase a person's desire to work effectively
- Comprehension of the benefits of social support in the workplace.

Section 6: Enhancing organizational communication, knowledge, and learning

In many organizations, communication is often inefficient, confusing, and even contradictory. Moreover, many individuals within these firms, including managers, possess poor communication styles. To improve communication company-wide, two conditions are necessary. First, management need to become effective communicators, capable of providing information that is clear, concise and consistent. Second, managers need to be able to model effective communication skills, including the ability to deliver information in a timely manner, and be able to listen to and act on the concerns of their subordinates.

Learning involves the willing uptake of information; nevertheless, too often, training is mistaken for learning. The assumption that if employees are presented with a particular type of training, they will learn from it is only valid if the training is geared towards the needs of the individual, so that he or she is motivated to learn. Consequently, workplace training should be conducted with the needs of the employee in mind, and include elements that are useful for improving his or her general lot and that address real, everyday issues. Moreover, conditions that enhance the transfer of learning from applied training, such as organizational and supervisory support, are vital if training is to be effective. Despite the emphasis placed on formal training, because a large amount of workplace learning occurs informally, it is also important that managers respect and encourage informal interactions between employees, recognizing that the most effective transfer of knowledge occurs through these informal interactions. Mentoring, in which a person with expertise in a given field is partnered with a less experienced staff member, represents an excellent form of informal training. When these relationships are encouraged, it is possible for people to learn experientially, directly and in-situ, from someone who understands his or her field to a high degree. Moreover, because the mentor can readily recognize and rectify mistakes, the learning process can be accelerated.

What you should look for:

- understanding of why communication practices in many organizations are inefficient or confusing
- knowledge of the most effective methods for enhancing communication in an organization
- increased comprehension of the "learning organization", and the company-wide value inherent in informed employees
- awareness of the shortfalls of workplace training, and the best ways to make training effective, so that employees are able both to learn and to implement their knowledge to the benefit of their organization
- understanding of the value of informal learning for transmitting tacit knowledge between employees and enhancing organizational human capital.

The Changing Face of Work Practice and the New Costs and Challenges for Employers

Introduction

Since the early 1980s, the ways in which companies and their employees relate have changed substantially. To begin with, the economically driven workplace modifications prevalent in the 1980s and 1990s have resulted in increased work hours, shorter holidays, and an increasing amount of outsourcing. These changes have done little to enhance employee well-being, and have resulted in high levels of workplace stress, illness, and employee dissatisfaction, and the consequent rise in health-related costs to employers. At the same time, changing sociological, economic, and political demographics have resulted in a different workforce, providing a new set of challenges to organizations. In the light of these changes, many employers are attempting to change the way in which they relate to their employees.

This section summarizes some of the recent trends in corporate attitudes, offers a review of several opinions regarding the genesis of these changes, and provides examples of best practice and tips for practical application.

Section guide

In Chapter 1, "The Changing Economy, Work Practices, and Culture", you will learn about economic rationalism practices in the 1980s and 1990s and why they were largely unsuccessful; the changing demographics of the workplace, including the increasing representation at work of women, older workers, and minorities; and regarding the recent organizational trends of temporary employment and outsourcing, and how they can negatively impact the workforce. Chapter 2, "Work Intensification, Increasing Healthcare, and Other Costs", explains why managerial attitudes and "quick fix" attempts to increase productivity have resulted in work intensification; why work intensification has led to an increase in work hours and why working longer hours does not equal an increase in productivity; how increased work intensity has led to an elevation of stress in the workplace, why stress is related to illness, and how stress in the workplace is costing businesses; and why workplace conditions that encourage physical inactivity are costly to the organization over the long term. In Chapter 3, "The Worker-Friendly Organization", you will read about flawed managerial assumptions regarding employee productivity; work–life balance, and why it is important both for organizations and individuals; and telecommuting, a popular programme that is often touted as a solution to work-life imbalance. Lastly, we will examine "The Current Role of Human Resources Management", looking at flaws in current human resources departments and where human resources managers should be directing their focus.

Reading objectives

By the end of this section you should have a clearer understanding of:

- economic rationalism and its applications, such as downsizing, layoffs, and outsourcing
- why downsizing attempts have been largely unsuccessful
- how the economy has changed in recent times to become information based
- how the workforce has changed over the last 25 years to encompass greater numbers of women, older workers, and minorities, and the problems faced by these employee subsets
- the trends towards temporary employment and outsourcing, and the potentially negative consequences for individual and organizations of these actions
- why work has become more intense, and why people are working longer despite a decline in productivity
- the consequences of workplace stress, and other modern workplace outcomes, for individuals and firms
- why certain managerial assumptions regarding productivity are no longer valid
- the problem of work–life imbalance, why this imbalance is counterproductive for employees and organizations, and how firms can use programmes like telecommuting to enhance the work–life balance
- the problems with organizational human resources management, and what human resources departments should be doing.

The Changing Economy, Work Practices, and Culture

KEYWORDS   Average, economy, downsize, excess, market, trend.

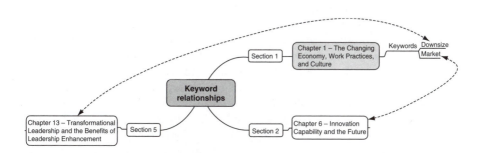

IMPORTANT CONCEPTS   Economic rationalism, workplace changes.

Part 1: Economic rationalism

The 1980s and early 1990s will no doubt be remembered for the economic rationalization that dominated many firms' business strategies. The purpose of economic rationalism was to maximize shareholder return over the short to medium term, by increasing organizational efficiency and reducing costs, in an economy driven primarily by manufacturing and product-based industry (Lazonick, 2003). One strategy employed in the name of economic rationalism, and employed as an almost "panacea" by companies facing poor growth, financial difficulties, or as the result of shareholder pressure for greater returns, was downsizing[1] (Collins & Harris, 1999), a process that involves the reduction of an organization's workforce in order to reduce operational costs. Despite the popularity of downsizing in the 1980s and 1990s, a large body of academic and practitioner research has shown that in the majority of cases downsizing is ineffective (Wagar, 1998). According to Wagar, many downsizing efforts have failed to meet organizational objectives because they are not carefully thought out or adequately linked to the strategic plans of the organization. This failure, in the opinion of Guastello and Johnson (1999), is almost entirely human-centred; for the most part senior managers overseeing downsizing efforts often fail to account for human resources issues during and after the process, or utilize poor strategies for retaining human capital (such as training investments, and technical and leadership expertise). More importantly if management, through archaic command and control or compartmentalized managerial style, is responsible for the organizational malaise that leads to a decision to downsize, it is unlikely that the downsizing process will repair this deficiency. Nevertheless, the temptation by senior managers to attempt to repair their mistakes through cost-cutting is strong: even in cases where downsizing has been shown to be unsuccessful, many organizations will repeat the process (Guastello & Johnson). According to Guastello and his coauthor, though in the longer term following downsizing a firm is likely to suffer, this failure is due primarily to short-term, favourable reactions by the stock market to announcements of labour-force reductions, resulting in performance bonuses for senior management, whose pay scales are often linked to the company's short-term economic performance. Nevertheless, researchers have found that short-term stock market gains do not last: among the majority of companies that downsized in the United States in the 1990s, stock prices in the two years following downsizing lagged comparable firms by between 5 and 45 per cent, and in more than half of cases, the prices were behind the general market by 17–48 per cent (Dolan, Belout, & Balkin, 2000). Moreover, in the United Kingdom, 51.8 per cent of companies that engaged in labour-force reductions between 1982 and 1993 showed a substantial reduction in productivity growth in the five years following downsizing efforts (Collins & Harris).

Other researchers have also shown that downsizing is seldom an effective solution to poor financial performance. Apart from the likelihood that lack of

---

[1] A more in-depth discussion of the impact of downsizing, both on employees and on employers, can be found in Section 4.

company ability is, in fact, often the result of mismanagement, a flaw that is unlikely to be repaired by downsizing, the human consequences of labour-force reduction can lead to a distinct lack of organizational productivity. According to Dolan *et al.* (2000), when a workforce is reduced, the productivity of the "survivors" is lessened for two distinct reasons. First, because labour-force reductions are often carried out without adequate liaison with human resources departments, those targeted for redundancy are not always the people that an organization wants to lose: employees with the most marketable skills will often leave the organization engaging in downsizing, in an attempt to secure a more stable position, or be "head hunted" by rival firms, creating an intellectual-capital gap. Second, remaining workers are saddled with an increased workload, having to do the work of departed employees often without adequate managerial support (especially if managers are preoccupied with the downsizing process), resulting in increased worker stress and burnout, and a consequent drop in productivity. Dolan *et al.* have also reported that the elevated stress levels of remaining workers following downsizing can lead to a "survivor syndrome", resulting in elevated feelings of fear, anxiety, depression, guilt, sadness, anger, poor conduct, career ambiguity, and a preoccupation with the future. As is discussed in greater depth in Section 4, when workers are unhappy, perform-ance suffers substantially, along with a reduction in employer loyalty, organiz-ational commitment, organizational citizenship, and employer–employee trust (Guastello & Johnson, 1999; Wagar, 1998).

Given the demonstrated lack of a relationship between downsizing and productivity, and the negative human costs to firms that attempt to downsize, with hindsight it seems strange that senior management would consider it as a viable business strategy. Nevertheless, as we have seen, downsizing justi-fication was widespread, and was most likely the result of a combination of flawed organizational management and prevailing economic thought, fuelled by a production-centred economy. These reasons notwithstanding, the huge impact of technology since the early 1990s on society and the economy has further reduced the justification for economic rationalism, by changing the way in which work is performed (Lazonick, 2003). According to Lazonick, the Internet revolution of the 1990s saw the emergence of the new "tech" or "knowledge" economy, after which some 60 per cent of all the work performed became information based (with a corresponding decline of over 50 per cent in manufacturing industries, such as oil refining and mining, in management and secretarial positions, and in farming, which in the last 100 years has changed from occupying 36 per cent of the population to less than 5 per cent (Porter & Bostrom, 1996)). Lazonick believes that this shift towards inform-ation or knowledge work has resulted in an increased focus on the develop-ment of innovative, everyday products. Thus, whilst earlier economic models motivated management to reduce their workforce in an attempt to increase productivity and reduce costs (in return for stock market gains), the "tech" economy requires that organizations attract highly skilled and educated workers in order to compete in a market dominated by the continued deployment of new, innovative products.

Changes in the type of work performed in recent times have certainly influenced the way in which organizations react to market pressures. However, Manders and Brenner (1999) have argued that whilst the methods have changed, the fundamental reasoning of profit maximization remains the same. They suggest that the tech revolution has allowed the emergence of "globalization", in which previously regionalized companies have expanded into world market forces representing industry monopolies and oligopolies. According to Manders and Brenner, this shift has been made possible largely through the appearance of "universal users", a new "breed" of global consumers, whose demand for new technological products crosses political and sociological borders, requiring that companies focus on a worldwide market. Consequently, to address the massive rise in research and development (R & D) costs required to fuel a global thirst for innovation, many organizations have attempted to reduce their spending on costly business requirements (for example, manufacturing, warehousing, and so on) by contracted to a "core" company, surrounded by a series of satellite companies or collaborative partners (who take on the "costly" roles previously handled by the core or parent company). This has resulted in new production means, such as co-makership (in which a central company performs the R&D, the design, and sales, whilst subsidiaries, or collaborative partners, manufacture the product), "just in time" production (in which a company maintains a flexible workforce in order to produce their products only when required), and an increasing reliance on subcontracting and outsourcing. Therefore, in the opinion of Manders and his colleague, this contraction is simply a modern effort at achieving the cost-cutting and productivity gains attempted by firms that downsized in the 1990s: according to Belout, Dolan, and Saba (2001), outsourcing has become, in effect, the new form of downsizing.

IN ACTION #1

Tangible and intangible assets in modern business

In many organizations worldwide, throughout the 1980s and 1990s, we saw a growth in "economically driven practice". Effectively, this meant that industry and workplace decisions were made, increasingly, by executives who took their cues directly from accountants. This strategy was represented by an increasing trend towards downsizing, layoffs (both voluntary and involuntary), cost-cutting, "streamlining", outsourcing, and the use of casual or temporary employment contracts.

Many accountants would argue that these initiatives are a necessary part of the modern organization: that the modern economic community requires a vigorous and impartial hand to keep organizations lean and competitive. However, recent research suggests that this way of thinking is flawed, because it ignores the most important indicators of organizational performance: intangible assets. In fact, whilst other professionals are paying increasing attention to the importance of intangible assets for proper financial functioning in organizations, accountants are failing to either recognize or address their impact.

The changing economy and the growth of the intangible asset

Traditional accounting practices are most applicable to manufacturing, in which let's say, a certain number of widgets are manufactured over a given time period. In these cases, the variables associated with the cost of widget manufacture are relatively simple, and can be calculated, for instance, by tallying the costs of raw goods, labour, manufacture, and shipping, against market price. In circumstances such as these, in order for a company to realize a profit, reduce waste and maximize efficiency, accountants are invaluable.

However, in a modern economy, whilst manufacturing is still big industry, information transfer and trading has dominated marketplaces at an increasing rate. Whilst manufactured goods are eminently tangible (that is, they can be measured, counted, and readily valued), information (an ephemeral catchall that includes ideas, patents, intellectual capital, innovation, knowledge, code, concepts, and so on) is distinctly intangible; that is, information cannot be readily quantified, especially with regard to its value. Nevertheless, intangible assets are highly valuable, often making up the majority of a company's market worth. An excellent example is that of Microsoft, one of the most successful and wealthiest organizations in the world, which has an estimated tangible to intangible asset ratio of 3:23. Unlike traditional manufacturing-based companies, Microsoft does not produce objects, but rather, it develops ideas and creates a product (that is, software) that has no physical dimensions and whose value is only determinable by its usefulness or innovativeness. Were Microsoft to sell its "hard" assets (for example, buildings, computers, infrastructure), it would realize only a small proportion of its estimated worth. The intangible assets represented by the ideas and knowledge of its employees, the code resident in its machines, and the patents on this code, make up the bulk of Microsoft's fortune.

Nevertheless, in attempting to value intangible assets, accountants are met with some major challenges. Most obviously, intangible assets are difficult to quantify, and whilst it is possible to operationalize (that is, make concrete) qualitative concepts, this process is relatively awkward. For example, in psychology, there have been attempts to operationalize pain. Pain is ephemeral in its nature; it can't be readily measured, weighed, or counted. However, by tying an actual observable event to the appearance of pain, attempts can be made to measure it in a quantitative way; for instance, by gauging how much pain killer a person requires, or rating how loudly they shout when a painful area is touched. As can be gathered, these techniques are far from perfect, and only serve to measure several of the many tangible phenomena that could be associated with an intangible one. In fact, given the number of variables associated with pain, it would be very hard to develop a definitive measure. Given the troubles faced by psychologists, who regularly deal with and have substantial experience in the operalization of intangibles, it is only natural that accountants, who are trained to deal with measurable, concrete phenomena, find it extremely difficult to assess intangibles.

The problem

Despite the increasing dependency on intangible assets in modern business, industry is faced with two distinct problems. First, accounting practices have not kept pace with marketplace changes (such as the emergence of intangible assets as market drivers) and, for the most part, modern accountants' approaches to book keeping are much the same as they were hundred years ago (except for a concession to modern tools). Second, in most large companies, the CEO's brief is to increase share value. Unfortunately, most shareholders have two regrettable conceits: they tend to require that company-value gains be short term, and they like to consider themselves the most important (or sometimes only) organizational stakeholders. Consequently, when a CEO fails to realize immediate or short-term share value gains, he or she is often disciplined or removed outright. The conundrum here is that share values are themselves highly intangible, but a company's value is most often measured based on its economic performance over a given timeframe. Whilst these calculations are most often performed by economists, they base their results on data supplied by accountants.

Part 2: The changing workplace

Whilst technology has helped to change the way in which organizations do business, computers, information technology, and the knowledge economy have not been the only reasons for changes in the workplace (Lavoie, Roy, & Therrien, 2003). According to Sue, Parman, and Santiago (1998), in their review of changing work practices in the United States, changes to the way in which we work have been accompanied by a coincident change in who is working; with the most important changes reflected in a substantial increase over the last 15–20 years in the number of women, older workers (no longer leaving the workforce at usual "retirement age"), and minorities in the workforce. McGrattan and Rogerson (2004) have suggested that the increasing participation of women in the workforce has been one of the most influential workplace demographic changes in recent times. They have reported that whilst the employment-to-population ratio for men has fallen by 12 per cent over the last fifty years, women's employment during this time has risen by 87.1 per cent, especially in women aged between 25 and 34 and in women with children: in fact, since 1950 the proportion of working mothers has increased by close to 450 per cent, with a corresponding increase in the number of households in which both partners work.

Women in the workplace

Relatively recent social changes have meant that women have gained increasing access to education and training previously only available to men, with the pool of qualified workers growing in proportion to the number of qualified women (Preston & Burgess, 2003). Consequently, in line with the increasing need for skilled workers required by an information-driven economy, the rise in female employment has favoured women who are highly educated or skilled (Fitzenberger & Wunderlich, 2004). According to Fitzenberger and his colleague, in industrialized countries such as the United Kingdom and Germany there has been a strong increase, over time, in the demand for highly-skilled women, with a corresponding decrease in low-skilled employment for both men and women. This trend is contrary to patterns of the mid-20th century, during which women were employed, for the most part, on a part-time basis in low-skilled jobs (Sakellariou, 2004), a change that, Sakellariou suggests, can be attributed largely to corporations' need for human capital, measured by education, training, and experience rather than by gender.

Nevertheless, the increasing numbers of women in the workplace have not necessarily resulted in workplace equality for women. Preston and Burgess (2003) have reported that in industrialized countries, although women are now overrepresented in terms of their qualifications and educational achievements, they still earn, on average, only 77.7 per cent of an equivalently employed male's salary. This gap, in the opinion of Preston and her coauthor, is the consequence of a lack of change in the structure of work, even though the makeup of the workforce, and the types of work performed have changed. Consequently, Preston and Burgess believe that many organizations still operate as though household income were derived by the stereotyped "single, male breadwinner" (even though this model represents less than 5 per cent of modern households (Barnett, 1999)), and that women are incapable of managing the demands of work and family coincidentally. This oversight, they suggest, has resulted in the continued overrepresentation of women in part-time work, and in careers such as nursing, clerical work, and teaching, and, due to the assumption that men must work full time and the consequent lack of flexible or part-time positions, has made it difficult for men to take on a home-based role. Kilbourne and Weeks (1997) have taken a more extreme position, suggesting that the lack of workplace gender equality is a result of biased social conditioning. They imply that despite recent changes in societal roles, and the increasing involvement of women in the workforce, the underlying patriarchal nature of many modern practices, such as economics, science, and the legal system, has created conditions in which women remain disadvantaged. This disparity has resulted in a division that extends beyond pay inequality, affecting job design, career choice, and encouraging the stereotype that women are, by nature, more competent in caring roles than in technological work functions.

The aging population

Although the increasing employment of women workers has certainly resulted in substantial changes to the workforce, Purcell (2000) believes that the changing age demographic among workers is of more reaching impact. The highly skilled, well-educated "baby boomer" generation is rapidly approaching retirement age which, according to Purcell, will have two dramatic consequences. First, the resultant loss of human capital will require that organizations, dependent on highly skilled labour, source new, equivalently qualified workers. However, alongside the aging baby boomer population there has not been a corresponding increase in the number of younger workers entering the workforce: from 1995 to 2005 whilst the actual number of persons aged between 25 and 45 has increased by 10 per cent, the number participating in the workforce has increased by only 1.2 per cent. Moreover, as the retirement age has been steadily declining in recent years, many baby boomers expect to retire before the age of 60 (Spiezia, 2002). At the same time, the downsizing efforts of many organizations in the 1980s and 1990s, which were often aimed at older workers through the encouragement of early retirement (Wagar, 1998), have led to a prevailing managerial attitude towards older workers (especially those aged over 60 years) as less valuable than younger workers, and a corresponding "ageist" stereotype of the older worker as slower, "behind the times", and less able (Rickard, 1999). Whilst this lack of foresight was unfortunate, many organizations, unable to replace the human capital of their retiring workers, are now being compelled to find ways to retain their existing workforce, by encouraging valuable older employees to work beyond retirement age through phased retirement plans (in which retirement is delayed through a transition to part-time or part-year employment) and the rehiring, on a part-time basis, of retired employees (Purcell). Nevertheless, as Spiezia (2002) has pointed out, many firms are still reluctant to invest in the hiring, training, or retraining of older workers, because of prevailing stereotypes about their productivity and efficiency, or because managers are concerned that the perceived threats inherent in hiring older workers, of imminent retirement, illness or death are a financial risk. This oversight will, in the opinion of Spiezia, result in a large deficit in organizational intellectual capital and produce substantial economic problems for firms who are unable to find alternative human resources.

The second problem of an aging population outlined by Purcell (2000), is that whilst workers are retiring earlier, they are also living longer. From an economic perspective, a larger populace of persons who are no longer able or willing to earn an income places an increasing burden on the remaining population, who are required to support retirees through increased taxation or other payments (Johnson, 2004). In 2000, the dependency ratio (that is, the ratio of working persons under the age of 65 to those who do not work and are aged over 65) in OECD countries was 0.4 (approximately three workers for each retiree), however, by 2040 this figure will increase to 0.74 (Spiezia, 2002), an almost one to one proportion of active workers to retirees, who will at that stage represent over 25 per cent of the total population. According to Purcell, many state-based social security or pension systems will be unable to cope with the financial burdens placed by such a large number of older people, especially in the light of increasing negative birth rates in developed countries, and given that people in the 21st century will live, on average, over 25 years longer than their 20th-century predecessors. To reduce the economic problems of increasing elderly dependency, Johnson has suggested that governments need to respond by liberalizing immigration laws to encourage the influx of qualified, younger workers, and by encouraging organizations to develop more creative methods for retaining older workers. Simultaneously, to ensure an adequate pool of experienced employees, organizations will need to overcome age biases, recognize the human capital inherent in their older workers, and change their recruiting drives to include the over 50s who have typically been regarded as a poor longer-term investment (Purcell).

Minorities

Another demographic shift in worker profiles over the last 25 years has been the increasing representation in the workforce of minority groups (Sue *et al.*, 1998). Nevertheless, black and other minority workers receive, on average, significantly lower pay than their white counterparts, and are overrepresented in low-skill occupations (Agesa & Monaco, 2004): although, in the United States, black workers make up 9.4 per cent of the working population, they represent 12.8 per cent of low-skilled workers but only 5.3 per cent of high-skilled employees (Agesa & Monaco). Moreover, minority employees are more likely than white workers to receive poorer work performance evaluations (Elvira & Town, 2001) and face a greater likelihood of being made redundant during downsizing practices (Elvira & Zatzick, 2002). This disparity, in the opinion of Agesa and Monaco, is driven by ongoing workplace biases, and is partly responsible for the increasing socio-economic gap in western countries between skilled and unskilled workers.

Part 3: Temporary employment and outsourcing

Despite evidence regarding the poor long-term success and survival rates of firms that downsize, and given both the recent changes to the way in which the economy is driven and the dramatic demographic changes of the work-force at large, it is surprising that many firms continue to behave as if the economic rationalism of the 1980s were still a viable business strategy. One unpleasant consequence of this hangover in economic thought has been a reduction, among management professionals and company boards, in the recognition of the value of human resources, an oversight that has resulted in another recent workplace trend: flexible-employment contracting (Storey, Quintas, Taylor, & Fowle, 2002), sometimes referred to as "precarious" (Benavides, Benach, Diez-Roux, & Roman, 2000), "non-standard", "contingent" (Allan, Brosnan, Horwitz, & Walsh, 2001) or "temporary" (Nollen, 1996) employment. Allan *et al.*, in their study of labour practices in 15,600 work places in Australia, New Zealand, and South Africa have reported that whilst employment before 1990 was typically represented by a nine-to-five, 40-hour per week, 52-week per year (with two to three weeks annual leave) job, changing worker demographics post 1990 (including the increased number of women workers, and the reduced prevalence of families with a single, male "breadwinner") and modifications to the economic structure of business (for example, globalization, "just-in-time production") have led to a steady increase in the use of flex-ible employment, including casual and part-time work; with many employers resorting to flexible employment practices in order to reduce or avoid the costs (for example, mandated benefits, health insurance, holiday pay, maternity leave, and so on) inherent in full-time, permanent employees.

In a study similar to that of Allan *et al.* (2001), Lee (1996) has pointed out that, between 1982 and 1992, flexible employment in the United States rose by 254 per cent, a figure he attributes to the increasing contraction of larger companies to a "core" business with escalating consequent specialization, outsourcing, and subcontracting in order to create a "production at will" environment, and these organizations' desire to reduce the increasing costs associated with the introduction of social-justice–based government policies. According to Lee, this represents a "bad reaction to bad policy". That is, whilst flexible employment strategies might reduce organizational costs over the short term, they result in negative long-term financial consequences; neither the employer nor the employees benefit long term from temporary employment because temporary workers are less likely than their permanent counterparts to take initiative, be motivated, or express loyalty to the organization; the resultant loss in productivity can have a substantial negative effect on company profitability. Likewise, Storey *et al.* (2002) have reported that because flexible employment involves short-term hiring practices, a predetermined contract termination and competitive renewal, there is little opportunity among temporary employees for advancement or job-role change, a trend which Storey and his colleagues believe has all but removed the notion of job security. In the opinion of Storey *et al.*, because of the temporary conditions inherent in flexible employment, employees seldom feel content or secure and are, therefore, unlikely to be innovative or creative in the workplace, or especially loyal to their employers. Simultaneously, many employers have neglected to recognize the negative effects of the working conditions of their temporary employees (cf., the psychological contract – see Section 2), typically by assuming that, because the employee is not permanent or full-time, he or she is of less value to the organization. According to Storey *et al.*, management has failed to realize that it is an employee's sense of commitment to what he or she does, and a consequent desire to be productive, that provides his or her value.

The lower workplace productivity of temporary employees resulting from feelings of insecurity and a lack of contentedness at work might also be the result of more tangible differences between permanent and flexible employees. Nollen (1996) has reported that because temporary workers are, on average, paid less than regular core employees, receive little or no training or other human capital development, and do not receive the benefits (such as paid leave, sick leave, or health insurance) available to their permanent colleagues, they are unlikely to be motivated to perform to the standard expected by their managers. In fact, Nollen refers to flexible employment as a form of under-employment, in which poor support, both social and supervisory, few advancement possibilities, little challenge, an unstable position, and very little perceived control over the work environment result in work conditions that seem almost designed to demotivate and demoralize employees. The low job satisfaction experienced by temporary workers is, therefore, a primary concern: according to a recent European Union report, 25 per cent of temporary workers report substantial job dissatisfaction, and little or no control over their work methods or pace of work, placing them at a greater risk of depression and other mental disorders than their permanently employed colleagues (*Temporary Agency Work in the European Union*, 2003). Equally, Benavides *et al.* (2000), who examined worker attitudes in Europe, have reported that psychologically there is little difference between the negative attitudes and consequences inherent to flexible employment and those of unemployment. As they have pointed out, "precarious" employment is psychologically and physically taxing, and can result in significantly increased levels of job dissatisfaction, absenteeism, and physical and psychological illness, much of which can be attributed to the increased levels of stress consequent to an unreliable and inconstant workplace. Consequently, Nollen believes that companies that display a lack of regard for their employees' psychological well-being by allowing them to work in the conditions generated by temporary employment have failed to understand the potential negative, longer-term economic and social effects of their employment strategies. Rather, he suggests, they should assess the actual costs resulting from a distinctly reduced level of productivity, against the perceived savings from reduced wages and benefits.

As we have seen, despite dramatic changes in both corporate practices and workplace demographics, and the repeated demonstration that many of the coincident, supposedly positive organizational interventions have consistently failed to increase company productivity or profitability, there has not been a major change in corporate attitudes regarding the needs of employees. One explanation for this failure is that, during this period, the processes that managers, I/O psychologists, and productivity consultants have traditionally used to assess, mollify, and motivate employees have become increasingly obsolete; because they were designed for a workforce dominated by white, middle-aged men, who had committed themselves to a lifelong career, these processes are no longer adequate to address the needs of a changing workforce (Sue *et al.*, 1998).

Best practice: Case examples of how it's being done

The aging population

As we have seen, the aging workforce presents problems at both an organizational and societal level. For organizations, the costs of replacing the human capital inherent in their older workers are becoming burdensome (Rickard, 1999). Nevertheless, it is possible for firms to find ways to retain and utilize the skills of their older employees. The European Foundation for the Improvement of Living and Working Conditions (*Ageing and Work in Europe*, 2004) has provided the following case examples of how an aging workforce can be better utilized:

Case example from Sweden: Older workers at Volvo-Torslandaverken: Staffing was reduced by 60 per cent. At the same time, car production rates increased. In an effort to manage the staff shortage, two departments for older workers were set up in 1994. Sixty persons who are older than 50 years or have medical difficulties are employed here. Ninety per cent of these have strain injuries. They do not work in cleaning, painting or other heavy tasks. Instead they perform service tasks or preparatory work for the assembly line. At the outset, Volvo's management counted on the older workers handling 75 per cent of commissioned production demands. Today they handle 90 per cent. To recruit a new, younger worker costs around 100,000 SEK. Early retirement for older workers is also costly. Thus, retaining these workers within the senior departments represents considerable cost savings. There is no direct competition with the younger assembly workers who have greater physical strength. The older, experienced workers can conserve their energies in dealing with more specialized tasks. In the beginning, the younger workers on the assembly line tried to find fault with the work of the older workers. However, this strategy was soon abandoned. The more experienced workers clearly knew how to build a car properly. And the younger workers could learn from them. A greater integration of ages in the work teams creates a sense of belonging, safety and well-being. The harmonious work situation strengthens workers' self-esteem and reduces sick leave. Short breaks and varied work schedules are also beneficial, allowing the older workers rest periods. The older workers do not have as high a pace of work as the younger workers but their work is cost-effective. The oldest senior worker was offered early retirement on reaching 59 years, but chose to remain at work. The management can be pleased with the success of their initiative.

Case example from Denmark: Retaining and attracting older workers: The Danish supermarket chain "Netto" is one of the largest Danish supermarket chains operating in Denmark and the rest of Scandinavia, as well as having a presence in Germany and the UK. The company has been very active in creating ways of retaining and attracting senior employees. Two main initiatives were undertaken: Senior policy: The supermarket chain has created a senior policy in order to attract and retain older employees. Hiring employees who represent each age category is believed to optimize customer satisfaction and profitability. Older customers like to deal with older employees. "Senior supermarkets": Netto has created three so-called senior supermarkets where at least half of the employees in the supermarket are over 50 years. This contrasts with the normal staffing in Netto's supermarkets where most of the employees are very young. After a period of implementation, the senior supermarkets have proven to fully measure up to the standards and profitability of the best supermarkets in the Netto chain. Personnel expenses are relatively higher in the senior supermarkets due to a greater degree of part-time and special arrangements but costs of sick leave are much lower in the senior supermarkets. Furthermore, the senior supermarkets perform excellently in Netto's customer satisfaction surveys. There are no plans to open more senior supermarkets. Rather, Netto intends to use the experience to create a higher age diversity in all its supermarkets in order to gain the advantages and benefits deriving from retaining older employees.

Temporary employment

Call centres have been labelled the "sweat shops of the 21st century" (van den Broek, Callaghan, & Thompson, 2004) due to poor working practices, long hours, highly rigid work schedules, elevated levels of workplace stress, and temporary-contract hiring policies. Consequently, they have one of the highest rates of staff turnover of any industry: some 95 per cent (*Best Companies: Best Practice*, 2004). Nevertheless, call centres and their employees represent the first (or only) point of contact between many large organizations and their customers and, as such, more organizations are beginning to realize that poor morale, motivation, and job satisfaction among call centre employees can have a negative impact on the satisfaction of their ctomers (Gollan, 2003).

In the United Kingdom, the Department of Trade and Industry (DIT) have profiled Kwik-Fit insurance (*Best Companies: Best Practice*, 2004), a major seller of motor insurance, whose principal sales are made through their call centre. According to their human resources director, the high level of customer complaints coupled with an unworkable level of turnover (and consequent costs of recruiting, hiring, and training) resulted in a recent overhaul of their workplace practices. By calling for and analysing staff suggestions for workplace experience, the HR department developed an action list for critical workplace changes which resulted in a drop in turnover from 95 to 50 per cent, a 200 per cent rise in company profits and a massive rise in staff morale, in less than a year.

Some of the workplace changes made by Kwik-Fit geared towards reducing work intensity, workplace stress and firm-wide costs included:

- An on-site, full-time concierge to help staff deal with personal needs, such as dry cleaning, making medical and dental appointments, picking up packages, and making show bookings and restaurant reservations
- The introduction of coffee cups with lids so that staff could have drinks at their workstations
- The introduction of a £1000 "signing bonus" for any staff member who recommended a friend or a former colleague for a position at Kwik-Fit who was subsequently hired
- The ability to take leave in hourly increments, so that staff could deal with small daily life needs (such as a medical appointment) without having to take an entire day off
- Major changes to the physical workplace environment, including natural lighting, a colour scheme designed to aid in stress reduction[2], and a "chill-out" area where employees could relax
- A scheme where directors spend time on the floor in the role of front-line staff, in order to expose them directly to the conditions dealt with by employees on a daily basis
- A direct mailing programme to the general manager, so that staff could voice complaints and concerns anonymously to the top level of management
- Free food in the company canteen once a month to help employees facing financial difficulties
- A social club, allowing employees to interact outside of work hours and that included lessons in salsa dancing, martial arts, and relaxation
- Offering longer-term contracts to encourage employees to remain with the company, and to induce an increased sense of employment security among call centre workers.

---

[2] See Section 6 to learn more about how the physical workplace environment, including colours, can have a major impact on the psychological well-being of employees.

Summary

The practice of economic rationalism in the 1980s and 1990s was intended to maximize shareholder return over the short to medium term by reducing costs and increasing efficiency. The main economic rationalistic strategy was downsizing: the reduction of workforce numbers in an attempt to reduce organizational costs. Downsizing was particularly common in organizations that experienced poor financial growth, financial difficulties, or shareholder pressure for greater returns. Nevertheless, research on the efficacy of downsizing practices has shown that it is a poor long-term strategy, resulting in longer-term harm to companies through the loss of human capital and intellectual resources, and an increased demand on the remaining employees (resulting, in turn, in raised levels of stress, illness, dissatisfaction, and turnover). This loss of human capital is particularly harmful to organizations, in the light of recent economic changes: the "knowledge-based" economy has resulted in more than 60 per cent of modern workers engaging in information-based work, and has led to an increasing demand for highly skilled workers.

Several other factors have changed the modern workforce. First, there has been a substantial rise in the number of women in the workplace in recent years, the result of greater equality, changing roles, and increased access to education. Nevertheless, women have not yet attained parity with men in terms of recognition or earning capacity: on average, women earn less than 80 per cent of the equivalent male salary. Likewise, there has been an increase in the number of older workers represented in employment. Companies that lost intellectual resources to downsizing practices in the late 20th century often have difficulties attracting skilled, younger replacement workers. Consequently, there is increasing demand for older workers to remain in employment past the traditional retirement age of 60, in order to shore up the loss of human capital needed to sustain the modern business. Lastly, whilst there has been a large increase in the number of minorities represented in the workplace, like women, they are often poorly treated. Typically, minorities are over-represented in low-skill occupations, and are less likely to be promoted over their white, male counterparts.

A final change in the modern workplace is the increasing tendency of employers to provide temporary employment in preference to permanent positions. Also known as contingent, non-standard, flexible, or precarious employment, temporary employment appears to increase firm flexibility, allowing employers to avoid mandatory costs, such as mandated benefits, health insurance, and holiday pay. However, whilst this strategy can reduce costs in the short term, it has been shown to be ineffective in the longer term, resulting in low employee satisfaction, loyalty and productivity, and high levels of employee stress and turnover, all of which can result in increased organizational costs and lowered effectiveness.

REVIEW QUESTIONS

1. Explain how the knowledge economy has largely replaced traditional, manufacturing-based economic practices.
2. Outline how the economic rationalism of the 1980s and 1990s affected workplace practices.

3. Describe how the nature of work and workers has changed since the 1980s.

4. What workplace changes have you noticed during your employment experiences over the last five years?

5. In your opinion, how have businesses coped with the increasing numbers of women and older employees in the workplace?

6. If you were in charge of hiring new employees, what measures would you put in place to ensure that older workers were considered for employment?

Mind-diagram summary

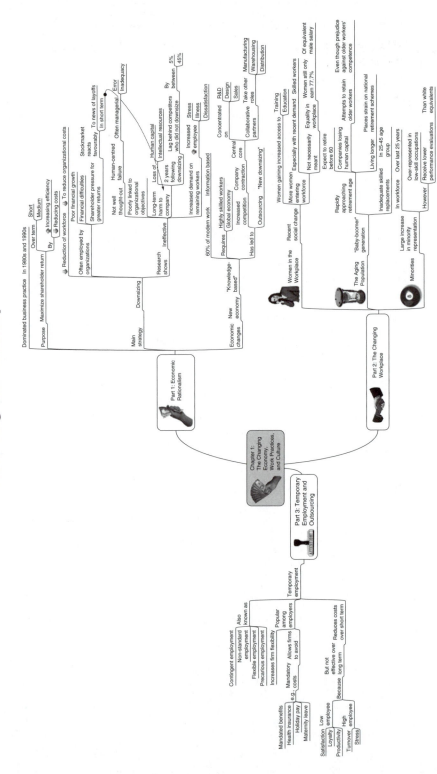

Chapter 1: The Changing Economy, Work Practices, and Culture

Part 1: Economic Rationalism

Main strategy — Downsizing
- Dominated business practice — In 1980s and 1990s
- **Purpose** — Maximize shareholder return
  - Over term
    - Short
    - Medium
  - By
    - Increasing efficiency
    - Reducing costs
      - To reduce organizational costs
  - Reduction of workforce
  - Often employed by organizations
    - Poor financial growth
    - Financial difficulties
    - Stockmarket reacts favourably — To news of layoffs — In short term
    - Shareholder pressure for greater returns
- Research shows — Ineffective
  - Not well thought-out
  - Human-centred failure — Often managerial
    - Error
    - Inadequacy
  - Poorly linked to organizational objectives
  - Long-term harm to company
    - Loss of — Human capital / Intellectual resources
    - 2 years following downsizing
    - Lag behind competitors who did not downsize — By between — 5% / 45%
  - Increased demand on remaining workers
  - Increased employee
    - Stress
    - Illness
    - Dissatisfaction

Economic changes — New economy
- "Knowledge"-based
- 60% of modern work — Information based
- Requires — Highly skilled workers
  - Concentrated on
    - R&D
    - Design
    - Sales
  - Central core
  - Take other roles
  - Collaborative partners
- Global economy — Increased competition
- Has led to
  - Company contraction — "New downsizing"
  - Outsourcing
  - Manufacturing
  - Warehousing
  - Distribution

Part 2: The Changing Workplace

Women in the Workplace — Recent social change
- Women gaining increased access to
  - Training
  - Education
- More women entering workforce — Especially with recent demand — Skilled workers
- Not necessarily meant — Equality in workplace
- Women still only earn 77.7% — Of equivalent male salary
- Even though prejudice against older workers' competence

The Aging Population — "Baby-boomer" generation
- Rapidly approaching retirement age
  - Expect to retire before 60
  - Companies losing human capital — Attempts to retain older workers
- Living longer — Places strain on national retirement schemes
- Inadequate skilled replacements — In 25–45 age group

Minorities
- Large increase in minority representation — In workforce — Over last 25 years
- Over-represented in low-skill occupations
- However — Receive lower performance evaluations — Than white equivalents

Part 3: Temporary Employment and Outsourcing

Temporary employment
- Contingent employment — Also known as
  - Non-standard employment
  - Flexible employment
  - Precarious employment
- Increases firm flexibility
- Popular among employers
- Mandatory — Allows firms to avoid
- Reduces costs over short term — But not effective over long term
- Because
  - Mandated benefits e.g.
    - Health insurance
    - Holiday pay
    - Maternity leave
  - Low employee
    - Satisfaction
    - Loyalty
  - High employee
    - Productivity
    - Turnover
    - Stress

Work Intensification, Increasing Health Care, and Other Costs

KEYWORDS Asset, contract, decrease, pressure, profit, spend.

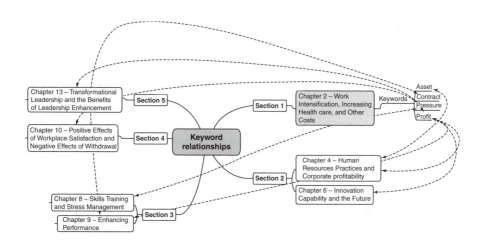

IMPORTANT CONCEPTS Productivity increases, organizational efficiency trends, work intensification.

Part 1: Work intensification and "quick fixes"

One consequence of organizational attempts to increase productivity, such as downsizing and outsourcing, has been the intensification of work. According to Green (2004), three major changes in workplace practices are responsible for work intensification. First, the "quick-fix" attitude of firms that reduce their workforce has meant that remaining employees are required to work harder to compensate for the loss of human capital. Second, technological changes in the workplace, such as the introduction of computers, have allowed managers to monitor work more strictly and control work flow more easily, resulting in greater automation of work tasks and a consequent reduction in the level of employees' perceived job control. Third, the increase in globalization and the consequent market pressures placed on firms to innovate have resulted in increased shareholder pressure for stock market performance. In many cases, the response of senior management to this pressure has been to compel their subordinates to reach unrealistic performance targets, a strategy that has substantially increased work pressures. Another response has been the linking of a manager or supervisor's subjective rating of employee effort to pay scales (Green). This strategy is based on the assumption that workers will be better motivated with the promise of fiscal rewards for increased performance, combined with the threat of a reduction in pay if targets are not met. As we will see in Sections 3, 4, and 6, because employees are more likely to be motivated by intrinsic factors (such as satisfaction and well-being) than extrinsic ones, this strategy is seldom effective and, in fact, can actually result in reduced productivity and increased organizational costs.

The desire by senior management for increased employee work performance has also seen the introduction of several attempts at organizational efficiency trends. One such process, "Total Quality Management" (TQM: Green, 2004), involves a restructuring of the workplace based on beliefs about worker efficiency; TQM is based on the concept of "lean production" and is supposed to "empower" workers by giving them greater discretion in the way in which they work (Batt, 1999). In the opinion of Green, however, TQM is too focussed on efficiency at the expense of employee needs.[3] This concern has been supported by Batt, who investigated the workplace effectiveness of 223 employees in a TQM-based workplace. According to Batt, in her investigation the introduction of TQM did not increase employee performance and actually created conditions that resulted in decreased workplace satisfaction. Another efficiency practice, self-managed work teams (Kirkman & Shapiro, 2001), in which managers are asked to allow employees to work together in a more integrated, self-determined manner, has apparently created more difficulties than those it was intended to solve. In the opinion of Kirkman and his co-worker, the growing diversity in the workplace, which has replaced traditionally homogenous workforces of countries like the United States, has led to increasing difficulties in the implementation of standardized work practices, despite the hopes of the financial consultants responsible for their implementation. According to Kirkman and

---

[3] See Sections 3 and 4 for an in-depth discussion of employee needs and corporate performance.

Shapiro, a failure to recognize the different cultural influences inherent in an organization can lead to the danger of "rubber stamping"; that is, the attempt to make an idea or practice that appears useful fit all workers, without consideration of individual differences. Consequently, whilst they can be highly effective, the main danger of systems like TQM and self-managed work teams lies in the reasons for their implementation: when used as a "quick fix" for more deep-seated problems within a firm, these systems invariably serve to distract management from organizational flaws with the promise of rapid improvements. Unless they are enacted in combination with a company-wide analysis, managerial training, and systematic attempts to repair poorly functioning processes, quick-fix approaches are unlikely to live up to expectations and can actually increase the pressures inherent in an already intense workplace environment.

Increasing work hours and overwork

One problematic consequence of work intensification has been the increase in hours worked: between 1992 and 1997, the average number of hours worked per US employee increased by 12 per cent (Green, 2004). Moreover, many salaried employees are required or encouraged to work unpaid overtime hours (70 per cent of employees who work more than 40 hours per week are not compensated for overtime (Cherry, 2004)). According to Cherry, whilst production was once clearly related to the number of hours worked (for example, a given worker could produce x number of units in a given amount of time), in a modern, information-driven economy the assumption that time at work is equal to effort (and therefore productivity) is seriously flawed. That is, because of the increasing complexity of tasks performed by highly skilled workers, the simple number of hours at work, or "face-time" (Potter, 2003), is a highly ineffective measure of productivity or efficiency. Nevertheless, the average number of hours worked per week in the United States has grown steadily since the 1970s: United States employees now work 50 per cent longer hours than their European counterparts, with 27 per cent reporting feeling overwhelmed by the amount of hours that they work (Gallinsky *et al.*, 2004). During this time the output of US workers (measured in hours worked) has increased by 40 per cent, but their actual productivity is actually 10 per cent less than their European equivalents (Potter). Moreover, the pressure to work longer hours is not limited to the United States: in his investigation of 21,000 worker records from EU member states, Cowling (2005) reported that employees in the EU were under increasing pressure to work longer hours. Cowling also pointed out that longer work hours in the EU were significantly related to occupation, industry, and gender. Those in high-pressure roles, including managerial, professional, and legislative jobs worked substantially harder than other workers; those in private industry worked longer than their colleagues in the public sector; whilst workers in smaller firms worked longer hours than those in larger businesses (business with more than 100 employees). As well, according to Cowling, the increased pressure on men to provide for their families resulted in their working significantly longer hours than their female counterparts, especially when job security was at stake (for example, during or following downsizing or outsourcing initiatives).

Although the trend to work longer hours does not appear to be abating, the belief that working longer hours is associated with increased production has been further discredited in the light of research that shows that overwork can actually reduce employee productivity. According to Gallinsky *et al.* (2004), when an employee is overworked there is a 20 per cent greater likelihood of mistakes, a 38 per cent increased probability of anger and resentment towards fellow workers (reducing quality of communication and team interaction). However, it is not only the number of hours worked that leads to problems: increasing job distractions such as telephone calls and e-mail can, according to a recent study by Wilson (*HP Guide to Avoiding Info-Mania*, 2005), result in a loss of concentration equivalent to a decline in IQ of 10 points, comparable to the deficit in mental functioning of an entire night's missed sleep. Moreover, many modern workers report being forced to concentrate on too many duties at once, making it difficult for them to focus adequately on any single task (Gallinsky *et al.*). Consequently, the increasing propensity for employee mistakes and the inability to concentrate, combined with a reduction in team performance, can all take their toll on the running of an organization: when employees are unproductive, the firm is not likely to perform well.

Part 2: Stress, illness, and organizational costs

Ironically, attempts to reduce organizational spending such as work intensification and the loss of employment stability have resulted in a substantial rise in work-related health complaints, and a consequent increase in costs to firms from increased health-related payouts and lost production time (Pousette & Hanse, 2002). In the psychological literature, the causal link between stress and illness has been well documented (for example, Pancheri, de Martino, Spiombi, Biondi, & Mosticoni, 1985; Schroeder & Costa, 1984); more recently, because workplace illness has begun to eclipse the shorter-term economic gains of downsizing and outsourcing, stress in the workplace has also attracted the attention of researchers. Ganster, Fox, and Dwyer (2001), for example, have documented a causal link between increased job demands and a reduced physiological capacity to deal with stress. According to these investigators, who studied the physiological stress responses of 105 nurses to workplace demands, when workers undergo extensive periods of high job pressure, the brain's adrenomedullary response becomes diminished; this reduces its ability to regulate the release of catecholamines (adrenaline and noradrenaline) required to normalize the stress response. Simultaneously, the increased adrenocortical activity increases cortisol (a catabolic steroid) levels; when cortisol is elevated excessively immune function can be compromised, making an individual more prone to illness. In fact, stress in the workplace can result in more than reduced immune efficiency. Swan and Cooper (2005) have reported that workplace stress can result in widespread affective and physical problems, with 48 per cent of surveyed British workers reporting chronic irritability, 44 per cent experiencing lack of sleep, 36 per cent suffering from regular headaches, 35 per cent indicating exhaustion, and 28 per cent diagnosed with depression. Nevertheless, Ganster *et al.* have reported that a person's perceived control over his or her work environment can buffer substantially against the effects of stress. In fact, according to Ganster and his colleagues, by increasing a worker's perceived control in the workplace, health care costs associated with the effects of stress (such as absenteeism, illness, tardiness, low motivation, and poor productivity) can be reduced significantly.[4] However, although such precautions can easily be taken to protect workers from the effects of stress and, consequently, reduce stress-related organizational costs, few firms appear to be taking these preventative measures: Jusko (2002) has reported that lost productivity time due to stress-induced illness in US workplaces comes to over US$250 billion per annum, a figure backed up by European research that estimates the annual cost in the Netherlands at €12 billion (*Work-Related Stress*, 2005) and £4 billion in the United Kingdom (Swan & Cooper). In the opinion of Jusko, these problems are, unfortunately, "invisible to employers", who in attempting to cut costs through layoffs, temporary employment, and outsourcing remain unaware that these processes actually increase workplace stress, adding to long-term organizational costs. One of these costs, according to Jusko, stems from stressed workers performing at subnormal levels, or simply not performing, when they are at work. This relatively new phenomenon, labelled "presenteeism" (Chatterji & Tilley, 2002), which has been blamed for up to 75 per cent of missed work time, occurs as the label suggests "on the job". The pressure for employees to be at work for longer hours and to take less time off has resulted in many workers attending work even when ill, reducing their productivity dramatically, and placing others in danger of contagious illness that can further reduce workplace performance ("The high cost of 'presenteeism' ", 2002): an ironic consequence of the managerial assumption that time at work equals productivity.

Part 3: Physical inactivity at work

Another health-related workplace problem that has resulted in a substantial rise in costs to employers is obesity, brought on by an increasingly sedentary lifestyle (at home and at work) and an increasing propensity to snack in the workplace (Conlin, 2002). Because, in many workplaces, there is little encouragement or opportunity to exercise, and as workers are spending more time at work (leaving little time to exercise in their spare time), it has become difficult for many employees to maintain a normal weight. According to Conlin, the health problems associated with obesity, such as heart disease, hypertension, diabetes, and musculoskeletal problems, cost (in the United States) in the realm of US$117 billion annually to lost productivity. Moreover, as Conlin has pointed out, despite the relatively simple and inexpensive intervention options available to employers to help employees maintain or lose weight (such as subsidized gym memberships, personal training, nutritional counselling, or even intelligent office design), the huge annual organizational costs associated with obesity suggests either that few employers are aware of the problem or that they

---

[4] See Section 4 for a discussion of how perceived control over work variables can act as a stress buffer.

are failing to take preventative action. Nevertheless, by investing in employees' health, organizations can make dramatic financial savings, often exceeding those expected from more traditional cost-reducing exercises such as workforce reduction (Riedel, Lynch, Baase, Hymel, & Peterson, 2001). In fact, according to Bolin, Jacobson, and Lindgren (2002), firms that make even minor attempts to address the health concerns of their employees can reduce costs and increase productivity.

Best practice: Case examples of how it's being done

Increasing work hours, work intensification, stress, and organizational costs

The corporate culture of long working hours, coupled with the managerial notion that productivity can only be measured accurately through face time, is pervasive (White, Hill, McGovern, Mills, & Smeaton, 2003). As we have seen, the modern "knowledge" economy has made the belief that time spent on the job is equal to productive output fairly irrelevant. Nevertheless, pressure to work increasing hours, and work intensification as a reaction to demands from senior management or shareholders, can result in reduced productivity, increased work stress and consequent illness, and soaring organizational costs (Cowling, 2005). In their report on work-life benefits and flexible working, the DTI highlighted the case of "Artline Solutions", a technology supply firm that was facing serious problems as a result of their workplace culture (*Work-Life Balance and Flexible Working: The Business Case*, 2004). According to the DTI, Artline Solutions had an extremely long-hours culture, requiring managers and other workers to be at work in excess of 10 hours a day. Moreover, the company had an inefficient management structure under which managers were poorly trained and unable to adequately delegate responsibility which, combined with long work hours, resulted in substantial productivity losses through staff sickness and absences (losing in excess of 45 days per year to absenteeism). Consequently, communication within the company was poor and customer service lacking, leading to increasing levels of customer complaints and a loss of business to competing firms.

Following a process of consultation with an external firm, including one-on-one interviews with all employees, Artline Solutions were able to identify the organizational problems that were reducing their ability to function; work intensification was one of the priority issues. To counter these problems, the management with the full involvement of the staff, introduced several interventions to change the way in which the organization functioned. Over the following year, staff absenteeism dropped from 45 to 8.5 days per year, communication improved dramatically, customer satisfaction rose substantially, and company profitability increased. Some of the interventions made by Artline Solutions included:

- After identifying time management and poor communication as a problem, staff and management attended workshops to help address these issues.
- A rota system was introduced allowing staff to vary their working hours depending on personal commitments. This included the ability to change

start and finish times and to work from home. Following its implementation, the majority of staff members took advantage of the programme, with a corresponding increase in job satisfaction.

- A formal HR department was formed to concentrate on staff training and development.

- To reduce any resistance during the transition, managers who were reluctant to elicit customer feedback were given extra training, and technical staff were trained in teamwork to increase collaboration and innovation, and to reduce their tendency to blame others for problems.

Points for action: Practical recommendations for change

Increasing work hours, work intensification, stress, and organizational costs

The UK DTI have made the following recommendations for organizations that would like to address the increasing costs associated with work intensification and work stress (*Best Companies: Best Practice*, 2004):

- Make sure employees are adequately recognized and rewarded for their contributions. This will enhance job satisfaction by letting people know that they are valued, even if and when they are required to work longer. In many cases, simple recognition of a job well done will encourage employees to work harder with higher-quality results.

- Promote learning and skills acquisition in workers, even if it is not directly associated with the job at hand. Again, encouragement of interests and investment in human capital can increase employee well-being, reduce stress, and reduce ongoing costs to the firm from illness and absenteeism.

- Set up effective systems for transferral of knowledge within the organization, both vertically and horizontally. As well, effective employee consultation practices should be developed: by making sure that managers are aware of feelings and attitudes in their subordinates, they are more likely to be able to take action to prevent small problems from becoming exacerbated.

- Empower employees by giving them as much control over their jobs and environments as possible. In doing so, stress and its effects can be mediated.[5]

- Train managers to understand that management does not necessarily involve direct line-of-sight supervision. When managers are able to let their employees work without direct supervision they are more likely to recognize that simple time at work is not an effective assessment of productivity.[6]

---

[5] See Section 4 for a more in-depth discussion of the mediating effects of perceived control on workplace stress.
[6] See Section 7 for a thorough examination of effective leadership and management.

■ Provide as much employment security as possible. One of the direct drives for employees to work long hours is fear of job loss. By providing job security, employers let employees get on with their work without worrying about problems like job loss or redundancy.[7]

Summary

Changes to working practices have also led to the "intensification" of work. Work intensification is often the result of "quick-fix" attitudes in which a workforce is reduced to make short-term savings, but requires that remaining employees work harder to fill the gap. As well, technological changes have allowed managers to more easily monitor the work of their subordinates, and control work flow, reducing employees' perception of job control, and increasing the actual workload; whilst increased globalization has resulted in mega-corporations in which shareholder pressure for company performance results in growing managerial pressure on workers to perform at increasingly higher levels. At the same time, organizational efficiency trends, such as Total Quality Management, and Self-Managed Work Teams, whilst potentially useful for increasing productivity, have done little to increase employee well-being, and often result in an increased workload.

Work intensification has been paralleled by an increase in work hours, often based on the flawed assumption that "face-time" is equal to productivity. Nevertheless, researchers have shown that increased hours at work can actually reduce employee productivity, by raising the likelihood of mistakes and reducing the ability of workers to concentrate on their tasks. Moreover, the increased stress consequent to greater work hours and intensity has resulted in a higher level of workplace illness, resulting in massive organizational costs through absenteeism and presenteeism.

Lastly, longer work hours in physically inactive jobs have led to a rise in the number of overweight workers, resulting in greater organizational costs from illnesses such as heart disease hypertension, diabetes, and musculoskeletal problems. Although these problems can be easily remedied through, for example, the introduction of sponsored exercise programmes, organizations seldom take any such initiative and, as a result, face increasing health care costs.

■■■■■■■■ REVIEW QUESTIONS ■■■■■■■■

1. Explain work intensification and its possible negative consequences, with particular reference to your own workplace experiences.

2. Examine the relationship between work intensification and the rise in organizational costs regarding health care.

3. What other workplace changes over the past twenty years have resulted in a negative organizational financial burden?

---

[7] Consult Section 4 to understand how individuals have a limited set of cognitive resources in the workplace, and how fear of job loss taxes these resources reducing both ability and productivity.

4. In your opinion, how well are contemporary organizations prepared for the likelihood that over the next fifteen years they will have a problem recruiting highly skilled employees?

5. In your experience, what changes have you observed in the workplace that have led to increased organizational costs?

6. Document any personal experiences relating to overwork or work intensification and stress or ilness.

Mind-diagram summary

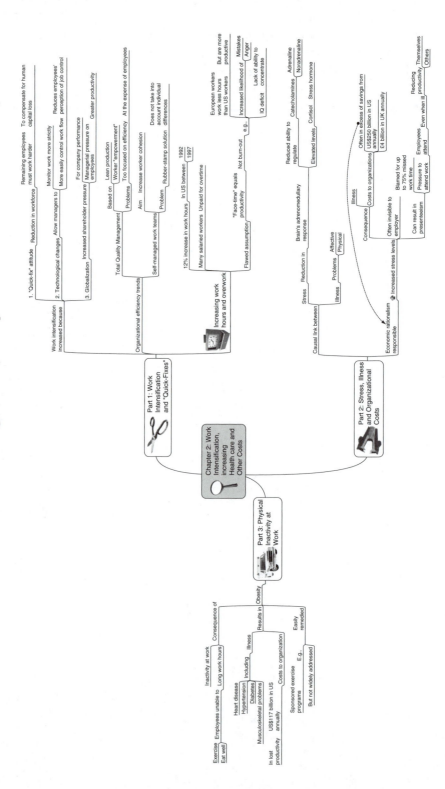

Chapter 2: Work Intensification, increasing Health care and Other Costs

Part 1: Work Intensification and "Quick-Fixes"

Organizational efficiency trends

Work intensification increased because
- 1. "Quick-fix" attitude
  - Reduction in workforce
    - Remaining employees must work harder
    - To compensate for human capital loss
- 2. Technological changes
  - Allow managers to
    - Monitor work more strictly
    - More easily control work flow
    - Reduces employees' perception of job control
- 3. Globalization
  - Increased shareholder pressure
    - For company performance
    - Managerial pressure on employees
    - Greater productivity

Total Quality Management
- Based on
  - Lean production
  - Worker "empowerment"
- Problems
  - Too focused on efficiency
  - At the expense of employees

Self-managed work teams
- Aim
  - Increase worker cohesion
- Problem
  - Rubber-stamp solution
  - Does not take into account individual differences

Increasing work hours and overwork

- 12% increase in work hours
  - In US between 1992 / 1997
- Many salaried workers
  - Unpaid for overtime
- "Face-time" equals productivity
  - Flawed assumption
  - Not burn-out
  - e.g.
- European workers work less hours than US workers
  - But are more productive
- Increased likelihood of
  - Mistakes
  - Anger
- IQ deficit
  - Lack of ability to concentrate

Part 2: Stress, Illness and Organizational Costs

Causal link between
- Stress
- Illness
- Reduction in
  - Problems
    - Affective
    - Physical

Brain's adrenomedullary response
- Reduced ability to regulate
  - Catecholamines
    - Adrenaline
    - Noradrenaline
  - Elevated levels
    - Cortisol
    - Stress hormone

Economic rationalism responsible ◄ Increased stress levels
- Increased stress levels
  - illness
    - Consequence
    - Costs to organizations
      - Often in excess of savings from
      - US$250 billion in US annually
      - £4 billion in UK annually
  - Often invisible to employer
  - Can result in presenteeism
    - Blamed for up to 75% missed work time
    - Pressure to attend work
      - Employees attend
      - Even when ill
        - Reducing productivity
          - Themselves
          - Others

Part 3: Physical Inactivity at Work

Obesity
- Consequence of
  - Inactivity at work
    - Employees unable to
      - Exercise
      - Eat well
  - Long work hours
- Results in
  - Illness
    - Including
      - Heart disease
      - Hypertension
      - Diabetes
      - Musculoskeletal problems
  - Costs to organization
    - US$117 billion in US annually
    - In lost productivity
    - E.g.,
      - Sponsored exercise programs
      - Easily remedied
      - But not widely addressed

The Worker-Friendly Organization

KEYWORDS Absenteeism, health, physical, policy, security.

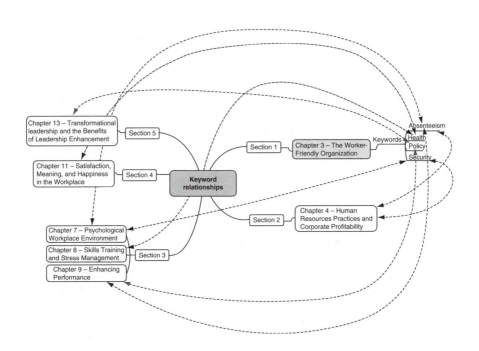

IMPORTANT CONCEPTS Work–life balance, social responsibility.

Part 1: Flawed assumptions of productivity

In the opinion of Porter and Bostrom (1996), workplace practices inherited from the industrial age have left modern industry with three flawed premises. The first, "the labour theory of value", assumes, like the observations of Cherry (2004) (see Chapter 2), that labour is a key factor in productivity (that is, more labour equals greater productivity). This notion has, in modern times, resulted in the managerial error of measuring productivity by the amount of perceived labour performed. However, as we have seen, the perception that more time spent at work is equal to greater labour, and therefore increased productivity, has become invalid: in an information-based economy, it is no longer a simple process to determine a person's productivity based on the amount of time he or she spends on a given task, because intellectual output cannot be measured in an easily quantifiable way. Unfortunately, in many organizations, individual merit, rewards, and promotions are often based on this unsound premise, forcing employees desiring workplace recognition to spend longer at work, even though this will not increase their productivity (Porter & Bostrom). Second, modern workplaces still commonly expound the protestant "work ethic", made dominant following the industrial revolution, that "idle hands do the devil's work" (Porter & Bostrom). Porter and his co-worker believe that in a modern economy this supposition is flawed because it leads to the conclusion that those without paid work are somehow "less worthy", and that an employee's leisure, personal, or family time represents a luxury that, in effect, steals production time from the employer. This results in a begrudging attitude among employers regarding paid vacation, sick leave, and other benefits for their employees. The third flawed assumption is that consumerism is the basis for a strong economy. Post industrial era, whilst production-based economy was driven by the manufacture and consumption of goods, according to Porter and Bostrum, the information-based economy is guided by innovation and the encouragement of ideas; consequently, that a person simply works to obtain money for the purchase of goods has become less of a priority in the modern world.

By pointing out that modern firms are still dominated by ideological hangovers from the industrial revolution, Porter and his coauthor (1996) have highlighted a major problem: although society, the way in which we work, and the type of people who do that work have all changed, organizations are often still directed and managed as if these changes had not occurred. As we have already discussed, a major social and economic consequence of outmoded organizational thinking has been the increase in workplace stress and lifestyle-related illnesses. However, at a more personal level, many people are no longer content to work under a paradigm that assumes that the worker is in some way indebted to the employer, and that this debt must be paid, even at the cost to a person's personal well-being (Wax, 2004). Consequently, the cognitive dissonance experienced by employees who value their personal relationships, and who also want to advance their careers, has led to a new buzz word in human resources: work–life balance (Schmidt & Duenas, 2002).

Part 2: Work–life balance

According to Schmidt and Duenas (2002), the increasing numbers of dual-income families in which both partners work a greater number of hours per week than did their parents means that in excess of 66 per cent of people now have trouble balancing their work and home lives.[8] Unfortunately, because of the predominant attitude that "face-time" at work equals productivity (Porter & Bostrom, 1996), when people make efforts to redress this imbalance (for example, by taking more regular leave or refusing to work overtime), they are often punished indirectly for their perceived lack of dedication through the reduced likelihood of seniority, promotion, or benefits (Schmidt & Duenas). Moreover, in the opinion of Schmidt and Duenas, this disincentive to reduce the precursors of workplace stress (such as overwork and work-life dissonance) has made it almost inevitable that stress-related illnesses will continue to increase.

The social and economic problems brought on by longer work hours, workplace stress, and reduced health notwithstanding, the prevalence of work-life imbalance, and its negative financial consequences, has attracted the attention of both researchers and firms. Wax (2004), for example, has suggested that workplaces need to be more sensitive to the needs of their employees; according to Wax, there is a greater need for highly skilled employees in the modern workplace, and it is necessary for these people to interact effectively in order for an organization to work successfully. However, current limitations, such as hierarchical company structures, in which employees must effectively compete amongst one other in a tournament-like fashion for a limited number of senior positions, do not engender cooperation (Wax). In other words, when employees are forced to compete for advancement, and when managers assume that company loyalty and employee productivity can be measured by the amount of time an employee spends at work, it is unlikely that the organization will operate successfully, but there is a substantially increased likelihood of employee dissatisfaction. Consequently, Wax believes that it is essential for managers to understand the consequences of this "rat race", by realizing that non-economic gains, such as workplace satisfaction and a consequent lower employee turnover, can, in fact, be profitable. Moreover, by intervening to decrease reliance on escalating rewards, a hierarchical company structure, tournament-style promotion, and by increasing awareness of the work-life imbalance, senior management can go a long way towards enhancing employee well-being.

Flexible working and family-friendly policies

One way that employers and employees can find equilibrium between the needs of the firm and employees' desires for a greater work–life balance is through flexible working practices. Organizations are seeking greater flexibility in the way they operate, whilst employees are calling for a better quality of life, with the reduction of working hours seen as the highest priority (Naegele, Barkholdt, Vroom, Andersen, & Krämer, 2003). In fact, according to Naegele *et al.*, in

---

[8] Other researchers have put this figure at closer to 80 per cent (Stevens, Brown, & Lee, 2004).

Europe a half of all surveyed employees would like to reduce their working week by at least 10 per cent, over 20 per cent of workers would take a three-month sabbatical without pay, whilst in excess of 14 per cent of full-time employees have made efforts to move to part-time work.

Researchers are of the opinion that the reduction of individual working hours can be achieved through several programmes, without necessarily reducing employee productivity (*Work-Life Balance and Flexible Working: The Business Case*, 2004). Flextime (that is, arrangements that allow employees greater control over the times and hours that they work), for example, is, among employees, one of the most requested flexible working programmes (49 per cent of surveyed employees regarded flextime as the most likely solution to their work-life imbalance, Stevens *et al.*, 2004), closely followed by reduced working hours per week (some 36 per cent), a compressed working week (34 per cent), and the ability to work from home (29 per cent: see "Telecommuting" below). Other plans include annualized hours, task-based working, term-time working, job sharing, and part-time work, each of which can be introduced at little or no cost to the organization (Woodland, Simmonds, Thornby, Fitzgerald, & McGee, 2003).

Some of the positive consequences of workplace changes geared towards enhancing the work–life balance have been investigated by Poelmans, Chinchilla, and Cardona (2003). In their examination of 1530 HR managers in Spain, they found that "family-friendly" policies, including child care, parental leave, and flextime, resulted in increased employee retention, greater affective commitment, increased productivity, better satisfaction with work–home life balance, and reduced absenteeism and turnover intention. Nevertheless, Poelmans *et al.* warned that the simple presence of work-life policies in an organization did not automatically lead to their uptake or use; outmoded company culture, or resistance from managers and colleagues can impair the implementation of worker-friendly policies, no matter how noble the intention. In should be noted, however, that Poelmans *et al.* reported a return rate of their data-collection instrument of only 8.5 per cent, reducing the validity of their claims.

The results of a similar, but more robust, study to that of Poelmans *et al.* (2003) were reported by Berg, Kalleberg, and Appelbaum (2003). Following a two-year investigation of 4374 employees from the steel, apparel, and medical industries, they found that a combination of managerial recognition that work and life imbalances can impair workplace performance and productivity, and company-wide strategies to reduce this inequity (for example, a reduction in involuntary overtime, lower working hours, and increased supervisor support for work-life policies) resulted in increased work–life balance, enhanced job satisfaction, and a consequent reduction in employee turnover and absenteeism. Likewise, following their study of work-life satisfaction in 3361 employees of organizations with reportedly good work-life policies, Roehling, Roehling, and Moen (2001) reported that the existence and successful implementation of flextime policies resulted in a significant increase in employee loyalty and a resultant decrease in turnover. Nevertheless, as with the findings of Poelmans *et al.* and Berg *et al.*, Roehling and her colleagues cautioned that the successful effects of these policies were only visible in the presence of adequate managerial and supervisory support for their implementation and uptake.

Since around the mid-1990s, there has been a substantial increase in the offering of flexible work policies (Naegele *et al.*, 2003) however, for the most part, these have been limited to part-time work availability. As we have seen, employees are keen to use flexible working programmes when they are available; for instance, according to Stevens *et al.* (2004), uptake of offered programmes such as flextime and working from home is in excess of 50 per cent. Nevertheless, in the United Kingdom, only one in four workplaces have made flexible working, apart from part-time work, available to their employees, with less than 9 per cent of employers offering four or more practices (for example, part-time, flextime, compressed work week, reduced hours, working from home) (Woodland *et al.*, 2003). Furthermore, Woodland and his colleagues have reported that 49 per cent of employers who offer flexible working restrict its use to only some employees, typically those who are more senior. Nevertheless, of more pressing concern is the lack of support for flexible working from managers and front-line supervisors (Clarke, 2005). In her report, Clarke indicated that whilst the HR departments of many organizations were attempting to implement flexible working policies, several specific problems were limiting their effectiveness. First, the prevailing corporate culture that equates time at work with productivity erodes the belief that those working reduced, compressed, or flexible hours are really working "hard enough". This results in a lack of support for flexible working programmes from senior management, and influences the perceptions of line managers when evaluating staff who choose to take up flexible work offerings, reducing the likelihood of progress within the organization. Third, Clarke has identified a gap in the ability of front-line managers to supervise their flexibly working staff: over 45 per cent were unable to understand the reasons behind flexible working, believing that their subordinates were trying to "cheat the system". Unfortunately, when there is a lack of organization-wide support for flexible work programmes, it is unlikely that adequate training will be given to the managers who are responsible for the success or failure of the programme. Consequently, because they feel that it might be damaging their careers, many employees feel unable to ask for flexible working, even if it is already available within an organization (*Part-Time Is No Crime: So Why the Penalty? Interim Report of the EOC's Investigation into Flexible and Part-Time Working, and Questions for Consultation*, 2005). As the employees most in need of flexible work are often parents with young children, this schism between company policies and prevailing company culture, results in discrimination against those employees who are not "unencumbered by family or other responsibilities", or those who simply choose to have a life outside of work (Swan & Cooper, 2005).

One flexible working policy that is widely available is part-time work. Part-time work practices, like the flexible working processes described earlier, are often advantageous to the employer, because they allow a firm to maintain a more flexible workforce: some 81 per cent of UK employers offer part-time work to their employees (Woodland *et al.*, 2003). Nevertheless, despite its availability, part-time workers, like other contingent workers, are often disadvantaged compared with their full-time colleagues. Moreover, part-time workers are overrepresented by women, who are frequently limited in career choice to hotel, catering, banking, cleaning, or education industries, and who typically earn 40 per cent less than their male equivalents (Woodland *et al.*). As well, for men, part-time work is seldom available, even if desired: of the 7.4 million part-time workers in the United Kingdom, men make up only 12 per cent (*Part-Time Is No Crime*, 2005). Further, like other forms of contingent work, part-time workers receive 40 per cent less training than their full-time colleagues, resulting in a lack of human capital investment that can affect future employment: the longer a person engages in part-time work, the less likely that their wages will increase, even if they return to full time work (*Part-Time Is No Crime*). Lastly, in the EU, 14.1 per cent of part-time work is involuntary, resulting in little opportunity for advancement (*Part-Time Work in Europe*, 2005). According to the European Foundation for the Improvement of Living and Working Conditions, part-time employees are often excluded from supervisory posts, even if they have appropriate qualifications: compared to the 25 per cent of full-time employees in supervisory positions, only 12 per cent of male and 8 per cent of female part-time workers achieve managerial roles (2005).

It is important to note that whilst a large amount of attention has been drawn to family-friendly policies and work–life balance in large businesses, the majority of OECD employers are small-medium enterprizes (SMEs); in the United States only 20 per cent of firms employ in excess of 100 people, with over 70 per cent of organizations employing less than 20 persons (Potter, 2003), whilst in Canada only one per cent of businesses employ over 100 workers (Belout *et al.*, 2001). However, Dex and Scheibel (2001) have pointed out that employees of SMEs are as concerned about work–life balance as workers in larger businesses. In their study of 10 UK SMEs, reportedly representative of UK industry, Dex and her colleague indicated that when work-life policies (for example, extended familial leave, child care, flextime, supervisor support for work-life practices) were successfully implemented, employees reported greater job satisfaction and worker turnover decreased, a finding that imitates those of other researchers (cf. Berg *et al.*, 2003; Poelmans *et al.*, 2003; Roehling *et al.*, 2001). Nevertheless, according to Dex and Scheibel, policies and practices that encourage work–life balance are more likely to be found in larger businesses because many SMEs consider these practices too costly: whilst most managers in SMEs are aware of the benefits of successful work-life policies, their implementation is often considered only from a purely economic approach: that is, whether work-life practices will result in a visible profit for the organization, whether they will cost the organization, or whether there is a perception that they will increase firm performance. Needless to say, given that SMEs make up the majority of OECD employers, a large proportion of employees might be missing out on the benefits of work-life equilibrium, with a consequent reduction in SME productivity and performance.

In her review of work–life balance trends in industry over the last 20 years, Barnett (1999) has pointed out that despite the benefits of work-life prac-tices, many organizational attempts to address employee work-life imbalance have been unsuccessful or poorly implemented. To redress this disequilibrium, Barnett has proposed a work-life integration model, in which an employer takes responsibility for the well-being of the employee's work-life system (that is, a greater sphere that includes his or her spouse and offspring). In this system, the employer recognizes that an employee has a life beyond work, and that problems balancing this life with work demands can reduce his or her work performance. Consequently, by addressing a person's needs beyond a strict work environment, the employer can reduce role stressors, and improve worker job satisfaction and performance: choices are made to maximize the well-being of the employee's work-life system by, for example, allowing a greater level of control over work roles and decisions, and reducing excessive time demands, such as work hours, commuting and travel. In concordance with Barnett's recommendations, Schmidt and Duenas (2002) have described several corporate practices that can encourage balance in everyday work and life and, consequently, reduce the toll of workplace stress. For instance, they have suggested that companies make an effort to detect and document the patterns of absenteeism, health problems, and illnesses within their organization and then identify, with the aid of the workforce, the most likely causes of these problems. Consequent actions to improve the status quo can include the improvement, expansion, and delivery of existing health-related policies and practices, or the introduction of new ones: employee flextime, in which a staff member is more able to control his or her work schedule (including start and finish times, goal setting and completion, and team interaction), or other time-related changes such as a compressed workweek (with a three-day weekend to allow employees time to catch up on personal affairs), or the introduction of telecommuting (see below). In a more extreme stance, Windsor (2001), who suggested that the recent reduction in corporate responsibility for the well-being of employees (a consequence of profit maximization and wealth creation practices such as downsizing) has caused substantial employee dissatisfaction, has recommended that employers view their employees as important, intangible assets, each of whom represents an opportunity for organizational wealth creation. In doing so, corporations can increase their reputations (both internally and externally) as excellent places to work, attract motivated, skilled employees, and stimulate long-term performance increases from existing employees.

Although work-life policies are not always well implemented, when they are instigated successfully, the benefits are not limited to employees. According to Clarke (2005), organizations that have effectively introduced and maintained flexible working programmes have seen greater employee retention (27 per cent), increased employee motivation (70 per cent), and more effective recruitment (50 per cent). Similarly, the DTI (*Flexible Working*, 2004) have reported that 71 per cent of businesses with flexible working programmes have better employee relations, 68 per cent have seen an increase in employee commitment and loyalty, 68 per cent have seen a reduction in staff turnover, whilst 50 per cent have experienced increased productivity as a result of reduced absenteeism. As well, in firms who provide four or more flexible working programmes, profitability is greater than their immediate (non-flexible working) competitors, with 76 per cent reporting that the programmes required little or no spending to implement (*Flexible Working*).

Workplace balance

Balance in the workplace is about recognizing the reality of the mind/body link. For years psychologists have documented the physical and psychological benefits of regular physical activity (Adams, 1999). However, it's not necessary to be an athlete, or even a committed exerciser to enjoy some of these benefits. Unfortunately, in excess of 30 per cent of Americans and Australians can now be classified as sedentary (that is, people who perform no measurable physical activity), whilst close to 50 per cent are overweight or obese (ABS, 1998; *Physical Activity and Health: a Report of the Surgeon General*, 1996). This is exacerbated by the fact that only 10 per cent of people get the recommended minimum of daily activity required for basic health. Why is it so difficult for people to be active? Well, office-based life doesn't help. Many people drive to work, park in the office carpark, walk no more than 100 metres to the lift, sit down and stay seated until it is time to drive home. Lunch is often taken at the workplace, and is frequently a poor nutritional choice. The long hours worked by many also discourage exercise, so that people must exercise early in the morning or later in the evening, something which, in itself, is unbalanced, because it interferes with social and family activity. Nevertheless, only 60 minutes of accumulated daily physical activity can enhance physical and psychological health (*Physical Activity and Health*, 1996). To address this, many organizations are installing both active and passive mechanisms for providing physical activity by employees (for example, Brophy Marcus, 2000; Conlin, 2002), including sponsored gym memberships, time during the day to exercise, workplace team sports, in-house group exercise provision, and financial encouragement to use public transport or cycling in preference to driving. Other ideas for companies planning new premises include situating car parks further from the workplace, and providing fewer lifts or escalators. Remember that physically and psychologically healthier people are a definite asset to an organization. They are more productive, less often absent, more confident and happier than their unfit or overweight counterparts. However, it's quite hard for most people to commence or maintain any form of exercise programme. They need encouragement, but more importantly, the physical activity has to be very easy to access.

Telecommuting

One type of flexible working that has received a lot of attention in recent times is telecommuting, defined as: "working remotely from the employer or traditional placed work" (Madsen, 2003); "boundaryless work performed where it makes the most sense", such as from a home office, satellite offices, on the road, or in neighbourhood telework centres (Potter, 2003); or the "substitution of all or part of the daily commute with the use of a communications channel" (Ellen &

Hempstead, 2002). According to Raines and Leathers (2001), in 1999, 19.6 million US employees engaged in some form of telecommuting, whilst over 50 per cent of companies employing more than 500 persons offered telecommuting as an alternative to regular work schedules. In more recent times, the massive increase in home computer ownership and broadband Internet connection, coupled with the rise of information-based jobs, has allowed the incidence of telecommuting to escalate: some 65 per cent of all US jobs are now amenable to teleworking at least on a part-time basis (Potter), a figure that appears to be backed up by the presence of an estimated 50 million US home offices (Ellen & Hempstead). Moreover, increased fears about travel safety since the US terrorist attack in 2001 have meant that the popularity of telecommuting has increased, especially as a replacement for work travel (Potter). In fact, the increasing popularity of telecommuting as an alternative to regular work has led some theorists to predict the collapse of the traditional workplace, even going so far as to imagine a future in which telecommuting will make the concept of the city as a central workplace redundant (Ellen & Hempstead).

As a strategy to increase work–life balance, telecommuting appears to be at least moderately successful. For instance, according to Raines and Leathers (2001), employees given the opportunity to telecommute on a regular basis reported that their more flexible work hours and schedules resulted in an improved quality of work, social, and home life. Similarly, Madsen (2003), in her study of telecommuting among 172 employees from seven Minneapolis companies, reported that teleworkers experienced significantly lower work-life conflict and perceived their health levels as substantially higher than their non-telecommuting co-workers. Other telecommuting benefits include a more positive outlook towards work, and a better work–life balance, especially among employees with children (Ory et al., 2004), increased employee loyalty (Paul & Anantharaman, 2004), greater job satisfaction with a consequent feeling of better recognition for workplace contributions (Schwartz, 2000), reduced absenteeism (Pousette & Hanse, 2002), a lowered rate of employee turnover (Batt, Colvin, & Keefe, 2002), and a surplus of time: telecommuting can save an hour a day in average commute times, or in excess of 90 minutes in high-density areas (Potter, 2003).

Telecommuting can also be advantageous to firms. For example, according to Potter (2003) and Madsen (2003), organizations that have successfully introduced telecommuting programmes have seen a decrease in absenteeism (gaining the equivalent of 22 work days a year per telecommuting employee from time that would have been lost to employees' family or personal needs), and a concurrent increase in productivity of between 10 and 40 per cent: 54 per cent of telecommuting employees reported that they worked greater or equal numbers of hours than they did when at the office, whilst still being able to manage the personal or family affairs that would have kept them out of the office, and 47 per cent estimated that they were more productive when working from home. Moreover, companies that offer telecommuting programmes are more popular among job seekers (Madsen), making them more competitive recruiters, as well as remaining appealing to their existing employees: Potter has estimated that for each worker retained through telecommuting policies a company saves close to US$8000 in direct and indirect turnover costs. Lastly, for each day an employee works at home, a company is likely to benefit from a 22 per cent productivity increase, equating to US$1850 annually per employee for 50 days worked at home (Potter). It is worth noting, however, that productivity gains from teleworking are most likely when an individual telecommutes one to three times per week (Madsen). This allows an increase in the balance of work and home life, but enables the employee to maintain a visible presence in the office, and allows management to adjust over time to the concept of absent but productive workers.

Its benefits notwithstanding, telecommuting is not without problems. As we have seen earlier, being out of the office can conflict with the modern managerial tendency to assess an employee's productivity based on his or her face-time (Porter & Bostrom, 1996). Consequently, a principal concern of tele-commuting workers is that, because they are out of sight of direct supervision, their productivity will be underestimated, resulting in a lack of advancement (Raines & Leathers, 2001), a problem that is magnified for female workers (Rogier & Padget, 2004). As well, because the workplace is a principal source of friendship and social interaction for many people (Potter, 2003; Spiezia, 2002), telecommuting can result in greater social isolation; consequently, because social interaction and support is a primary buffer against stress (Fairbrother & Warn, 2003), telecommuting practices could have an opposite effect from their intended goal of work-life stress reduction. Telecommuting can also be elitist: Ellen and Hempstead (2002) in their investigation of data collected by the US Census Bureau have reported that although telecommuting is offered by over 37 per cent of employers, only between 1 and 5 per cent of employees are in a position to telecommute. Apart from fears of work penalization and social isolation, Ellen and her colleague have indicated that only employees who are relatively senior, who are better educated and more affluent, and who work in professions that do not require regular office face time (for example, consulting, sales, public relations) are able to take advantage of telecommuting programmes. Moreover, the methodology behind telecommuting programmes can affect their success: according to Madsen (2003), because of the current popularity of telecommuting, programmes are often introduced without adequate prepar-ation, design, or evaluation. Consequently, many employees participating in these programmes find themselves unsupported and isolated from the workplace mainstream or, due to lack of training in time management or goal setting, are simply unable to motivate themselves outside of the office environment (Madsen). Accordingly, to reduce the likelihood of telecommuting problems, and to achieve its potential productivity benefits, Madsen has recommended that organizations take care to design a programme properly before its imple-mentation, paying particular attention to its evaluation and the ongoing support of telecommuting workers. Potter concurs, suggesting that the "line of sight" management prevalent in many firms is counterproductive. He recommends that for a telecommuting programme to be successful, organizations must train not only their telecommuting staff but also their supervisors and managers, stressing the importance of continued support for their subordinates, and encouraging a shift from the predominant management by enforcement to management by results.

Their problems notwithstanding, work–life balance efforts that give employees greater control over when and where they work, such as flextime and telecommuting programmes might, according to Beers (2000), eventually completely replace the traditional "nine to five" work day. Quoting 1997 data, Beers has reported that more than 27 per cent of US employees vary their work hours to some degree from the customary format, a rise of over 15 per cent since 1985. More recently, this figure has been estimated at closer to 40 per cent (Almer & Kaplan, 2002).

Nevertheless, despite flexible working efforts, such as telecommuting and flextime, to increase work–life balance and improve HRM, as we have seen throughout this chapter, organizations are frequently failing to address HR issues, often with negative outcomes for both the employer and the employee.

Part 3: The current role of human resources management

A large proportion of this book focuses on the importance of human beings in the workplace. This information is aimed at guiding corporations to realise the worth of their human or intangible assets (otherwise known as human resources). As we will see, organizations that focus on the well-being of their human resources perform substantially better than their rivals. However, given the importance of human resources to the performance and productivity of an organization, it is remarkable that HRM is often treated as a necessary evil of having employees, whilst HR departments are frequently regarded as backwaters of corporate functioning, in which nothing of particular value to the organization is done (Belout *et al.*, 2001).

Traditionally, HRM has been concerned with tasks such as recruiting, staffing, orientation and training, performance appraisal, career management, restructuring, and relocation (Tziner, 2002). Tziner argues that whilst each of these activities is highly important for the effective running of an organization, HR departments are seldom given the budget or power needed to adequately oversee the implementation, evaluation, or evolution of their mandates. It is ironic therefore that although modern companies spend vast amounts on R&D for areas that they believe will increase fiscal return, HRM (which performed effectively can substantially improve company profitability) seldom receives much in the way of funding and is often the target of economic cuts (Harrison & Kessels, 2004). In fact, in an increasing number of cases, the organizational enthusiasm for outsourcing has resulted in the contracting out of HR departments themselves (Belout *et al.*, 2001). As we will see, given the role of HRM in the productivity and profitability of an organization this bias can be a damaging oversight.

With the reduction of spending on HRM, in many organizations HRM has become primarily concerned with tasks that equate to little more than employee book keeping, with little effort made to encourage employee loyalty (Belout *et al.*, 2001; Richbell, 2001). For example, according to Belout *et al.*, in Canada, HRM is often poorly connected to the motivation of employees;

the assumption being either that employees should be responsible for their own motivation or that simple financial incentive or compensation schemes are motivation enough (Belout and her coauthors have criticized monetary-based compensation schemes as shallow, being too focused on remuneration at the expense of satisfaction,[9] and biased, in that they are often weighted towards more senior employees). HRM has also been co-opted as the first step in employee downsizing or outsourcing efforts (Richbell): often when an organization is considering reducing its workforce the HR department is approached to create a list of employees considered less desirable or expendable.

What then should be the role of HRM? According to Belout and her colleagues (2001), HR managers should be expanding their traditional roles to incorporate a link between human resources and the firm's business models. In this way, an organization's business plan becomes related to the performance and productivity of its employees, rather than assuming that the company will function independent of employee concerns. As well, HR managers should be concerned with providing innovative solutions (beyond simple remuneration) to increase employee productivity, by addressing employees' work–life balance and the quality of the work experience; should address the building of employee citizenship and the alignment of employer and employee interests; and should encourage the proper uptake and utilization of HRM policies by front-line managers and supervisors (Belout *et al.*). Moreover, HRM needs to further concern itself with the development of an organizational learning culture, the promotion of a clear and consistent vision throughout the firm, and the development of managerial and leadership ability (Harrison & Kessels, 2004).

As we have seen so far, the consequences of economically driven decisions about human resources have been financially unpleasant for many firms. We have also seen that "worker-friendly" organizations make for happier employees. Nevertheless, whilst these "human resources" are extremely important for the effective functioning of an organization, HR departments are typically relegated to token activities, such as payroll, or employee reduction schemes. In the next and following chapters, we will investigate further how "happy" employees can benefit the productivity and profitability of an organization, how firms can enhance their HRM, and how companies can extend beyond their human resource departments to capitalize on their intellectual capital.

Best practice: Case examples of how it's being done

Work–life balance

Achieving a good balance between work and life is a struggle for most employees and, given the lack of initiative taken by many organizations, often a low

---

[9] As we will see in Sections 3, 4, and 6, effective motivation requires more than the promise of a simple extrinsic reward. Intrinsic rewards such as job satisfaction and feelings of worth and support are substantially stronger motivators than fiscal rewards.

priority for firms (Barnett, 1999). Nevertheless, the business benefits for organizations that implement an effective work–life balance practice are numerous (Landauer, 1997). One firm, Millenium Bright Kid Company, recently singled out by the DTI for their excellent work–life balance practices (*Work-Life Balance and Flexible Working: The Business Case*, 2004), has found that concentrating on the work–life balance of their employees increased their profitability substantially. As a childcare provider, Millenium Bright found that they had difficulty recruiting well-qualified employees and had problems with staff retention, due to relatively high job stress and long working hours. Following the successful implementation of work-life policies, Millenium Bright reported better company-wide communication, a better working culture, a drop in staff turnover from 27 per cent to less than 10 per cent (saving the company over £12,000 in direct recruitment costs), and an increase in the retention of existing staff from 65 to 84 per cent. As well, the increased quality of communication meant that managers were better able to concentrate on staff development.

To achieve these changes, Millenium Bright introduced the following changes to their work practices:

- time off in lieu for any overtime worked by staff
- the introduction of staff training during working hours, to reduce intrusion into employees' private lives
- an increase in holiday time for longer-term staff
- a day off for each staff member on his or her birthday (beyond regular leave).

As well, to determine the continued efficacy of their work-life policies, Millenium Bright introduced an ongoing evaluation process. This included:

- continued feedback from staff and managers
- analysis of the number of sick days taken and of ongoing staff turnover.

Flexible working and telecommuting

As we have seen so far, both flexible working and telecommuting programmes can have positive effects on employee job satisfaction and health, and organizational productivity and profit (Schmidt & Duenas, 2002). In their analysis of UK-based companies who had successfully introduced and maintained flexible working programmes, the DTI (*Flexible Working*, 2004) highlighted the efforts of three organizations: Bristol Myers Squibb, Dutton Engineering, and Innocent.

Bristol Myers Squibb, a manufacturing firm in Britain's north west, wanted to increase their retention of qualified staff who had become parents. Because of their previously poor parental packages, this organization had faced difficulties keeping key employees who chose to have a family, especially those engaged in field work, either through resignation or through transfer to competing firms. Following the successful development of flexible working programmes aimed at working parents, Bristol Myers Squibb were able to increase retention of staff with families by a substantial margin. As well, the company has estimated a saving of around £30,000 per retained employee. Changes included:

- the introduction of a standardized request process for flexible working
- padoption leave
- helpline services for employees seeking assistance with childcare and eldercare
- the reduction of hours and the introduction of term-time working for field-based employees
- an online programme to provide work-life resources
- a career-break scheme.

Dutton Engineering, a smaller company based in south-east England, found that by making their working arrangements more flexible, staff productivity and company efficiency increased by an "incredible" margin, resulting in a rise in their market competitiveness. Rather than introduce parental leave schemes, Dutton Engineering contracted with each of its 50 staff to work a given number of hours per year, with a reserve of 160 hours to take account of problems such as sickness, medical appointments, and peak production times.

Dutton Engineering also introduced:

- A process whereby working hours were determined by customer demand rather than managerial expectation. This allowed the company to increase production when needed, but allow employees to take time off when work pressures were slower
- Changing the work requirement from hours worked to successful project delivery. Consequently, employees could work how they pleased on the proviso that products were delivered to the customer on time and to a high standard of quality
- When goals were met, employees were free to take time off for personal activities. This allowed workers to feel rewarded for a "job well done".

Innocent, a fruit smoothie company in England's South East with only 27 employees, chose to allow their employees to work in the way that each felt was best suited to his or her needs. Effectively, because each employee had a different way of working to his or her optimum, management at Innocent decided to let employees choose how they worked.

Some of the practices initiated included:

- Allowing workers to choose their working hours. For example, people who enjoyed getting up early and also leaving work early were able to start before the traditional 9 am, while those who preferred to start later were able to stay beyond normal closing of 5 pm. This was enacted without a "formal" flextime system – staff simply turned up and left when they wanted.
- Employees were encouraged to work from home or telecommute when they felt the need for time away from the office.

- Staff were encouraged to pursue interests outside of work, and requests for time off work to followup with these activities were usually granted. For example, one employee was able to work a four-day week so that he could study on Fridays, another was given a 6-week break in order to travel.
- A "hobby fund" has been introduced to help people pay for interests outside of work, and the company now offers free yoga classes to employees.

Benefits to Innocent included:

- A very high level of employee loyalty and job satisfaction, with minimal employee turnover, has been achieved.
- Innocent has become one of the fastest growing food and drinks companies in the United Kingdom, and has won several awards for its flexible working practices.

Points for action: Practical recommendations for change

Work–life balance

The Families and Work Institute (Gallinsky *et al.*, 2004) have several recommendations for employers wishing to improve the work–life balance situation of their employees. These include:

- basing any workplace changes on empirical research (such as the studies reviewed in this text)
- training supervisors to support employees in succeeding on the job
- allowing employees continued access to learning, including job-specific and general-life skills (for example, time management, interpersonal communication)
- allowing employees greater flexibility over the times and hours that they work
- letting employees have a say in managerial decision-making, and acting on their suggestions
- considering employees as individuals, not simple producers, who have interests and strengths outside of their direct job roles, and encouraging a balance between work and life
- reconsidering how work is performed by addressing the following:
  - focus: allowing employees uninterrupted time to concentrate on tasks without interruptions
  - job pressure: attempting to replace work pressures that are stressful (such as strict or unrealistic deadlines) with those that are stimulating (such as having control over a project)
  - low-value work: making sure that employees are able to concentrate on the important aspects of a project, rather than being distracted by low-level, day-to-day tasks

- accessibility: encouraging communication practices and time management so that people make themselves available to their colleagues when they are needed
- working during holidays: employers should discourage workers from taking work on vacation and should encourage them to take holidays regularly, and for longer periods. Holidays should allow employees to feel rested and recharged so it is important that work is reallocated when a person is on vacation (so that they will not waste their holiday dreading the pile of work waiting for them on their return).

Flexible working and telecommuting

In order to successfully implement flexible working at the place of work, the European Foundation for the Improvement of Living and Working Conditions (Naegele *et al.*, 2003) have suggested that organizations restructure the way in which the working week is perceived. That is, rather than counting the actual number of hours worked by a given employee, his or her work output can be measured by task completion. For example, in a system that determines worker effort by the number of hours worked there is little scope for job flexibility, because variations can only be made to working hours at a relatively basic level (for example, part-time work, job sharing, overtime payments, flextime). However, once work is measured on a task completion basis, there is the potential for almost unlimited job flexibility. In these cases, the employer and employee negotiate the time that will be required for a task to be completed, as well as the resources that will be available to the staff member during the task, with the only proviso being that the task be finished in a given time period to a given level of quality. It is then up to the employee to determine in what manner he or she will work on the task. Options can include:

- homeworking or teleworking
- working around team or resource availability
- choosing working hours that most suit the employee

According to Naegele *et al.* (2003), this style of working is beneficial to the employer as well as the employee. Allowing employees to choose how and when they work on a given project can ensure far greater commitment to that project, because workers are assessed on the quality of their completed work, rather than the number of hours clocked. As well, giving employees freedom to work flexibly on a project allows their supervisors to concentrate on keeping the project on track, rather than keeping count of hours worked. In this way the focus is on the actual work done, rather than implied or perceived work.

Summary

Unfortunately, many modern work practices have been inherited from earlier periods of history, resulting in several flawed modern work premises. First, the labour theory of values assumes that amount of labour is the key force in production. Whilst this premise is valid in manufacturing, the modern "knowledge-economy" is based on information work, which is very difficult to quantify. Consequently, when managers assume that amount of work is the main predictor of productivity, they risk irrelevance. Second, "work ethics" assume that leisure time is less important than work time, resulting in a culture of excessive work and endemic, low job satisfaction. Finally, the assumption that consumption is required for a strong economy has little value in a knowledge economy, in which innovation represents a better measure of organizational success.

Largely because of these flawed assumptions of productivity, work–life balance has suffered in the modern workplace. With the majority of employees unable to balance the pressures of their work and life, staff morale and productivity have been reduced, resulting in widespread organizational problems. Two potential solutions for better work–life balance are flexible working and teleworking. Flexible working is a process in which an attempt is made to balance the needs of the employee and the employer, and include options such as flextime, reduced working hours, a compressed working week, working from home, annualized hours, task-based working, term-time working, job sharing, and part-time work. Whilst the benefits of flexible working can include reduced absenteeism and turnover, increased organizational profitability, and employee productivity and job satisfaction, it is often difficult to implement; a prevailing corporate culture based around the notion that productivity requires time at work often results in a lack of support for flexible working initiatives from managers and supervisors, as well as reluctance from employees to be seen as not working hard enough. Teleworking, in which an employee works remotely using a technological solution to connect to the office, has also been successful in increasing work–life balance. Again, whilst there are many benefits to both the employer and employee from teleworking, it often suffers from the same implementation problems as flexible working schemes.

Finally, HRM has not kept up with the changing needs of employees in modern organizations. Traditionally, HRM departments were involved purely in personnel decision-making, and were not connected to the notion of employee well-being. Nevertheless, there has been substantial call for HR managers who can address work-life imbalances by increasing access to flexible working and enhancing work quality.

REVIEW QUESTIONS

1. Describe five actions that you could take as a manager or employer to increase the well-being of employees, and outline how these actions can increase both employee well-being and organizational performance, financially and otherwise.

2. What is work–life balance, and how can it be improved in the workplace?

3. What are the potential, positive outcomes of the effective application of work–life balance policies?

4. Describe some of the difficulties faced by both organizations and employees regarding the successful implementation of work–life balance.

5. As an HR manager, how would you go about helping employees find a balance between work and life, without reducing organizational performance?

6. How might you argue the potential organizational benefits of implementing an effective work–life balance programme to the board or your CEO?

Mind-diagram summary

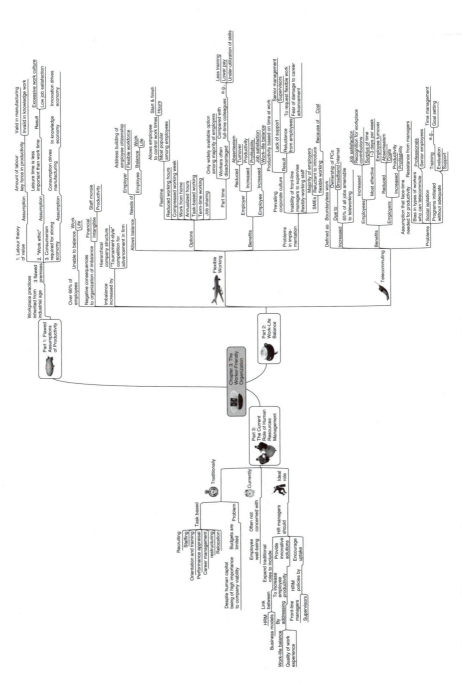

Chapter 3: The Worker-Friendly Organization

Part 1: Flawed Assumptions of Productivity

- Workplace practices inherited from industrial age
  - 1. Labour theory of value — Assumption
    - Amount of labour key force in productivity
      - Valid in manufacturing
      - Invalid in knowledge work
  - 2. "Work ethic" — Assumption
    - Leisure time is less important than work time
      - Result — Excessive work culture / Low job satisfaction
  - 3. Consumerism required for strong economy — Assumption
    - Consumption drives manufacturing
    - In knowledge economy
      - Innovation drives economy
- Over 66% of employees — Unable to balance Work / Life
- Negative consequences to organization of imbalance — Financial / Intangible
- Imbalance increased by
  - Hierarchical company structure
  - "Tournament-style" competition for advancement in firm
  - Staff morale
  - Productivity

Part 2: Work-Life Balance

- Address building of employee citizenship
  - Flexible workforce
- Allows balance — Needs of — Employer / Employee — Balance Work / Life

Flexible Working

- Allows employee to control work times
  - Most popular among employees
- Flexitime
  - Start & finish — Hours
- Reduced working hours
- Compressed working week
- Work from home
- Annualized hours
- Task-based working
- Term-based working
- Job sharing
- **Options**
  - Part time
    - Only widely available option among majority of employers
    - Workers often disadvantaged — Compared with full-time colleagues — e.g. Less training / Lower pay / Under-utilization of skills
- **Benefits**
  - Employer
    - Reduced — Turnover / Absenteeism
    - Increased — Productivity / Profitability
  - Employee
    - Increased — Job satisfaction / Work-life balance
    - Productivity based on time at work
- **Problems in implementation**
  - Prevailing corporate culture
  - Inability of front-line managers to supervise flexibly-working staff
  - Majority of employers — SMEs — Reluctant to introduce flexible working
  - Lack of support
    - Senior management
    - Supervisors
    - Reluctance from employees — To request flexible work — Because of — Cost / Fear of damage to career advancement

Telecommuting

- Defined as — Boundaryless work
- Increased — Due to
  - Ownership of PCs
  - Broadband Internet
  - 65% of all jobs amenable to teleworking
- **Benefits**
  - Employees
    - Job satisfaction
    - Recognition for workplace contributions
    - Surplus of time
  - Employers
    - Most effective 1–3 days per week
    - Reduced — Employee turnover / Absenteeism / Costs
    - Increased — Productivity / Profitability
- **Problems**
  - Resistance from managers
    - Assumption that face-time needed for productivity
    - Bias in types of workers who can telecommute
    - Professionals / Senior employees
  - Social isolation
  - Programs initiated without adequate
    - Training
    - e.g. Time management / Goal setting / Evaluation / Support

Part 3: The Current Role of Human Resources Management

- **Traditionally**
  - Task based
    - Recruiting
    - Staffing
    - Orientation and training
    - Performance appraisal
    - Career management / restructuring / Relocation
  - Problem — Budgets are limited
- **Currently**
  - Often not concerned with
    - Employee well-being
  - Despite human capital being of high importance to company viability
- **Ideal role**
  - HR managers should
    - Expand traditional roles to include
      - Employee well-being
    - To increase employee productivity
    - Provide innovative solutions
    - Encourage uptake
      - HRM policies by
        - Front-line managers
        - Supervisors
  - HRM — Link between
    - Business models
    - Quality of work experience
    - Work-life balance
    - By addressing

Enhancing Corporate Performance

Introduction

The primary aim of many organizations is to increase performance and profits. Habitually, performance indicators have included economic progress, acquisitions, and growth. However, as the following review will show, corporate practices such as human resources, effective management and vision are directly related to productivity and financial performance.

Section guide

In Chapter 4, "Human Resources Practices and Corporate Profitability", you will learn how HR practices have a direct impact on organizational performance, and about techniques that have been used to enhance human resource management (HRM). Chapter 5, "Strategic Principle, Vision and Mission", describes the necessity of company-wide awareness of goals, combined with a clear understanding of how these goals will be accomplished. Lastly, in Chapter 6, "Innovation Capability and the Future", you will read about the organizational importance of investment in non-financial resources and realization of human capital for increased company innovation, and ways for enhancing innovation in the firm by enhancing the position of the individual within the organization.

Reading objectives

By the end of this section you should have a clearer understanding of:

- how effective HRM can be a key ingredient in organizational success
- methods for more effective HRM

- why a company-wide vision is important, and why it is even more important that everyone in that company is aware of the vision, and is using the same version!
- how the notion of a "company" is changing
- why a traditional "profit-centred" organizational approach is not always in an organization's best interest
- why innovation is important to organizational success
- how investment in human capital can enhance innovation.

Human Resources Practices and Corporate Profitability

KEYWORDS   Absenteeism, asset, behaviour, competitors, profit, security, spending.

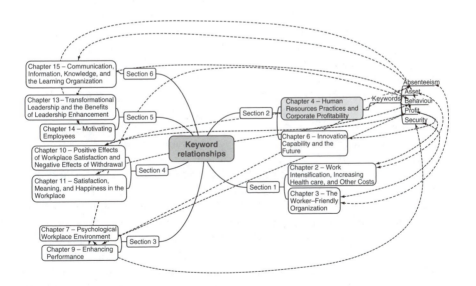

IMPORTANT CONCEPTS   Employee satisfaction, intangible assets.

In the first three chapters we looked at how the economy has changed over the last twenty years to incorporate knowledge and information as valuable resources that can have economic worth. We also examined how social and demographic changes, combined with changes in the way that employers and employees perceive the work relationship, have led to the introduction of a wide range of worker-friendly policies. Whilst these policies and practices undoubtedly enhance employee satisfaction and increase individual productivity, they also have a wider, organizational effect. In this chapter we will investigate how effective HRM and other company-wide practices can actually increase organizational profits.

Part 1: Human capital and the intangible asset

Organizations represent the sum of their components. As we have seen, many modern organizations are, in fact, knowledge producers; nevertheless, in these firms, despite their real economic performance, the tangible value of this knowledge is not easily measured. Consequently, according to Wang, Dou, and Li (2002), in an organization that bases its decisions on conventional accounting-based analyses, it is very difficult for senior managers to understand how spending on human resource development can lead to real financial gains for the organization. Wang and his colleagues believe that this problem is based on the modern-day use of accounting practices, originally developed in 1919 by the DuPont organization to decentralize financial control; whilst these practices were very successful for measuring financial performance in a relatively simple manufacturing environment, they were not designed for the more complicated problem of managing human resources because, simply put, people and the skills and knowledge that they bring to an organization are a lot more complicated to manage than machines. In other words, in the manufacturing environment of the early 1900s, financial decisions could be made by analysing the costs of raw goods, machinery, labour and maintenance, and distribution, and then determining a market price based on overall costs, market demand, and competitors' pricing schemes. Given that each of these variables was easily quantifiable, this process for measuring economic performance, return on investment, and determining financial strategy was relatively simple. However, in modern companies that produce knowledge-based products (for example, software), many operating variables become difficult to measure quantifiably. For example, in an organization that sells technology products, the ability to provide effective customer after-sales service might be a key market distinguisher. However, to develop strong customer support and to be able to measure its effectiveness requires attention to a much greater number of variables than when evaluating financial returns in manufacturing (for example, training of support staff, customer experience, resources available to support staff in dealing with customer enquiries, satisfaction of support staff, technical aspects of the support system, rapidity of support resolution, customer satisfaction), the majority of which cannot readily be quantified: simply put, customer support represents one of many aspects important to the successful running of a modern organization, and yet it remains difficult to quantify. Consequently, in the opinion of Wang *et al.*, whilst senior managers continue to rely on accounting practices that cannot be used to measure the financial effects of intangible variables, organizations will not be able to successfully innovate in a knowledge economy. Unfortunately, this lack of understanding regarding human factors in economic performance has been reflected in the accounting and economic literature.

Nevertheless, the "knowledge economy" appears to be here to stay. To illustrate, since 1900 the amount of labour needed to produce a given unit of manufacturing output has dropped by an estimated 1 per cent per year (Karp, 2003); mechanization, computerization, and modern methods have all but replaced human labour in modern manufacturing, but the production means for both mechanization and technological advancement in manufacturing are the result of another type of labour: innovation produced by organizational investment in intellectual capital and largely responsible for the ability to compete in a modern marketplace. Thus, whilst older manufacturing-based organizations regarded their money, machines, and factories as capital, modern firms are valued based on their intellectual or human assets which, although intangible, are recognized as a major source of their capital wealth, and influence their market and share value (Karp). Like Wang *et al.* (2002), Karp believes that intellectual capital, which can include intellectual assets, human capital, intangibles, knowledge and learning, is a difficult commodity for accountants and mangers to understand, because it is hard to measure and is often based on diffuse concepts such as know-how, training, intuition, and collaboration. Consequently, there is a growing disparity between knowledge companies' actual market value and their physical assets as recorded on accounting balance sheets, resulting in an average organizational market value four times greater than its book value (Karp): intellectual capital, therefore, can make up to 50 per cent of the value of modern manufacturing companies, and over 90 per cent of the value of e-commerce companies. Karp has also pointed out that intellectual capital is non-rival, meaning that unlike tangible resources which can only be deployed individually and take resources from rival assets, intellectual capital can be widely deployed at the same time for multiple uses (for example, software running on many machines simultaneously versus use of a single computer); thus leveraging of intellectual capital is limited only by the size of a given market.

Intellectual capital, therefore, is extremely valuable, but remains extremely difficult to account for through traditional means. In the opinion of Karp (2003), despite the inability of accounting models to explain intellectual capital, its cultivation is key to the economic development of most modern firms but this development is hampered by outmoded management models that are reliant on conventional accounting: less than 15 per cent of managers understand how to measure intellectual capital. In other words, whilst modern managers are beginning to understand that the market values their company on the strength of its intellectual capital, they are unable to realize or increase its worth because they cannot quantify it. In order to pass this hurdle, Karp believes that managers must realize that an organization's intellectual capital is dependent on the firm's social capital which, in effect, represents an organization's ability to harness the value of its employees. Thus, by investing in its HRM, a company stands a strong chance of increasing both social and intellectual capital.

According to Bartel (2004), research in the manufacturing sector has shown a strong, positive relationship between HRM and organizational performance. However, in the services industry (which makes up the majority of modern employment, the greater part of which is knowledge based), research demonstrating this relationship is lacking. The economic research that has addressed this issue has concluded that when other variables are accounted for, variations in performance between organizations are due not to human factors (because they were not measured) but rather to a "black box" phenomenon (Bartel). Unfortunately, this sort of conclusion is representative of organizations that are unable to see the value of investment in human resources. That is, as Karp (2003) pointed out, accounting-based practices make their practitioners unable to account for variables that cannot be readily quantified: accountants would rather envision a "magical" black box to explain intangible variables and their effects than expand their research focus to examine the potential causes of these "variations". As Bartel has indicated in her own research, in which she investigated economic performance differences between 160 branches of a large bank in Ontario, branch performance was significantly associated with HR practices. These included employees' perceptions of performance feedback, manager characteristics, and an employee reward and recognition system at the branch. Similarly, in an earlier case study, Bartel identified managerial differences between high-performing and low-performing branches: managers of high-performance branches were more people focussed, had more time for their employees, gave constructive and timely feedback, recognized achievement, and encouraged open communication between employees.

Consequently, it is certainly not impossible, or even particularly difficult, to explain the effects of qualitative variables, and certainly not necessary to invent "black box" solutions to account for human-based phenomena. Other recent contributions to the scientific and economic literature, as well as practitioner research and case examples, have made it very clear that, in organizations that effectively deal in knowledge, investment in human resources and the development of human capital have a very real positive effect on company profitability. In one such example, West and Patterson (1998), who conducted a seven-year longitudinal study of the HRM practices of 107 employers, have reported that HRM explained up to 20 per cent of the variability in company productivity and profitability. According to the investigators, employee skills utilization, one of the most important contributors to productivity, was enhanced substantially both by a combination of effective recruiting and selection in the hiring phase and through the creation of jobs that promoted autonomy, flexibility, and problem solving, and that allowed employees to use their existing skills in a creative, supported manner. Further, West and Patterson reported that by allowing employees to develop new skills, through the provision of training, and the successful introduction of coaching and, mentoring programmes, employee, and, in turn, company-wide, productivity was substantially increased. Similarly, HR practices that focussed on enhancing relationships in and out of the workplace, and that encouraged health and fitness, also had a strong effect on efficiency. To enact this change, West and Patterson have suggested that employers pay substantially more attention to their HRM, so as to encourage a workplace environment that utilizes favourable reward systems, increases employee involvement in decision-making, and promotes harmonization between employees and their relations with management. Similarly, following HRM interventions, a single-point increase (on a scale of 1 to 5) in employee commitment can increase monthly retail sales by 9 per cent (worth over £200,000 in one UK chain), whilst listed companies with committed employees can expect a 36 per cent greater three-year total shareholder return than organizations with low employee commitment (Tuffrey, 2003).

Guest, Michie, Conway, and Sheehan (2003) have also reported a strong relationship between HRM practices and company performance. Following their investigation of 610 HR managers from both manufacturing and service-based industries, Guest and his co-investigators reported a positive association between HRM practices (including feedback, rewards and benefits, flextime, and supervisory support) and reduced employee turnover as well as increased company profitability. They also found that effective HRM increased employee and organizational performance even when subjective variables, such as assessments of performance and employee feedback were included in their analyses. Guest *et al.* concluded that the effective deployment of human resources leads to organizational competitive advantage because the performance of the company as a whole is almost entirely dependent on the combined productivity and innovation of its individual employees.

According to Richard and Johnson (2001), who assessed the responses of 73 HR executives on company HR practices against firm performance, the development of effective HR practices is important to any company because, once developed, this investment in human capital represents a substantial company-wide asset; that is, because of their excellent human resources, these companies become a commodity that is hard to duplicate, has no direct substitutes and, because of its strong, enabled workforce, facilitates the increased pursuit of opportunity. In other words, Richard and his co-worker have posited that companies that invest time and resources in the development of HR performance, placing employee worth above the value of physical, technical, or financial resources, perform better than their competitors simply because they are so hard to emulate. However, given that the findings of Richard and Johnson were based on a 23 per cent return rate to a questionnaire of no established validity, their conclusions should be approached with some caution.

Cogan (2000), in a similar vein to Richard and Johnson (2001), has written that, historically, company management has viewed employees simply as a means to enhance customer satisfaction, with the expectation that staff satisfaction was the responsibility of the individual employee. Consequently, according to Cogan, in recent times there has been an increased level of absenteeism and staff turnover, directly related to increased employee dissatisfaction (on average, in industrialized countries, employees stay with a given firm for only three years before seeking a new job (Cogan)). Nevertheless, as we saw in Section 1, Cogan has indicated that these changing lifestyles and job expectations have led employees to look to organizations to provide an increased level of workplace satisfaction. Thus, because workplace satisfaction has been strongly correlated with productivity, in some organizations employers have been required to recognize human productivity as the key indicator of corporate success, and make appropriate investment in human capital to enhance worker satisfaction.

One way of enhancing employee satisfaction (with the expectation of enhancing company profitability through enhanced employee performance) is through the HR practice of effective performance appraisal. According to Roberts (2002), performance appraisal is most effective when, in order to develop a perception of fairness, it involves a high level of employee participation. Further, Roberts has suggested that to effect an evaluation that is both useful and perceived as just, it is important to develop a climate of trust and communication, to utilize goal setting and appropriate, timely feedback, and to ensure that the employee has understood the evaluation process and accepts it as useful. Moreover, allowing employees to self-rate, within a set of performance standards that are clear and specific, can also enhance the appraisal process. This suggestion becomes particularly important in the light of a report by Mani (2002), who has pointed out that as employee appraisal is often used as a principal criteria for layoffs, terminations, promotions, pay increases, and the assessment of training quality and equitable treatment, it is vital that it be conducted in a worthwhile and valid manner. In his investigation of satisfaction with work appraisal methods in 69 university staff, Mani reported that, in his sample, motivation was significantly enhanced by the perception of fair assessment as well as positive feelings (such as trust and satisfaction) by an employee towards his or her supervisor.[10]

In a particularly interesting article, Barrett (1999) has posited that the intangible value that a company assigns to its employees, and the recognition of the worth of these assets, will have a substantial impact on that company's economic success. However, to do so requires viewing the needs of employees in a different light. For instance, Barrett has proposed that the alignment of an employees' work and his or her personal passions can allow workers to regard the workplace as a means not just for a weekly paycheque but also for personal fulfilment. In other words, workers become committed to their workplaces, because they are provided with more than just a source of income. Barrett has described these workers as intellectual resources, because they represent motivated, stimulated persons who are committed to their employer; moreover, it is the company's ability to mine this resource that Barrett has labelled "cultural capital". According to Barrett, to begin manufacturing cultural capital, a company-wide values audit is necessary, in which traditional organizational values (such as economic reward) are questioned. Barrett has suggested that, during this process, company leaders address employee needs at a physical, intellectual, emotional, and even spiritual level. At the physical level, managers are required to address the basic issues of adequate financial compensation, a safe working environment, and the provision of correct tools and resources needed to get the job done. However, this represents only a basic investment in intellectual capital. To more readily realize potential cultural capital, employers need to address intellectual needs, such as the encouragement of ideas contribution

---

[10] For a much more in-depth investigation of workplace satisfaction, and individual productivity, see Sections 3 and 4.

and creativity; emotional needs, including effective communication, expressed appreciation, and empathic relationships between staff and managers; and spiritual needs, such as encouraging workers to feel that they make a difference in the company, and to align an employee's work with his or her passions.

After an evaluation of the ability of 100 *Fortune* 500 companies to mine their cultural capital, Barrett (1999) reported that 69 per cent of employee satisfaction in these corporations was directly related to a combination of the perceived quality of employees' relationships with management, and their ratings of managers' empowerment skills. Moreover, in the *Fortune* 500 companies rated as best to work for (highest reported levels of employee satisfaction), shareholder return averaged 23 per cent, 9 per cent higher than the US national company average of 14 per cent. Most noteworthy was the result that employee satisfaction accounted for 39 per cent of the variability in company financial performance. Given the large number of variables that affect a company's economic output, a single variable that can explain close to half of a company's profitability ought to be held in high consideration. Nevertheless, Barrett's research has shown that worker unhappiness and dissatisfaction are at a record high, twice the reported level of 40 years ago.

Because of the large economic gain to be made by organizations that employ satisfied workers and because of the strong relationship between employee satisfaction and a company's investment in cultural capital, in order to enhance a company's ability to harvest cultural capital, Barrett (1999) has documented what he believes to be seven levels of organizational development. Each of these levels represents a developmental level that, much like psychological developmental theory, must be overcome before progression to the next stage can occur. Thus, at each stage the organization becomes more complex and advanced in its internal and external actions and policies. The first stage, labelled "survival consciousness", represents a typical company concerned mostly with financial survival. In this state, company management focusses predominantly on the financial "bottom line" and remains insecure about future prospects. According to Barrett, in this phase employees are often seen simply as resources: useful, but not particularly valuable. In the second level, "relationship consciousness", more established companies begin to form more complex interactions with their customers, their employees, and their competitors. Nevertheless, at this stage, companies are often somewhat traditional in both their outlook and actions (many family companies remain at this stage), and are relatively inflexible, having instituted strict rules for workers without having first developed trust in their employees' abilities (especially to innovate). In the third stage, labelled "self-esteem consciousness", companies most often try to be the best in a given field. This, according to Barrett, is a dangerous period, because the company often tries its utmost to become highly competitive, with a constant emphasis on improvement. Whilst this can stimulate innovation and development, the cost of this philosophy is often a bureaucratic organization that pursues cost-effectiveness without considering the less tangible costs of its actions: for example, laying off low-end workers (that is, those considered dispensable) without concern for morale, or the increased workload placed on remaining employees. At the fourth level, "transformational consciousness", Barrett has described companies that have begun to pay attention to the intangible worth of their employees. In these companies, management is better able to perceive broader indicators of success (beyond simple economic performance), including concepts such as vision, mission, and values. Managers encourage employee participation and involvement in company affairs (especially the development of vision and values), realizing human capital by attempting to change perceptions of control to those of trust, punishment to incentive, and exploitation to ownership. At the fifth level, "organizational consciousness", an organization has become focussed on the development of employee satisfaction, having realized that satisfied employees contribute substantially to the company's economic worth and health. These firms attempt to align organizational values with the personal values of their employees, opting for values transparency and equality. Moreover, they attempt to foster employee growth, both professionally (by encouraging skills development and confidence) and personally, and attempt to develop a sense of internal (to the company) connectedness, increasing trust and promoting personal creativity and productivity. By the sixth level, "community consciousness", a company will have expanded its sense of duty beyond its employees and into the surrounding community, by developing external ties and relationships. This might include its employees' families and the external lives of employees, addressing physical, intellectual, emotional, and spiritual needs by asking employees directly what they need to feel satisfied in their lives, both in and outside of work, and acting on their responses. Finally, at the seventh level, "social consciousness", companies address their responsibility to the planet as a whole, assessing and minimizing their negative impact on future generations, and addressing their ethics, justice, and impact on human rights.

Other authors have expressed views similar to Barrett (1999) regarding the necessity for companies to operate beyond a bottom-line approach. Mayo (2000) for example, like Karp (2003) and Bartel (2004), has also suggested that the accountancy systems used by most modern businesses are out of date, and remain focussed on shorter-term profits to the detriment of their economic development. Similarly, as we have already discussed, according to Mayo most popular accounting systems are unsuitable for tracking the worth of intellectual resources. Mayo has suggested that, for modern accounting to reflect the finding that companies that value employee well-being are more likely to succeed financially, it is necessary that human resources be linked to the "bottom line". Consequently, Mayo has challenged companies to insist that their accountants assess an organization's true worth, by asking the question "what is left after the people have gone home?" In this way, *intellectual capital* (or *intangible assets*) can be defined as the value inherent in an organization that cannot be bought, upgraded, or sold. More specifically, this definition includes external structures (customer capital) such as brands, relationships, customer contacts, loyalty, satisfaction, image, market share, and reputation; internal structures (organizational capital) including knowledge, know-how, databases, patents, culture, systems, and methodologies; and human capital such as wisdom, judgement, individual competence and expertise, leadership, motivation, and team competence. Consequently, Mayo has calculated that the true market value of a company is, in fact, the product of its tangible assets (as represented in a formal balance sheet) and intangible assets, a figure similar to that reported by Karp (2003). This realization notwithstanding, like Karp, Mayo has warned that for an organization to appreciate the value of its intangible assets there must be a way of quantifying their value. Consequently, he has suggested that they be tracked by operationalizing their worth, and has provided several mechanisms for doing so. For instance, financial measures of inherent value can be made possible by evaluating the effect on firm productivity by consultants, the economic worth of long-term customer contracts, and/or the real replacement costs of people, systems, or knowledge bases. Similarly, the calculation of negative financial costs associated with the loss of key employees[11] or the lack of productivity that occurs when employees have a low level of motivation or commitment should be equally viable.

In line with the operationalization of intangible assets, Mayo (2000) has recommended that the professional growth of employees be quantified, by realizing that the development of individual employee skills can enhance company-wide value. This can be done, according to Mayo, by cataloguing a person's potential for growth, his or her ability to achieve, and what he or she brings to the workplace from other aspects of his or her life (such as skills, knowledge, and professional contacts). Similarly, a person's ability to lead, including his or her clarity of vision, and ability to communicate, as well as the organizational climate (in terms of individual freedom to be innovative, creative, and flexible), can also be valued with respect to an individual's quantifiable worth. Mayo has determined that this value can be calculated by statistical modelling: taking into account the intangible asset variables and linking them to financial performance outcomes. For example, in calculating individual intellectual capability, Mayo has suggested the development of a model that evaluates a person's personal capabilities, his or her professional and technical know-how, his or her network and range of professional contacts, and his or her values and actions that influence action, by linking these values to a financial performance indicator such as yearly turnover.

Mayo (2000) has also indicated that simple organizational modifications can be made to improve the value of human assets. For instance, individual motivation, according to Mayo, can be readily enhanced by matching people to roles that they find personally interesting and enjoyable. As he and other authors reviewed in this chapter have pointed out, employees that enjoy their work are more likely to be productive. Moreover, Mayo has advised that in any accounting of intangible assets, organizational management first appraise the corporate climate in order to determine whether the value of human resources is being adequately harnessed. This can be achieved, first, by evaluating whether individuals and teams are valued for their achievements or punished for their mistakes; this variable determines whether there is a cultural climate for learning and advancement. Second, when mistakes are made, it is necessary to establish whether they can be used as learning opportunities (as in an ongoing social experiment), or whether they represent an incentive to hide the results and

---

[11] See Section 4 for a more detailed discussion of estimating the costs of psychological withdrawal in the workplace.

to blame others. Third, management should question whether innovation is adequately encouraged and rewarded. If so, are people able to innovate without asking for permission? Fourth, it is necessary to understand if adequate resources are provided to allow both employees and management to complete the tasks set them in an efficacious manner. Finally, the firm must resolve whether knowledge is shared throughout the organization or whether it is guarded by individual departments: knowledge is only powerful to an organization when it is spread effectively to its constituent members.

On a positive note, Smith, Ockowski, Noble, and Macklin (2003), in their survey of 3400 private sector enterprises in Australia, have reported that many organizations are beginning to invest substantially in HRM as the result of the influence from the United States of a series of "new management practices" (NMPs). NMPs, according to Smith *et al.*, represent new ways in thinking about the role of management and its relationship to the workforce. In many of the NMP philosophies, the manager is seen more as a facilitator or guide for his or her subordinates (rather than as the traditional "boss") whose role is to encourage a situation in which employees can work with greater autonomy, support, and feedback and, in theory, help to increase both individual and company-wide productivity and profitability (Smith *et al.*). Unfortunately, many NMPs are delivered as a "one size fits all" package, in which a central philosophy is adhered to as the only method for organizational transformation. Nevertheless, according to the findings of Smith and his co-workers, the introduction of certain NMPs including Total Quality Management, the learning organization, and teamworking is highly correlated with an increase in training expenditure, particularly regarding the training of managers (especially supervisors and line managers); and focussing on behavioural and communications skills, a greater use of mentoring and coaching,[12] increased worker autonomy, and the increased use of team-based practices.

Whilst the majority of studies have focussed on the relationship between HR practices and organizational performance in large firms, other researchers have indicated that smaller companies can also benefit financially from investment in human capital. For instance, de Kok and Uhlaner (2001) in their investigation of 20 small Dutch companies found that SMEs that invest in their HRM can increase their financial performance to a degree similar to larger firms. Nevertheless, de Kok and his co-author, who defined HRM as "a process of attracting, developing, and maintaining a talented and energetic workforce to support organizational mission, objective and strategies", also reported that many SMEs are faced with a quandary when choosing to invest in human capital: whilst it is important for knowledge-based companies to attract highly skilled employees in order to compete, it is also necessary to be able to motivate and retain these employees, both of which require spending. With a high-commitment model of HRM, resulting in an employee base that is well paid and motivated, in an atmosphere of trust and open communication, SMEs can see substantial increases in their performance and competitiveness, with lower

---

[12] See Section 6 for a more detailed discussion of the benefits mentoring and coaching in the workplace.

costs resulting from absenteeism and turnover (de Kok & Uhlaner). However, de Kok and his colleague, who also found a positive relationship between company size and spending on HR practices, have warned that many SMEs are reducing their ability to innovate and compete by neglecting to invest in their human capital through failure to adequately train their staff and managers. In the opinion of de Kok and Uhlaner, a reluctance to spend money on HRM is a common failing of small business owners, and represents a lack of ability to plan for the long-term competitiveness of their organization; SMEs that hope to survive should, according to de Kok and Uhlaner, take a "resource-based view" by working towards developing a human resource base that is durable, difficult to substitute or replace, and that can differentiate an organization from its competitors. Nevertheless, because human capital investment is time-consuming and resource costly, small business owners require a long-term view, focussing on the eventual outcome rather than short-term costs.

Bosma, van Praag, Thurik, and de Wit (2004) have reported similar findings to de Kok and Uhlaner (2001): following an investigation of over 2000 small Dutch firms over three years, they concluded that SME success was highly dependent on the business founder's ability to recognize and invest in human capital for their business, and reported a high positive correlation between company profitability and formalized, well-developed HR practices. Further, business owners with higher levels of education, prior business experience, and former experience as an employee were more likely both to recognize the importance of human capital and to invest in its development through HR practices, resulting in greater organizational success.

Part 2: The organizational climate

As we have seen, HRM practices are significantly related to organizational profit. However, as we have also discussed, there is reluctance among many senior managers to invest in something that their accounting models cannot easily quantify. Consequently, not only are many organizational leaders loathe to invest in HR, they also place heavy demands on their HR departments to justify any spending directed their way (Batt & Valcour, 2003). As there are a large range of HRM possibilities, it is therefore quite important for HR managers to make sure that the practices they implement are likely to result in the right type of organizational climate: one in which savings resulting from HR practices are obvious, representing a tangible outcome from investments in intangible resources. In their investigation of this question, Batt and her co-worker (2003) evaluated a series of HR workplace practices against turnover, a distinct source of organizational costs. After assessing 557 employees, 71 per cent of whom were at a managerial or professional level, Batt and Valcour determined that lower quit rates were significantly related to HR practices. Specifically, they found that employees were much more likely to remain with the company when there was adequate work–life balance (for example, flexible scheduling, childcare), when they were given adequate benefits (for example, a high salary, job security, and access to career development), and when their jobs were designed to encourage productivity (for example, decision autonomy, coordination responsibilities, flexible use of technology, lower-than-average work hours, and balanced travel demands).

In fact, whilst HR practices (including flexible working) have been shown to be of distinct financial value to organizations (for example, through reduction in costs associated with turnover), these practices are really just a process that can enable a particular organizational climate to occur. As we have seen so far, and will continue to investigate in greater depth in later chapters, there are many ways of enhancing the organizational climate so that employees are more satisfied and productive. Nevertheless, given the need for many senior administrators to see tangible savings or increased company profits following investment in HR, it is important that they understand how the correct implementation of these practices, to form a specific organizational climate, can increase company viability. Consequently, several researchers have focussed their attention on defining and improving the organizational climate.

McMurray, Scott, and Pace (2004) have defined organizational climate as "member's collective perceptions about their organization" with respect to autonomy, trust, cohesiveness, support, recognition, innovation, and fairness. According to these authors, the literature shows that an individual's organizational commitment (that is, his or her loyalty and dedication to the organization), which has a direct bearing on his or her motivation, enhances the likelihood of increased tenure (with consequent lowered absenteeism), stimulates the individual's accomplishment of organizational goals, and is highly influenced by the organizational climate. To test this supposition, McMurray *et al.* measured the organizational commitment levels of 1413 employees from 3 global automotive companies based in 42 different countries. The investigators reported that when employees perceived the organizational climate to be healthy, they were significantly more committed to their employer. In contrast, among employees with negative perceptions of work conditions, supervision, compensation, advancement, relationships with colleagues, organizational rules, decision-making practices, and available resources, a laissez-faire attitude was substantially more common and there was a significantly greater chance of turnover.

In a similar investigation, Meyer and Smith (2000) reported that organizational climate, represented by employees' perceptions of both the firm's HRM practices and its commitment to HRM activities (including good employee attitude and retention and a sense that HRM spending is geared towards creating a caring environment rather than simply to increase productivity), was significantly related to employees' organizational commitment. In their research, Meyer and Smith indicated that affective commitment (Allen & Meyer, 1990) (that is, representing a person's emotional attachment to, identification with, and involvement in an organization) was the strongest predictor of an individual's likelihood to remain with a company, reducing the likelihood of turnover. Moreover, when they investigated this phenomenon in 94 employees from several US organizations, Meyer and his colleague found that HRM practices that increased affective commitment in employees were mediated by employee perceptions of organizational support and procedural justice. Thus, according to Meyer and Smith, when a firm invests in HRM practices that are focussed on career development, it has an opportunity to demonstrate its support and commitment to its employees which, in turn, is likely to foster greater employee affective commitment, resulting in lowered turnover, harder, more focussed work, greater levels of initiative, and increased company savings. Paul and Anantharaman (2004), who completed a similar investigation of 370 software engineers from 35 Indian companies, reported analogous findings. In their study, affective organizational commitment among employees was positively associated with perceptions of organizational climate and consequent job performance. HRM practices most likely to enhance perceptions of organizational climate and therefore increase organizational commitment, included work environment, career development, development-oriented appraisal system, and comprehensive training variables. More specifically, employee organizational commitment was greatly enhanced when HRM was aimed at creating a workspace with a pleasant physical infrastructure, strong support, an informal culture and good communication that emphasized career development as a form of ongoing commitment to the employee, that projected genuine interest in the development of the employee and his or her skills, and that included comprehensive training so that employees felt more confident to innovate and express creativity.

Another way of enhancing the organizational climate to foster greater commitment and reduce company expenses is for firms to make a long-term commitment to their employees (Kandel & Pearson, 2001). In recent times, US firms have begun to adopt a long-time Japanese workplace practice known as "lifetime employment" (LTE), in which an organization guarantees lifelong employment and discourages employee turnover by applying a pay scale that increases steeply with tenure. In their review of the literature pertaining to LTE, Kandel and his colleague reported that when employees cannot be dismissed at will they become less concerned with the threat of job loss, resulting in better relations between employees and management, increased employee eagerness to invest their time in human capital development, and a lower chance of sabotage. Moreover, organizations that commit to LTE are more likely to invest in the development of their employees (increasing human capital) by encouraging employee cross-training, worker initiative, local information gathering (to help utilize specific employee knowledge), self-regulation and autonomy, horizontal communication, and continuous improvement, and by developing cross-functional development teams and enacting profit-sharing schemes. Consequently, LTE is positively associated with organizational commitment, because employees feel that the firm is genuinely interested in their development and well-being, and also with substantially greater company productivity and profitability. According to Kandel and Pearson, because companies that practice LTE cannot fire their employees, they are forced to invest in ways to increase profitability that does not include workforce reductions. This can include increased attention to the financial benefit of investments in intangible resources, and can result in a labour force that is more adaptive and multiskilled, a more flexible manufacturing and innovation processes, and highly flexible contracts with suppliers and customers. Nevertheless, Kandel and Pearson admit that LTE practices are not necessarily viable for all employees in every company, and have therefore proposed a model in which companies invest in LTE with a core of skilled employees, surrounded by lower-skilled, more temporary employees. This, they suggest, represents a trade-off between the greater productivity of LTE firms and the greater flexibility inherent in a temporary workforce. However, without any research to test the real-world viability of their model, with respect both to company profitability and to employee performance, Kandel and Pearson's recommendations remain speculative.

Fostering a strong organizational climate appears, therefore, to be an effective way for firms to increase their profit margins by reducing the costs associated with employee dissatisfaction, such as absenteeism and turnover. This assumption can be further illustrated by comparison with organizations that have a poor organizational climate. On the one hand, for example, Hodson (2001), in his review of work practices, has highlighted the financial importance of participative organizations that attempt to encourage productivity through heightened worker involvement. Hodson has reported that in participative organizations, which encourage worker autonomy, rely on worker initiative, and have less need for tight forms of employee control, employees are motivated towards organizational citizenship behaviours (that is, greater commitment to the organization and its practices, higher productivity, and better interaction with co-workers) perceive a higher level of fairness within the organization, and are willing to invest time in the development of interpersonal and communication skills. Consequently, workers in participative organizations are less likely to have turnover intentions, or be regularly absent, resulting in higher company profitability. On the other hand, Hodson has pointed out that many firms have organizational climates that are either disorganized or unilateral. Disorganized workplaces have poor management structures in which managers fail to affect a system of production that is either workable or efficient. Likewise, disorganized workplaces have few constraints on managerial behaviour, resulting in chronic disorganization, rule by fiat, and a strong likelihood of managerial abuse of worker's rights. According to Hodson, this chaotic environment can lead to worker dissatisfaction, worker dissent, and resistance behaviours (including passive resistance such as "playing dumb", avoiding work, and withholding enthusiasm, and active resistance including social and machine-based sabotage, and informal group action against management or individual managers), a high level of hostility between employees and managers, a poor organizational climate, and a very low level of organizational commitment. Similarly, unilateral organizations, which emphasize one-way control in their normative framework, represent a challenge to participative work; unilateral firms often place a great deal of importance on direct supervision, automation of work, technological processes, and bureaucratic rules which restrict autonomy, often resulting in accommodation behaviours by employees (that is, strategies to minimize involvement in work without directly challenging authority, such as presenteeism, psychological withdrawal, or even neglect) (Hodson). Thus, whilst turnover is lower in unilateral than disorganized organizations, their employee productivity is typically low: because of the poor organizational climate, workers in unilateral firms are simply not motivated to work beyond the basic minimum required to retain their jobs.

In an economic environment of takeovers and retrenchments, a possible disruption to a strong organizational climate concerns management buyouts (Bacon, Wright, & Demina, 2004). Nevertheless, according to the findings of Bacon and his colleagues, when careful attention is paid to takeover strategy (including employee involvement in the process), HRM spending is actually likely to increase in an effort to retain valuable human capital by encouraging key employees to remain with the organization; a process referred to as a "soft" takeover. However, "hard" takeovers, which emphasize the role and power of investors over management, usually result in reduced HRM spending, a reduction in the quality of organizational climate, and a likely exodus of key employees and the consequent loss of human capital. As we saw in Section 1, companies that lose human capital following redundancies or the loss of key employees are not likely to perform well.

Best practice: Case examples of how it's being done

Human capital and corporate profitability

In their recent report, the Task Force on Human Capital Management (*Accounting for People*, 2003) highlighted the need for organizations to report not only their yearly financial activities but also their efforts to manage and cultivate their human capital. One such report from Unilever UK, a large consumer goods firm, has underlined this organization's apparent commitment to the development of its human capital, as well as its awareness of the organizational savings inherent in human capital investment. In their report, Unilever have outlined a "UK People Strategy" for increasing both proactive and reactive HR interventions in order to deliver their business plan. Unilever have identified four areas in which they have recently increased HR spending and focus: leadership, talent management, culture, and efficiency and effectiveness.

Under the "leadership" banner, Unilever have:

- committed to increasing leadership training for managers, including leadership teams which attempt to build relationships between managers and their subordinates, and increase manager self-awareness and behavioural/communication skills;
- introduced intensive, six-month leadership training programmes;
- introduced coaching programmes across all levels of management, as well as programmes that enable managers to act as coaches.

The efficacy of this programme was assessed internally by using company-wide surveys and 360-degree feedback for managers. Unilever have reported that since the introduction of their leadership programme, employee commitment and satisfaction has increased above the UK norm, resulting in a net decrease in turnover.

Unilever's "talent management" programme was aimed at "attracting, keeping and nurturing" employees identified as highly talented, with the aim of increasing overall effectiveness and company reputation as an employer of top-quality staff. To effect these ambitions, Unilever instituted:

- a graduate trainee scheme
- procedures for succession planning and identifying high potential
- open, internal job posting
- the possibility for fully supported overseas postings
- career counselling
- formal career breaks
- a flexible working policy.

To assess the effects of these initiatives, Unilever implemented formalized, documented reviews of the progress of each area, and a regular review of their performance by the company board. Unilever have reported that since its initiation the "talent management" programme has resulted in an increased graduate intake at management level, an increase in the perceived attractiveness of Unilever as a career option by graduates, and an increase in female managers.

Unilever's "culture" programme was aimed at increasing the company's employee diversity and at making the working climate more "fun". To implement these initiatives, they

- introduced a "code of business principles" or mission statement
- encouraged development of organizational citizenship behaviours
- developed a partnership initiative to encourage employee creativity through alignments with organizations and institutions external to Unilever
- commenced a formal employee reward and recognition programme.

A biannual employee survey was introduced to measure the impact and success of these programmes. Unilever claimed that, following the introduction of these programmes, they scored above the UK norm on cultural diversity, employee involvement in corporate decisions, and organizational openness.

Finally, the "efficiency and effectiveness" programme, which was put in place to develop "simple, uncluttered and transparent structures and processes", was aimed at corporate "leanness". To affect change in this area, Unilever attempted a policy of continual improvement, by harvesting human capital. This included a reward system to create "individual accountability", rewarding employee initiatives that resulted in net savings to the organization. Unilever have reported annual savings of £11 million based on these initiatives, and have won several awards for their management processes, especially in their manufacturing plants.

According to the UK DTI, Toughglass Ltd., a UK-based manufacturing organization, recently made substantial changes to its operating procedures in order to compete with other firms offering new technology (*High Performance Workplaces*, 2004). Whilst a part of this "upgrade" included new machinery and technology, the company also invested a substantial amount of time and resources in "up-skilling" their workforce and management in order to be more competitive. This investment in human capital included training and development in e-commerce, IT training and the latest industry improvements, as well as management and leadership training for managers (including behavioural and communications skills). Following their human capital investments, Toughglass were able to successfully expand their business into Europe, gaining over £2 million in new contracts. At the same time, over 90 per cent of their staff reported that the training and new management practices increased both their ability to do their jobs and their satisfaction at work.

The organizational climate

The DTI (*High Performance Through People*, 2005) recently showcased the performance increases of a UK consulting law firm, Pannone and Partners, following their attempts to enhance their organizational climate. According to Pannone and Partners' HR department, they have worked closely with senior management to develop an organizational climate that encourages loyalty and reduces turnover. One way this has been achieved has been by offering a high level of job security to their employees, by adjusting their client base to include both commercial and private clients to ensure a consistent revenue flow. Along with job security, Pannone and Partners have concentrated on employee satisfaction by making sure their employees have a good work–life balance, and have instituted a reward system that includes salary bonuses and extra time off for activities outside of work. The high level of employee commitment at Pannone and Partners has resulted in a very low level of turnover and made them highly popular among job seekers. As a result of their efforts, Pannone and Partners have become one of the fastest growing legal firms in the United Kingdom, performing well even when their competitors struggled to find adequate work, with a 22 per cent growth in profit in recent times.

Points for action: Practical recommendations for change

Human capital and corporate profitability

In a recent report by the Corporate Citizenship Company, Tuffrey (2003) has highlighted four steps for measuring the business benefits of HRM. According to Tuffrey, because HRM measurements are often limited and imprecise, it is necessary to attempt to formalize ways of measuring their impact, especially if there is managerial pressure to see a real fiscal return from HRM investment. Moreover, Tuffrey believes that an objective measurement process can help HR managers to understand the goals they are hoping to achieve through the intervention, making it more likely that they will see the process through.

Tuffrey's (2003) four steps when evaluating employee morale, motivation, commitment and performance, and business bottom-line benefits (such as productivity gains) include:

- Step 1 – Identify what impact, if any, the HRM practices have had on employees, especially with regard to opinions, attitudes, or behavioural changes. Measurement can include:
  - Staff turnover and wastage: the number of employees that leave the organization over a given time. This can be broken down by percentage of total workforce, or more precisely to include information on, for example, department, grades, season, tenure, gender, and cause.
  - Absenteeism, lateness, and presenteeism: measured as number of days lost against total working days, and analysed against overall or more specific demographics (for example, department, gender, and so on).
  - Recruitment: measurement of number of job applications (including internal applications) as well as cost or time savings in recruitment.
  - Productivity levels: depending on the type of work being measured. This is much simpler in manufacturing than in most knowledge work, but can be determined as successful completion of a task to a given standard in a given time period.
  - Quality of services: includes measurement of customer complaints (which can be an indirect measurement of staff satisfaction).
  Cost savings can often be estimated based on these metrics. For example, increasing staff retention can result in measurable savings in recruitment costs, lost skills, and organizational disruption.[13]

- Step 2 – Carefully consider the company definition of "good performance". For instance, there is no correct level of absenteeism, only a judgement of what should be correct. It is better to examine improvements over time and base future "best" levels on these trends.

- Step 3 – Initiate cost comparisons based on costs of achieving benefits (such as reduced turnover). In other words, compare the cost of implementing the HRM practices that reduced turnover against the real savings from the turnover reduction (making sure to account for all variables in turnover, rather than just the basic costs of recruitment and replacement – for example, training, lost time and productivity in other employees, lowered morale, and so on).

- Step 4 – Consider longer-term benefits to HRM spending. Whilst data might not be available for a full accounting-based audit of spending versus gains, at the very least a conceptual approach (that is, thinking through the likely benefits in order to help managers make decisions) should be implemented.

---

[13] See Section 4 for a more detailed discussion of how to estimate tangible costs based on intangible variables.

The organizational climate

Tuffrey (2003) has reported five HRM practices most effective for increasing staff retention and, consequently, achieving financial savings from reduced turnover. These include:

- Adequate pay – making sure that employees receive above the industry standard in order to reduce turnover intention. As well, regular pay rises, bonuses, or rewards (financial and other) enhance employees' feelings about the organizational climate and increase their affective commitment.

- Secure employment – reducing concerns about employment termination increases employee satisfaction, reduces conflict between employees and management, and increases affective commitment.[14]

- Interesting work – a varied and challenging level of work allows employees to feel that they are being adequately utilized in their jobs. Underutilization can lead to boredom, psychological withdrawal, increased absenteeism, presenteeism, and increased turnover intention.[15]

- Convenient location – long commutes or travel time have a negative impact both on the affective commitment of the employee and on his or her work–life balance. Organizations that are based outside of large population centres should consider recruiting only local workers or implementing a strong telecommuting programme.

- Flexible working arrangements – as we covered in depth in Section 1, flexible working can substantially increase employee satisfaction. Flexible working also enhances the organizational climate, increasing employee affective commitment and reducing turnover intention.

- Community involvement – organizations that develop real and long-term relationships with their surrounding community generally have employees with a more positive perception of the organizational climate, and have a stronger mission attachment, feeling that the company's values align more readily with their own. These employees are more committed to the organization and express a lower turnover intention.

Summary

Many managers find it difficult to quantify the value of intangible assets, because they continue to refer to outmoded accounting principles that imply that an organization is only worth the sum of its tangible assets. Nevertheless, an organization's intangible assets or intellectual capital often represent in excess of four times its physical worth. Moreover, effective HRM can account for up

---

[14] See Section 3 for more information about how stress over job loss can reduce an employee's ability to function effectively in the workplace, and how this impacts organizational performance.
[15] See Section 4 for a discussion of the organizational costs of psychological withdrawal in the workplace.

to 40 per cent of a company's profitability, especially when it is geared towards employee satisfaction, and helps to align employees' work and passions. The ability for HRM and other managers to "mine" this intellectual capital has been labelled "cultural capital"; that is, when employers address the physical, intellectual, emotional, and spiritual needs of their employees, they are better able to harness the inherent worth of their staff, leading to greater organizational performance through realization of value. Despite the difficulties faced by many organizations in effectively measuring their intellectual capital, it is most simply defined by the question "what is left when employees go home". In other words, intellectual capital represents the value inherent in an organization that cannot be readily bought, upgraded, or sold.

The organizational climate can have a large bearing on that company's ability to harvest its intellectual capital. Organizational climate refers to the members' collective perceptions about the organization, with respect to autonomy, trust, cohesiveness, support, recognition, innovation, and fairness. A strong organizational climate can result in tangible results, such as lowered organizational costs through reduced turnover and absenteeism, and in increased affective commitment from employees, effectively enhancing staff loyalty to the firm.

REVIEW QUESTIONS

1. Explain how human resource management contributes to company profitability.

2. Run through some of the recent changes that have forced companies to begin to recognize the value of effective human resources management.

3. What is intellectual capital? Why is it important to organizations?

4. Why is it often difficult for managers to appreciate the benefits of intellectual capital?

5. What experiences have you had in which conventional accounting practices have diminished your capacity to work to a high level of productivity?

6. Using personal experiences, explain the benefits of a good organizational climate.

Mind-diagram summary

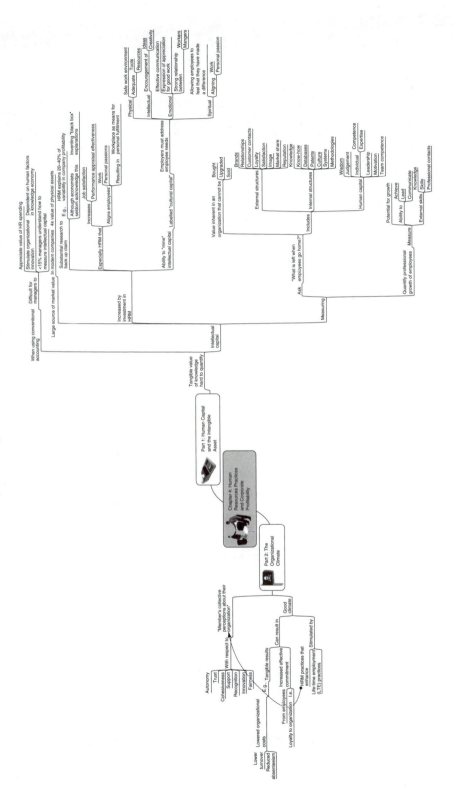

Chapter 4: Human Resources Practices and Corporate Profitability

Part 1: Human Capital and the Intangible Asset

Tangible value of knowledge hard to quantify

Intellectual capital
- When using conventional accounting
  - Difficult for managers to
    - Appreciate value of HR spending
    - Dependent on human factors in knowledge economy
    - Stimulate organizational innovation
    - <15% managers understand how to measure intellectual capital
- Large source of market value in modern companies
  - Substantial research to back up claim
    - 4x value of physical assets
    - HRM explains 20-40% of variability in company profitability
    - Although economists seldom acknowledge this
    - Inventing "black box" explanations
- Increased by investment in HRM
  - Especially HRM that
    - Increases
      - Job satisfaction
      - Performance appraisal effectiveness
    - Aligns employees'
      - Personal passions
      - Work
    - Resulting in
      - Workplace as means for personal fulfilment
  - Ability to "mine" intellectual capital
    - Employers must address employee needs
    - Labelled "cultural capital"
      - Physical
        - Safe work environment
        - Adequate
          - Tools
          - Resources
      - Intellectual
        - Effective communication
        - Encouragement of
          - Ideas
          - Creativity
      - Emotional
        - Expression of appreciation for good work
        - Strong relationship between
          - Workers
          - Managers
        - Allowing employees to feel that they have made a difference
      - Spiritual
        - Aligning
          - Work
          - Personal passion
- Measuring
  - Ask "What is left when employees go home?"
    - Value inherent in an organization that cannot be
      - Bought
      - Upgraded
      - Sold
    - Includes
      - External structures
        - Brands
        - Relationships
        - Customer contacts
        - Satisfaction
        - Loyalty
        - Image
        - Market share
        - Reputation
        - Knowledge
      - Internal structures
        - Know-how
        - Databases
        - Patents
        - Culture
        - Systems
        - Methodologies
      - Human capital
        - Wisdom
        - Judgement
        - Individual
          - Competence
          - Expertise
        - Leadership
        - Motivation
        - Team competence
  - Measure
    - Quantify professional growth of employees
      - Potential for growth
      - Ability to
        - Achieve
        - Lead
        - Communicate
        - Knowledge
      - External skills
        - Skills
        - Professional contacts

Part 2: The Organizational Climate

"Member's collective perceptions about their organization"
- With respect to
  - Autonomy
  - Trust
  - Cohesiveness
  - Support
  - Recognition
  - Innovation
  - Fairness
- Can result in
  - Good climate
- E.g. - Tangible results
  - From employees
    - Loyalty to organization i.e.
    - Increased affective commitment
  - Lowered organizational costs
    - Lower turnover
    - Reduced absenteeism
  - HRM practices that enhance
    - Life-time employment (LTE) practices
  - Stimulated by

Strategic Principle, Vision and Mission

Aims, company-wide, competitive, evolution, growth, mission, strategic, talent.

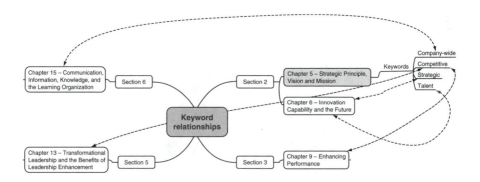

Corporate vision, collaborative relationships, employee motivation.

Effective corporate performance requires the ability to both define a current position and look towards the future. Whereas many companies engage in forecasting during incorporation (in the form of a business plan), this foresight is seldom continued. Loss of focus can impact on an organization's ability to grow, communicate, and understand where to concentrate its attention. Gadiesh (2001) has highlighted this problem, in his description of the importance of development and ongoing use of a strategic principle (in effect, a statement describing a company's philosophy, squeezed into a single catch-cry) to guide company strategy. He has suggested that such a statement can help to promote and guide action among employees company-wide, by providing a simple, single point of reference. According to Gadiesh, effective examples of strategic principles can be found in the catch-cries of highly successful corporations, such as America Online ("Consumer connectivity first – anytime, anywhere") or Wal-Mart ("Low prices, everyday").

Another way to develop an effective vision, according to Szulanski and Amin (2001), lies in finding a balance between organizational imagination and discipline. In their opinion, on the one hand, discipline represents the consistent application of rules in order to provide a practical methodology for corporate decision-making, programme development, and external dealings. However, Szulanski and Amin believe that decisions based entirely on a system of discipline are limited because they are founded on analysis without synthesis and on selection at the expense of generation. Moreover, because they rely on extrapolation from the past, decisions made from disciplinary bases often lack timely information and run the risk of being out of date. On the other hand, decisions based on imagination, according to Szulanski and Amin, are prospect oriented, in which one works back to the present from a projected future, and represent a process of harvesting from a myriad of ideas in order to find one that is applicable to a given situation. Nevertheless, like a disciplinary approach, an imaginative focus is not ideal: imagination can be limited by a lack of order, leading to disorganization through a loss of touch with reality. This disorganization, according to Szulanski and Amin, can dilute individual creativity, because no single idea can stand out above the group. As well, because imaginative solutions are often based on a fictional future, it can be easy to undervalue lessons from the past. In order to overcome the limitations of both the imaginative and disciplinary approaches, Szulanski and his co-worker have suggested a "disciplined imagination" decision-making paradigm, in which imaginative options are generated (allowing for creativity), but these options are evaluated using a disciplined, methodological approach. In this way a balance is found that allows a vision of the future without losing sight of the present.

Durkalski (2001) believes that an effective corporate vision comes from the modification of competition traditionally found within and between organizations, positing instead the value of collaborative relationships. According to Durkalski, the future is best appreciated not by company directors but by company employees, each of whom maintains a small investment in the firm's future prosperity. Durkalski has argued that by increasing this stake, employee commitment will also be increased and, consequently, the likelihood of a company's continued survival will be enhanced by dint of the improved productivity of its committed workers. To achieve this goal, Durkalski has suggested initiating a programme of profit sharing within a company, with a percentage of profits being passed directly on to employees. However, because motivation is not entirely monetary, Durkalski has also recommended that programmes, – such as the development of a more relaxed (less stressful) working environment in which communication lines are reinforced, training the workforce to be more effective and confident, taking training outside of the workplace by providing education to the families of employees, and investing in technology that increases efficiency without removing human communication elements – can all enhance an employee's sense of commitment and, consequently, a more coherent vision of a company's future.

Closely tied to the concept of vision is an organization's mission, often encapsulated in a mission statement. Unlike a company tagline, a mission statement is a clear and simple statement of principles that can help define an organization's values and envision its future (Brown & Yoshioka, 2003). A mission statement can also identify organizational objectives, give employees goals to direct organizational behaviour, and describe performance standards. Moreover, a strong mission statement can also affect an organization's bottom line: Brown and Yoshioka have identified a high correlation between an organization's values as defined through its mission statement and employee commitment. Specifically, following an investigation of 304 members of a non-profit organization, Brown and his colleague reported that when staff felt that there was a good crossover between their values and goals and those of their employer, there was a greater likelihood of job satisfaction and productivity, and an increased intention to remain with the organization. Moreover, those employees that believed in the company's mission felt happier in their work, irrespective of salary, especially when they felt that their job role aided the company in its mission. In other words, employees who feel that their own values are similar to those of their employer will be more productive and stay with the company, even when extrinsic motivators, such as pay, are low: a phenomenon labelled "mission attachment". However, Brown and Yoshioka have warned that an alignment between an organization's mission and the values of its employees can only be realized if the mission statement is available to and understood by the employees and, more importantly, that the activities of the company and its managers do not contradict the implied values inherent in the mission statement.

Aligning company activities with the supposed values and goals expressed in the mission statement brings up an interesting tangent: company and managerial ethics. Recent corporate "scandals" highlighted by the press, such as the problems at Enron, have placed many companies in the limelight for "unethical" accounting and management practices, mostly in the overstatement of their assets in an attempt to raise share value. According to Kantor and Weisberg (2002), when an organization or its management behaves in a manner that is perceived as unethical by its employees, it does substantial harm both to its organizational climate and to its employees' "mission attachment". In the opinion of Kantor and Weisberg, whilst most organizations have a written code of ethics (often contained within their mission statement), when managers act in contrast to this code there is a likelihood of a deterioration of relationships, raised mistrust, a negative impact on employee productivity, a stifling of employee creativity, ineffective information flow, and decreased employee loyalty. In an examination of this problem in 111 employees from an Israeli municipality finance department, Kantor and Weisberg found that the majority of employees perceived that both their ethical values and beliefs and their ethical behaviours were higher than those of their managers. Thus Kantor and his colleague concluded that whilst employees were more likely to be loyal and committed to their employers, managers were perceived to have behaved ethically; in fact this was not the case, making it very hard for employees to see their supervisors as role models. Of course, Kantor and Weisberg's findings were limited to a single organization; nevertheless, in the context of the high levels of competition-based pressure placed on many modern organizations, the assumption that unethical behaviour is prevalent in the actions of many managers and in many companies does not appear too far-fetched, reducing managers' viability as leaders, and resulting in a lowering of company performance by damaging employees' mission attachment.

Best practice: Case examples of how it's being done

Strategic principle, vision and mission

Tuffrey (2003) has highlighted the case example of a recent initiative by British Gas to increase employee satisfaction and mission attachment by offering free social works services to the local community. British Gas's call centre, based in Cardiff, Wales, employs around 2500 people who provide the first point of contact between the company and its domestic electricity and gas customers. Like many organizations, British Gas have found it difficult to retain staff in their call centre, with a turnover rate as high as 80 per cent (typically, staff complained of low motivation, part-time and shift working, and stress); consequently, it was in the company's interest to introduce measures to increase employee satisfaction in an attempt to reduce turnover.

In an effort to address their turnover problems, British Gas joined "Cardiff Cares", a community programme that provided volunteer services to improve the local community. Staff were encouraged to volunteer their time (during work hours) to assist in community projects, such as helping to clean the local watercourses. As well, managers were able to work with small local businesses to provide expertise in helping to prepare business plans and improve operations, and senior managers were encouraged to spend time in other departments to increase their knowledge, and management and communications skills. Employees who felt unable to volunteer their time outside of the organization were able to use company time to help raise money for charities, successfully raising more than £200,000 in the first year.

Following assessment of its initiative, using employee surveys and one-on-one interviews, British Gas reported that over 700 employees had become involved in volunteer and charity work (Tuffrey, 2003). Moreover, British Gas found that by increasing the mission attachment of their employees, satisfaction rose considerably, resulting in a greatly lowered turnover rate and substantial financial savings. As well, British Gas's reputation as a company that helps its local community increased dramatically, producing excellent press coverage.

Summary

The way in which an organization represents itself both to its members and to the outside world can have a great bearing on its ability to effectively motivate its staff to perform. One simple way of communicating the organization's purpose is through a representative strategic principle: an all-encompassing catch-cry that represents a company's philosophy and helps to guide employee focus towards a single, simple point of reference. Likewise, an effective vision, or the ability of an organization and its leaders to perceive and navigate its future, can help to encourage employee commitment. One way to clarify vision is through an effective mission statement: a clear and simple statement of principles that helps to define values, envision the future, and identify organizational objectives. In the presence of a strong mission statement, there is often a relationship between the values of the organization and those of its employees, resulting in greater organizational performance, a phenomenon referred to as "mission attachment". Lastly, whilst many firms spend a great deal of time and resources on developing an effective catch-cry and mission statement, there is often a lack of correspondence between their rhetoric and their actions. This dichotomy between stated principles and actual behaviour, especially when practised by senior management, represents a breach of ethical practice and can seriously damage the mission attachment of an organization's employees, reducing the likelihood that they will perform to their capabilities.

REVIEW QUESTIONS

1. Outline the differences between a strategic principle and corporate vision.

2. What is a mission statement and how can it affect employee performance?

3. In your workplace experiences, have you noticed a disparity between the stated ethics of the organization, and its actions, or the actions of your manager or supervisor?

4. What reasons might an organization have for acting in a way that is contrary to its stated mission or ethics?

Mind-diagram summary

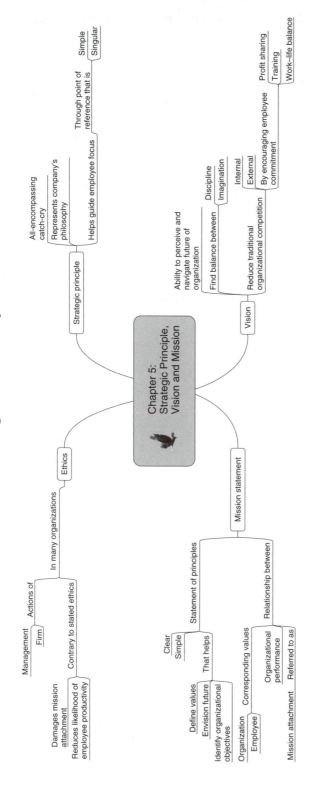

Chapter 5: Strategic Principle, Vision and Mission

Strategic principle
- All-encompassing catch-cry
- Represents company's philosophy
- Helps guide employee focus
  - Through point of reference that is
    - Simple
    - Singular

Vision
- Ability to perceive and navigate future of organization
- Find balance between
  - Discipline
  - Imagination
- Reduce traditional organizational competition
  - Internal
  - External
    - By encouraging employee commitment
      - Profit sharing
      - Training
      - Work–life balance

Ethics
- In many organizations
  - Actions of
    - Management
    - Firm
  - Contrary to stated ethics
    - Damages mission attachment
    - Reduces likelihood of employee productivity

Mission statement
- Statement of principles
  - Clear
  - Simple
  - That helps
    - Define values
    - Envision future
    - Identify organizational objectives
- Relationship between
  - Corresponding values
    - Organization
    - Employee
  - Organizational performance
  - Referred to as
    - Mission attachment

Innovation Capability and the Future

Employee satisfaction, market, profit, psychological contract, recruit, satisfied, strategic, talent.

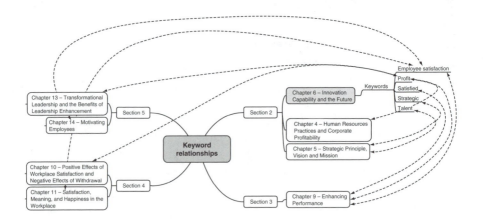

IMPORTANT CONCEPTS   Cultural capital, organizational development, intangible assets.

Vision and mission statements and strategic principles describe how a company will approach the future. However, whether an organization is actually capable of achieving this vision is of high import. Several authors have suggested that an organization's ability to innovate represents a primary means to achieving vision; nevertheless, as contrasting opinions demonstrate, there is no clear path to innovation. There remains, however, a consistent theme in the current literature describing innovation: the success of companies that focus on the assets inherent in their employees.

Part 1: Innovation, information, and human and non-financial resources

So far we have devoted quite a bit of time to the idea of the new, knowledge information economy. Basically, with the advent of new technology, industry has progressively moved away from raw products and manufacturing towards the development of innovation through new ideas, technology, and services (with a concurrent move towards globalized markets). As we have also discussed, conventional accounting is largely unable to deal with many of the economic issues associated with corporations that are largely knowledge based; consequently, the field of information economics, which pays closer attention to non-financial resources, has begun to gain more attention from economists, senior managers, and company heads, in order to better understand the financial futures of firms and the link between innovation and corporate performance.

According to Mandeville (1998), "information is a descriptive term for an economically interesting category of goods which has not hitherto been accorded much attention by economic theorists"; however, he also states that information has assumed a central importance in economic transactions, despite its inherent intangibility. One reason for the increasing importance of information as a major economic factor is that technology, or "knowledge or information applied to doing things" (Mandeville), is a crucial aspect of corporate growth through innovation; that is, innovation or technological change represents a change in the way "things" are done, or allows us to do completely new "things". Nevertheless, in conventional economic theory, technology is often considered as if it were a tangible, material good, such as a blueprint for a particular gadget. Consequently, conventional economists often define innovation (especially in technology) simply as a process for coming up with new or refined blueprints for creating "better" products. However, in the opinion of Mandeville, the "blueprint" aspect of technology is extremely small. Rather, technology is the totality of information that allows something to be done, from descriptions in a blueprint, to skills teachable only by example, to purchasable information, to techniques that represent the tacit learning and knowledge of a firm's employees. Further, if it is understood that technology represents all of the information that allows a firm to actually do what it does, then it must also be understood that massive spending on R&D will not necessarily lead to innovation and invention. Rather, R&D spending can only produce information which must be supplemented by other information before "things" such as inventing can be done. Some of this necessary information can include, for instance, information embodied in the hardware of associated technology, information suggested by users of a given product, software needed to make hardware work, information required to affect organizational change, information related to marketing, market feedback, or understanding user needs, and information obtained through the process of learning by doing. Consequently, innovation represents a broad informational process (of which R&D represents a small part) that needs to be understood as both information flow and information creation.

If innovation in technology is the consequence of information flow and creation, it can also be viewed as a social process that requires the successful interaction of a large number of participants in order to function (Mandeville, 1998). For example, new technology is often dependent on the flow of information both between and within firms, and the development of new information to piece this information together into a cogent pattern. Thus, innovation is more than the development of new ideas; in actuality it represents the shaping of information from a raw, intangible form into a more tangible product. In other words, in an information economics model, innovation involves creating meaning from vast reserves of information, in a collective, social manner that requires learning, collaboration, and evolution of thought, rather than simply a "one-off" technical process. This encompasses a spectrum of information from highly intangible or uncodified material, such as undeveloped ideas or tacit knowledge, to highly codified "commodities" such as patent specifications, blueprints, or technical and trade papers. Thus, according to Mandeville, given that information cannot be exhausted (the more the users, the more it grows), and given that the cost of production of information is independent of the scale of its use (unlike traditional manufacturing), it pays for organizations to share information in order to stimulate innovation.

In the close to a decade since Mandeville's (1998) ideas, other authors have stressed not only the importance of understanding the role of information in innovation but also the need to capitalize on human resources in order to enhance information quality and availability. Webster (2001), for example, has reported that when firms invest in their human capital, through training, improved management, and practices that increase employee satisfaction and productivity, they are gaining, in effect, a product that does not degrade over time, but continues to appreciate in value. This value can be utilized in many different ways: for instance, harnessing the expertise of field engineers in the ongoing development of a technology, or treating maintenance workers as expert users of a given system. However it is used, employees' knowledge of the way in which a given firm, technology, or service operates is invaluable for an organization's continued ability to innovate, and the more skilled the employee, the greater his or her worth. Webster has gone so far as to suggest an analogy between the value of employees and land: land is more valuable when it has characteristics that are both scarce and desirable. Likewise, the more useful an employee's knowledge towards the future development of an organization, the greater the need to invest in his or her improvement, and the higher the motivation to put practices in place that will make sure that he or she does not consider leaving the organization. Moreover, to successfully utilize the knowledge and skills inherent in employees, and to aggregate and develop information that allows for innovation, it is extremely important that organizations have managers and a management system that allow for successful motivation and stimulation of those employees. In fact, according to Webster, because employees are actually much more valuable to an organization than its tangible investments (such as machinery), but substantially more complex to "operate", a very high priority should be given to extensive training of managers in order to increase their ability to motivate and to inspire loyalty and productivity in their subordinates. Cooke (2002), in his recent article, has taken a similar viewpoint; in his opinion, employees with operational and technological knowledge represent a highly valuable commodity because they have information that cannot be easily obtained or replaced and that is vital for innovation. Nevertheless, according to Cooke, managers frequently fail to realize this value by underutilizing their staff. Because managers have a tendency to underplay day-to-day activities in preference to the "big picture", the intellectual resources of their subordinates are often taken for granted: it is assumed that they can be replaced as easily as other "technology", and because their abilities are not leveraged beyond a basic application, their opinions and ideas are not sought out (Cooke). In other words, when managers assume that employees should just fulfil their basic job role and do not include them when attempting to find new directions or applications for the firm's products or services, they remain ignorant of their employees' actual (or untapped) value. This managerial behaviour results in an increased likelihood of intentional and unintentional turnover: managers will "let go" employees whose value is unappreciated and, because they are underutilized, employees will be less creative, curious, and innovative, will not contribute to solving organizational problems, and will be more likely to leave the firm, taking their human capital value with them to other organizations (Cooke). Thus, like Webster, Cooke suggests that organizations invest both in training for management so that they can access the firm's intellectual capital, and provide incentive for workers to reduce their turnover intention, with the understanding that human capital cannot be easily acquired or copied and takes a substantial investment of time and resources to develop.

The need to invest in human capital, and in mechanisms for extracting and applying knowledge and information to stimulate innovation is, according to Kort, Verheyen, and De Waegenaere (2003), a principal determinant of the future economic survival of modern organizations. Like other authors reviewed in this section, Kort *et al.* have posited that over the last decade the determinants of firm performance have changed dramatically, so that physical assets are no longer the major source of financial return. Rather, an increased demand for continual quality improvements and innovation requires the acquisition, retention, and motivation of highly skilled employees, and highlights the need for firm investments in human capital. In fact as Kort and his colleagues believe that existing theories of the firm, such as financial forecasting based on asset balance sheets, are no longer valid, they have suggested instead that it is necessary to determine an optimal level of investment in human capital in order to predict organizational performance. To this end, their financial model, based on an analysis of existing economic models, predicts that firms that invest in their human capital will increase (to an optimum point) productivity, profitability, and innovating ability. Conversely, corporations that do not invest in human capital will lose existing human resources and fail to attract new human capital, resulting in eventual failure. A similar conclusion has been reached by Black and Lynch (2004), who, following an examination of recent US census data on over 3000 private firms, have reported evidence of a "new economy" in the United States, and concluding that in recent times there has been a substantial change in US business practices, most notably an increase in human capital investment in order to stimulate innovation. In their analysis, Black and Lynch defined human capital investment as the strong implementation of HRM practices, especially those that increased managerial competence (for example, quality management, encouragement of innovation) and that leveraged the tacit knowledge of non-managerial employees (for example, introduction of incentive-based compensation for employee contributions that led to company profit) by increasing employee involvement in problem solving and in identifying opportunities for company growth and innovation. Similarly, Laursen and Foss (2003), in their analysis of 4000 Danish firms, reported that HRM practices that helped to mine human capital were significantly related to increased firm innovation. Specifically, Laursen and his co-investigator found that interdisciplinary workshops, systems for the collection and implementation of employee proposals, job rotation, effective delegation of responsibility, integration of work functions, and performance-related pay (for example, rewarding a shop-floor employee for suggesting process improvements by giving him or her a share of the company savings resulting from the suggestion) resulted in improved innovation and, consequently, firm financial performance. Moreover, according to Laursen and Foss, these practices worked best when combined in a holistic package; that is, a system that encourages employees both to increase their human capital and allows them to use that human capital more extensively in problem solving (that is, the ability to use new and existing skills), increases organizational innovation because it actually makes use of a wider range of the resources available to the company (rather than simply relying on financial indicators to drive strategy).

Managerial "buy-in" to HRM and other practices geared towards innovation increases are, in the opinion of Hadjimanolis (2000), essential to their success. Hadjimanolis has defined innovation as "the management of... activities, central to the long-term survival of the firm, ranging from the continuous improvement of existing products, processes and services through the introduction of new ones to activities designed to enter new fields", and has suggested that managers utilize a resource-based view, in which business strategy is determined through an understanding of a firm's resources (that is, assets that are tied semi-permanently to the organization and that include physical, human, technological, and reputational resources, and the employment and utilization of skilled personnel), capabilities (that is, features of the firm and managerial skills in forming organizational routines that lead to competitive advantage over competitors), and competencies (the successful interaction of resources and capabilities). To support this position Hadjimanolis, in his examination of innovation success in 25 Cypriot SMEs, reported that strategies for the accumulation and development of organizational resources and capabilities, combined with managerial skills and capabilities and the utilization of knowledge-based resources that are unique to the firm and hard to copy, are strong predictors of organizational innovation success and represent a principle factor in firm survivability. Cummings (2000) has also indicated that the skills required by managers and entrepreneurs to enhance organizational innovation are vital. Unfortunately, as he has also pointed out (and as we have already seen), these skills are unlikely to be taught in the typical MBA programme. In fact, according to Cummings, an understanding of conventional economics is not sufficient to manage a workforce, because people require more than financial incentives and deadlines to motivate them. In illustration of this point, Cummings has pointed out the similarities between successful entrepreneurs and psychologists, drawing parallels in their ability to motivate, to listen, to inspire, and to enact change. Interestingly, as Cummings notes, many entrepreneurs are themselves less motivated by money than they are by challenge and the need to implement a vision (for example, many start-up directors trade sweat equity for a modest salary). Consequently, Cummings has argued that, at a base level, most workers are more stimulated by the desire to achieve than by the desire to earn.

Said, HassabElnaby, and Wier (2003) have also reported a strong link between non-financial measures, and innovation and firm performance. According to Said *et al.*, non-financial measures such as employee and client/customer satisfaction (which are positively correlated with firm financial performance and market value), and managerial practices that emphasize the importance of non-financial information result in innovation-oriented business strategies, and a substantial increase in the firm's economic performance. Said and his colleagues, who investigated a series of financial (annualized market-adjusted stock returns and returns on assets) and non-financial (ratings of improvement in customer satisfaction, quality and performance, and input from employees) measures over a four-year period in 1441 firms and another 1441 matched control organizations, concluded that organizations that combined financial and non-financial measures in assessing performance and planning strategy performed better than those that only used financial measures. Because non-financial measures provide a greater depth and range of performance feedback, are less subject to manipulation, and are less dependent on managerial judgement than balance sheets and cost allocations, Said *et al.* believe that they can provide managers with a better quality of information than financial measures alone. Moreover, when managers use non-financial information to help shape strategy, they are utilizing the firm's intellectual resources (by acting on the information and tacit knowledge of employees), justifying spending on human capital acquisition and improvement and stimulating innovation. Equally, Lawson and Samson (2001) have posited that the framework for innovation in organizations lies in a given company's ability to harness its competency base, to develop a strong level of creativity and idea management, and to encourage flexibility in its organizational structure. Nevertheless, Lawson and Samson have pointed out that, without employee participation, these innovations are unlikely to occur. In fact, in the opinion of Lawson and his colleague, employees are the only source of innovation available to a company; that is, computers and workplace designs are not, in themselves, capable of coming up with or implementing ideas; rather, it is the willing contributions of motivated, satisfied staff that drive advancement, a process that is highly dependent on competent management. Thus, according to Lawson and Samson, there is a strong, direct correlation between managerial practices that improve employee satisfaction, and innovation capability and organizational success. Hull and Kaghan (2000) have also highlighted the importance of management in harnessing innovation. They have reported that because innovation has, over the last fifteen years, moved to become an organizing principle throughout many areas of the firm (that is, beyond R&D and board level decisions on R&D spending), greater attention is now being focussed on the importance of competent management of the firm's technical and professional human resources. Thus, whilst the previous role of management was to organize for company efficiency, based on the premise that competitiveness involved the most effective and efficient supply of products or services, modern managers are required to drive company innovation to compete in a global market (Hull & Kaghan). To do this requires that individuals within an organization have the ability to act as agents for the firm which is, in turn, dependent on their ability to have control over the decisions and directions behind innovative change, their role within the organization, and their capacity to act. Hull and Kagan believe that each of these freedoms, and the ability of the company to innovate by harnessing its intellectual resources, is largely dependent on the attitudes, leadership, and motivational abilities of its managers.

Whilst many authors have propounded the value of company-wide innovation, and intangible asset recognition, it is still necessary to have specific mechanisms for realizing these goals. Obviously, there are many variables associated with organizational innovation; however, as we have already seen, most sources agree that employee satisfaction is the key to organizational success, because satisfied employees are more likely to hold the success of the company for which they work in esteem. Although specific mechanisms for enhancing workplace satisfaction will be explored in greater depth below (see Section 4), one mechanism, the psychological contract, which has recently received literary attention, is pertinent to our current discussion. Heron and Thompson (2001), for instance, who have defined the psychological contract as an employee's perception of his or her obligations to an organization (and vice versa), believe that it represents one of the most important variables in a person's perception of opportunity, security, and development in his or her workplace. According to Heron and his co-author, the terms of the psychological contract are seldom stated explicitly, but have a substantial impact on a person's view of his or her work, and on his or her perception of the fairness of treatment within the organization. Consequently, without adequate attention to the terms of a psychological contract, individual performance can be negatively affected. As Heron and Thompson have pointed out, even the most conventional of accountants will agree that poor employee productivity negatively affects a company's economic indicators.

In order to enhance company productivity through the recognition of the psychological contract, Flannery (2002) has suggested that employers understand that it is the terms of this agreement that, in the employee's opinion, often make his or her job worthwhile (such as perceived opportunities for advancement, security, and personal growth). Therefore, according to Flannery, each employee's psychological contract should be discussed and regularly re-evaluated with his or her manager, so that management can provide an ongoing effort to develop a strong fit between an employee's expectations and his or her actual role. Moreover, in Flannery's opinion, by ignoring a person's expectations, or by failing to provide adequate training, education, time, or resources (both during and outside of work hours), an employer is likely to reduce actively an employee's enthusiasm and, consequently, his or her productivity.

The importance of the psychological contract has also been emphasized by Kickul (2001) in his report on employee attraction and retention practices in small business. According to Kickul, a large proportion of turnover in small to medium-sized businesses is due to the perception, by the employee, of a loss of trust. In order that employers be better able to realize the value of the psychological contract to employees, Kickul has developed a comprehensive list of items that should be addressed when it is discussed, including the categories of autonomy and growth, financial benefits, rewards and opportunities, job security and work responsibility, and work facilitation.

IN ACTION #3

Corporate evolution – taking it one step further . . .

"Corporate evolution" is another buzz phrase, but what does it mean? Well, it can mean replacing outmoded concepts and practices with ones that work. In psychological terms, this is known as exchanging "maladaptive" cognitions and behaviours for "adaptive" ones. Nevertheless, corporate evolution can encompass very much more. For example, in his excellent paper "Why the Future Belongs to Values Added Companies", Richard Barrett, a United States-based management consultant, described seven levels of corporate evolution. In Barrett's model, the lowest level of operation is profit-driven activity, whilst the highest includes a balance of intellectual, emotional, physical, and spiritual activities, coupled with a desire to improve not only the lives of employees and the surrounding community but also the planet as a whole. Barrett cites several organizations that are already operating at this level. Not surprisingly, these organizations are doing very well financially, and command enormous respect at an individual (employees and clients) and societal level (community, economic community, government). According to Barrett, organizations like these encourage the development of complete, satisfied human beings who can achieve their goals within the workplace. Here the workplace becomes more than just a place to "go to work" and "earn money", it becomes a place in which to realize human potential.

Part 2: Embracing change (or not)

So far we have reviewed a lot of evidence to suggest that the changing of traditional workplace roles is beneficial for both employees and employers. We have also seen that there is a growing trend, especially in the United States, towards investment in human capital, and methods for realizing the worth of that capital. However, there is still a widespread reluctance to embrace change. For example, O'Neill (2001) has reported that since the 1950s accounting practices have dominated both the economic and social decisions of senior managers and corporate leaders, dictating organizational nature and direction, and allowing managers to define disruptive changes within their organizations as rational and purposeful, even when they ignore intangible processes and assets. Consequently, O'Neill believes that traditional accounting models assign a zero balance to philanthropic endeavours, placing any rationale that does not present a clear tangible value on a balance sheet in this category. In his case study of BHP, a global mining and steel production company, O'Neill has pointed out that recent company-wide changes spearheaded by the new CEO and CFO have had a negative impact on the company's longer-term viability. In 1998 and 1999, basing their company "initiatives" on economic rationalism models, BHP's new leaders implemented a massive cost-saving programme, which resulted in the shedding of some 26,000 workers worldwide (almost half the company's employees), and the sales and closure of a large proportion of the company's physical infrastructure. Whilst BHP shares made modest gains following these changes, they did not consistently climb above pre-downsizing values, and BHP is now struggling to compete as a major producer. According to O'Neill, the principal failure of the new BHP leadership was to attempt to improve BHP's value by concentrating purely on its physical worth. Their portfolio management model, with "clearly defined" goals for making BHP a world player, did not include any specific methodology aimed at line managers. Consequently, divisional and operational managers were required to "enact savings initiatives" without any clear understanding of how or where these savings should be made, resulting in an enormous loss in human and intellectual capital as employees were let go to meet economic performance targets. This philosophy effectively devalued BHP's "soft" assets, such as employees and their knowledge and abilities, damaging the company's organizational capabilities, learning abilities, and creative capacity, possibly irreversibly. Unfortunately, because the CEO and CFO did not understand that when they responded to shareholders' demands for organizational profit increases using traditional economics and accounting models, other stakeholders vital to these profit gains (that is, employees) were affected in such a way as to damage the company's ability to be profitable in the long term.

Sull (1999), in his analysis of why successful companies lose their competitive edge, has also suggested that it is traditional thinking, especially adherence to traditional economic models, that reduces a company's impact. He has posited that companies that remain rooted in tradition are unable to take appropriate action when faced with change. Among his examples of traditional corporate thinking, Sull has cited the economic crisis of Firestone, the American tyre company, when faced with the import of European radials. Because this company had followed a strategy that, until that point, had allowed them to dominate their market, they took little action at the introduction of a new, better technology and, consequently, came close to financial ruin. Similarly, traditionalism can cause problems when everyday processes become dogmatic routines.

For example, Sull has referred to the example of McDonalds, an organization that has such a rigid operations procedure that there is virtually no room for individuals to take any initiative. Consequently, in recent times as people have started to eat less fast food, McDonalds has not had the innovative capacity to modify their marketing tactics and has lost market share. Nevertheless, the dangers of traditionalism notwithstanding, Sull has also warned against change that is too rapid. Rather, he has counselled an evolutionary strategy, in which innovation is allowed to appear randomly, and is then tested in the real world. He has suggested that during this process, companies pay more attention to the processes that hinder them rather than the questions of what they should do.

Best practice: Case examples of how it's being done

Innovation, information, and human and non-financial resources

In their report on increasing organizational performance through attention to human resources, the DTI (*High Performance Through People*, 2005) have highlighted several case studies of organizations that have increased profits through awareness of their human resources and information processes within the firm. One such organization: Bacardi-Martini Limited, an alcoholic beverages company in the United Kingdom, has achieved large savings by focussing on enhancing communication processes between employees and management, so that managers can access the tacit knowledge and abilities of their workers. To affect this goal, Bacardi-Martini implemented three key changes:

1. First, every three months, senior executives now spend a day on the shop floor where they observe activities and listen to employee suggestions and complaints. Employees are encouraged to be open and honest, and managers are trained in communication skills to increase the value of the exercise. Employee suggestions are then fed directly into business plans, increasing non-managerial employee participation in business-related decisions, and enhancing the organizational climate by helping employees feel as if their contributions make a difference to the company as a whole.

2. Second, three formal communications channels have been put in place:
   (i)   a monthly discussion between the HR department and employee representatives about day-to-day issues, with the aim of enhancing workplace conditions and processes
   (ii) a yearly survey, designed to determine employees' views on company direction, leadership, performance, strengths, and weaknesses
   (iii) a monthly employee satisfaction survey, designed to assess morale.

3. Finally, Bacardi-Martini has introduced a dedicated innovation team that works with each department to identify new or improved processes that could increase company performance. Employees and managers from the individual departments are encouraged to report their ideas and innovations to this team, who then make representations to senior management.

According to internal reports from Bacardi-Martini (*High Performance Through People*, 2005), their attempts to lever their human capital through the effective use of information have been successful. Since introducing changes to their internal communications they have seen cost reductions by reducing waste and increasing efficiency on production lines, and in sales, warehousing, data management, purchase, quality assurance, personnel, plant services, and stock control. This has resulted in annual savings of £4.4 million in production process efficiency and service level improvements in warehousing of 12 per cent.

The DTI (*High Performance Workplaces*, 2004) have also showcased the recent successes of PizzaExpress, a large restaurant chain in the United Kingdom, following initiatives to increase innovation by harnessing existing human capital. PizzaExpress formed a working group that included employees from as many aspects of the business as possible. The group's brief was to help facilitate two-way communication between shop-floor employees, line managers, and senior management, encouraging employees to voice their concerns, suggestions or queries, and delivering these ideas to the company board. At the same time, to keep employees updated on management decisions, board-level plans were summarized into a newsletter format and distributed regularly to staff. Some staff ideas put into practice have included better customer relations procedures and a recycling programme to reduce Pizza-Express's waste. According to PizzaExpress, their initiatives have substantially increased staff morale, allowing employees to see that their ideas and suggestions are having an influence on company policy. Moreover, PizzaExpress has expanded into one of the largest restaurant franchise operations in the United Kingdom, a level of success that they attribute, in part, to their ready access to the expert knowledge of their employees.

Points for action: Practical recommendations for change

Innovation, information, and human and non-financial resources

In their report on innovation in the United Kingdom, the DTI (*Competing in the Global Economy: The Innovation Challenge*, 2003) have made several research-based recommendations for enhancing innovation. These include:

- Management skills – company innovation is largely dependent on managers' abilities to utilize the organization's human capital. To do this, managers need to be experts in communication, dispute resolution, time management, and logistics. If managers are able to make it easier for employees to do their jobs, and are able to encourage performance from their subordinates, there is a greater likelihood that their firm will be better able to innovate. As well, managers need to be given discretion to reward outstanding performance, without having to follow a bureaucratic process.

- Highly trained, motivated workforce – simply put, when employees are well trained and are motivated to perform, they are more likely to be innovative in the workplace. Investment in human capital expansion is therefore of high importance, as is the development of effective managerial processes, and flexible working to increase employee satisfaction and mission attachment. It should also be noted that training in skills that are not directly related to an employee's job description, such as communication, time management, interpersonal and teamworking, and creativity skills have a substantial indirect effect on productivity and innovation.

- Flexible workplace practices – allowing workers to increase their work–life balance and work flexibly (for example, telecommuting, reduced hours, compressed work week, and so on) has a direct impact on employee satisfaction and loyalty. These are in turn related to increased innovation in the organization.

Summary

Innovation has been bandied as the new driver of organizational performance. However, innovation is really a product of information: information represents the basis for innovation through collaborations between people and systems that allow for technological change. In fact, technology is little more than a way of doing things more effectively and is, for the most part, based on the availability of effective information. In this paradigm, R&D represents only a small aspect of innovation. Instead, innovation stems from access to a spectrum of information, from intangible or uncoded concepts such as undeveloped ideas or tacit knowledge, to tangible or coded information, such as blueprints, software, or patents. Thus, if innovation stems from the flow and quality of information, systems to enhance the quality and flow are paramount. One such system is effective HR spending, specifically on programme that lead to highly trained managers capable of effectively mining human capital for the acquisition, access, and cultivation of information; and on policies and actions that enhance employee satisfaction, increasing motivation to encourage the flow of information. Unfortunately, human capital is largely ignored or underutilized, and managers poorly trained or incapable of understanding the value of human capital in innovation. Thus, despite the weight of evidence demonstrating the link between effective HRM and corporate innovation and performance, many organizations remain focussed on outmoded accounting principles that assign a zero value to philanthropy, assuming that money spent on employees has little or no relationship to an organization's ability to innovate.

REVIEW QUESTIONS

1. Describe why work/life programmes are being used increasingly in human resources management.

2. Explain the concept of cultural capital and outline why it is important to contemporary organizations.

3. Outline how an organization can improve the value of its human assets, and the likely benefits of these actions.

4. How is innovation related to HRM practices?

5. What examples have you seen in which an organization has effectively increased its level of innovation by focussing on its employees' needs?

6. Despite the documented link between corporate performance and effective HRM, what stops organizations from addressing their HR problems?

Mind-diagram summary

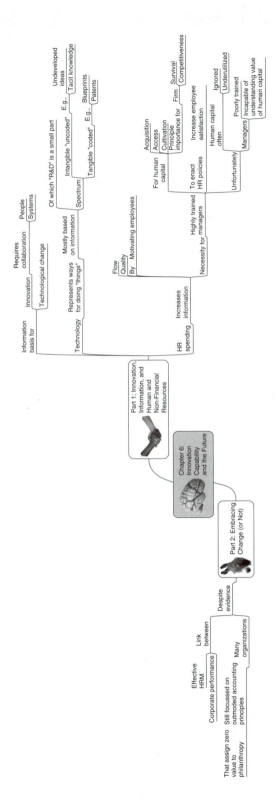

Chapter 6: Innovation Capability and the Future

Part 1: Innovation, Information, and Human and Non-Financial Resources

- Information basis for
  - Innovation
    - Requires collaboration
    - Technological change
      - People
      - Systems
  - Technology
    - Represents ways for doing "things"
    - Mostly based on information
      - Spectrum
        - Of which "R&D" is a small part
        - Intangible "uncoded"
          - E.g.,
            - Undeveloped ideas
            - Tacit knowledge
        - Tangible "coded"
          - E.g.,
            - Blueprints
            - Patents
  - HR spending
    - Increases information
    - Quality
      - Flow
      - By
        - Motivating employees
    - Necessity for managers
      - Highly trained
        - For human capital
          - Acquisition
          - Access
          - Cultivation
          - Principle importance for
            - Firm
              - Survival
              - Competitiveness
        - To enact HR policies
          - Increase employee satisfaction
      - Unfortunately
        - Human capital often
          - Ignored
          - Underutilized
        - Managers
          - Poorly trained
          - Incapable of understanding value of human capital

Part 2: Embracing Change (or Not)

- Despite evidence
  - Link between
    - Effective HRM
    - Corporate performance
  - Many organizations
    - Still focussed on outmoded accounting principles
      - That assign zero value to philanthropy

Developing Individual and Team Performance in the Workplace

Introduction

So far we have examined the importance of the recognition of cultural and societal change, as well as the necessity for innovation at a corporate level in order to remain competitive. As well, we have seen how employee satisfaction is a necessary and important part of corporate progress: without positive HR management and practices, firms risk alienating their employees and reducing organizational performance. Consequently, to increase employee satisfaction in the workplace and to enhance organizational performance, a balance of corporate and individual action is required. In this section we will investigate how organizations can work to improve their performance by understanding and attending to the needs, psychological and otherwise, of their workforce.

Section guide

Chapter 7, "Psychological Workplace Environment", examines how issues like employee empowerment, voice, and an individual's perceptions of control are extremely important for workplace performance, and looks at ways to enhance perceived control over workplace variables; we will also evaluate different types of high-performance work systems for their ability to increase empowerment. In Chapter 8, "Skills Training and Stress Management", we will investigate the negative consequences of feelings of little or no control over workplace environment, such as stress and burnout, and assess various methods, including training, holidays and work–life balance efforts for reducing the effects of stress.

In Chapter 9, "Enhancing Performance", we will look at the relationship between organizational commitment and performance, how incentives can be used to increase this commitment, the positive effects of changes to the physical workplace environment, and how teams and teamwork can enhance individual and company performance.

Reading objectives

By the end of this section you should have a clearer understanding of:

- the importance of workplace empowerment and employee voice
- why a person's perceptions of control over workplace variables is so important to his or her success at work, and what happens when this perceived control is absent
- how to increase a person's perception of control over factors in the workplace
- the various types of high-performance work systems and their benefits and drawbacks
- stress, its origins, and how to reduce both stress and its negative effects
- the different types of organizational commitment and how they relate to individual performance at work
- why conventional bonus schemes are flawed, and how to implement more-effective reward schemes to increase performance
- the notion of teams, how they work best, and under what circumstances they can help organizational performance.

Psychological Workplace Environment

KEYWORDS Absenteeism, chance, convention, discretion, empowerment, engagement, latitude, membership, modification, moral, owner-ship, security, self-manage, wage.

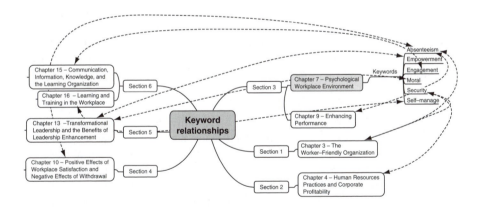

IMPORTANT CONCEPTS Occupational and workplace stress, perceptions of control.

In Sections 1 and 2 we looked at how the notion of work has changed, positive and negative ways in which firms have responded to this change, and how organizations can use HRM to enhance their productivity and profitability. In this section, we will examine in greater depth how the workplace psychological environment has a direct effect on employees' motivation, organizational commitment, and productivity, and what can be done to improve workplace conditions to enhance employee performance.

Part 1: Empowerment, employee voice, and ownership

Empowerment has become yet another of the many buzz words or jargon surrounding modern business practices. In a way this is unfortunate, because the overuse of a word can reduce its perceived validity, and given that empowerment is one of the most important variables in employee productivity (Paul, Niehoff, & Turnley, 2000), it is important that HR and other managerial professionals consider it valid. Defined as a "process of passing autonomy and responsibility to individuals at lower levels in the organizational hierarchy" (Paul *et al.*), empowerment is a powerful motivator, because it allows employees to feel that they have a measure of control over their working lives. As we will see later in this section, the perception of control over one's environment is a key factor in reducing stress, and increasing satisfaction with the status quo.

In fact, in high-empowerment workplaces, there is a greater likelihood of higher-quality products and services, lower rates of absenteeism and turnover, and better decision-making and problem solving, all of which increase organizational effectiveness and which make the goal of empowered employees an attractive prospect for senior managers (Paul *et al.*, 2000). These benefits have also resulted in empowerment being considered as "trendy" among management consultants, resulting in the profusion of modern corporate paradigms such as Lean Production and Total Quality Management (Smith *et al.*, 2003). However, according to Paul *et al.*, achieving empowerment in the workplace is not as simple a process as proponents of these systems would have us believe. Rather, Paul and his colleagues have suggested that to achieve a goal of employee autonomy from excessive managerial controls, managers must ensure that all employees (even those at the lowest levels of the organization) have ready access to the information and knowledge they need in order to be able to act independently, the power to act and to make decisions about their work (within a given framework) without consulting a supervisor, as well as access to reward schemes that are tied to both business results and continued growth in worker capability and contribution. Nevertheless, as Paul and his co-workers have pointed out, simply providing access to information and allowing employees to make decisions does not lead to empowerment; instead, successful workplace empowerment requires that management also examine and modify a wide variety of organizational practices. First, according to Paul and his colleagues, jobs should be designed to further employees' abilities to be involved in decision-making and to take control of their own work practices. That is, regular contact with co-workers and management to discuss ideas and suggestions, encouragement for employees to determine their own goals and requirements for their tasks and projects, and latitude to make decisions regarding project involvement, time, resources, collaborators and deadlines, "empower" employees by encouraging ownership of their work. Second, attention needs to be given to organizational design, such as the reduction of the number of levels within an organizational hierarchy alongside the encouragement for individuals to be able to make decisions at all levels of the organization. This means that firms should reduce or remove the "chain of command", allowing workers the leeway to make decisions pertinent to their jobs without needing to defer to a supervisor. In this way, supervisors take on the role of coach or facilitator, providing expert information and support for their subordinates, rather than spending time telling workers what they can or cannot do. Likewise managers take on a broader job role, with less distraction from daily hassles, and with a correspondingly greater sphere of decision-making autonomy. Consequently, a "flat" organization increases employee empowerment by making each member of staff an active part of the organization, rather than the end point in a hierarchy, with the ability both to make decisions and contribute to the day-to-day running of the organization. Third, empowerment can be stimulated by restructuring monetary reward systems to include stock ownership programmes, which allow employees real (albeit limited) ownership of their firm, and profit- or gain-sharing programmes, which reward employees for their successful efforts by sharing organizational windfalls. Fourth, like any other attempted workplace change, managerial training is paramount to the success of any empowerment programmes; managers need to understand why empowerment is beneficial for the organization. Likewise, because empowerment requires that managers take on roles of encouragement, information provision, and counselling, they also require training in interpersonal skills, active listening, and feedback. In this way, managers participate in transformational leadership, becoming motivators rather than book keepers.[16] Fifth, organizations encouraging employee empowerment need to focus on communication practices that are two way, clear, and honest. This presupposes a level of organizational ethics in which a firm contracts to keep its promises to employees, whether written, spoken, or simply implied. Effective communication also requires training in interpersonal skills, for both managerial and non-managerial staff; without the understanding of how to communicate effectively, it would be unrealistic to expect communication that is clear or honest. Lastly, Paul *et al.* have recommended that firms wishing to enhance employee empowerment practice good employee relations, including positive HRM practices such as flextime, cross training, attention to work–life balance, and training. As we have already seen, when employees feel that their employer is invested in their well-being, they respond with increased organizational commitment and citizenship; a process which represents an embodiment of trust within the organization.

Like Paul *et al.* (2000), other authors have cautioned that the organizational changes required to implement or maintain real employee empowerment

---

[16] See Sections 5 and 6 for more information regarding leadership styles, transformational leadership, and employee motivation.

involve substantial organizational change, and are by no means simple. Unfortunately, this complexity means that many organizations that attempt "empowerment programmes" do so in a manner that is poorly executed or flawed. For example, Yates, Lewchuk, and Stewart (2001), in their investigation of feelings of empowerment in 2424 employees of major car manufactures in the United States, concluded that when many large organizations initiate "empowerment programmes", their focus is not on increasing employee autonomy or decision-making power, but rather exclusively on increasing fiscal performance by following economically driven programmes such as "lean" and "just in time" production. Under these schemes, employees are arranged into semi-autonomous teams, but are responsible for meeting management-set targets without consultation on defining these objectives. In fact, according to Yates and her colleagues, following the introduction of lean production "empowerment" schemes, workers often report very low feelings of empowerment, but do describe an increase in work hours and intensification, and a reduction in "voice" (that is, the ability to participate in decisions that affect the overall running of the firm); issues which Yates *et al.* interpreted as the consequence of employees being held accountable for the successful achievement of managerial objectives, without being consulted on the way in which these goals are achieved. Yates *et al.* have described this process as a "Trojan horse" by which senior management misuse the notion of empowerment to increase production at the cost of employee satisfaction, a strategy that could have negative consequences for the firm. As Godard (2001) pointed out in his investigation of high-performance work systems in Canadian organizations, systems like lean production, which claim increased employee empowerment but actually restrict worker autonomy, have a negative effect on the productivity and performance of the firm. Consequently, senior management with the intention of modifying organizational practice to enhance employee empowerment should carefully assess the claimed benefits of a programme before its implementation.

Whilst ineffective empowerment schemes can have negative consequences, the importance of the large number of variables in achieving increased employee empowerment means that even effective empowerment schemes are not automatically successful. In their study of 57,561 employees from 42 countries, Hui, Au, and Fock (2004) reported that whilst empowerment activities are generally accepted as an excellent way for organizations to increase employees' job performance, satisfaction and motivation, especially in front-line service employees, they can only work if employees are able to accept their newfound discretionary abilities and are motivated to take on a more directive role. One factor that is, unfortunately, often overlooked when implementing empowerment programmes is the impact of cultural differences, both within organizations and between countriess an oversight that can reduce their effectiveness. According to Hui and his colleagues, a key concept in cultural differences is power-distance effects, or the "extent to which people expect and accept power to be distributed unequally among different levels of organizational hierarchy". On the one hand, in low power-distance cultures, such as the United Kingdom and the USA, there is a high level of power sharing between supervisors and subordinates, and employees are generally willing to take a more directive role in their work. On the other hand, persons in high power-distance cultures, like Japan and Mexico, are less comfortable taking an authoritative role unless their position specifically authorizes it. Thus, in low power-distance cultures, employees find it difficult or awkward to share decision-making with their superiors and are reluctant to take a more direct role in their work. Thus, to avoid unease, a lack of acceptance, and reduced job satisfaction, Hui *et al.* have reported that it is important that managers be highly sensitive to cultural differences when attempting to initiate empowerment processes. Nonetheless, according to the findings of Hui and his co-workers, even in high power-distance cultures, employee job performance and satisfaction can improve when empowerment programmes are properly implemented, because employees feel more able to contribute to the ongoing success of their organization.

IN ACTION #4

Meaning and empowerment

The notions of "meaning" and "empowerment" have major implications for workplace satisfaction. It should be obvious that when people are invested with a sense of meaning in their work, they perform at higher levels, maintain greater interest, and feel more committed. Unfortunately, many workplaces are dull, and the nature of the work repetitive, even (or especially) in corporate environments. Nevertheless, people who feel in control of their environment also feel as if they have choice in that environment, and choice engenders personal responsibility! So, given the reality of dull, repetitive jobs, how can we endow meaning? At a basic level, a person needs to feel that what he or she does in an organization has some value. Many people turn up to work each day, knowing that they are just another cog in the corporate machine: the message here is "you are replaceable, and you have no real value to our organization." Couple this with over-controlling supervisors, a bureaucratic company structure, little or no positive feedback, no ability to enact change and a lack of autonomy, and it it's not really surprising that most people hate their jobs or, at best, are simply ambivalent (given the principles discussed above). So, by allowing staff some decision-making abilities, giving them positive feedback about the value of their contributions and listening to what they have to say and then acting on it can dramatically enhance a person's sense of value.

As we mentioned earlier, employee voice, or employees' ability to express concerns, dislikes, suggestions, and recommendations to management, and to be involved in company decision-making processes, is an important aspect of empowerment. When an employee feels that he or she is able to be heard within the organization, and that his or her suggestions can have an impact on the way things are done, there is a substantial increase in job satisfaction, with a corresponding decrease in quit rates. According to research conducted by Batt and her colleagues (2002), who investigated employee voice in 363 telecommunications industry workers, facilitation of employee voice within an organization increased employee satisfaction, reduced turnover, and enhanced problem solving and productivity, especially in a team-based environment. Batt *et al.* reported that a team-based collective voice resulted in increased opportunities for workers to solve problems and improve production processes, leading to an increase in positive employee behaviours, a reduction in turnover and absenteeism, and greater productivity, especially when teams were self-managed, semi-autonomous, and were given considerable responsibility for making day-to-day decision without having to consult management. Batt and her co-workers also pointed out that high-commitment HR practices used in combination with enhanced voice mechanisms, such as higher pay, firm-specific training, promotion opportunities, and job security, further contributed to employee performance. Nevertheless, Batt *et al.* cautioned HR departments against practices that contradict high-commitment processes. For example, Batt and her co-workers have cited research involving HR reduction practices including downsizing, outsourcing, contingent staffing, and subcontracting, which indicated that these practices have a substantially undermining effect on any attempts to increase employee voice. In fact, Batt and her colleagues reported that the damage to employees' trust in their employer, based on HR reduction practices, resulted in substantially increased turnover rates and a corresponding rise in organizational costs that negated any savings from empowerment programmes and/or commitment-enhancing HR practices.

In a similar study to that of Batt *et al.* (2002), Delbridge and Whitfield (2001) examined employee perceptions of job influence and consequent organizational participation. Using 1998 data collected by the British Workplace Employee Relations Scheme, which assessed 28,323 employees from 2191 UK firms with more than 10 employees, Delbridge and his co-investigator (who defined employee participation in decision-making as "a process which allows employees to exert some influence over their work and the conditions under which they work") found that employees in establishments that offered a successful employee voice scheme were significantly more likely to perceive a greater level of influence over their jobs and show a greater level of organizational commitment. Moreover, a substantially increased effect was observed in organizations that allowed non-managerial employees access to and influence over managerial decisions, especially when there was a broad level and range of involvement, than in firms using schemes that focussed on employee influence only at the point of production (that is, only with regard to their direct job duties/influence).

It appears, however, that many organizations struggle with being able to give more discretionary power to their employees. For example, Gollan (2003), in his investigation of employee voice among 30 call centre workers at the Eurotunnel call centre, reported that management practices typical of call centres and other organizations with a strong front-line worker presence are seldom concerned with employee empowerment, especially with regard to the ability to voice concerns or suggestions. According to Gollan, despite a corporate mission that purported to encourage employee voice, employees at Eurotunnel felt that they had very little influence over managerial decisions, were widely dissatisfied with their management's inability to listen, act, or communicate, and felt that management did not keep them apprised of information relating to decisions made higher up in the organization. Consequently, employees reported feeling very low levels of empowerment, especially with regards to voice, and expressed a strong turnover intention, a finding that was reflected in the high turnover rates experienced by their employer.

As we have seen, when management is unable or unwilling to listen to, or give credence to, employee suggestions and concerns, they run the risk of alienating their workforce, invoking low levels of perceived empowerment among employees, reducing employee productivity, and increasing organizational costs through increased turnover rates. Moreover, as we saw in Section 2, a failure to recognize the value of employee contributions reflects a lack of ability to mine human capital, reducing the potential innovativeness and profitability of the organization. However, the use of relatively simple workplace practices to enhance employee empowerment and voice can remedy these problems and increase organizational commitment and trust. One such system has been developed in Denmark, a country with a strong history of employee involvement in the workplace (Triantafillou, 2003). Danish HR development models, which focus on increasing the ability for employees to participate in workplace development and day-to-day decisions, include a process known as employee development dialogue (EDD), defined as a "systematic, periodic, planned, and well-prepared dialogue between an employee and her/his direct supervisor – ideally in a way that the two persons enter the conversation as equal partners" (Triantafillou). According to Triantafillou, organizations and their employees can use EDD to determine employee needs regarding assessment, planning, tutoring, self-development, goal formation, and organizational strengthening, providing employees with a map of future possibilities for development within the organization. EDD sessions typically begin with a frank discussion between an employee and a supervisor in a private space, in which the supervisor presents a non-judgemental assessment of the employee's efforts. The employee then presents his or her views and evaluation of the superior's efforts, and his or her personal ambitions and grievances regarding job tasks, colleagues, prospects of promotion, and issues outside the workplace (such as family grievances). The supervisor listens actively, and provides practical suggestions and feedback whilst maintaining interest and concern and avoiding hostile or judgemental comments. The supervisor then acts on the employee's concerns to the best of his or her ability. According to Triantafillou, whilst EDD requires training for both participants, particularly for the supervisor, it is a highly effective means for enhancing employee empowerment because it provides workers with an excellent method for voicing concerns and desires, and the ability to make a contribution to the day-to-day running of the workplace.

Another system for increasing employee voice, through greater involvement in firm-wide decision-making, is employee ownership, a process that has become popular in the USA, the United Kingdom and the European Union based on the managerial assumption that it will increase employee motivation and company performance (Pendleton, Wilson, & Wright, 1998). In fact, following their investigation of organizational commitment in 234 employees from 4 employee-owned companies, Pendleton and his colleagues reported that employee ownership schemes did increase positive employee attitudes, such as feelings of involvement, integration, and affective commitment, but only when employee voice was increased as a result of the action. Specifically, Pendleton *et al.* indicated that employee ownership schemes succeeded in increasing both employee organizational commitment and productivity when employees achieved a substantially greater level of participation in organizational decision-making following their implementation. However, Pendleton and his co-workers reported that many such schemes fail because opportunities for employee voice do not eventuate. In other words, without increased opportunities for employees to feel that their actions affect organizational direction, employee ownership does not influence employee empowerment because employees do not feel that the "ownership" means anything. Ironically, Pendleton *et al.* have pointed out that in many employee-ownership schemes, the only way in which employees can feel a benefit is by selling back their shares to the company for a financial profit, losing whatever decision-making powers those shares entitled them to.

On a side note, in his book on enhancing satisfaction and meaning in the workplace, Csikszentmihalyi (2003) also propounded the importance of employee voice for enhancing feelings of empowerment. According to Csikszentmihalyi, the need for meaningful work is a fundamental human drive, but meaningful work can only be achieved when an employee feels that he or she is able to contribute to the workplace in a way that is recognized and lauded. Consequently, when employees feel that their ideas and opinions are not valued or even attended to, they are unlikely to perceive their jobs as meaningful, and either will withdraw psychologically, resulting in increased absenteeism and lowered productivity, or will quit. Either way, the organization loses financially.

Part 2: Perceived control and stress

An important aspect of a person's feelings of empowerment is his or her perceptions of control over the immediate environment. As we have already discussed, when someone perceives a high level of control over his or her surroundings, he or she will be more comfortable and less likely to be negatively affected by environmental stressors. The stress-reducing effects of perceived control have been studied in the laboratory since the early 1960s; however, more recently investigators have reported that the stress-buffering effects of perceived environmental control are equally valid in the workplace (McKnight, Ahmad, & Schroeder, 2001). McKnight *et al.*, for instance, who collected data from workers in 100 different manufacturing plants in three countries, reported that workers' positive perceptions of control over their work environment, in terms of working hours, goal setting and realization, and structure of the physical environment, significantly enhanced physical and psychological well-being. Moreover, the investigators reported that employee morale, an important variable in worker satisfaction and productivity, was enhanced significantly by the closeness of the relationship between employees and their supervisors. McKnight and his colleagues hypothesized that the quality of this relationship also helped to reduce the effects of stress[17] by increasing a person's ability to perceive their environment as less threatening.

In their report on the perception of control in the workplace, Bond and Bunce (2001) assessed the responses of 937 government workers on measures of occupational stress, job control, self-rated performance, well-being, and sickness and absence. They found that increased perceptions of job control (defined as an individual's personal feelings of control over work rewards, goals, and time) were significantly related to enhanced ratings of both happiness and health and a reduction in occupational stress. Bond and Bruce reported that, following reorganization of the workplace to allow workers more ability to regulate their own work environment (that is, increasing perceived job control), mental health and self-rated performance increased significantly, whilst reported sickness and absence rates were reduced. Likewise, Spector (2002), in his review of perceived employee control in the workplace, reported that perceived job control, in terms of time, goals, and reward, was the most important buffer against the negative effects of stress (that is, mental and physical illness, absenteeism, reduced performance, and depression). His survey of American workplace trends indicated that workplace stress is commonplace, resulting in both short- and long-term illness, and costing the US economy in excess of US$150 billion per year. Spector concluded that large organizational savings can be made by paying attention to employee perceptions of workplace control.

Other investigators have reported similar findings linking perceived job control with a reduction in workplace stress. For example, Jimmieson (2000), who measured workload, role conflict, work control, self-efficacy, psychological well-being, job satisfaction, somatic health, depersonalization, and negative affectivity in 100 telecommunications workers, reported that moderate and high levels of stress at work resulted in psychological, physiological, and behavioural problems. However, according to Jimmieson, by increasing a person's perception of job control which, in turn, was enhanced by increased self-efficacy (that is, situational specific self-confidence), these effects could be moderated. Moreover, people with high self-efficacy, also showed better somatic health and were more satisfied in their work. Clemmer (2002) in his article on the effects of empowerment in the workplace, echoed this sentiment, suggesting that perceived control, moderated by sufficient resources to successfully complete one's job, can decrease workplace stress, and increase motivation.

Fairbrother and Warn (2003) have posited a causal model indicating that illness is a consequence of stress, identifying perceived control as a pivotal variable in stress reduction. Fairbrother and his colleague, who investigated perceived control and stress in 100 naval officer trainees, reported that the workplace factors that lead to stress, such as conflict, poor leadership behaviour, low quality of social environment, work overload, and role-based factors, reduce an individual's perception of control. However, this perceived control also represents the primary means for a person to regulate his or her interaction

---

[17] See the section on support and meaning in the workplace in Section 4 for a more thorough review of this phenomenon.

between the self and the workplace, and the attainment of desired job outcomes. Thus, according to Fairbrother and Warn, without the perceived ability to advance oneself in the workplace, or to buffer the demands of everyday work, stress becomes inevitable, the consequences of which include rigidity of thought, reduced job satisfaction, increased desires to quit the workplace and consequent turnover, a loss of interest in work, reduced initiative, responsibility and capacity to perform, and a loss of concern both for colleagues and for the organization.

Pousette and Hanse (2002), who examined the responses of 1124 white- and blue-collar workers on measures of control, health, absenteeism, and stress, also reported a causal link between job control and stress. They reported that stress, absenteeism, and poor health were positively related to a low perception of perceived control which, in turn, originated in a poor fit between an employee and his or her environment. According to the investigators, in their sample, job control was moderated by job autonomy, in which a person was given sufficient latitude to control the timeframe, workload, and rewards associated with his or her work, and skill discretion, where a person was given the opportunity to utilize and enhance his or her skills. As a result, when job autonomy skills discretion and, consequently, perceived job control were low, the likelihood of a stress-related illness increased. In contrast, when a person felt that his or her job autonomy and skills discretion were reasonable, job satisfaction increased, whilst the likelihood of a stress-related illness decreased. In a related, cross-sectional study, de Jonge, Bosma, Peter, and Siegrist (2000) described the effects of job strain on their sample of 11,636 Dutch workers. They reported that when job strain, defined as the combined negative effects of high job demand, low perceived control, job dissatisfaction, and psychosomatic distress, was rated as high, there was a stronger consequent likelihood of illness. Furthermore, according to the investigators, when workers perceived an imbalance between effort and reward, there was an increased probability of emotional exhaustion, job dissatisfaction and/or health problems. Interestingly, de Jonge *et al.* have suggested that this imbalance could stem either from high perceived effort with low reward, low effort with low reward, or even high effort and high reward, if the employee did not believe that the level of reward was comparable to his or her level of effort. However, the effort–reward imbalance reported by de Jonge and his colleagues was moderated by a combination of high job demands and high perceived control, a permutation that allowed for an environment of motivation, learning, and growth. In contrast, a situation in which high job demands were combined with low perceived control resulted in an adverse strain reaction, often culminating in illness and/or burnout.

In the same vein, Demerouti, Bakker, de Jonge, Janssen, and Schaufeli (2001), in their investigation of 381 employees of an insurance company, reported that burnout was strongly related to perceived demands in the workplace. They found that when employees had little latitude for decision-making, but had high demands on their resources (for example, time, skills) there was a substantial increase in psychological strain, often followed by reduced physical and psychological health. As well, low decision latitude combined with a low demand resulted in boredom and a consequent reduction in work activity and productivity, leading to an actual reduction in job skills over time. Nevertheless, according to Demoerouti *et al.*, when decision latitude was both increased and combined with a moderate demand on personal resources, motivation and performance also increased, culminating in a phenomenon labelled by the investigators as "active learning". In this state, workers were highly motivated because they were not only able to use their existing skills in a challenging and stimulating manner, but also able to enhance those skills (and learn new ones) without feeling overpressured to perform. Similarly, when organizational support, in the form of high standards, personal control, and a feeling of belonging, is lacking, employees are likely to feel more stressed (Singh, 2000). According to Singh, without adequate attention, this stress can lead to burnout, in which an individual looses all interest in his or her job and, consequently, interest in the organization. Following his investigation of burnout tendencies in 306 customer service representatives, Singh reported that, as burnout approaches, quality of performance was reduced significantly, and employee turnover (an expensive prospect in terms of rehiring, retraining, and loss of morale) increased. To prevent the onset of workplace stress and its progression into burnout, Dunn (2001) has suggested that employers take responsibility for evaluating the causes of organizational stress, and take pains to remedy it. According to Dunn, this evaluation process should question several possible precursors to workplace stress, many of which are directly related to the employee's perceived control over his or her work: whether an employee's personal style is compatible with his or her environment and role, whether he or she is capable, whether his or her job role is clear, if both the employee and his or her manager understands the employee's job role, whether he or she is willing to work, whether performance expectations have been communicated and understood adequately, and if there is a good relationship between the management and the employee. Moreover, Dunn has suggested that this assessment be followed by attempts to establish both the reasons for employee unwillingness and dissatisfaction, and to determine the proper job-role match for each employee, even if this involves finding a better match (in collaboration with the employee, his or her colleagues, and the management) within the organization. Lastly, in Dunn's opinion, management should provide the proper training, where necessary, through coaching and mentoring, to allow an employee to improve his or her skills and knowledge and feel more control over his or her work role; by providing constructive feedback, and rewarding initiative, Dunn has posited that most employees can become more motivated and, consequently, more committed and valuable to an organization. In this vein, in Dunn's view, the goal of transforming employees into self-motivated, accomplished, and powerful individuals enhances the overall worth of an organization, and can enhance productivity and financial success dramatically.

The relationship between job control, stress, and illness has also been studied by Elovainio and co-workers (Elovainio, Kivimaeki, & Helkama 2001; Elovainio, Kivimaeki, & Vahtera 2002), who evaluated the effects of perceived organizational justice on health, job control, and occupational strain in 688 white-collar workers. They reported that the worker's perceptions of occupational justice (that is, how fairly they felt that they were treated within their organization) had a significant effect on perceived job control and that a reduction in job control increased the likelihood of illness. In other words, according to Elovainio *et al.*, when an employee felt that he or she was being treated unfairly, his or her perception of control over job-related variables such as time pressures, production demands, and goal achievements was reduced, and the consequent stress increased his or her chances of absenteeism, illness, and burnout. Conversely, employees with a higher perception of fairness felt more control over job-related variables and were reported to be healthier both physically and psychologically, both by occupation and by gender.

Part 3: Enhancing the perception of control: Psychological contracts, time, and self-actualization

Given the strong link between increased stress and lack of perceived workplace control, and noting the high costs to industry associated with stress, increasing workers' perceptions of control in their jobs is likely to be financially beneficial to firms. Researchers have pointed out several factors that mediate perceived control, including the psychological contract, workplace time, and workplace meaning.

As we discussed in Section 2, the psychological contract represents an unwritten, perceived agreement between the employee and employer, in which each party has expectations about how the other should behave. From the employee's perspective, this can include such things as positive HR practices, advancement opportunities and access to training, work–life balance, utilization of skills, involvement in workplace decision-making, and job security (Flannery, 2002). From the employer's perspective, the psychological contract can include perceptions regarding levels of commitment, punctuality, productivity, professionalism, and enthusiasm. When either party breaches the "terms" of the contract, there is a likelihood of negative consequences, including a reduction in trust and commitment, and financial penalties in the form of reduced productivity and performance, and increased absenteeism and turnover (Flannery); however, as we have seen, when employers take care to honour their part of the psychological contract, their employees are likely to be more productive, resulting in greater organizational performance. Moreover, when employees perceive an equitable balance in the psychological contract, they are more likely to feel a greater measure of control over their work environment (Flannery).

IN ACTION #5

Enhancing employee performance – advice to employers

A well-functioning organization is the product of its healthy, committed, and motivated employees. Nevertheless, when your employees are not well adjusted, they will reduce the operational ability of your firm. In the psychological literature, when people have a strong perception of control over their immediate environment, they are psychologically healthier and perform better. Conversely, when there is little perceived control, people become stressed, anxious, and unable to make effective decisions. These findings extend into the workplace so, if your employees feel that they have some say in what they do and what happens to them, they will be better able to do their jobs. Some of the things that can be done to improve perceived control include: modification of the physical environment so that it better suits the individual; relaxation of strict working hours, such as allowing employees to determine when they are the most productive and to modify their working hours around these times; allowing employees to have more say in their job roles, and making these roles more flexible (for example, job swapping) so that people can extend their skills and learn new ones; encouraging employees to develop and manage their own goals, including project acquisition, completion timeframes, allocation of resources, collaboration and outcomes; and allowing workers to have more say in the type and frequency of work incentives – not everyone is motivated by money, and rewards are most successful when they are contingent on high performance.

As an employer, it is unlikely that you will be able to actually implement these changes, it is up to your managers to make this happen. Nevertheless, it is your responsibility to make sure that your management team has your support as well as the tools and wherewithal to deliver these products. If they are unable, unwilling, or simply don't know how to make these changes, they won't happen and your employees will remain stressed and unproductive. This brings up a related point: are your managers capable, and are they actually able to manage? More importantly, are they leaders or simply administrators? Remember that it's easy to forget that managers are also employees and, therefore, share many of the same needs, ambitions, and problems (often more so, because of the increased stress that often goes with management, an issue that is not easily ameliorated by the salary or prestige associated with the position).

Another important variable to consider is whether your employees are able to perceive any meaning in their work – that is, do they have a sense of purpose? It would stand to reason that an employer who was concerned with the ongoing viability of his or her organization would also be concerned with whether his or her staff shared this concern. However, remarkably, many employers actually believe that the weekly paycheque is enough to provide this investment. Nevertheless, a large body of research indicates that when workers feel needed, can perceive meaning in their work, and feel that they are making a difference, they will work harder and better, and not be stressed about it (a paycheque does not provide this for most people). The message here is simple: if you don't give, you don't get, and if your employees don't feel that you care about them, they won't care about you, or your firm and its future.

The relationship between the psychological contract and perceived control in the workplace has been well illustrated by Liao-Troth (2001). According to Liao-Troth, on the one hand, the psychological contract is, from the employer's perspective, transactional, in which hard work is rewarded by higher pay and advancement, and relational, in which job security is dependent on employee loyalty and tenure. On the other hand, employees perceive the status of the psychological contract based on benefits received from the employer. These include: compensation (such as salary) and other perquisites, often intangible, such as recognition, support, stimulation, meaning, and fun; good faith and fair dealing, representing the interpersonal interactions between the employee and the firm; intrinsic job characteristics, such as the level of personal satisfaction from a particular job; and working conditions, including safety, resources, and other intangibles like socialization, belongingness, team interaction, and employee voice. In the opinion of Liao-Troth, breaches of the psychological contract have a distinctly negative impact on organizational commitment, or the "degree to which an employee feels obligated to an employer", because employees are likely to feel a reduction in control over their work environment, resulting in increased stress. Also, because (as we have seen) organizational commitment is strongly positively associated with an individual's intention to remain with an organization, these breaches can also increase turnover. To further explore this assertion, Liao-Troth examined attitude differences regarding the psychological contract and organizational commitment between paid and volunteer workers in a sample of 108 medical centre employees. He reported that the integrity of the psychological contract was important to both groups of workers, and that affective commitment was largely dependent on employees' perceptions of their employer's performance in terms of the psychological contract. Moreover, employees who felt a greater level of control over their working environment were more likely to also feel good about the state of their psychological contract, with a corresponding increase in their levels of affective commitment towards the organization. It is interesting to note that, in terms of the importance of the psychological contract for perceiving a greater level of workplace control, Liao-Troth did not find any significant differences between paid and volunteer workers. This suggests that many factors beyond monetary remuneration are at work in employees' psychological contracts with their employers,[18] a likelihood supported by Levin (2002), who reported that companies that concentrate on maintaining their part of the psychological contract with their employees perform consistently better than those who violate the contract by breaking implicit promises to their workers.

Employee perceptions of control over their working practices, and the importance of the firm's behaviour in honouring the psychological contract to encourage this control, have been further highlighted by Amoore (2004). In her article on organizational risk, Amoore has pointed out that companies can do irreparable harm to the relationship with their employees by ignoring the psychological contract. According to Amoore, whilst senior management might view organizational change, such as restructuring of employment, working practices, or the boundaries of the firm, as positive, it is likely that without adequate consultation and communication of their intentions employees will view these changes as a violation of the psychological contract, mostly because of the perceived reductions in control inherent in the change processes. For example, whilst management consultants and senior management might view downsizing and the use of contingent labour as a means to make the firm more lean and flexible, the resultant confusion is likely to leave employees uncertain of their job security, hours, and pay, with a consequent lowering of perceived control and morale. Likewise, whilst "new management practices"

---

[18] As we will see in Section 4, there are many positive consequences of workplace satisfaction that are not dependent on monetary compensation.

such as Total Quality Management, flexible working practices (lean production, just-in-time production), or customer orientation might be viewed by management as effective cost-cutting and streamlining methods, Amoore has suggested that without proper concern for the effects on employees, the increased individualization, self-monitoring, and surveillance inherent in these practices are likely to result in work intensification, confusion, and a further loss of perceived control. Consequently, to reduce the chances of lowering employees' perceptions of workplace control, senior management should pay careful attention to the likely impact of workplace change on the psychological contract: as we have seen, activities that illustrate an employer's commitment to the psychological contract serve to increase perceived control and affective commitment, improving worker productivity and performance; whilst those that detract from this commitment are likely to lead to worker withdrawal, increased stress and resultant illness, higher turnover, and the consequent organizational costs.

Another way to enhance employees' perceptions of control in the workplace is by addressing issues of time. The modern concept of time is a relatively recent phenomenon: prior to the industrial revolution, human conceptions of time followed an agrarian calendar, with sunrise, sunset, the cycles of the moon, and the changing of the seasons determining optimum times for events such as sowing or harvesting crops (Hoppe, 1999). Consequently, it was only during the industrial age, along with the development of machinery that allowed mass production of goods but which required constant attention and predictable schedules, that the idea of punctuality appeared. This era also saw the development of more sophisticated timekeeping machinery in the form of accurate clocks and watches, which resulted in both a greater awareness of the passing of time and the need for punctuality. Moreover, according to Hoppe, the subsequent information age has brought substantially more time pressures to bear. Not only are we expected to be prompt, but we are now required to account for our time, between the time pressures of work, home, and social lives. Simultaneously, people have become more and more aware of leisure time, with the evolution of greater numbers of pastimes to fill our entertainment needs when we are not working. In fact, Hoppe has argued that for many people working time has become, to a greater or lesser extent, the time spent in order to afford leisure time. Time, especially leisure time, has therefore become a rather precious commodity, with a substantially greater awareness of both its passing and its use (Hoppe). It is, therefore, noteworthy that employees are under increasing pressure to work longer hours despite the fact that, unlike their parents and grandparents, most workers no longer sell their time but, rather, trade what they produce with their time (Hoppe), a notion that makes the traditional nine-to-five workday somewhat redundant. Nevertheless, as we saw in Section 1, increased workplace time pressures have a substantial impact on the ability of employees to balance their work and home lives, with many employees feeling unable to control the time pressures in their lives. Consequently, control over the amount of time spent at work, or travelling to and from work, represents an important aspect of workplace empowerment, and is a strong mediator of the perception of control over workplace pressures. In this vein, Berg, Appelbaum, Bailey, and Kalleberg (2004), in their review of employee control of working time in various countries, have reported on the difficulties faced by many employees in managing to control their time. According to Berg and his colleagues, in the majority of countries, save several European countries (such as Sweden and France) whose governments have imposed limited work week laws, employee time spent at work is largely in the hands of the employer: it remains up to employers to develop and implement flextime, and other work–life balance policies that can help employees to manage the time pressures of their work. However, as we have seen, work–life balance remains a distinct problem in many organizations; even when policies are in place to help workers balance work and life pressures, they are seldom adequately implemented, resulting in negative financial consequences for firms that fail to act appropriately. Again, as we have already discussed, when work–life balance policies are well researched, developed, monitored, and assessed, there is a high likelihood of corporate savings based on raised employee productivity and satisfaction, combined with reduced turnover, largely because employees perceive a greater measure of control over their working time. Nevertheless, the perceived availability and usability of these programmes remains the key element to their success. For example, in her examination of 483 biotech employees from hi-tech US firms, Eaton (2003) pointed out that employees who perceive that company-initiated work–life balance programmes are readily available and usable also demonstrated significantly greater levels of organizational commitment and productivity. Moreover, when adequately utilized, programmes that encouraged employee control over time, such as flexibility of working hours, and the pace of work, contributed substantially to employees' overall perceptions of workplace control.

In Section 1 we discussed work–life balance and the types of HR practices that organizations can enact to improve employee satisfaction in the workplace, and in Section 4 we will examine the positive and negative effects of workplace satisfaction. However, in our present discussion of perceived control and empowerment, which are largely based on a person's psychological state, it also makes sense to look at some of the psychological effects of workplace processes, especially given the premise that employees who feel fulfilled and psychologically satisfied are also likely to perceive a greater level of control over their work environment and a consequently higher level of empowerment. One paper that has linked workplace practices with psychological control was that of Rubery and Grimshaw (2001), who examined how information communication technologies (ICTs) could enhance job quality. According to these authors, job quality, which is related to feelings of fulfilment in the workplace, is determined by workplace variables that affect workplace satisfaction, perceptions of control, and workplace behaviours, such as turnover intention, absenteeism rates, and organizational citizenship. These variables can include: the skills involved in daily job activities and the opportunity to use those skills; the degree of autonomy at work; the perceived fairness of management systems; freedom of association with groups outside of the organization (such as unions); job security; the level of responsibilities in the job balanced against stress levels associated with those responsibilities; work intensity and work–life balance, including encouragement to develop interests outside of or unconnected with work; the opportunities that the job provides for skills development and enhancement, and the ability over time to move into roles that are more satisfying, more secure, and better paid; and opportunities afforded for contributing towards the creative activities of the organization, both in terms of problem solving and the use of personal initiatives. Consequently, Rubery and her co-worker concluded that when a job is designed to enhance job quality, employees are able to fulfil their personal needs to a far greater extent and, consequently, perceive a far greater level of workplace control and a stronger level of empowerment. Similarly, Hundley (2001), in his study of 1316 self-employed and organizationally employed workers, reported that, for the most part, self-employed persons are more likely to feel satisfied in their work and life than equivalent organizationally employed workers because of correspondingly greater feelings of control over their work activities. Specifically, according to Hundley, self-employed persons felt more empowered and in control of their work environment because they perceived fewer constraints or routines in their work, and felt that they had a greater level of task and job autonomy, increased ownership, and were more able to use and develop their existing skills and learn new ones than their regularly employed counterparts. In other words, Hundley's self-employed participants were able to fulfil their "innate" needs for self-expansion and growth to a greater extent than organizational employees because they had a greater level of control over what they did and how they did it.

The need for variables that enhance the perception of control in the workplace is also highlighted by examinations of the negative consequences of restrictive workplace. For example, Hsieh and Hsieh (2003), who investigated the effects of job standardization on 412 employees, reported that when jobs are not perceived as fulfilling, there is a significant decrease in perceptions of job control, accompanied by a rise in burnout. In particular, in jobs in which there was a formalization of roles, where there was excessive scrutiny by supervisors, and in which there were rigid rules and procedures, employees reported feeling unmotivated, disempowered, and confined, with a resultant increase in conflict with the management and a reduction in affective commitment towards the organization. Likewise, in an ongoing longitudinal investigation of voluntary turnover, Price (2001) has found that when jobs are routine, provide little autonomy, and offer little opportunity for involvement, skills utilization or advancement, employees feel substantially less control over their work, and are significantly more likely to experience low affective commitment and seek an alternative employer. Like Hsieh and Hsieh, Price concludes that perceptions of control in the workplace are highly dependent on employees' ability to participate in work that is challenging, engaging, and in which they have a measure of autonomy over how and when their work is performed.

On a related note, in his discussion of needs in everyday life, Csikszentmihalyi (2003) has posited that human needs are substantially greater than the basics of nourishment, shelter, emotional support, and simple work. Like Maslow who proposed a pyramid of self-actualization (Ronen, 2001), Csikszentmihalyi has suggested that to achieve true satisfaction, humans require the ability in work and in life to use and challenge their existing skills, and to be able to be exposed to the things that they find the most interesting. According to Csikszentmihalyi, when employees feel that they can control their work environment, they are more motivated to seek out new challenges and, consequently, are able to feel more fulfilled in their work roles. This equates to finding meaning in life through meaningful work, a topic that we will explore in greater depth in Section 4.

Part 4: Control and performance: High-performance work systems

In recent times, so-called high-performance work systems (HPWS) have received a lot of attention, particularly in management consulting circles. Typically, HPWS claim to increase worker empowerment and the perception of control in the workplace, by giving employees greater autonomy and access to increased participation in decision-making (Godard, 2001). Nevertheless, as we have already seen, simply introducing workplace changes does not guarantee positive outcomes; in many cases well-intentioned interventions can have negative consequences to both the organization and its employees. Consequently, before implementing change, it is extremely important that senior management conduct a proper analysis of the type of changes to be made, the proposed benefits of the change, the necessary conditions required for change, and the best methods for undergoing change. In this section we will examine the various types of HPWS and look at their effects on employee control.

According to Tomer (2001), HPWS, also known as high-involvement or high-commitment work systems, are typified by a different relationship between the employer and employee than in conventional workplaces. This relationship is designed to improve individual performance through better management of human resources, allowing individual employees to more readily contribute to the success of the organization. Consequently, ideal HPWS are characterized by employment security, selective hiring of new personnel, self-managed teams, decentralization of decision-making, comparatively high compensation (contingent on firm performance), extensive training (including job rotation), transparent communication, and a reduction in status distinctions and barriers, such as dress, language, office arrangement, and wage differentials across levels. Furthermore, in the opinion of its practitioners, because of these enhanced measures, HPWS reduce employee turnover, and increase employee productivity and corporate financial performance, especially when these HR practices are "bundled" so that they are geared towards employee empowerment, involvement, and multiskilling (Tomer). Nevertheless, despite these potential positive outcomes for the organization and its employees, Tomer has identified several issues that explain why the implementations of HPWS are rarely completely successful. First, as we examined in Section 1, decision-making in firms is too often guided by economists, using mainstream economic principles that were designed to explain behaviour in control-oriented (rather than non-hierarchical) organizations, where there is a clear relationship between the principal (that is, managers) and the agent (that is, employees). These systems work on the basis of trying to encourage workers to perform tasks that they find onerous; that is, based on the assumption that financial compensation or rewards should be enough to motivate employees when they dislike their jobs. Again, as we have discovered throughout the text so far, people are often not satisfied with this type of compensatory relationship and require more, in the form of challenge, knowledge, or personal fulfilment, to be adequately motivated. Second, alongside their conventional management systems, many firms employ only the most conventional HRM systems (Tomer), which amount, simply, to personnel management. According to Tomer, personnel managers are interested in organizational factors such as employee recruitment, selection, training, development, performance appraisal, compensation and labour relations, but seldom concern themselves with practices that encourage employee empowerment through greater involvement in decision-making, increased latitude in control over their time, work, and resources, the encouragement of greater work–life balance, or through development of employee interests, skills and ambitions. This failure, in Tomer's opinion, results in a failure to realize the competitive advantages that result from an empowered workforce.

IN ACTION #6

High-performance work system terminology

High-Performance work systems (HPWS) are often touted as corporate saviours by their practitioners. However, the catch-cry contains several distinct approaches, some of which are more successful in increasing organizational performance than others and a substantial amount of jargon. Aspects of HPWS include:

- Participatory Work Organization (PWO): Systems that are designed to allow a greater level of participation by non-managerial employees in everyday decision-making. Includes self-managed teams and workplace-level employee involvement programmes.

- Commitment Enhancing Human Resources Management (C-HRM): HR practices that are designed to increase affective commitment towards an organization. Includes intensive training, work–life balance programmes, profit sharing, job security, selective recruitment, and dissolution of status discrimination between workers and management.

- Quality of Work Life (QWL): Programmes that are designed to increase employee perception of quality in working life and job satisfaction. Often a combination of PWO and C-HRM functions.

- Total Quality Management (TQM): A system that espouses increased empowerment through the management of quality in an organization. Includes greater distribution of information and substantial management training.

- Lean Production (LP): A process that is supposed to increase organizational performance through the division of tasks to teams that are responsible for achieving preset targets in an efficient manner.

- Self-Managed Teams (SMT): A system designed to reduce organizational hierarchies by placing many managerial functions under the control of semi-autonomous groups, that are responsible for the planning, implementation, and completion of tasks. Ideally, SMTs are also in charge of developing their own performance standards, setting and meeting deadlines, and deciding which resources they require for successful project completion.

With these potential pitfalls in mind, in order to make HPWS work effectively Tomer (2001) has suggested that organizations wishing to implement HPWS pay attention to three important areas. First, they need to update their economic systems to include behavioural economics, which recognize that human input into any system is more complicated than the simple, traditional "carrot and stick" motivation systems used by many organizations. Using behavioural economic principles, firms can begin to understand that to adequately access their human capital, they need to invest time and resources into developing systems that actually help to enhance employee satisfaction, well-being, and empowerment. Second, organizations need to recognize that HPWS HRM practices will only increase firm financial performance when employees possess knowledge and skills that managers lack (that is, human capital), when employees are motivated to apply these skills and knowledge through discretionary effort, and when the firm's business strategy can only be achieved when employees apply this effort. In other words, HWPS work better when managers are able to lever the human capital and tacit knowledge of their workforce by providing an environment that encourages employee involvement and participation in organizational processes and when these processes are geared around employee participation. In these cases, HPWS lead to greater employee perceived control over their work, higher involvement, and higher affective commitment to the organization. Third, senior management should be aware that their investment in HPWS processes effectively means an investment in fulfilling the higher needs of their employees, so that workers are able to choose a level of effort that maximizes their utility. This requires an effective match between the individual and the characteristics of his or her job and the organization, the existence of clear, meaningful goals within a job and within the organization, and careful attention to the nature and enforcement of the psychological contract. These precautions notwithstanding, Tomer warns that HPWS are not simply a mater of plugging in best technology or methodological practices to an organization but, instead, require a transformation of the relationship between an employer and employees. Nevertheless, according to Tomer, this transformation is seldom easy because it requires relatively high, initial organization-wide training costs, and is often impeded by the difficulties of satisfying short-term oriented investors, as well as managerial inertia and resistance resulting from conservative values and beliefs, combined with uncertainty about what is required from them in a HPWS environment.

Godard (2001), in his examination of the effects of HPWS on employee reactions in 508 Canadian workers, has confirmed many of Tomer's (2001) recommendations. Prompted by the recent attention towards HPWS and managerial assumptions regarding their effectiveness, Godard evaluated his participants on a wide range of variables, including feelings of belongingness and empowerment, as well as self-esteem, fatigue, job satisfaction, organizational commitment, motivation, and citizenship behaviour, and their relationship to various types of so-called HPWS or advanced work practices (AWP), including Total Quality Management, "just-in-time" and lean production, team-based work, team autonomy, and job rotation. As a result of his findings, Godard reported that conventional assumptions about the effectiveness of AWP were largely over-simplified. According to Godard, whilst moderate implementation of many types of AWP had mostly positive implications for employers (including increased profitability) and for employees (greater job satisfaction, self-esteem, motivation, commitment, and organizational citizenship behaviour), higher levels of implementation resulted in a reduction of these positive benefits, because of higher levels of stress generated by the systems. However, Godard believes that this stress was generated by an imperfect application by management of the ideas behind HPWS; effectively, in an attempt to increase productivity, senior management had put in place practices, such as semi-autonomous teams, with corresponding levels of increased responsibility and greater accountability, but without providing employees with either the tools to achieve their new goals, or the authority to make any real changes. That is, management were still setting achievement goals, but had placed the responsibility for how they were to be realized on workers or teams, without allowing them any control over their projects. This means that many of the functions performed by managers, such as project, resource, and time management, became the responsibility of employees on the assumption that this extra responsibility was equal to empowerment. According to Godard, this oversight neither empowers nor motivates employees but, rather, overwhelms them with work over which they have less control. Likewise, when these extra pressures are introduced without adequate backup from positive HR practices (such as training, guidance, leadership, and access to information and resources) that allow employees to better cope with their new discretionary responsibilities, employees invariably feel overworked, stressed, and are likely to become demotivated, unproductive, and dissatisfied. Consequently, Godard concluded that whilst the principles of various HPWS are probably sound, unless they are applied in a way that actually enhances employees' abilities to participate in workplace decisions, increasing the perception of workplace control and enhancing feelings of empowerment, they can lead to negative consequences for both the firm and its employees. Moreover, because they are likely to increase work intensity without a corresponding increase in empowerment, Godard warns particularly against LP systems, the natures of which are geared towards streamlining organizational processes to supposedly increase performance, and also cautions senior management against HPWS implementation simply because they are "trendy".

In a study similar to that of Godard (2001), Preuss (2003) concluded that the success of HPWS is dependent on the quality of information made available to employees. Following his investigation of the responses of 935 registered nurses from several hospitals on measures (including work design, TQM implementation, work-specific knowledge, access to information, and quality of that information), Preuss reported that the introduction of TQM, which is supposed to allow employees access to greater amounts of information to enhance decision-making only increased productivity if employees had the appropriate skills, knowledge, and job flexibility to make on the spot decisions. According to Preuss, because information is dynamic (that is, variable according to situation and need), simply increasing employee access to information does not guarantee its uptake. Rather, an employee's ability to use and interpret information is dependent on his or her training, skills, prior knowledge, and freedom to act without permission from a supervisor. Thus, the only way to increase the value of information in an organization is to ensure that employees are highly skilled and given the latitude to use those skills when required, and to ensure that the information given to employees is of high quality, rather than simply increasing its quantity. Furthermore, unless employers are willing to provide workers with the training they require to be able to adequately interpret the information being given to them, it is unrealistic to assume that they will know what to do with it, and more likely that they will feel less in control of their work environment, with the consequence of greater stress and its associated problems. Preuss concluded that although TQM is touted as a system for increasing employee empowerment through greater access to information, it is largely inadequate because it does not provide a mechanism for increasing employees' ability to interpret that information. In other words, by increasing the amount of information that an employee must deal with without first making sure that the information is of high quality, and that the employee is capable of understanding, interpreting and acting on the information, organizations are actually reducing the ability of employees to perform, by reducing feelings of control and virtually guaranteeing a consequent rise in stress.

In another study of the efficacy of HRM practices implemented as a part of HPWS, Black and Lynch (2001) examined 1994 data collected by the US Census Bureau from over 3000 private firms. After the creation of a mathematical model to determine precisely which HR practices were most effective, Black and her colleague found that the most important factors for increased workplace productivity lay not in the individual practices themselves, but in the way in which they were implemented. For example, productivity increases following the introduction of profit-sharing schemes were effective only when they were extended to all non-managerial employees. Likewise, HPWS themselves did not raise employee productivity. Rather, it was the increased perceptions of employee voice and sense of control following successful HPWS implementation that raised employee effectiveness. That is, the findings of Black and her co-worker suggest that it is not the particular HPWS that leads to change, but rather the conditions that are created by their application. For instance, when managers are trained to listen more effectively and act on what they hear from their subordinates, they are better able to mine human capital, and use it in collaboration with employees to increase organizational performance. This is analogous to psychotherapy, in which it is not necessarily a particular therapeutic technique that leads to positive behaviour change, but rather the conditions engendered by the therapist–client relationship (such as freedom to express one's problems to someone who can listen non-judgementally) that allow for the possibility of change. Consequently, systems like TQM, which are often touted as panaceas for solving organizational problems, do not really perform as advertised. Instead, it is the change in condition allowing greater employee latitude in decision-making and voice that make them effective. In fact, like Godard (2001), according to Black and Lynch, when TQM programmes are enacted without a consequent increase in employee perceptions of control, it is likely that organizational performance will actually decline. With this in mind, senior management should think carefully about the likely outcomes of a HPWS before its implementation.

Best practice: Case examples of how it's being done

Empowerment, employee voice, and ownership

In their report on involving employees in the workplace (*Partnership Working and Involving Employees*, 2005), the UK DTI cited the case example of Proper Cornish Ltd., a UK food manufacturer who has recently won a high-performance workplace award for their changes to the way employees are involved in company-wide decision-making. According to the DTI, prior to the work-practice modifications, Proper Cornish suffered from a high rate of absenteeism and staff turnover as the result of staff dissatisfaction with the long hours required by management to meet production deadlines. To counter these problems, senior management introduced communication groups among the firm's 165 staff, to allow a better discourse between employees and directors and to establish the cause of the company's problems and employees' dissatisfaction. This process identified pay and performance issues, as well as working conditions and the physical environment, as sources of malcontent among staff. By allowing employees a voice, much of the dissatisfaction that centred on an "us and them" division between management and employees was dissipated. Moreover, following employee suggested changes, staff turnover was reduced by over a half, and absenteeism was reduced from 18 to 7 per cent. This increase in attendance resulted in a rise in production levels to 98 per cent, and resulted in savings of £3000 per week over previous overtime payments required to make up the time lost to absenteeism. In order to maintain these positive effects, a regular staff "health check" survey was established to determine employee suggestions and dissatisfactions.

Points for action: Practical recommendations for change

Empowerment, employee voice, and ownership

In order to manage expectations and increase empowerment in the workplace, Paul *et al.* (2000) have made the following recommendations:

- So that employees are able to feel a sense of empowerment in their work, jobs should be designed from the outset to
  - allow individuals at all levels of the organization to be involved (at least to some extent) in decisions involving their day-to-day occupation as well as those decisions that affect the entire organization
  - allow individual employees discretionary control over aspects of their work, including say in the type of tasks allocated to them, the timeframe for task

completion, the resources available to them, and the people with whom they will collaborate.

- The organization should be restructured to enable:
  - Modification of reward systems to include employee stock ownership options (making sure that all levels of the organization have access to an equitable level of distribution), and profit or gain sharing, so that employees are able to share in the benefits that their industry has generated for the firm
  - training of managers so that they understand the value of empowerment in the workforce without feeling threatened; so that they are able to adequately give advice, counselling, and distribute accurate, timely information; and are able to learn transformational leadership styles[19] to counter maladaptive techniques learnt on the job
  - increased communication throughout the organization, so that firms are able to communicate information to their employees in a manner that is clear and honest; so employees are able to engage in two-way discourse with senior management; and so that the organization is able to honour its promises to the workforce
  - positive HR practices within the organization, including participation and empowerment programmes; employee wellness programmes; work–life balance programmes; greater employment security; career and other training; the opportunity to develop multiple skills; and diverse career paths (rather than simple progression through the company hierarchy), in order to develop a more trusting and supportive work environment, and increase both employer and employee loyalty.

- Lastly, management should take pains to avoid breaches of the psychological contract by managing employee expectations, including:
  - addressing unrealistic expectations through realistic job previews and more accurate descriptions of job roles and duties, and candid, frequent discussions between employees and more senior managers
  - periodic employee opinion surveys (not just at employee exit) to address employee needs and harness human capital, that involve open-ended questions and that are evaluated by both managers and other employees
  - the establishment of focus or discussion groups of eight to 10 people representing different aspects of the business, in order to highlight ideas, expectations and problems, and to communicate these issues to senior management
  - adequate training of HR managers, interviewers, and public relations employees in interviewing skills, to allow accurate information about the state of employee morale to be gathered
  - the revision of organizational publications so that they offer a clear and consistent message, and do not lead employees to have unrealistic opinions regarding the state of their psychological contracts.

---

[19] See Section 5 for a more in-depth discussion of transformational and other leadership styles.

Control and performance: High-performance work systems

Tomer (2001) has suggested that for HPWS to be effective, management needs to consider and implement the following factors:

- Increasing employment security, so that workers are able to commit without concern over future employment prospects. This represents a two-way process: the employer provides a commitment to the employee, whilst, for the most part, the employee shows a greater level of loyalty in return.

- Being more selective in hiring new personnel. It is important that new recruits are well matched to the conditions the firm is attempting to put in place. This can be achieved simply by a greater level of discussion and transparency during the hiring phase, so that both parties have a comprehensive understanding of what each expects of the other. This discourse will also help to reduce breaches in the psychological contract following commencement of employment.

- Teams should be encouraged to be self-managing. This means that team members should be free to make decisions relating to the completion and success of their projects without direct supervision or interference.

- Decision-making should be decentralized. Rather than all company edicts coming from a central office or department, sections, teams, and individuals should be given discretionary powers to make decisions regarding their projects, without having to get permission from a superior. This allows for a greater sense of control over workplace variables, reduces stress, increases satisfaction, and enhances performance.

- Compensation should be increased to reduce employees' desire to look elsewhere for employment. If compensation is increased based on organizational performance (for example, profit sharing), employees are likely to align their interests with those of the firm. However, these benefits should be sufficient, and equitable throughout the organization; unequal or inadequate amounts can encourage resentment and dissatisfaction.

- The firm should invest in extensive training for its employees to help them perform their jobs more effectively. Training should be focussed both on job-specific tasks and on more general skills (such as communication and interpersonal interaction). As well, employees should be encouraged to develop skills in their interests outside of the workplace that, although potentially unrelated to their job roles, can have a positive spillover effect into work life.

- There should be a reduction in status distinctions and barriers within the organization, including:
  - a lessening of hierarchies including the dismantling of as many levels of management as possible
  - more relaxed dress codes
  - use of less formal language and titles
  - a more equitable and sociable office arrangement
  - less wage differentials across the organization.

- Information regarding organizational performance (financial and otherwise) should be freely distributed within the organization to all employees.

- Recognition that, at a senior level, each of these recommendations (although costly to implement) is likely to substantially increase company performance in the longer term; especially if a programme is implemented in a way that is well planned, clearly communicated, and regularly assessed.

Summary

Empowerment represents the "process of passing autonomy and responsibility to individuals at lower levels of the organizational hierarchy", and can result in employees perceiving an increasing amount of control over their working life. Effective empowerment results in increased quality of products, services, decision-making and problem solving, whilst reducing absenteeism and turnover; and is the result of effectual job design, organizational planning, effective reward systems, and strong management. Unfortunately, the "buzz word" nature of empowerment has led to a plethora of programmes that promise employee empowerment, but deliver work intensification by actually reducing the ability to make autonomous decisions or control workplace variables. Employee voice, an aspect of empowerment, represents the ability of employees to express their concerns, dislikes, suggestions and recommendations within the organization, allowing a level of involvement in the process of organizational decision-making. Like empowerment, a valid employee voice can result in increased opportunities for employees to solve problems, increasing their productivity, and is vital for job satisfaction.

Another aspect of empowerment is the perceived control of the work environment. Typically, humans experience greater stress when they feel unable to manipulate the variables within their environment. Thus, a perception of control reduces stress, enhances satisfaction, and saves money through lowered illness, absenteeism, burnout, and turnover. The perception of control can be increased through attention to several workplace factors: principally the psychological contract, unwritten agreement between the employer and employee that represents expectation about how the other party should behave. When the psychological contract is honoured, employees feel that they have a greater level of control over their work and responsibilities, are likely to be more productive, and have a greater level of affective commitment to their employer. However, breaches of the psychological contract can result in lowered commitment and trust, and raised absenteeism and turnover, reducing organizational profitability.

In recent times, attempts to increase performance through greater employee perception of control have resulted in so-called high-performance work systems that claim to increase worker empowerment by giving employees a stronger hand in decision-making access and autonomy. Researchers have demonstrated that these systems can increase organizational performance and employee satisfaction, but only when they are "bundled" together in a package that includes employment security, self-managed teams, the decentralization of decision-making, high levels of financial compensation, extensive training, transparent communication, and a reduction in the status of organizational distinctions and barriers. Needless to say, attempts to increase workplace performance that fail to encompass this "package" can lead to lowered employee satisfaction and performance, by actually increasing workload at the expense of control and autonomy. Systems such as "just in time" and "lean" production, whilst often touted as empowerment systems, are often representative of this failure.

REVIEW QUESTIONS

1. Describe empowerment, and highlight its importance for employee performance.
2. How do perceptions of control moderate stress?
3. Summarize the techniques that can help to increase a person's perceptions of control in the workplace.
4. Outline the benefits and drawbacks of the various types of high-performance work systems.
5. Describe experiences in which you have experienced workplace stress, and what, if any, you were able to do to reduce it.
6. Think back to a time when you felt "empowered" at work. What were the conditions that increased your feelings of empowerment and control?

Mind-diagram summary

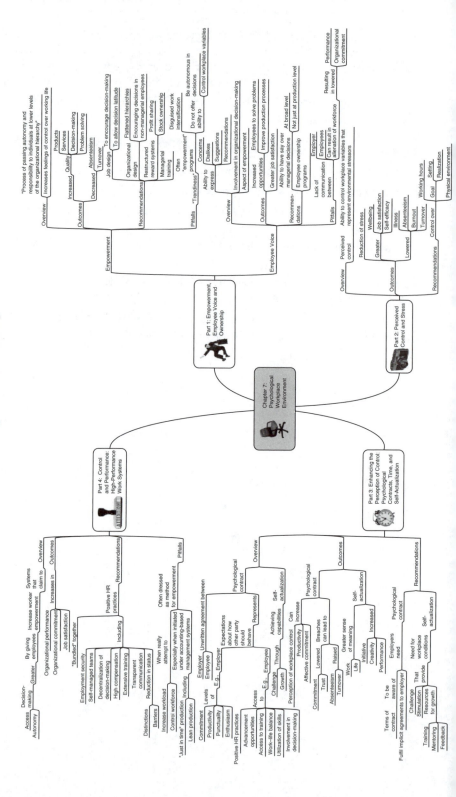

Chapter 7: Psychological Workplace Environment

Part 1: Empowerment, Employee Voice and Ownership

Empowerment

Overview
- "Process of passing autonomy and responsibility to individuals at lower levels of the organizational hierarchy"
- Increases feelings of control over working life

Outcomes
- Increased
  - Quality
    - Products
    - Services
  - Decision-making
  - Problem solving
- Decreased
  - Turnover
  - Absenteeism

Recommendations
- Job design
  - To encourage decision-making
  - To allow decision latitude
- Organizational design
  - Flattened hierarchies
  - Encouraging decisions in non-managerial employees
- Restructured reward systems
  - Profit sharing
  - Stock ownership
- Managerial training

Pitfalls
- Often "empowerment" programs
- "Trendiness" of programs
  - Disguised work intensification
  - Do not offer ability to
    - Be autonomous in decisions
    - Control workplace variables

Employee Voice

Overview
- Ability to express
  - Dislikes
  - Suggestions
  - Recommendations
- Involvement in organizational decision-making

Outcomes
- Aspect of empowerment
  - Increased opportunities
    - Employees to solve problems
    - Improve production processes
  - Greater job satisfaction
  - Ability to have say over managerial decisions

Recommendations
- Employee ownership programs
  - At broad level
  - Not just at production level

Pitfalls
- Lack of communication between
  - Employer
  - Employees
- Can result in alienation of workforce
  - Resulting in lowered
    - Performance
    - Organizational commitment

Part 2: Perceived Control and Stress

Overview
- Ability to control workplace variables that represent environmental stressors

Outcomes
- Reduction of stress
- Wellbeing
- Greater
  - Job satisfaction
  - Self-efficacy
- Lowered
  - Illness
  - Absenteeism
  - Burnout
  - Turnover
- Control over
  - Working hours
  - Goal setting
  - Realization
  - Physical environment

Recommendations

Part 3: Enhancing the Perception of Control: Psychological Contracts, Time, and Self-Actualization

Overview
- Psychological contract
  - Represents
    - Unwritten agreement between
      - Employer
      - Employee
        - E.g. Employer
          - Expectations about how other party should behave
        - E.g. Employee
- Self-actualization
  - Achieving capabilities
  - Can increase
    - Productivity
    - Affective commitment
    - Perception of workplace control

Outcomes
- Psychological contract
  - Breaches can lead to
    - Commitment
      - Trust
      - Lowered
    - Absenteeism
      - Raised
    - Turnover
- Self-actualization
  - Greater sense of meaning
    - Work
    - Life
  - Initiative
  - Creativity
  - Increased
    - Performance

Recommendations
- Psychological contract
  - Employers need
    - To be aware of
      - Terms of contract
      - Fulfil implicit agreements to employer
- Self-actualization
  - Need for workplace conditions
    - That provide
      - Challenge
      - Stimulation
      - Resources for growth
        - Training
        - Mentoring
        - Feedback

Part 4: Control and Performance: High-Performance Work Systems

Overview
- Increase worker empowerment
  - By giving employees
    - Access
    - Autonomy
    - Decision-making
  - Greater
    - Organizational performance
    - Organizational commitment
    - Job satisfaction
- Systems that claim to
  - "Bundled" together

Outcomes
- Increases in
  - Employment security
  - Self-managed teams
  - Decentralization of decision-making
  - High compensation
  - Extensive training
  - Transparent communication
  - Reduction in status
    - Distinctions

Recommendations
- Positive HR practices
  - Including
    - Barriers
      - Increase workload
      - Control workforce
        - "Just in time" production
        - Lean production
    - Commitment
      - Productivity
      - Punctuality
      - Enthusiasm
    - Positive HR practices
      - Access to
        - Advancement opportunities
        - Access to training
        - Work-life balance
        - Utilization of skills
        - Involvement in decision-making
      - E.g. Employee
        - Challenge
        - Growth
        - Through
          - Work
          - Life

Pitfalls
- Often dressed as method for empowerment
- Especially when initiated under accounting-based management systems
- When really attempt to

Skills Training and Stress Management

KEYWORDS   Compensation, cope, day to day, mental health, physical health, pressure, workload.

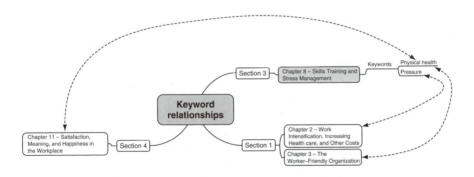

Keyword relationships

Section 3 — Chapter 8 – Skills Training and Stress Management

Keywords — Physical health, Pressure

Chapter 11 – Satisfaction, Meaning, and Happiness in the Workplace — Section 4

Section 1 — Chapter 2 – Work Intensification, Increasing Health care, and Other Costs; Chapter 3 – The Worker–Friendly Organization

IMPORTANT CONCEPTS   Disease prevention, stress management.

Perception of control over one's environment represents one of several variables in the enhancement of individual performance. Obviously, when someone feels in control of his or her immediate surroundings and actions, there is a corresponding sense of relaxation and satisfaction. However, in order for a person to function effectively in any environment, he or she must also be both physically and psychologically healthy, and be able to function consistently in an environment free of long-term exposure to high levels of stress. Unfortunately, as we have seen, many workplaces encourage stress and poor health because of ignorance or apathy. In order to address this problem, the following section summarizes techniques available to reduce stress and enhance health and, consequently, performance in the workplace.

Part 1: Stress, health, and morale

In a recent literature review of the effects of disease prevention and health promotion on workplace productivity, Riedel *et al.* (2001) reported that the most important moderator of job performance was morale. Morale, according to these authors, can be increased substantially when companies invest in the well-being of their employees, such as including employee health priorities in business objectives and linking employee satisfaction and performance to financial indicators. In fact, Riedel and his colleagues reported that in the Fortune magazine's top 100 companies to work for, all of which were rated highly on employee morale and performance, particular attention has been paid to the recognition of employee well-being. Nevertheless, according to Riedel *et al.*, these top companies represent a minority; most companies ignore issues of employee morale, or fail in their attempts to enhance performance and morale because they are addressed inadequately. For instance, many companies fall short of realizing the magnitude of a given problem (such as dissatisfaction, stress, or low morale), assuming that prevalence is directly related to a calculable financial cost (for example, assessing the amount of workplace stress by calculating the number of days off taken per year), without taking into account the large number of other variables that contribute to these problems (for example, workplace stress will be manifest in many ways that cannot be directly calculated, such as demoralization, reduced productivity, low motivation, and recalcitrance). Moreover, Riedel and co-workers have reported that, in terms of lost performance, lifestyle issues such as smoking, poor diet, sedentary behaviour, obesity, elevated blood pressure, and stress are most likely to reduce an individual's capacity to perform at work, but that these variables are seldom recognized by organizations as threats to financial performance.

Stein (2001), who has examined the effects of various methods for reducing occupational stress, has pointed out that job stress is most often the culmination of pressures in the workplace, such as tight deadlines, heavy workloads, poor communication, frustration, a lack of resources, and a poor comprehension of work roles. Occupational stress outcomes, according to Stein, are manifest by an increase in psychological problems, injuries, disease, absenteeism, and violence, as well as a reduction in productivity, and cost the US economy in excess of US$120 billion annually. Furthermore, in the workplace, stress levels are highly variable, depending on the coping resources available to the individual. For example, the characteristic "hardiness", which represents a person's ability to self-regulate stress, along with other coping techniques, helps to determine whether an individual will experience a given stressor as mild, moderate, or severe. Stein believes that when stress is mild or moderate, it can actually serve as stimulus or motivation, a state referred to as "eustress". Nevertheless, when an individual's ability to cope is overwhelmed and stress levels become severe, physical and psychological manifestations (see above) can become apparent. However, the negative effects of stress are not inevitable: Stein has reported that there are several techniques to reduce the impact of stress, even when coping is overwhelmed. For example, human factors such as relaxation training or regular exercise can reduce the impact of stress. Nonetheless, according to Stein, in addressing stress it is more effective either to improve a person's ability to really deal with stress, therefore lessening its impact, or to reduce or remove the causes of stress. In the latter case, positive HR practices, such as attempting to enhance communication between employers and employees, providing a physically calm and pleasant work environment, providing training for managers in the reduction of workplace stress, and increasing an individual's perception of job control, can be highly effective. In the former case, according to Stein, the character trait of hardiness, a moderator of the intensity of reaction to stress, can be reinforced both by aligning a person's work with his or her abilities, interests, skills and talents, and by compiling a list of the events that he or she finds stressful and documenting the effects of stress-reduction interventions. In doing so, a person can learn about the things that he or she finds most stressful, and then systematically learn the most effective methods for dealing with or eliminating the stress inherent in those variables.

Rowe (2000) has suggested a similar process to Stein (2001) of training and awareness in addressing the effects of workplace stress on health, satisfaction, and productivity. According to Rowe, who evaluated stress and coping in 113 workers, to understand the sources of stress one must understand the context and circumstances from which the stress originates. In this way, interventions to reduce its effects can be more readily implemented. Moreover, Rowe has indicated that successful coping involves developing a resiliency to stress by learning to interpret potentially stressful events as manageable. Thus, when a person is threatened by a potential stressor, he or she can learn the most effective method of coping, and can then repeat this behaviour in future, stressful situations, a process similar to the notion of self-efficacy (Martin & Gill, 1991), in which a person develops increasing confidence for a given event by repeated successful exposure. Rowe has also suggested that, in the workplace, coping can be developed by encouraging transformational coping (hardiness) by reinforcing a person's existing coping behaviours, and by providing specific skills training in the form of relaxation training, and training in coping and communication skills. According to the findings of Rowe, for this stress-reduction training to remain effective, regular "top-up" sessions at six-month intervals are necessary. The benefits of training and retraining notwithstanding, Rowe has pointed out that unfortunately, many workplace environments actually encourage stress, because of role uncertainty, inadequate training, poor support and communication practices, interpersonal conflict, and heavy job demands; each of these problems reduces a person's perception of environmental control and, therefore, makes him or her more vulnerable to the effects of stress.

A corollary to the suggestions of Rowe (2000) were the findings of Bekker, Nijssen, and Hens (2001), who posited that, despite the benefits of stress-coping skills training in the workplace, the majority of this training, when it occurs, is aimed at the needs of men. According to Bekker and her colleagues, who examined work stressors, coping strategies and training effects in 63 health care trainees, the impact of stress in the workplace is often gender specific, because of the multiple roles that many women are required to play in balancing their work and home lives. Consequently, Bekker *et al.* have suggested that gender-specific training be incorporated into stress training programmes. Nevertheless, whilst their comments appear valid, it is worth noting that it is likely that stress is interpreted differently by each individual, not just by women or other minority groups. As such, the recommendations of Bekker *et al.* do not seem to go far enough. That is, rather than introducing "one size fits all" or "one size fits some" stress-prevention training, it would appear valuable to implement training that can be customized to the needs of the individual: much like the recommendations of Stein (2001), who suggested that each individual catalogues the events and situations that are stressful to him or her, and then applies interventions in a methodological way in order to find the most successful coping techniques. Of course, the efficacy of such a programme would be likely to be enhanced substantially were it to occur under the supervision of someone, like a psychologist, who understood the process, rather than through the inefficient mechanism of trial and error.

Part 2: Stress, vacation, athletes, and balance

One way postulated to mediate the effects of stress is the proper use of vacation. According to Westman and Etzion (2001), absenteeism, itself the product of workplace stress and job-related tension, is often used by employees as a coping mechanism for reducing stress; by taking time off, many employees are able to "catch up" with their daily lives. However, Westman and his colleague have reported that by taking regular vacations, workplace stress can be reduced significantly, with corresponding reductions in absenteeism and burnout. However, these buffering effects are limited to a six-week period; consequently, Westman and Etzion have suggested that, ideally, to reduce both stress and absenteeism, employees take more regular, shorter breaks, such as a 10-day break every 4 to 6 weeks, the increased costs of which are easily returned based on the employee's consequent increases in productivity. Hayward (2001) has made a similar suggestion in his article on the stress-reducing effects of vacation. According to Hayward, work-related stress costs the UK economy in excess of £10 billion per year or, approximately, £500 per worker per year. Despite the demonstrable buffering effects of regular vacation on stress, Hayward has cited work-related statistics for the United Kingdom that mimic those of the

United States: workers are taking fewer holidays, for less time, and are remaining contactable whilst on vacation, thanks to modern accoutrements such as laptops and mobile phones. To combat these intrusions, Hayward has suggested that, for a vacation to be successful in reducing the outcomes of workplace stress, it be well planned so that no contact with the workplace will be necessary during a person's absence. This includes leaving work and work tools (for example, laptops and mobile phones) behind, wrapping up duties efficiently before leaving, and effectively delegating duties to others for the duration of absence to avoid a large workload on return.

According to Loehr (2001), another important way of dealing with stress in the workplace and, correspondingly, for increasing physical and psychological well-being is to learn from the skills of high-level athletes, who routinely deal with extreme stress and difficulties. As Loehr has pointed out, most people are only connected "from the neck up"; that is, they assume that high performance is purely a mental state. However, as has been discussed above, best performance is seldom achieved under conditions in which health is less than optimal. In fact, according to Loehr, on the one hand, many business people engage in activities that actively reduce their health, such as smoking, poor diet, inactivity, and obesity, and place themselves in high-stress environments, without developing adequate coping skills. On the other hand, athletes realize that it is important to find a balance between physical and psychological energy expenditure and renewal. Consequently, in preparation for an important competition, athletes train more and compete less (whereas business people train less and compete more) and take time to recover between events; if athletes train too hard, they become overtrained and can no longer compete effectively. Loehr has indicated that to achieve balance, athletes pay careful attention to getting adequate sleep, proper nutrition, and learning to relax (to reduce competition anxiety), as well as training hard, both physically and mentally, to be in full form when they need to compete (and, as well, competing only when necessary). In comparison, most business people do not get enough sleep, eat poorly, are highly stressed, do little or no physical or psychological training, and compete at every opportunity (often under someone else's volition), leaving little in reserve. Nevertheless, many business people are placed under stresses of time, endurance, and performance that are, in many ways, equivalent to those of high-level athletes. Consequently, in Loehr's opinion, it is hardly surprising that they become ill, discouraged, or burnt out.

To achieve an athlete's balance in business life, Loehr (2001) has proposed a four-level training pyramid, commencing with physical capacity, in which a business person engages in physical training to become fit; as many researchers have pointed out, physically fit persons are healthier, both physically and mentally (Adams, 1999). To succeed at the physical level, Loehr has recommended getting plenty of sleep, engaging in behaviours that are known to be healthy (for example, healthy eating, and so on), recovering adequately between tri-weekly aerobic training sessions, and training with weights at least twice a week (to increase muscular strength, joint integrity, and bone density). The second level, emotional fitness, involves working on the ability to form close relationships, to communicate effectively, and to regularly experience positive emotions. According to Loehr, like an athlete, a person who is emotionally fit is able to feel pleasure in commencing a difficult task, because he or she is confident of having both the physical capacity and the emotional reserves required to attempt and complete it. The third level, mental capacity, entails the development of cognitive relaxation and visualization skills, as well as mental "toughness" (that is, the ability to keep at an unpleasant or aversive task). Loehr has reported that many successful athletes work regularly with sports psychologists to develop their ability to imagine an event accurately before it happens, so as to be better prepared. Likewise, they develop their mental toughness so as to be able to continue to work, train, or compete even when tired, stressed and/or in pain; Loehr believes that business people can also benefit substantially from this type of training. The final level, spiritual development, involves finding a sense of purpose, and taking joy in everyday life, including mundane tasks (like training). By working on the ability to take pleasure from everyday events, Loehr believes that business people can find meaning even in small things, and can substantially enhance both their happiness and well-being.

Best practice: Case examples of how it's being done

Stress, health, and morale

In his case study of ergonomics programmes at Scottish and Newcastle Plc. (S&N), a large UK brewing, leisure and retail company with almost 27,000 employees, Butler (2003) reported that a stress audit of all S&N companies by the University of Manchester Institute of Science and Technology had identified an "institutional stress problem". According to the results of the stress audit, occupational stress was common in both "blue collar" and "white collar" workers, across all company sectors and levels. As a result of this report, the occupational health and safety arm of S&N instituted company-wide stress awareness training for employees, so that they could learn about the causes and outcomes of stress, and take measures to prevent them. The company identified over 3400 employees who could benefit from the training, and conducted group-based training sessions (limited to eight persons per group). Moreover, managers throughout the company were surveyed regularly using a stress-needs analysis survey, comprising a semi-structured interview, in order to determine managers' needs regarding assistance in dealing with occupational stress. This led to the introduction of a guidance manual and training seminars aimed at reducing the risks associated with stress.

Although the company has yet to report any cost-benefit data following their interventions, early signs have been encouraging (Butler, 2003). Evidence collected to date has suggested that greater awareness, especially among managers, that occupational stress is prevalent throughout the organization, combined with methods for recognizing and reducing the causes and effects of stress, have increased organizational performance by reducing absenteeism, time off for illness, and burnout-related employee turnover.

Summary

Unfortunately, on the one hand, many of the factors associated with the modern workplace are conducive to poor health. Stress, smoking, inactivity, poor diet, obesity and the lack of perceived control have all been identified as substantial health risks. On the other hand, healthier workers show greater levels of productivity, morale and satisfaction, and lower rates of illness and absenteeism. To increase the health of employees, researchers have suggested that organizations introduce programmes that encourage regular exercise and health awareness, as well as training in relaxation and interpersonal skills in order to lower stress. Another way of countering workplace stress and reducing illness is through the provision of regular vacation time. Ideally, workplace breaks should be shorter and more frequent: 10 days every 6 weeks. Of course, unless an employee's tasks are covered adequately during his or her absence, the return to work, and consequent workload increase, is likely to induce greater stress. Lastly, it has been suggested that organizations learn from the habits of athletes in order to provide a better balance for their employees' physical, emotional, and mental needs. This includes attention to physical aspects in order to provide adequate physical fitness, better sleep, and a good diet; emotional fitness, encompassing effective communication, the ability to form healthy relationships, and experience of regular positive emotions; mental capacity, in which skills focussing on mental toughness and successful visualization are developed; and the encouragement of spiritual development in employees: when people are able to better find meaning in everyday life, achieve a greater sense of purpose, and take pleasure from daily living, they are more able to feel balanced, allowing for healthier, happier employees.

REVIEW QUESTIONS

1. Explain how stress is related to illness.
2. Describe the sorts of training that can be used to reduce the effects of stress and explain how they work.
3. What is the point of having healthy workers, and how might they be more effective at work?
4. How does vacation or regular breaks influence employee performance, and why is it important that workers be encouraged to take vacation?
5. Can you think of a situation in which a company might increase its profitability by providing more holiday time for its employees?
6. Think back to an experience in which you could not wait to take a break from work. How might you have performed better if you had been provided with greater coping resources, such as fitness and relaxation training or expertise in mental toughness?

Mind-diagram summary

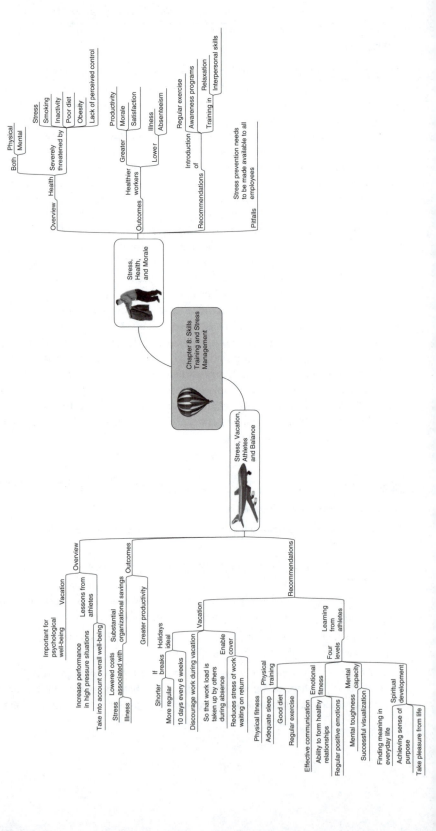

Chapter 8: Skills Training and Stress Management

Stress, Health, and Morale

- **Overview**
  - Health
    - Both
      - Physical
      - Mental
    - Severely threatened by
      - Stress
      - Smoking
      - Inactivity
      - Poor diet
      - Obesity
      - Lack of perceived control
- **Outcomes**
  - Healthier workers
    - Greater
      - Productivity
      - Morale
      - Satisfaction
    - Lower
      - Illness
      - Absenteeism
- **Recommendations**
  - Introduction of
    - Regular exercise
    - Awareness programs
    - Training in
      - Relaxation
      - Interpersonal skills
- **Pitfalls**
  - Stress prevention needs to be made available to all employees

Stress, Vacation, Athletes and Balance

- **Overview**
  - Vacation
    - Important for psychological well-being
  - Lessons from athletes
    - Increase performance in high pressure situations
    - Take into account overall well-being
- **Outcomes**
  - Stress
    - Lowered costs associated with
      - Illness
  - Substantial organizational savings
  - Greater productivity
- **Recommendations**
  - Vacation
    - Holidays ideal
      - Shorter
      - More regular
      - 10 days every 6 weeks
    - If breaks
    - Discourage work during vacation
      - So that work load is taken up by others during absence
    - Enable
      - Reduces stress of work cover waiting on return
  - Learning from athletes
    - Four levels
      - Physical training
        - Physical fitness
        - Adequate sleep
        - Good diet
        - Regular exercise
      - Emotional fitness
        - Effective communication
        - Ability to form healthy relationships
        - Regular positive emotions
      - Mental capacity
        - Mental toughness
        - Successful visualization
      - Spiritual development
        - Finding meaning in everyday life
        - Achieving sense of purpose
        - Take pleasure from life

CHAPTER 9

Enhancing Performance

KEYWORDS Absenteeism, behaviour, competitive, contract, duty, employee motivation, employee performance, employee satisfaction, equitable, intrinsic, policy, profit, satisfied, supervise, teamwork.

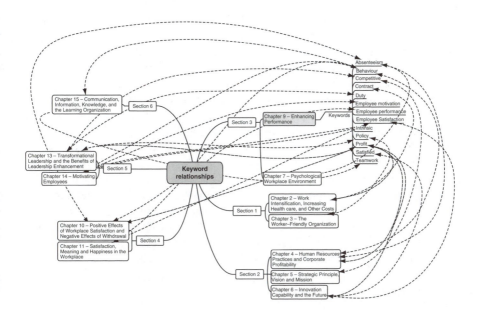

IMPORTANT CONCEPTS   Positive psychology, positive leadership.

Part 1: Performance and commitment

Individual performance enhancement in the workplace should, according to Csikszentmihalyi (2003), be the primary goal of any employer. After all, motivated, capable, interested, and creative workers are the best assets a company can have, especially when they are devoted to achieving organizational goals. We have already looked at some of the best practices for increasing employee empowerment and perceived workplace control and noted that greater levels of employee affective commitment towards an organization leads to greater firm performance. In this section we will review a selection of papers that describe methods for enhancing organizational commitment in order to increase performance at work.

According to Bergmann, Lester, De Meuse, and Grahn (2000), employee commitment is composed of organizational and professional commitment. Professional commitment is represented by a person's feelings and attitudes towards their profession – "an individual's belief in and acceptance of the goals and values of a profession, a willingness to work hard on behalf of the profession, and a strong desire to remain in a profession" – whilst organizational commitment represents a person's cognitions and desires regarding the organization for which he or she works. Bergmann *et al.* have stated that whilst high levels of individual professional commitment are valuable to an organization, it is the level of organizational commitment that can help to determine job performance and to reduce the costs associated with absenteeism and turnover. In their study of the responses of 450 nurses on measures of satisfaction with HRM policies, empowerment, and organizational and professional commitment, Bergmann and his colleagues reported that organizational commitment was increased in relation to employee tenure; rank within the organization; satisfaction with organizational policies, including whether the company met the needs of its employees and the sensitivity of the employer towards contemporary trends regarding employee benefits and corporate policies (for example, work–life balance and ethical practices); and advancement and growth opportunities. Moreover, the more empowered the employees felt, the greater their level of organizational commitment. Professional commitment, on the other hand, was related to HR practices that remained relatively stable across a given profession, such as salary and advancement opportunities, but was not a strong predictor of organizational commitment.

IN ACTION #7

False professionalism

Define professionalism for yourself. If, like many people, you think that professionalism is defined by appearance, a good suit, the haircut, prompt arrival at work, a strong division between work and personal life, control of emotion, meeting imposed deadlines, playing the game, and always respecting the rules, chances are your organization needs work. Let me explain why. Each of the items and characteristics in the above list implies rigidity. They imply a pre-existing set of rules that are not to be questioned. They hint at conformity, lack of initiative, and toeing the line. OK, so many people would applaud these qualities because they promote discipline and reliability. Perhaps these things are desirable in the military, where the ability to follow orders is considered paramount. But the modern company is far from the military: a company with rigid rules, no initiative, and a lack of creativity has little chance of competing. In fact, in a recent article, Steiner (2001) argued that current definitions of professionalism in corporate communication can transform dynamism and heterogeneity into dogmatic structure, in which there is little room for originality.

So if professionalism isn't about rule following or appearance, what can it be? A modern definition of professionalism should determine what behaviours and actions are most beneficial for the modern work environment. It might include things like: situational behaviours, specific results across a broad range of job situations and personal interactions, abilities to work with a team, to look after oneself, to manage effectively, to inspire others, to balance work and a personal life (or to blend the two successfully), to be autonomous, to be able to ask questions, and to be able to set and achieve goals. It might also include a person's attitude to given situations: Are they obstacles or challenges? Are they sources of stress, or interesting possibilities? Are they opportunities for personal growth, or excuses for failure? Moreover, such a definition could also include a person's skills and his or her ability to enhance those that already exist, to learn new skills, and to seek out opportunities for discovering more about the self, and what's needed to realise this self-expansion. Professionalism should be about communication, and the joys of successfully and dynamically communicating with other people or organizations, in a way that leaves both parties with a sense of mutual recognition, achievement, and success. Lastly, professionalism should incorporate creativity, its encouragement, and its realization in all situations, in the workplace and in personal life.

Consequently, as we have seen throughout this text, one of the key elements for enhancing both individual and organizational performance is HR practices. However, commitment to an organization can only be enhanced by particular types of HRM. For instance, in his review of high performance work organizations in UK aerospace, Thompson (2002) concluded that there was a strong relationship between effective HR practices that related to the elevation of individual performance by promoting feelings of personal identification with the workplace and organizational financial performance. Likewise, van Knippenberg (2000) has pointed out that it is personal identification with an organization that elicits a sense of belonging in employees, and enhances both an individual's motivation and his or her performance. According to van Knippenberg, a person's social identity is related to how greatly he or she recognizes that his or her personal characteristics are shared by those of a group. That is, the more highly a person imagines this group cohesion to be, the more he or she will agree with the attitudes, behaviours, and perceptions of the group. Further, the greater a person's group identification, the greater will be the motivation to fulfil the group's goals, because the individual's goals will have become subsumed by those of the group. Therefore, van Knippenberg has reported that when an organization expects a high level of performance from an employee, it is more likely that he or she will perform to these standards when he or she not only believes in the institution but also maintains the perception of a level of personal volition (control) over his or her actions. Each of these factors is likely to increase affective commitment towards the organization.

According to research by Waclawski (2002) involving 3583 bank employees from 235 bank branches in the north eastern United States, lack of attention to HR practices that address organizational cultural variables, including employee attitudes norms, and core beliefs, is one of the key reasons for lack of success in attempted large-scale organizational change. Waclawski has reported that 75–90 per cent of organizational change attempts fail largely because those alterations are dependent on behavioural changes (such as willingness to contribute, and greater organizational commitment and citizenship behaviour) in organizational members, including leaders, managers, and employees. However, behavioural change is a complicated process that is highly dependent on an individual's motivation to make changes. Consequently, in organizations that encourage group identification by paying close attention to the social cohesion of their members and the alignment of their values with the personal beliefs of employees, there is substantially greater motivation to make these modifications. Moreover, this change is especially important among leaders and managers: as Waclawski has pointed out, if organizational members responsible for modelling effective behaviour do not believe in or model these characteristics, it is highly unlikely that their subordinates will take on desired qualities.

Part 2: Incentives, reward, and reinforcement

Workplace incentives, varying from monetary bonuses, to recognition awards, to simple "pats on the back" are widely used by management in an effort to increase employee performance. Nevertheless, management often initiate incentive schemes without having much understanding of employee motivation (Gibbs, Merchant, van der Stede, & Vargus, 2004) and without bothering to determine whether their schemes are effective for increasing employee productivity. Whilst we will examine theories of employee motivation in greater depth in Section 6, in this section we will look at the more effective types of rewards and incentives for increasing employee performance and productivity.

According to Gibbs et al. (2004), conventional bonus schemes are often flawed because they are based on quantitative measures that are poorly related to the dimensions of an individual's job. For example, employee bonuses are often determined by complicated formulae based, for instance, on the amount of time spent on a project or on the gross amount of revenue generated over a given time period. Unfortunately, given the complexity of most of the modern jobs, these variables do not adequately represent employee effort, performance, motivation, or drive. Moreover, the complexity of these formulations often makes it difficult for employees to achieve their bonuses, particularly when factors outside their control (like budget overruns, lack of resources, poor communication, or the unavailability of co-workers) have confounded their best efforts. Consequently, when a bonus is paid the resultant monetary reward is unlikely to motivate more desirable employee behaviour, such as creativity, initiative, or commitment. Moreover, the complexity of the process combined with the number of variables outside of the control of the employee can actually act as demotivators, further reducing positive employee behaviours. In their study of 1057 full-time employees to determine the efficacy of more subjective variables in assessing incentives, Gibbs and his colleagues found that by accounting for subjectivity in employee performance, such as managerial and supervisory opinions of performance, as well as employees' opinions about how well they achieved their goals, employees were more satisfied with their pay, and more productive than employees whose performance was assessed in the traditional, quantitative way. Moreover, successful subjective assessments also led to a greater level of trust between employers and employees. Consequently, in the opinion of Gibbs and his colleagues, the rigid reward or bonus structures common to many workplaces are not effective for increasing employee perform- ance, and could actually have a negative effect on satisfaction and productivity. A similar conclusion was reached by Batt *et al.* (2002), who reported that bonus schemes that relied purely on monetary rewards without concurrent positive HR practices, such as training, promotion opportunities, and work–life balance enhancement programmes, did not achieve greater employee commitment, loyalty, or performance, especially when the bonus scheme was complicated and quantitatively determined based on factors often outside of the employee's control.

IN ACTION #8

Motivation and reward

One way to encourage people to use their time well is to give them control over it. Researchers suggest that people who perceive a greater level of control and autonomy in structuring their immediate environment are substantially more motivated to achieve. This is a basic psychological principle, and implies that a person who feels that he or she has not been forced to complete a task is more likely to willingly complete that task. Moreover, if successful completion of that task *at a high level* is rewarded, then even greater motivation to achieve can be stimulated. In this case, not only does a person feel that he or she has a choice in the undertaking of a project, he or she also chooses the level of commitment to that task, and reward becomes contingent on high-level completion rather than just completion.

The concepts of reward and recognition form the basis of cognitive-behavioural psychology, and have been in place for over forty years. The principles are simple, but are often not addressed in the workplace. Put simply, when a person is rewarded for a behaviour, that behaviour is more likely to be repeated. Slightly more complex are the principles of positive and negative reinforcement. These state that when a person is rewarded with something that is interpreted as pleas- urable (for example, money, praise, recognition, promotion, esteem) immediately after an event, there is a greater likelihood that that event will be repeated. The key to positive reinforcement is recency, that is, that the reward follows the event as quickly as possible, so that the two events become paired. Conversely, negative reinforcement represents the feelings matched to an event that *removes or ameliorates* an unpleasant situation or affect (for example, pain, frustration, stress, humiliation). A classical example of positive reinforcement would be a rat being rewarded with a piece of food for pressing a lever. In business, positive reinforcement could be effected by recognition, by a supervisor, for the high performance of an employee (if it is timely!). Negative reinforcement can be illustrated by the use of aspirin for a headache: the act of taking the aspirin is reinforced by the fact that the headache (unpleasant) goes way. In business, this principle can be applied to enhance motivation by removing unpleasant obstacles (again in a timely fashion), such as environmental and situational stressors (for example, miscommunication, stress, uncomfortable workspace).

In a similar vein to Gibbs *et al.* (2004), Fessler (2003) has reported that most accounting-based management systems assume a discrepancy between work and incentive to work, requiring that employees be encouraged to work through some sort of financial incentive above their regular wage. However, according to Fessler, many employees are actually intrinsically motivated to work; that is, they find reward in their jobs through completing everyday tasks or through involvement with co-workers, projects or other challenges. In fact, the perceived attraction of a task increases the likelihood of job performance: that is, when someone likes doing something, they will work harder at it and perform better. Consequently, when managers assume that employees must be coerced to work effectively, they can actually reduce the intrinsic pleasure taken by employees in their work, essentially reducing performance by lowering task attractiveness. To further investigate this phenomenon, Fessler assessed task performance in various scenarios among 98 university undergraduates. He found that incentive-based compensation (such as monetary bonuses) did not always increase task performance. In fact, participant effectiveness was moderated by the attractiveness of the task: when a task was perceived as appealing, performance increased, but when incentive-based compensation was introduced, tasks were perceived as less desirable and performance was significantly lowered. In other words, the introduction of an external reward for a task that was already considered as attractive led to participants feeling less motivated to perform that task, because the external reward suggested that the task was only worth doing for a monetary incentive, rather than for its own sake. In the light of these findings, Fessler has argued that managers, rather than assuming that workers require external motivation in the form of financial bonuses, should focus on increasing task attractiveness so that employees are more inclined to participate in tasks for their intrinsic reward, and in doing so, increase employees' levels of job satisfaction and performance.

Muhlau and Lindenberg (2003), in a large-scale study involving 4567 US workers and 3735 Japanese workers from 52 US and 46 Japanese car manufacturing plants, respectively, reported that efficiency wages or bonuses were only effective when they were paid in combination with other forms of motivation, such as the encouragement of intrinsic rewards, an increase in the quality of relationships between workers and supervisors, and the availability of promotion opportunities. According to Muhlau and his colleague, typically, senior managers attempt to motivate employees in a way that Muhlau and Lindenberg have labelled an "incentive model". In this model, employers assume that by paying higher wages or bonuses for achieving a certain level of efficiency, they will increase the attractiveness of the organization both to job seekers and to current employees, and will increase workforce morale and increase productivity by encouraging reciprocity (that is, higher pay in exchange for a greater commitment from the employee). As well, this theory supposes that employees will work harder because they are afraid of losing their highly paid position if caught shirking. Nevertheless, Muhlau and Lindenberg have suggested that the incentive model is naïve, because it assumes that wages are the only motivational factors. Instead, they have proposed a "relational signalling model", which suggests that "principal–agent conflicts at the workplace are resolved by harmonizing the conflicting objectives of labour and management rather than by altering economic incentives". Thus, when an organization attempts to motivate its workforce purely through economic incentive, it signals that the relationship between the employee and employer is purely economic, leaving out more complicated human factors such as trust, intrinsic drive, and commitment. In other words, on the one hand, when an employer implies that the only interest in employee motivation is monetary, employees will respond with a lowered level of commitment, because they do not perceive any encouragement for a more meaningful relationship between themselves and the employer. On the other hand, when an employer invests time and resources in, for instance, employee development, enhancing the work–life balance, improving the physical environment, or reducing workplace stress, employees will perceive that the organization has their interests at heart, and will respond with greater affective commitment and higher performance. Consequently, according to Muhlau and Lindenberg, incentive models of efficiency wages are flawed because they fail to take into account human factors: as we see time and time again, people require more to motivate them in the workplace than extrinsic fiscal rewards.

In a related study, Drago and Garvey (1998) investigated the effect of conventional incentives on workplace helping behaviour. Following their study of 839 employees from 23 workplaces in Australia, Drago and his colleague found that employee helping efforts (such as cooperation, collaboration, team work, and mentoring) were actually reduced by workplace incentives such as pay rises, conventional bonuses, and tournament-style promotions, but were increased by activities that led to task variety and increased interpersonal interaction. Thus, according to Drago and Garvey, conventional incentives actually increased competition and antipathy between employees, because workers ended up rivalling one another for a limited number of rewards. Instead, when employees were able to engage in varied, more interesting tasks that required greater levels of cooperation, they were more likely to assist one another independent of any external reward. Nevertheless, because in most workplaces, the only way to attain higher rank and salary, and consequent increases in work complexity, is through limited, competitive promotion, most organizations regulate the amount of cooperation between their employees to the minimum required to meet individual, rather than company-wide, goals. Thus, conventional reward processes can actually reduce workplace productivity by decreasing employees' desires to cooperate with their colleagues. In a similar vein, in their review of incentive-enhancing preferences, Bowles, Gintis, and Osborne (2001) indicated that managers can increase workplace performance by simply paying greater attention to factors that encourage interaction, collaboration, and commitment, without needing to resort to financial-based incentives. Instead, Bowles *et al.* believe that managers should focus on aligning the desires and objectives of individual employees with those of the organization. This can be achieved by designing jobs to be compatible with the individual in a given position (Bowles *et al.*). That is, rather than simply defining an employee's role and expecting him or her to perform just because he or she is expected to, aspects of the job should be designed to appeal to that person's interests and ambitions. For example, a person who enjoys interacting with others should be placed in roles that allow regular interactions. In this way, the attractiveness of job tasks is increased, with a corresponding raise in job satisfaction and a greater likelihood of higher performance: the employee becomes intrinsically motivated so that extrinsic, monetary rewards become less necessary.

The problems with conventional, accounting-based reward systems notwithstanding, bonus schemes are still widely used in an attempt to motivate workers. In these circumstance, most commentators agree that, monetary or not, for rewards to motivate they must be contingent on high performance. Eisenberger and Rhoades (2001), for example, have suggested that conventional rewards are not particularly motivating; in everyday management, rewards, such as financial incentives, are often given for conventional behaviour (that is, not aimed at rewarding creativity or initiative) and are, therefore, utilitarian and non-motivating. Rather, Eisenberger and his colleague have posited that if they are to be used, rewards should be given to reinforce creative behaviour and in order to prime employees for greater creativity, and that these rewards need not necessarily be monetary to be effective.[20] However, according to Eisenberger and Rhoades, for a reward to be effective, it must be both unexpected and contingent on a creative process. Further, in the workplace environment, when an employer rewards contingent to high-level performance, the employee is more likely to perceive greater personal control because he or she retains the option of whether or not to attain that level of performance or even to decline the reward. In the opinion of Eisenberger and his colleague, because this flexibility increases the employee's level of perceived control, it is likely to enhance his or her sense of self-determination. Consequently, when the creative process is both rewarded and optional, the motivation to be creative can become intrinsic: that is, creativity becomes its own reward.

Rewards can also enhance performance in a team environment, both individually and in the team as a whole. Kerrin and Oliver (2002) have suggested that effective team building is based on both its structural elements (that is, flexible work roles, multiskilling, and self-contained tasks) and its process elements

---

[20] Praise and recognition can be powerful motivators – for a more comprehensive discussion of reward and motivation, see Section 5.

(that is, effective corporate behaviour, the pooling of information, and joint problem solving). They have also suggested that rewards in a team environment can be highly motivating to team members but, based on the principles of team building, are more effective when the use and distribution of the reward is left up to the team. However, Kerrin and Oliver have warned that it is important to pay attention to what is actually rewarded; in their opinion, people adapt to a system very quickly and will exploit good intentions. Thus, for example, if a team (and its individual members) is rewarded consistently for attaining a particular financial target, it will do only what is necessary to reach that target, setting, in effect, self-imposed limitations.

A person's own desire for improvement can also serve as a strong reinforcing factor. Shatte, Reivich, and Seligman (2000), in their report on promoting corporate competency, have espoused the benefits of "positive psychology" in helping individuals reach a state of optimism and hope, rationality and realism, future mindedness, and resilience and performance. These authors have argued that because humans are extremely efficient information processors, in order to better deal with large amounts of information taken in daily, over time they develop a series of mental shortcuts. Nevertheless, people often develop mental heuristics that are flawed and which can result in maladaptive coping. In these cases, according to Shatte *et al.*, psychological techniques, such as rational emotive therapy cognitive behavioural therapy (which help to identify and reduce irrational or nonsensical thought processes), as well as self-disputation and focussing skills, can substantially improve an individual's mental processing, and allow him or her to function at a much more effective level. Lloyd and Atella (2000) have also cited the benefits of positive psychology, which they have described as a methodology for attaining optimum human functioning. According to these authors, optimum human functioning is comprised of a person's effectiveness, and his or her health, happiness, virtue, and strength. However, to be proficient in each of these areas requires a working environment that is low in stressors, the possession of strong coping skills, the opportunity (in the workplace) to pursue life goals, and effective, inspirational leadership. Lloyd and his colleague believe that the most effective leaders inspire by helping their charges to improve themselves physically, intellectually, emotionally, and spiritually, by providing the conditions necessary for health, communication, intellectual challenge, personal fulfilment, and a sense of everyday meaning.[21] In such cases, reward is encapsulated in the ability to be able to align personal beliefs and a need for fulfilment, with everyday work.

Part 3: Ergonomics and physical environment

Despite the documented positive effects of reward on performance, as has been mentioned, the physical environment in which a person works can also affect his or her performance. Ergonomics, the practice of designing a workplace to reduce stress and enhance well-being, has received substantial attention in recent

---

[21] A more thorough discussion of leadership can be found in Section 5 below.

years. Beishon (2000), for example, has reported that effective ergonomics requires modification of the work environment to suit the individual. According to Beishon, when environmental demands become too high, there is a negative impact on psychological and/or physical health, and a consequent reduction in performance; early maladaptations to a poor environment, for instance, are manifest in neck or back pain, as well as in viral complaints. The physical solution, according to Beishon, involves both the ready availability to employees of health activities such as personal training, yoga, or access to a gym, the encouragement (or reward) of their usage and the modification of the physical workspace to be, for example, a multi-function zone, in which the individual can work standing or sitting and in different locations, depending on his or her mood. However, in Beishon's opinion, the token ergonomic efforts taken by many companies, such as adjusting the height of computer monitors to make typing more comfortable, do not enhance the environment, they simply remove a little discomfort, a process analogous to treating a symptom without assessing its cause.

One way to address the ergonomics of a workplace effectively is to pay attention to the ambient environment. Hedge (2000), in his assessment of workplace ergonomics, has stressed the importance of environmental conditions such as lighting, heating, and air quality. Hedge has reported that the ideal operating environment is heated to 22 degree celsius, with a relative humidity of 25 per cent, is lit brightly, but without glare, using uplights or ambient lighting, and provides air quality that is substantially higher than that of the typical office. Similarly, Baughan-Young (2001), in his review of the research pertaining to the psychological effects of colour, has suggested that worker productivity can be substantially affected by the colour of both a room and its decorations. According to Baughan-Young, people who are naturally more cautious work better in surroundings that are coloured "coolly" (for example, blues and greens), whilst more outgoing people respond better to "warm" colours (for example, reds and oranges). Moreover, a room's colour can be conducive to certain types of activities. On the one hand, cool colours "speed time" by providing a calmer environment better suited to activities that require high levels of concentration. In fact, according to Baughan-Young, these colours reduce nervous system activity at a physiological level; in these surroundings, individuals are less stimulated by the environment, paying less attention to their surroundings and more to their work. On the other hand, rooms with warm colours "slow time" because people become more physiologically aroused, consequently paying more attention to their surroundings; these rooms are better suited to work that requires stimulation, such as creativity and brainstorming (thus, warmer colours are well suited to meeting rooms). Baughan-Young has also noted that despite the positive effects of colour on certain psychological states, a "colour break" is required at regular intervals, so that the individual does not become too habituated; likewise, all-white environments understimulate the eye, leading to ocular fatigue and, consequently, physical and psychological malaise.

The benefits of an ergonomic environment notwithstanding, according to Duffy and Salvendy (1999), organizational and individual effectiveness are best ameliorated when an ergonomic environment is married to a high quality of company-wide communication (combined with a managerial perception of the necessity of effective communication), and a reward system that reflects the achievements of both individuals and teams. In this case, the ergonomic environment reduces stress and enhances performance, setting the appropriate conditions for collaboration and communication, and allowing for improvements to an individual's performance to filter into the organization as a whole.

Part 4: Teams and teamworking

To a large extent, many of the studies and articles that we have examined so far have indicated that encouraging and increasing performance in the workplace is dependent on the ability and willingness of employees to collaborate in meaningful and productive ways, such as in teams. Whilst the concepts of teams and teamwork are by no means new, they have received substantial attention in recent times both in the business world and by researchers. Many of these authors have claimed that teamworking in the workplace is a powerful means for increasing both individual and organizational productivity; however, they have also pointed out that determining an environment that encourages teamwork requires the measured input of senior management, and substantial training for team participants and their supervisors. In the following section, we will examine the various recommendations put forward for enhancing teamwork and getting the most out of teams.

In his meta-analysis of 122 case studies regarding the use of different types of organizational teams, Hodson (2002) described the particular importance of employee participation for organizational productivity, especially in a team environment. According to Hodson, the best conditions for teamwork occur when teams are self-managed and semi-autonomous, and when they are composed of groups of 5–10 persons, each of whom has a specific role. Self-managed teams are responsible for planning, undertaking, and completing their own projects in a manner and time frame decided within the group, and to a performance standard that they have developed. Further, they do not need to defer to, or obtain permission for actions (up to a certain level) from a manager or supervisor, but remain responsible for the success or failure of their activities; consequently, supervisors take a less direct role as a facilitator of ideas, a go-between with senior management, and/or an aid in situations where the group needs expertise outside of that of its members. Ideally, when teams are self-managed and semi-autonomous (that is, operating independently of other groups, and not dependent on their input for their activities), there is a substantially greater level of participation, commitment, satisfaction, and meaning derived from individual participation in the team. Further, each member should be able to contribute in a way that has a bearing on the outcome of a project, and feel a corresponding sense of ownership and empowerment (Hodson).

Nevertheless, Hodson (2002) has cautioned against two particular organizational practices which, in his opinion, are likely to damage team success. First, it is common for teamwork programmes to be developed in which teams are self-managed and autonomous in name only. In these cases, management decides which projects a team should work on, their available resources, the project's completion date, and the standards to which it must adhere. Nevertheless, the team is still held both responsible and accountable for the project's outcome. Such cases present two real dangers to team and employee performance. First, employees are likely to feel that their workload has intensified (meeting deadlines that they have little control over) without any sense of gain; as we have seen, when the perception of workplace control is reduced or removed, there is a substantially greater likelihood of stress and stress-related illnesses. Second, teamwork (that is, a group of people collaborating with one another to achieve a common goal) is likely to be reduced because there are few positive incentives for members to work together to achieve an outcome: rather than feeling empowered by having control over a project and the level of input needed for its completion, employees feel resentful towards their managers and overworked and unmotivated (Hodson). The second concern expressed by Hodson echoes those of researchers in HPWS (Godard, 2001; Tomer, 2001; White *et al.*, 2003): "trendiness". Because workplace teamwork has received a lot of attention in recent times, it is common for managers to implement "teamworking" programmes without adequate thought or planning into how they will work, particularly regarding team autonomy. Moreover, when teamworking is introduced in an effort to increase organizational productivity, it is also often accompanied by cost-reducing exercises, such as lay-offs. The contradictory message given by management of increased expected productivity gains alongside reduced job security and reduced funding is unlikely to be successful. Unfortunately, according to Hodson, because teamworking is often introduced without pause given to the factors required for its success, it seldom succeeds, resulting in a return to traditional management styles, and a reluctance to try other HR practices that are likely to increase organizational performance.

Similar recommendations and concerns have been made by Tranfield, Parry, Wilson, Smith, and Foster (1999). According to these authors, a team is "a small number of people with complementary skills who are committed to a common purpose, performance goals, and approach for which they hold themselves mutually accountable", whilst a high-performance team "has all the conditions of teams, but also having members deeply committed to one another's personal growth and success". Nevertheless, Tranfield *et al.* believe that simply restructuring existing groups into "teams" is not adequate to increase organizational performance; instead, the process must include a well thought-out design and purpose. Thus, when teams are assembled in a way that encourages free action, an organization can expect increased responsiveness, a better integration between employees and the organization's goals, and increased innovation, as the result of groups working together over time to build better products or services. In effect, a well-actualized team comprises a form of collectivism that demonstrates a shared purpose, can be pursued through a series of interdependent roles, and that uses mutual adjustment as its principal means of coordination. This is an excellent way of harvesting human capital, because employees are directly contributing to the development of a service or product using their tacit skills and abilities. Moreover, when the team becomes semi-autonomous and self-managing, there is a reduced need for complic-ated management systems, because accountability is pushed down the chain of command, culminating at the people actually doing the work. This can result in substantially greater feelings of ownership, commitment, and responsibility (Tranfield *et al.*). Nevertheless, like other sources we have encountered, Tran-field and his coauthors have warned that unless organizations restructure to allow teams to work independently of a chain of command, there is a likeli-hood of work intensification and a reduction in employee job satisfaction and productivity. In this vein, Tranfield *et al.* have described three team conditions. The first, empowerment, is met when the team is able to function autonomously and without direct managerial control. In this condition, employees have access to the resources required to complete their tasks, and are primarily respons-ible for meeting those tasks in a timely and effective manner. This leads to a stronger corporate culture in which workers take on a wider range of tasks, skills, and responsibilities in order to meet challenges faced by the team, whilst reduced supervision results in a less-adversarial relationship between employees and management. The second and third team structures, lean production and project teamworking, do not often meet the conditions of empowered teams. According to Tranfield *et al.*, the lean production methodology behind lean teams results in a highly standardized work structure that is closely monitored. The result, groups that are directly supervised to meet tight schedules over which they have little control, does not encourage team functioning or productivity, but does lead to work intensification and stress. Likewise, project teamworking, which aims to reduce operational timelines by packaging tasks into tightly coordinated projects, has similar effects to lean production methods: rather than encouraging initiative and creativity, it limits employee decision-making latitude and results in increased pressure, with lowered productivity.

Some of the problems regarding the uptake, continued use, and success of teams have been further examined by Batt (2004). In her review of the literature, Batt found that the introduction of self-managed teams to hierarchical organ-izations does help to reduce the need for supervision by placing supervisors in a coaching role, and encouraged worker commitment and increased productivity by allowing workers with tacit knowledge regarding a process or system to use that knowledge effectively. However, Batt also found that the continued use of teams was highly dependent on financial and political processes within the company that were often unrelated to team performance. To examine this issue further, Batt assessed 1191 US employees from a former Bell telecommunic-ations company on their perceptions of job satisfaction, security, and decision discretion, as well as their managerial level and team participation opportun-ities. She reported that both managerial and non-managerial employees who were able to work in self-managed teams reported a significantly greater level of discretionary decision-making ability, as well as greater job satisfaction and feelings of job security. Nevertheless, Batt also reported that the introduction of self-managed teams often fails in organizations because nervousness about its possible outcomes leads to a lack of "buy-in" from managers and employees. Specifically, because self-managed team systems are often introduced without adequate employee preparation and education, and because teams are usually trialled on a voluntary basis, concern about the consequences of participation, as well as inadequate time or other resource availabilities, results in low participation interest. Consequently, the trial is deemed unsuccessful, reducing the likelihood of its reintroduction.

According to Crossman and Lee-Kelley (2004), one of the principal factors for the success of self-managed team programmes is trust. In their case study of a UK software company, Crossman and his colleague found that when employees felt trusted by their superiors to carry out their work independently, they were much more likely to cooperate with fellow team members, and reported greater personal and team productivity. Moreover, when the team was free to make decisions related to their tasks without deferring to their supervisor, and were able to rely on the supervisor to support those decisions, the team functioned more effectively and was able to meet task deadlines more often and to a higher quality. Lastly, teams were more effective when members were able to remain in a given team for longer periods. This had the effect of forging relationships and increasing trust between team members, allowing them to work more effectively. This effect was also increased by direct support and coaching from a supervisor to help team interaction, smooth out disputes, and offer information and resources that team members were unable to provide.

Consequently, team structures that encourage individual thinking, mutual interest and collaboration and that provide the resources to act independently of direct supervision appear more effective than traditional work structures. There is no great mystery to this outcome; as we have seen throughout this book so far, when firms pay attention to human needs and manage their employees as people rather than automatons, there is a much greater likelihood that their workforce will respond with greater commitment, productivity and loyalty. However, as we have seen, too often organizational policies are based on outmoded accounting-based systems, which seldom take into account human factors. One example of "teamworking" which failed to address these human variables was described by van den Broek *et al.* (2004), who assessed the attempted implantation of teams in Australian and Scottish call centres. Based on interviews with both call centre workers and managers, van den Broek and her colleagues reported that in these call centres, despite the division of employees into "self-contained teams", there was no evidence of the task interdependence or autonomy that allowed for the decentralized decision-making that typifies a self-managed team. Rather, "team members" were allocated their tasks for the day by a supervisor, whose main responsibilities involved making sure that the "team" met its daily quotas. Moreover, although team members met their supervisor on a regular basis to provide feedback that was supposed to be directed to senior management, they reported feeling pressured to contribute ideas that they believed were seldom acted on, resulting in disappointment and dissatisfaction with the team environment. Also, in an attempt to improve team performance, teams were encouraged to compete against one another for token prizes such as plastic trophies. Team members described these competitions and other attempts at team motivation (such as high-street discount vouchers, bright colours on the walls, and a "welcome to the team" video from the CEO) as a "joke", and reported that these efforts only served to make them feel isolated and dissatisfied. Employees also reported that one unpleasant side effect of these competitions was the increased peer pressure to participate in "meaningless activities" by their colleagues, increasing the work intensity of an already distressingly dull job. Some workers even described how their co-workers would report any perceived "slacking" to the supervisor, in the hope that they would be rewarded for identifying any gaps in the team's performance. Needless to say, this did not increase collaboration or goodwill between team members, and had a negative impact on productivity.

Best practice: Case examples of how it's being done

Incentives, reward, and reinforcement

One example of a successful company-wide incentive scheme has been described by Knez and Simester (2001), who assessed changes at Continental Airlines, one of the largest US airlines. According to Knez and his colleague, firm-wide incentives that involve schemes such as profit sharing and employee ownership can be particularly effective in increasing employee performance, because they encourage employees to align their interests with those of the organization. In the case of Continental Airlines, which before 1995 was consistently rated as the worst-performing US airline, with the lowest financial performance (and several near bankruptcies) and the highest levels of customer complaints in the industry, the company was required to initiate some sort of scheme to increase employee performance, or face insolvency. Although several authors have recommended against efficiency wages as a primary means of incentive, senior management at Continental introduced a $55 monthly bonus for every employee for each month that Continental met its perform- ance targets, with an extra $100 for each month that the airline was ranked first in the United States. However, Continental also simultaneously intro- duced a major overhaul of its timetabling systems and software, allowing for a greater level of efficiency; a comprehensive scheme for training managers for better communication with their subordinates, increasing the ability for employees to make suggestions, recommendations and complaints; and a system that allowed managers to communicate staff proposals to senior manage- ment, so that ideas and propositions could be used to increase company-wide performance.

According to Knez and Simester (2001), following the introduction of these schemes, Continental's performance increased dramatically, resulting in its consistent ranking as one of the United States's top airlines. Increased company performance was attributed to a substantial reduction in sick days, absenteeism, and turnover, as a partial consequence of the bonus scheme which, whilst costly, began paying for itself within three months of its implementation (through reduced costs from staff absence and turnover, increased bookings, and rebook- ings from other airlines that were required to accommodate their passengers following delays or other problems). In the opinion of Knez and his co-worker, the success of Continental's programme was the result of four factors. First, performance goals were introduced on a sliding scale, with bonuses being paid immediately after the scheme's introduction. This allowed a form of behavioural shaping to occur, in which employees were able to observe that small changes to their work practices resulted in almost immediate reward. Over time, the performance targets were raised in order to continue to increase individual performance levels. Second, the combined introduction of the bonus scheme and the more efficient timetabling resulted in what Kenz and Simester labelled an "employee attribution bias"; that is, employees were unsure whether it was the new timetabling, or their increased efforts to achieve the bonus that was responsible for the company's upturn. Consequently, employees preferred to assume that it was their efforts that had contributed to the Continental's success, resulting in a greater feeling of empowerment and control, and reinforcing their new efforts. Third, the increased ability of senior management to access the ideas and proposals of staff resulted in the introduction of a large number of changes that increased the airline's effectiveness. Lastly, once management were better trained to encourage communication with their subordinates, the pre-existing structure of the airline, in which many workers were already partitioned into semi-autonomous groups or teams (for example, flight attendants, pilots, baggage handlers, caterers, and so on), allowed for a higher level of self-management among teams, resulting in a greater sense of control over their work roles and the outcomes of their projects. Because these teams were able to make decisions relevant to their daily roles without direct or excessive supervision, team members served to motivate one another to reach performance targets.

Teams and teamworking

In their case study of a large car assembly plant in the north UK midlands, Tranfield et al. (1999) reported a substantial financial recovery following the successful introduction of self-managed teams. According to Tranfield and his colleagues, prior to restructuring, the plant was inefficient, had been losing money for some time, and faced closure by its parent company. To counteract this problem, senior management initiated a complete reorganization of the plant's work practices, by reducing the hierarchical management structure and grouping employees into 12 separate zones responsible for products, manufacturing, management, and culture, each of which was comprised of 12 semi-autonomous teams, with a team leader, chosen for long tenure with the company, responsible for that team. Simultaneously, the previous seven levels of management were reduced to five, with supervisors and foremen taking roles within each team as facilitators and coaches. Following this successful change, the company reported a substantial reduction in employee turnover and absenteeism, a rise in productivity, and increased efficiency, resulting in performance gains that allowed the plant to remain open, and workers to retain their jobs. Tranfield et al. have attributed the success of the restructure to the ability of workers to have a direct influence over conditions and decisions relating to their daily tasks, rather than simply taking orders from a foreman. This allowed employees to make substantial contributions, based on their knowledge and experience, to the way in which products were designed and manufactured, and enabled a substantially greater level of innovation, combined with increased efficiency. Moreover, the increased ability to contribute to and control workplace variables resulted in greater job satisfaction, and increased organizational commitment, with a corresponding decrease in turnover, absenteeism, sick days, and presenteeism.

Points for action: Practical recommendations for change

Teams and teamworking

Teams have been shown to be extremely successful in increasing organizational performance. According to Che and Yoo (2001), self-managed teams are most successful under the following conditions:

- Team members should be allowed to interact over a long period of time, both frequently and consistently, in order to develop longer-term relationships, including trust, reliance, and cooperation.

- Teams should be empowered to make day-to-day decisions related to their assigned projects without deferring to supervisor, and encouraged to show initiative in problem solving in order to increase their productivity.

- Team members should be encouraged to monitor and support one another. This reduces the need for outside supervision and helps the team to become more autonomous.

- Team members should work together to come up with cooperation-enhancing schemes, including group incentives, where the team is rewarded as a whole following successful completion of a task; this helps to make group members more reliant on one another to achieve success.

Summary

The way in which a person feels about his or her employer has an impact on performance. This "organizational" commitment encompasses an individual's beliefs, feelings, and attitudes towards the organization, his or her willingness to work on behalf of the organization, and a strong desire to remain (with the organization). Needless to say, a higher level of organizational commitment leads to greater attachment to the organization, willingness to help the organization, and raised productivity. HR practices go a long way towards enhancing organizational commitment. However, it is often assumed that organizational commitment can be increased through the use of simple incentive schemes, which assume that employees are only motivated by external rewards, and which ignore intrinsic drives. Moreover, bonuses and other financial incentives are often based on complicated calculations that involve economic indicators and work variables that are often outside of the employee's control, resulting in a system that is often perceived as unfair and restrictive. Instead, successful reward schemes encourage commitment, productivity, and job satisfaction by taking into account human factors, such as desires for stimulation, recognition, progression, utilization of skills, creativity, and initiative.

The workplace environment, both physical and subjective, can also impact employee commitment, satisfaction, and productivity. For instance, ergonomic design of the physical environment can reduce stress and increase performance by allowing the employee to feel more comfortable. Examples include attention to the ambient environment (temperature, lighting, and colour), recreational facilities, and the workplace layout. The subjective environment, including the ability to work effectively with others is also paramount. Teamworking, or the ability to collaborate with others to achieve a common goal, increases initiative, innovation, job satisfaction, and productivity. Nevertheless, teams are not simply collections of people. Rather, they should represent heterogeneous groups that are semi-autonomous, self-managed in their responsibility for project success or failure, and with access to adequate resources to achieve desired outcomes. Unfortunately, the "trendiness" of teamworking has resulted in the overuse of the concept without adequate planning, assessment, decision-making latitude, training, or resources, and resulting in overworked, stressed employees who certainly do not feel able to contribute to the group.

REVIEW QUESTIONS

1. Define affective commitment, and determine how it is related to individual workplace performance.

2. Explain why conventional bonus schemes are unlikely to motivate employees.

3. What factors would you take into account when designing a reward scheme for your employees?

4. If you were redesigning the physical workplace environment to increase employee performance, what sort of modifications would you make?

5. With regard to a positive personal experience, give an explanation of how teamworking increases performance at work.

6. What are the ideal conditions for self-managed teams? Why does the introduction of teamworking in organizations often fail?

Mind-diagram summary

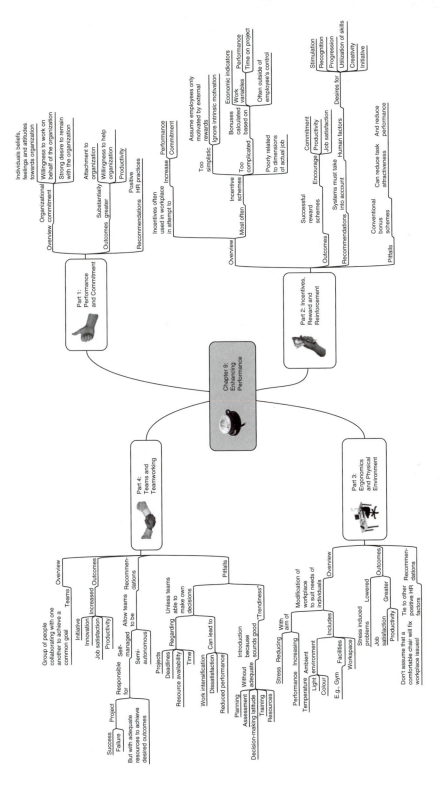

Increasing Workplace Satisfaction and Productivity

Introduction

In previous sections we have examined studies describing both corporate and individual workplace performance enhancement. Many of these articles have described the necessity for employee satisfaction in order for organizational performance to increase. Furthermore, these studies have demonstrated that when an employee is satisfied and stimulated, his or her work productivity also increases dramatically. Consequently, the following section examines ways to enhance satisfaction at work.

Section guide

In Chapter 10, "Positive Effects of Workplace Satisfaction and Negative Effects of Withdrawal", we will revisit some of the issues associated with workplace reduction schemes, like downsizing, and their effects on workplace performance and employee effectiveness. Issues such as workplace stress will be re-examined, and ways to mediate the stress of work covered. One way to reduce workplace stress and increase both satisfaction and performance is workplace support, especially from a supervisor; another is the ability to participate adequately at work. We will also look at performance evaluations and their effects on workplace satisfaction. Chapter 11, "Satisfaction, Meaning, and Happiness in the Workplace", covers the importance of subjective variables, such as job satisfaction, in the economic performance of organizations, and suggests that economists should follow the lead of psychologists in broadening their research areas to include subjective factors. We will then examine the relationship between meaning at work and job satisfaction, as well as the strong links between happiness at work, health, and well-being.

Reading objectives

By the end of this section you should have a better comprehension of:

- work conditions that are likely to result in stress and burnout
- the importance of job satisfaction for workplace happiness
- how workplace support, especially from a supervisor, can increase job satisfaction
- how a greater depth of participation at work can increase workplace satisfaction
- the financial importance of workplace satisfaction to firms
- the need for meaning, and its relationship to workplace activities
- the link between happiness and health.

CHAPTER 10

Positive Effects of Workplace Satisfaction and Negative Effects of Withdrawal

Absenteeism, citizenship, data, employee performance, economist, profit, qualitative, workplace satisfaction.

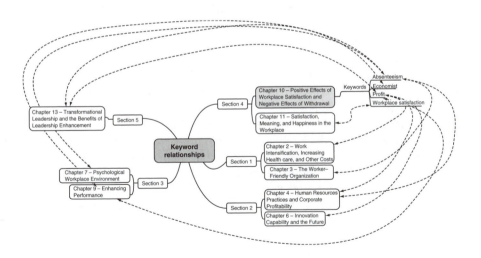

Affective commitment, organizational citizenship, social support, supervisory support.

Part 1: The story so far

In the 1990s, popular stop-gap solutions to poor corporate performance, such as downsizing, layoffs and outsourcing, were to an extent successful. However, the extent and definition of this success has been questioned by several authors. Whereas these techniques were undoubtedly lucrative for temporarily increasing share prices (by reducing costs and increasing profit margins), as we have seen so far, they were thoroughly unsuccessful in their effects on company morale, worker productivity, and employee satisfaction: in the longer term, many of these solutions did more harm than good, by leaving companies stripped of their intellectual capital. Moreover, these organizations were often left with disenfranchized core employees, and a front-line that often consisted almost entirely of temporary staff (Kerr, 2003). In his recent case study of the problems and challenges of changing the fortunes of ailing organizations, Kerr has pointed out that one of the principal problems of layoffs is that the majority of those who are laid off represent workers from the "bottom end" of a company; in other words, the people made redundant are the people that actually do the majority of the work. Consequently, following layoffs organizational morale suffers substantially, especially when the remaining workers are required to complete both their own jobs and those of the removed staff. This labour shortage, according to Kerr, invariably leads to the necessity to hire temporary staff, often at greater cost than retaining the original staff, and at a loss of team cohesiveness, in order for the organization to continue to function satisfactorily.

An alternative to mass layoffs, according to Kerr (2003), is to increase motivation and effectiveness in organizations by training management to set high goals for employees, and then to communicate these goals effectively. This communication must be two-way, so that employees understand what is expected of them and so that managers can make decisions based on employee and organizational needs. Thus, in assessing a company's problems and attempting to make changes, rather than removing and disenfranchizing employees (in Kerr's view employees represent the most important parts of an organization), Kerr has espoused the importance of getting to know workers individually, and of understanding their attitudes, opinions, and ideas: information that reflects the existing systems in the company, and the fundamental aspects of everyday organizational functioning. This perspective allows management to determine what the organization would like to be done differently, and how to figure out why it has not been done already.

In the modern economic climate, the threat of job loss, according to Probst (2002), can dramatically reduce a person's ability to perform. Probst has theorized that each individual has only a limited set of cognitive resources (whether for work or for other activities); the threat of job loss taxes these resources, reducing the amount available for effective work. According to Probst, when a person is content in the workplace, his or her cognitive resources are distributed between on-task activities such as the work being performed and off-task activities such as socializing, the combination of which utilizes the majority of available cognitive resources. When another demand, self-regulation (that is, worrying about a potential loss of work), is introduced the resultant increase in anxiety limits the amount of cognitive resources available for on-task behaviours. To compensate, a person might increase the quantity of his or her work, but at the cost of quality; however, because he or she is no longer focussed on issues such as safety (the resources previously devoted to these functions are now taken up by self-regulatory processes), the likelihood, for instance, of accident and injury is increased, and the capacity for effective work diminished. Sverke and Hellgren (2002) have also commented on performance loss as a consequence of the global trend towards downsizing and flexible contracting; they have argued that the temporary economic gains inherent in these actions are rapidly offset by a consequent loss of productivity. Like Probst, Sverke and his colleague believe that even minor workplace uncertainties, such as the anticipation of a stressful event (for example, redundancy) or even the subjective perception of a loss of job features (such as reduced autonomy, tighter deadlines, or reduced support), can reduce performance.

The stresses associated with potential job loss notwithstanding, job stress can lead to more than just a reduction in performance and productivity. According to Taris, Peeters, Le Blanc, Schreurs, and Schaufeli (2001), the perception of workplace inequity (that is, a lack of appreciation, empowerment, or influence in the workplace) is also a strong predictor of burnout. Further, when an employee is burnt out, the desire to work, and consequent performance drops to levels that are often unacceptable to both the employee and employer, resulting in willing or unwilling employment termination and substantial organizational costs (in terms of rehiring and retraining, as well as affected morale in other staff). Following their investigation of 271 Dutch teachers, Taris and his colleagues reported that increased workplace stress, whether due to threat of layoff, reduced satisfaction, or conflict, corresponded to an elevated likelihood of burnout, as measured by scores on its three dimensions: depersonalization, emotional exhaustion, and lack of personal accomplishment. As a result of their findings, Taris et al. theorized that, because stress is a subjective response, it is a person's coping resources (both internal and external) that determine whether an event is perceived as stressful or not. However, when an employee invests energy to his or her workplace, but perceives a reduction in rewards, the resultant inequity reduces coping and increases stress that, if left unchecked, will most likely result in burnout. The findings of Taris and his co-workers have been mirrored by those of Zivnuska, Kiewitz, Hochwarter, Perrewe, and Zellars (2002), who assessed tension (stress) and performance in 270 hotel managers. They found that although moderate work tension was beneficial to performance, high or low tension levels decreased productivity and performance significantly, and resulted in either illness and burnout (at a high level) or withdrawal and boredom (at low levels), with resulting increases in staff turnover. Consequently, Zivnuska et al. have posited an inverted U-curve model for the interaction between workplace tension and performance.

Whilst burnout is often perceived as an inconvenience for employers, it is also the source of substantial economic cost. Sagie, Birati, and Tziner (2002) in a recent analysis of the costs of psychological withdrawal, such as burnout, have reported that although this behaviour has traditionally been seen as a nuisance, it is expensive, both directly and indirectly, to a company. Sagie and his colleagues, who have developed a set of formulas for calculating the direct and indirect economic costs of withdrawal, have reported that the direct cost of a person's loss (to his or her team, project, and subordinates) represents only a portion of actual expenses. Other variables, such as the effect of burnout on an employee's clients and customers, morale within the workplace, possible influences on other employees (in terms of increased stress and possible burnout) and consequential further loss of clients and customers, and the costs of rehiring and retraining also need to be considered. In fact, according to Sagie *et al.*, the expenses associated with reducing or preventing psychological withdrawal in the workplace, such as stress reduction, work–life balance, and wellness programmes, are likely to be substantially less than the costs consequent to it. Similarly, Pauly *et al.* (2002), who attempted to quantify the indirect costs to firms of regular absenteeism resulting from stress, burnout, or illness, reported that productivity gains from programmes or medical interventions that reduce absenteeism are likely to be substantially higher than the hourly or daily wage costs of temporary workers required to fill the shortage created by absent employees. Corollary to these models are the findings of Chan, Gee, and Steiner (2000), whose examination of the Fortune magazine's "Top 100 Companies to Work For" (an annual rating of how well organizations look after the well-being of their employees) showed that these organizations performed better financially than comparably matched firms that were not recognized for their attention to employee well-being. In other words, as the models of Sagie *et al.* and Pauly *et al.* predict, organizations that pay attention to the needs of their employees are likely to be more profitable than those that do not. As Andrikopoulos and Prodromidis (2001) have pointed out, the qualitative factors traditionally ignored by mainstream economists, who espouse a theory of the firm that is material, monetary, and representative of a system of relations and constraints, are extremely important in the modern economy for successful organizational performance. In fact, according to Andrikopoulos and his co-worker, a combination of internal and external qualitative factors, such as high-quality interpersonal relations and a strong attachment by employees to the organization, give rise to synergistic effects in production that can substantially increase economic performance in firms, and must be taken into account in any comprehensive, modern economic theory.

Part 2: Satisfaction, workplace support, and performance

How then does one increase a person's satisfaction in the workplace and, in doing so, reduce stress and enhance performance? One way is to recognize the existing workplace factors associated with stress and burnout (Taris *et al.*, 2001). Another is to take measures to reduce stress by creating an inspirational workplace environment (Demerouti *et al.*, 2001). However, according to Baruch-Feldman, Brondolo, Ben-Dayan, and Schwartz (2002), the most effective measure is to enhance support in the workplace. In their investigation of 211 traffic police, Baruch-Feldman *et al.* found that those with strong social support were more satisfied in their work and were less likely to experience burnout. Moreover, when social support was broken down by family support and supervisory support, it was found that both dimensions improved well-being, but that family support was more effective in reducing burnout, whilst supervisor support helped to ameliorate work satisfaction and productivity.

Rhoades, Eisenberger, and Armeli (2001) have also examined means for reducing psychological withdrawal (such as burnout) and increasing satisfaction in the workplace. They assessed 367 workers from four different workplaces, on measures of affective commitment, psychological withdrawal, and employee turnover, and reported that a person's perception of organizational support (POS) was the most important variable in reducing withdrawal. According to Rhoades *et al.*, POS was increased by rewards, the perception of just procedures, and supervisor support in the workplace which, in turn, increased a person's affective commitment to the organization. Rhoades and her colleagues formulated this relationship as a model, in which an increase in favourable work experiences (such as rewards, support, and recognition) elevated POS, whilst POS simultaneously ameliorated affective commitment and reduced psychological withdrawal and turnover. Corollary to this, workers with high POS reportedly developed a stronger sense of obligation to the organization and its ongoing welfare, a phenomenon labelled by Rhoades and her co-workers as "reciprocity". Thus, according to Rhoades *et al.*, employees continually assessed the readiness of an organization to reward action and initiative and, in turn, rewarded the organization with their loyalty, born of increased satisfaction with their role at work. In a similar investigation to that of Rhoades *et al.*, Wayne, Shore, Bommer, and Tetrick (2002), who studied the responses of 211 employee–supervisor dyads, reported that the quality of leader–member exchange was the most important variable in increasing a person's POS. Moreover, when a supervisor used performance-contingent rewards to encourage behaviours, but avoided non-contingent punishment, employees reported fewer symptoms of stress and, consequently, were more satisfied with their work and more likely to stay with the organization.

According to Ellinger, Ellinger, and Keller (2003), supervisory support is key to both organizational success and individual satisfaction, especially given that more and more activities traditionally completed by HR personnel, such as employee selection, assessment, development, and retention, are commonly placed in the hands of supervisors and line managers. Ellinger and her colleagues have cited a large body of research showing that supervisory coaching can have positive consequences for employee satisfaction and performance; however, they have also warned that the ability of supervisors to act in a supporting or coach-like role, and to guide their subordinates in career and skills development, is dependent on the supervisor's coaching skills. Unfortunately, as Ellinger *et al.* have pointed out, whilst HR roles are commonly handed to supervisors, the supervisors are seldom given effective training in the skills necessary to provide adequate support to their charges. To further examine this issue, Ellinger and her co-workers evaluated the responses to measures of supportive coaching behaviour, job satisfaction and employee performance from 425 employees and 67 supervisors in a large US warehousing firm. They found a strong relationship between supervisors' coaching skills and application as perceived by their subordinates, and employees' job satisfaction and work performance. However, Ellinger *et al.* also reported that whilst many supervisors believed that they were acting in a coaching role, employees did not see this behaviour as coaching, or even as support. Rather, many supervisors did not have the necessary skills to provide adequate support, and were not actually providing developmental aid to their subordinates even though they believed that they were. Consequently, Ellinger and her coauthors concluded that in many organizations, supervisory support is more a case of rhetoric than reality, and recommended that, given the strong relationship between a supervisor's supportive abilities and employee performance and satisfaction, organizations devote substantially more time and resources to the adequate training of supervisors and line managers in strong coaching skills. Bhanthumnavin (2003), who investigated perceived supervisory and organizational support, self-reported work effectiveness, and self-efficacy among 355 matched supervisor and subordinate pairs from Thai health centres, reported similar findings. According to Bhanthumnavin, in his sample, employee perceptions of supervisory support, especially with regard to emotional and material support, were significantly related to increased subordinate perform-ance, but only when supervisors possessed the skills necessary to provide that support.

In another investigation of the relationship between supervisory support and workplace effectiveness, Cromwell and Kolb (2004) looked at uptake of learning at work. According to these authors, US firms pay upward of 3 per cent of their annual payroll on workplace training, but only between 13 and 15 per cent of this employee training results in workplace transfer of knowledge. However, Cromwell and her co-investigator hypothesized that this learning transfer fails to occur mostly because of inadequate support for the application of newly learnt skills by supervisors and line managers. Nevertheless, following their evaluation of 63 supervisors and their direct managers in a north-eastern US university who participated in a training programme over 12 weeks, Cromwell and Kolb reported that learning transfer can increase dramatically when employees are given sufficient encouragement by their supervisors and colleagues. Specifically, when trainees perceived a greater level of supervisory and peer support there was a correspondingly greater application of learnt knowledge and skills in the workplace. In other words, simply having the support of a superior can substantially increase a person's ability to successfully apply learned skills to their work. However, Cromwell and Kolb, like Ellinger *et al.* (2003), pointed out the importance of adequate supportive skills among supervisors, without which they would be unable to provide the encouragement required for effective learning uptake.

IN ACTION #9

How to excel as a supervisor

As a supervisor, your relationships with your subordinates are, quite probably, your most important motivational assets. If your interactions with your staff are strained and impersonal it is unlikely that they will see you as a leader, or attempt to assist you in your, let's face it, difficult and demanding job. By encouraging a healthy, supportive dialogue between you and your charges, you are making your job easier and encouraging people to work better, both for themselves and for the organization. Think about it in simple, human terms: if you had to work in an environment that you perceived as oppressive or openly hostile, for a supervisor who you felt was uncaring, indifferent, or actively obstreperous, chances are that you wouldn't be very productive. When you hear stories from people about how terrible their work is, of their unsympathetic boss, or how they can't wait to leave their job, you can pretty much guarantee that that person has a poor relationship with his or her supervisor. So how do you enhance these relationships? First, it's not necessary to be everyone's best friend, but it is necessary to win people's respect. Put simply, most people respect others who say what they mean, do what they say, are good at what they do, and who inspire confidence. Second, recognize that you are the one expected to start the ball rolling: if you don't make the effort, your subordinates certainly won't. One more thing: it's not just supervisor/supervisee relationships that are important. When people can go to work knowing that they can interact with likeminded, supportive, friendly co-workers, they will be much more motivated to perform.

One example of the effects of a lack of supervisory support on employee satisfaction and performance has been illustrated by Ensher, Grant-Vallone, and Donaldson (2001), who investigated the effects of workplace discrimination among 366 non-professional US employees. According to Ensher and her colleagues, discrimination by supervisors and managers is still a large problem in many US workplaces, with distinctly negative consequences for both employees and, as a result of their lowered performance and satisfaction, the firm. After assessing the responses of their sample to measures of job satisfaction, perceived discrimination by co-workers, supervisors and the organization, organizational commitment, and organizational citizenship behaviour, Ensher *et al.* reported that when supervisors were actively unsupportive through discriminatory behaviour, there was a significant decline in employee job satisfaction, organizational commitment, and organizational citizenship behaviour. Given the negative consequences (such as increased absenteeism and turnover) of lowered job satisfaction and organizational commitment, Ensher and her colleagues recommended that organizations take pains to provide diversity awareness training, combined with formal and informal mentoring programmes, for supervisors and managers in order to reduce discrimination and increase supportive behaviour.

In addition to supervisor support, the notion of extended organizational commitment to employees' health and well-being, whilst considered outmoded by many social commentators, is, according to Larson and Sasser (2000), one of the most effective tools for enhancing job satisfaction and performance and reducing stress and burnout. As Larson and Sasser have pointed out, it is the employees (not the management) of a given organization who are responsible for customer retention and satisfaction. In fact, Larson and his co-worker stated that "highly satisfied employees exhibit a series of positive behaviours which allow them to do a better job of delighting their customers". Thus, according to these authors, more-satisfied employees are more loyal to their company, and a large base of long-term, stable employees engenders a sense of trust from customers who are, in turn, more likely to remain customers. Koys (2001), who assessed 774 employees and 64 managers on measures of employee satisfaction, organizational citizenship behaviour, and employee retention and turnover, has mirrored this sentiment. He has reported that, in his sample, increased organizational effectiveness (defined as managerial ability, clear communication of goals and expectations, and the effective reward of high performance) led to a significant increase in organizational citizenship. Moreover, Koys has reported that high levels of organizational citizenship, comprised of civic virtue, courtesy, sportsmanship, altruism and conscientiousness, were shown to increase employee satisfaction and customer satisfaction, as well as company profitability.

Tansky and Cohen (2001) have gone so far as to claim that organizational support, in the form of human resources, is the sole source of sustainable advantage in organizations. They believe that in a modern economy, a flexible, adaptable, responsive, and motivated workforce is essential in order to compete through steady innovation. Nevertheless, employee effectiveness is highly influenced by the firm's role in employee development, especially when managers and supervisors take the roles of mentors, coaches, and counsellors to enhance employee development. Unfortunately, according to Tansky and her colleague, managers are only motivated to support the development of their subordinates when they themselves feel supported in their own career growth, a fact that highlights the importance of adequate organizational support. In fact, following their evaluation of the responses of 262 supervisors and managers in a major Midwestern US hospital to measures of organizational commitment, perceived organizational support, satisfaction with employee development and perceived self-efficacy concerning their coaching skills, Tansky and Cohen found that managers who invested time to help their subordinates only did so when they felt strongly supported by their firm. Thus, when organizations invest time and money in the career development of managers, including opportunities for career counselling, training, tuition reimbursement, and job rotation, managers respond not only with increased organizational commitment and effectiveness, but also by taking a more direct role in the development of their charges. Tansky and Cohen have reported that when this "direct role" is encouraged through training in coaching behaviour, problem solving, communication, listening, leadership, and counselling, subordinates will benefit from increased job satisfaction, whilst their employers profit from greater employee effectiveness, increased performance and productivity, and reduced absenteeism and turnover.

One factor in the perception of organizational support among employees is trust (Chami & Fullenkamp, 2002). In their review of trust and efficiency in the workplace, Chami and Fullenkamp have drawn attention to the need for two-way trust, defined as "a confident reliance on the integrity, veracity, or justice of another", between an organization and its employees, in order to maintain a successful business. Citing the problems of the post-Soviet-era Russian economy, Chami and his co-author have pointed out that when there is a lack of trust between a principle and agent (in this case a lack of trust by the citizenry in the ability of the government to intervene in corrupt business practices), both parties suffer. With regard to modern businesses, in which a network of managers, employees, suppliers, and outsourced agencies, manufacturers and distributors must interact in a trustworthy manner in order to achieve a successfully mutual objective, trust becomes a highly valuable commodity. However, as Chami and Fullenkamp have reminded us, the objectives of a shareholder-controlled board, under which most companies' main objective is the enhancement of profit, and the goals of the organization's other stakeholders (such as employees, clients, customers, and allied firms) are not always aligned. In fact, Chami and his coauthor have gone so far as to suggest that, largely, the objectives of shareholders and the board are actually irrelevant to the real-world relationships required for an organization to be successful, because they ignore the importance of trust among the various stakeholders. According to Chami and Fullenkamp, paramount to the understanding and implementation of trust in the workplace is the notion of mutuality and reciprocation: in effect, when an employee's loyalty and commitment is reciprocated, in the form of, for instance, organizational and managerial support, there is a corresponding increase in job satisfaction, and a consequent increase in firm-wide performance.

In order to achieve a high level of performance within a firm, Chami and Fullenkamp (2002) have reviewed three organizational philosophies. The first, which they have labelled "leaner and meaner", describes the economist-led firm in which decisions are made primarily from an accounting-based perspective to increase the organization's end profit. In this model, the organizational leaders assume that there is no mutual interest or altruism between the firm and its employees: workers are simply paid for their time and expected to provide a service in return. This lack of attention to any human factors, according to Chami and his coauthor, results in an extremely low level of organizational commitment among employees, who then operate at a minimal level of productivity in order to maintain their jobs, resulting in a poor overall level of organizational performance. The second model, which describes the paternalistic firm, involves treating employees as a part of a larger family by placing absolute trust in their activities. Whilst this model has its benefits, Chami and Fullenkamp have criticized its effectiveness on the grounds that absolute trust can be taken advantage of by employees, who have little motivation to work more effectively just because their employer believes that they will: merely placing trust in one's employees without also providing a reason to work to a greater capacity is unlikely to produce expected results. The final model reviewed by Chami and his collaborator combines the trust of the paternalistic organization, with incentive to work to a higher standard. In this model, employees are motivated to work for several reasons: they are trusted to do their work without excessive managerial intervention, are supported by their supervisors in what they do, but are also rewarded, in the form of profit sharing or share ownership, for high performance. In this way, employees feel a sense of control over their work environment and a greater level of job satisfaction, and are motivated to perform to a higher level.

Perceived organizational support certainly serves to enhance satisfaction in the workplace. However, Sandberg (2001) has suggested that employers go further, positing the necessity for time-off from regular "work" to allow creative thinking to occur. According to Sandberg, the majority of employees are overwhelmed by information, and are often interrupted by workmates, telephone calls, e-mails, or overzealous supervisors, leaving little time to actually think about what they are doing. Thus, she has suggested allowing a minimum of 15 per cent of work time to be devoted, simply, to uninterrupted thinking. Using this philosophy, Sandberg has speculated that it is possible to convince accountants that production is not always tangible (that is, measurable in terms of physical output) and that ideas (the more the better) rather than time are money. However, quality ideas require time to think and this, in turn, requires rethinking the way in which a typical day is structured. Consequently, Sandberg favours the modification of the standard nine-to-five day, in order to cater to an employee's most productive times. Moreover, she has suggested that employees be encouraged to make, and be rewarded for making, the most of natural thinking time (that is, time when the body is occupied but the mind is free to wander), such as commuting, walking the dog, or even showering.

Schweitzer (1998) also supports the idea that the conventional workplace needs to change, but he also believes that this change is necessary in order to continue to attract effective employees. According to Schweitzer, modern business is threatened not by economic change, but by generational change. He has pointed out that many younger, educated people are questioning whether the traditional style of work is, in fact, worth their while, with many opting for careers that allow them to work when and how they wish (for example, knowledge workers who "telecommute"); these people are not prepared to sacrifice their personal standards and ways of living for a corporate ideal, especially when these same corporations are demanding more and giving less in return. In fact, some 82 per cent of younger workers, when questioned, prefer the idea of working for themselves (Schweitzer). According to Schweitzer, the solution lies in building fluidity into job definitions, engendering commitment to an organization by providing more than a pay cheque. By allowing people to trade jobs in order to learn new skills, providing access to ongoing training in the things that interest them, and giving them the ability to try new things, Schweitzer believes that people can achieve challenge, meaning, and stimulation in a supportive environment within the workplace. Similarly, Schweitzer has recommended that more consideration be given to matching a particular person to a job, and keeping that job flexible rather than making a person fit a predefined role. In this way a person can see himself or herself as a unique contributor to the organization, rather than as a replaceable "cog in the works". Finally, by blurring the distinction between work and play, people are more likely to enjoy the work that they do: after all, as Schweitzer rightly points out, why should work be dull and serious?

Part 3: Satisfaction, workplace participation, and performance

Another suggestion for increasing the perception of organizational support is to enhance the complexity and perceived meaning of a given job (Sandburg & Vinberg, 2000). In this model, job design is treated as a "real-time" experiment in which learning and practice are combined, in collaboration between the employee and the employer, to tailor a job to the needs and interests of the employee. Sandburg and Vinberg have also suggested that technology in the workplace be considered in the same light; that is, that it represent a tool to enhance the workplace and to make work more flexible, rather than another excuse for increased rigidity, restriction and control, and a consequent reduction in POS.

Effectively, increasing a person's involvement in designing his or her job roles represents a subset of workplace participation. Conceptually similar to the ideas on empowerment and perceived control that we covered in Section 3, increased workplace participation represents a way to enhance job satisfaction and performance through relatively simple changes to the way in which employees are treated within the organization, so that they are able to feel that they have some say both in the way they do their jobs and in the way that the organization views their work. Zwick (2004), for example, who evaluated data from 2085 shop-floor employees, reported that management-led initiatives to increase employee participation through efforts such as increased involvement in decision-making and work processes, and greater control and autonomy in their regular jobs, increased worker productivity significantly. Zwick believes that by introducing self-managed teams and autonomous work groups, and by reducing organizational hierarchy, the increased ability for employees to participate in their everyday work allows for a substantially greater level of self-esteem, pride in their work, work enjoyment, and job satisfaction. Zwick has explained these changes as a simple human need: the act of participation enhances feelings of being a part of something important, and allows employees to feel needed, both of which are fundamental human drives, the satisfaction of which can result in the responses of increased employee performance and organizational commitment.

The need to feel needed and important in the workplace and its relationship to job satisfaction has also been investigated by Thoms, Dose, and Scott (2002). According to their review of the literature, high workplace performance and job satisfaction are associated with self-management, but only when attention is given to levels of accountability (that is, the responsibility of a given person to make sure that his or her actions are successful) and trust between an employee and those to whom he or she is held accountable. Following their investigation of 284 employees on measures of job satisfaction with levels of responsibility and with their supervisors and co-workers, their level of accountability to managers and co-workers, and trust levels in management and supervisors, Thoms and his colleagues reported that job satisfaction was significantly greater in employees who trusted their immediate supervisor and management as a whole. More importantly, Thoms *et al.* showed that satisfaction was increased among employees who felt that their supervisor and co-workers were aware of their work. In other words, Thoms *et al.* have demonstrated that when employees were held accountable for the quality and outcomes of their work, were able to trust the people who held them accountable for that work, and who felt that their work was acknowledged and respected, they felt more important and, therefore, a greater satisfaction with their role at work. That is, people who feel that their participation at work has a noticeable effect and who feel noticed and valued for what they do also feel better about their work and more satisfied with their jobs.

Guest and Peccei (2001) have defined participation in the workplace as an operalization of partnership between employers and employees in terms of principles, practices and outcomes. Following the analysis of responses to measures of workplace partnership by 82 managers and 65 employees from UK businesses, Guest and his co-worker showed that partnership practices, such as direct employee participation in workplace decisions and practices, as well as greater attention to job design and quality were significantly related to positive organizational outcomes (such as higher employee contribution, better employment relations, and improved organizational performance), and employee outcomes (including increased job satisfaction and satisfaction with the state of their psychological contract). Guest and Peccei have recommended that in order to take advantage of the financial and qualitative benefits subsequent to partnership practices, organizations take pains to implement a combination of programmes to integrate employer and employee interests, such as the execution of financial reward schemes that encourage feelings of ownership (such as stock rights and profit sharing), the direct involvement of employees in day-to-day activities and decisions, and the judicious use of HPWS.

Organization-based self-esteem (OBSE), a measure of how confident employees feel about their ability to do their work and a strong predictor of job satisfaction, is also a direct consequence of opportunities to participate usefully in a workplace setting, and the ability to feel valued for those contributions (Brutus, Ruderman, Ohlott, & McCauley, 2000). According to Brutus *et al.*, who examined 261 managers from 4 different companies who had enrolled in MBA programmes, on the one hand, managers with high levels of OBSE used their own self-concept to guide their career development through their focus on learning and development, and felt greater levels of career development regardless of the amount of perceived challenge in their work. Low OBSE managers, on the other hand, tended to rely on outside sources (such as the attitudes of their co-workers) to form opinions and shape their actions and, therefore, only felt that they were able to develop when they perceived greater levels of job challenge. That is, whilst high OBSE employees felt confident to guide their own development, low OBSE workers used their perceptions of job challenge to determine whether they needed to learn or grow, often becoming stagnant because of their inability to take personal responsibility for their learning. Consequently, to increase managerial competence by encouraging self-led development, Brutus and his colleagues have recommended that organizations invest substantially in helping managers to increase their OBSE in order to see themselves as capable and of value to the organization. This can be done by allowing managers to expand their capabilities, by increasing their ability to contribute to the organization in valuable ways, such as increasingly important job assignments, formal education, and relationship-based strategies including coaching and mentoring, both with their subordinates and with their superiors (to provide support during the transition to increased responsibilities). Importantly, to increase OBSE without the damaging effects of perceived failure, managers should be given these increased responsibilities in a risk-managed environment, drawing on the manager's current strengths and expertise and encouraging increasingly independent decisions. In fact, in the opinion of Brutus and his co-workers, managers should be encouraged and given the latitude to make decisions within their sphere of experience without having to seek approval from higher-up, to be able to communicate with their superiors and subordinates providing regular upward feedback, and be allowed to reward their subordinates for successful performance. The benefits of highly competent and confident managers are transparent: as Brutus *et al.* have pointed out, when managers feel that their participation is of value to the organization as a whole, their increased satisfaction and performance will have a trickle-down effect on their subordinates.

In his evaluation of the relationship between job satisfaction, participation, and performance, Kim (2002) has reported that participation by both managers and employees is vital to satisfaction in the workplace. According to Kim's review of the literature, the ability to participate meaningfully at work increases job satisfaction because people who feel that their work is of value to their organization are more likely to be intrinsically motivated to perform. Moreover, participatory factors such as task clarity, skill utilization, task significance, and social interaction all help to increase job satisfaction, however, the actions of an employee's immediate supervisor in enabling that employee to feel that his or her work is adequately participatory are also paramount. According to Kim, when supervisors act in a way that is supportive, caring, and non-controlling, encourage skill development and the voicing of concerns, and provide feedback that is positively focussed and mostly informational in content (a process labelled "participatory management"), employees are more likely to feel that their participation is both supported and meaningful, increasing their intrinsic motivation to work and enhancing their job satisfaction. To validate the findings of previous researchers, Kim analysed data on 1576 employees from the 1999 Clark County employee survey on variables including participative management style, employee participation in strategic planning, effective supervisory communication, and job satisfaction. He found that job satisfaction was significantly higher among employees whose supervisors had a greater participatory management style and who possessed clearer communication abilities, and among those who were better able to participate in strategic planning processes. Kim also reported that among these employees there was a lower incidence of absenteeism and turnover, and recommended that organizational commitment to change processes should encompass management training programmes that focus on the development of managerial participatory styles and communication ability.

The importance of workplace participation in job satisfaction can be illustrated by the research of Nachbagauer and Riedl (2002) on the influence of career plateaus on job performance, commitment, and satisfaction. Nachbagauer and his colleague have asserted that career plateaus, in which employees find that they are no longer able to rise within an organization or to participate in a manner that they find satisfactory, represent an increasing problem in hierarchical organizations and firms that employ outsourcing and downsizing. Following an assessment of the responses of 155 faculty and 77 teachers from an Austrian university on measures of task satisfaction, individual development, affective organizational commitment, working hours, and self-assessed perform-ance, Nachbagauer and Riedl found that when employees perceived their work as stagnant, and felt unable to participate adequately, job satisfaction decreased significantly. Moreover, lack of promotion or other types of recognition of work quality resulted in both reduced job satisfaction and affective commitment and, in many cases, was seen as a breach by their employer of their psychological contract, further reducing satisfaction. To avoid these problems of stagnation and lack of recognition, Nachbagauer and his co-worker have recommended that management pay careful attention to factors that increase the ability of employees to participate, including increases in job rotation, project work, task variety, training, and flexibility in job design. They have also recommended dual track promotions in hierarchical organizations, with one side devoted to managerial appointments, and the other reserved for increased levels of involve-ment, responsibility, and complexity, but without a managerial component. This provides talented employees the ability to progress within their fields and the firm, without taking on the added responsibility of management, or losing the capability to work on projects that interest them.

Their success notwithstanding, attempts to instigate increased workplace participation have been varied. According to Poutsma, Hendrickx, and Huijgen (2003) who analysed data collected from 10 European countries on employee participation, participatory schemes are mostly moderated by a combination of financial and cultural differences and, on the whole, employee participation is poorly implemented in the majority of workplaces. For instance, profit sharing, a popular method of enhancing employee participation through increased reward, was only found to be present in the United Kingdom and, to a lesser extent, France, and was used for the most part not as an HR-driven initiative to enhance employee satisfaction but as a tax-efficient reward scheme. Likewise, share ownership, another participatory strategy, was only readily available in countries like the United Kingdom, in which the share market plays an important role. Consequently, this type of participatory scheme is not available in the state-run companies common to many mainland European countries. Direct particip-ation, in which employees are encouraged to take part in decision-making processes that affect the company, and to be more autonomous in their work practices, is also highly culturally driven, and is more common in countries that have more advanced social policies, like Ireland and the Netherlands, than in more disorganized countries like Spain and Italy. As would be expected, companies that encourage direct participation are more likely to be innov-ative, and have the support of senior and middle management in implementing employee participation; these companies also tend to perform better than both their non-participatory competitors and similar firms in less socially aware coun-tries (Poutsma *et al.*). Lastly, employee participation through representation, such as trade unions, was found to be much more common in countries like France and Spain, in which trade unions still hold a large amount of power over the actions of government and private industry. However, unlike direct participation schemes, employee representation does not tend to be associated with high-level company performance. With respect to their findings, Poutsma and his co-workers believe that whilst employee participation in the workplace is extremely important both for employee satisfaction and for organizational performance, to date many companies and the governments of their respective countries are only paying lip-service to the notion of employee involvement, despite the potential gains to be had. In fact, with the exception of forward-looking countries like the Netherlands, in many countries, employee particip-ation is often seen either as a way of reducing company tax burdens or as the exclusive domain of trade unions and their representatives.

Part 4: Performance evaluations and job satisfaction

Performance evaluations or job appraisals, in which supervisors or managers attempt to assess the performance of their subordinates, have also been linked to job satisfaction by several investigators. In fact, according to Boswell and Boudreau (2000), the quality of job appraisals is a strong predictor of employee attitudes towards their supervisors, satisfaction with their job, and the appraisal process itself. Typically, performance evaluations fall under one of two categories (Boswell & Boudreau). The first, evaluative, involves the gathering of inform-ation on the employee for use in mostly administrative decisions, such as determining salary, promotion decisions, retention or termination decisions, recognition of individual performance, identification of poor performance, or layoffs. Typically, because this type of evaluation does not assess qualitative variables, but rather seeks to quantify an individual's performance, evaluative appraisals are not particularly useful for providing developmental critique to an employee, with their use actually contributing to the potential for employee frustration and disappointment (Boswell & Boudreau). The second type of evaluation, developmental, is used to gather information pertaining to an employee's job development and progress. Typically this type of appraisal is more qualitative in nature and helps to identify training needs and an indi-vidual's strengths and weaknesses, as well as to provide performance feedback and to determine appropriate transfers and assignments. To further investigate the relationship between performance evaluations and employee satisfaction, Boswell and her colleague looked at the responses of 129 employees from a production equipment facility, on measures of performance appraisal satisfac-tion. Following analysis of their data, Boswell and Boudreau found that the use of developmental appraisals was positively associated with employee satisfaction with their appraisals and with their appraiser. Evaluative appraisals, however, were associated with lowered satisfaction with the appraisal, the appraiser, and with their job, a finding that Boswell and Boudreau explained by pointing out the conflicting and contradictory messages given through evaluative appraisals: because evaluative appraisers attempt to quantify a person's performance, but are not able to give that person useful critique regarding development or assess their needs or frustrations, the appraisals are often interpreted by employees as invasive and non-constructive. In other words, rather than feeling as if their employer were interested in their development, employees undergoing evalu-ative appraisals tend to feel scrutinized, resulting in lowered trust, and reduced job satisfaction and organizational commitment. Thus, whilst Boswell and her co-worker recommend the use of appraisals, where necessary, as an effective organizational tool, they also suggest that employers take care in how they are used: rather than evaluating employees simply to determine if they are doing their job effectively, they should include aspects that are important to the employee, such as career development, training, and other issues affecting job satisfaction. In a similar investigation Pettijohn, Pettijohn, and d'Amico (2001), who evaluated responses by 115 salespeople from franchised US car sales firms on measures of appraisal criteria, job satisfaction, and satisfaction with appraisals, reported that appraisal satisfaction was linked to whether the evalutaion focussed on what Pettijohn *et al.* labelled "input" variables. These input variables, similar to the aspects of developmental appraisals identified by Boswell and Boudreau, focus on providing positive feedback through insights into employee satisfaction, knowledge, and commitment to the firm, as well as evaluation of employee focus and employee needs regarding training, coaching, and career development. Thus, according to Pettijohn and his co-investigators, when performance appraisals are used as tools to help employees understand how they are doing and how they could improve, rather than mechanisms for evaluating whether targets have been met, employees are likely to respond with greater enthusiasm, commitment, job satisfaction, and improvements in performance.

Another important aspect in the efficacy of performance evaluations is their perceived fairness. According to Elvira and Town (2001), when evaluations are seen as unfair or unjust, employee job satisfaction can actually be reduced. After investigating 316 personnel records from a large US corporation with nation-wide employees, Elvira and her colleague found that interpretations of subordinate performance by supervisors were highly dependent on race. Specifically, black employees were much more likely to receive negative or poor performance evaluations than their white counterparts, particularly on the subjective variables relating to feedback and career development championed by Pettijohn *et al.* (2001) and Boswell and Boudreau (2000). Elvira and Town have also reported that, to make matters worse, given that the majority of supervisory positions are filled by white employees, issues of race in performance evaluations represent a substantial problem, with black and other minority workers consistently feeling that their performance evaluations are unjust, and resulting in substantial job dissatisfaction and poor organizational commitment among many minority employees.

One way for managers and supervisors to provide performance appraisals that focus on employee development and that are less likely to be influenced by bias is to use computer-based tools (Miller, 2003). Miller has reported that software tools can simplify the appraisal process in two ways. First, automatic monitoring, such as measuring the number of given work units completed over time, can be used to quantify performance, allowing for a more objective evaluation. Whilst this type of monitoring does not provide the necessary subjective information for a balanced appraisal, it can be used to provide direct feedback to employees so that they can self-monitor their performance, use the information to identify and improve areas that require development, and collaborate with their supervisor on goal setting, task achievement and measurement standards. Nevertheless, Miller has also pointed out that this type of monitoring, when used specifically as a surveillance practice, can result in distinctly negative consequences regarding employee satisfaction. That is, when employees feel that electronic monitoring is being used to "spy" on their work practices and performance level, their notions of trust in their employer, satisfaction with the state of their psychological contract, and organizational commitment are all likely to suffer. The second type of software tool, recommended by Miller for enhancing the performance evaluation process, involves programmes that reduce a manager's workload in producing formal evaluations, by providing templates, or standardized forms that can be customized for specific needs. These programmes can greatly reduce the time required to generate a report, allowing supervisors more time in which to address subjective variables, including career development, and employee satisfaction issues. Likewise, web or intranet-based tools can allow employees to self-rate and participate anonymously in the evaluation of their colleagues, allowing managers to get a broader range of information on their charges, and HR professionals to better identify training needs, and competencies among teams, individuals, groups, and departments.

Best practice: Case examples of how it's being done

Satisfaction, workplace support, and performance

One example of successful workplace support and employee performance involves Walter Dorwin Teague Associates (Teague), a large and established industrial US design firm (Reed & Clark, 2004). Because a large proportion of their 130 staff were approaching retirement age, management at Teague were concerned that they would lose important human capital. As well, an increased level of support and interaction between senior and junior employees was required. To effect this change and ensure that important knowledge remained with the firm when key staff retired, a voluntary mentoring scheme was set up, pairing experienced, older workers with younger employees with less than five years experience at the company. Employees were screened so that the most appropriate matches could be determined, resulting initially in three paired mentoring relationships. Moreover, supervisors were encouraged to develop mentoring relationships with their charges, and supported in developing the necessary coaching skills in order to provide greater levels of support. Teague have reported that since the initiation of the programme, several younger employees have developed considerably, with a substantial increase in their learning and performance. As well, junior employees have reported an increase in workplace satisfaction as a result of these relationships.

Satisfaction, workplace participation, and performance

Business Link, a part of the British Department of Trade and Industry (*Employing People Guidebook*, 2005), have profiled Escrick Park Estate, an

English country house that operates as a multifaceted business. In order to increase employee participation, Escrick Park directors encouraged a staff participation programme that included weekly strategy meetings in order to allow employees to participate directly in the development of ideas and strategies for the business. As well, outside of meetings, employees were encouraged to voice opinions, give ideas and feedback, and make suggestions about business practices. Management were also persuaded to make a strong effort to incorporate these ideas into their workplace decisions, so that staff felt that their contributions were valid and could make a difference to the way in which the organization was run; and to communicate back to employees which ideas had been acted on, and why, to avoid disappointment and letdowns. Since the implementation of their participation programme, Escrick Park have reported substantial increases in their sales, as well as successful modifications of their internal systems for centralized budgeting to allow staff ideas to be acted upon, even if a department had already made several changes in a given time period.

Performance evaluations and job satisfaction

Anglesey Sea Zoo, a popular tourist destination in the United Kingdom, recently implemented an updated employee appraisal programme to help with flagging staff motivation and workplace satisfaction (*Employee Appraisals*, 2005). This programme involved the development and implementation of an evaluation system that sought to involve both employees and their supervisors in rating their performance (on a scale of one to four) to resolve mismatched expectations. Moreover, the appraisals themselves were conducted in a neutral environment (rather than in the supervisor's office) and emphasized two-way feedback. This feedback included discussion regarding not only whether performance objectives had been met, but also (and more importantly) other employee-related issues, such as training needs and workplace satisfaction, so that both the supervisor and employee were able to generate a list of the employee's goals and needs. Consequently, this process was aimed at assessing a person's skills, rather than the person themselves. Assessment results were fed back to both the employee and higher management, and any issues identified during the meeting were worked on as soon as possible. As well, supervisors were given training and support in order to develop and enhance the skills required to adequately debrief a subordinate, and were also encouraged to assign plenty of time for the appraisal so that neither party felt rushed. Since implementing their new assessment programme, Anglesey Sea Zoo has reported a decrease in turnover, and their employees have reported that they are more satisfied in their work.

Points for action: Practical recommendations for change

Satisfaction at work: Support and performance

The Health and Safety Executive (*Work-Related Stress*, 2004), in their report on workplace stress, have made several suggestions for increasing performance and reducing stress by encouraging adequate support at work. Their recommendations include:

- ongoing support and encouragement of staff, even (and especially) when things go wrong
- making sure that employees are balancing their work and life
- investigating flexible working options such as flexible hours or working from home, for each employee
- taking individual differences into account so that projects are tailored to the capabilities of each worker
- making sure that communication practices between supervisors and subordinates are of a high level, and providing training, where needed, to enhance this communication
- communication should involve talking regularly with employees to make sure that they are clear about their goals and the company's objectives, and that supervisors understand what employees need to do their jobs to the best of their abilities, and are able to identify and repair potential problems
- support can also include listening to individual ideas for improvement of job performance, or production or other processes, and acting on those recommendations.

Performance evaluations and job satisfaction

In their report on performance evaluations, Business Link (*Performance Evaluations*, 2005) have recommended that organizations include both professional performance measurement and personal performance evaluation when assessing staff. On the one hand, professional performance involves assessing levels of achievement on objective indicators such as sales figures, production outcome, and financial performance. However, these variables should be supplemented by regular subjective feedback, such as weekly progress meetings, in order for management to keep in touch with a project's progress, and to identify any support gaps or employee needs. Personal performance evaluations, on the other hand, should be used on a regular basis to determine whether an employee is developing in the way that he or she had hoped. Rather than assessing whether an individual is meeting targets, this assessment is aimed at identifying how the employee feels about his or her work, colleagues and skills, and what can be done to enhance his or her satisfaction and performance in the workplace. Business Link recommend that personal performance evaluation should follow four stages:

1. setting objectives, so that both supervisors and employees are clear on what is expected of them in their work roles;
2. managing performance, including providing employees with adequate tools, resources, training and support in order to be able to meet their objectives and perform at the highest level possible;
3. carrying out regular appraisals, to figure out what an employee thinks and feels about his or her work, to identify areas that need improvement, and to determine what can be done to improve satisfaction and performance;

4. providing rewards or remedies, making sure that employees are recognized (in the form of formal or informal rewards and recognition) for their achievements, and encouraged to meet their goals through ongoing support, and positive critique and feedback.

In thier report on employee appraisal methods, ACAS (*Employee Appraisal*, 2005) have recommended that organizations take the following steps when evaluating staff:

- Seek commitment and support from all levels of management.
- Consult with management before the introduction of appraisals to make sure that they understand, and are supportive of the programme.
- Make sure that appraisals are not used in isolation, but rather are strongly tied to policies and practices throughout the organization, especially in human resources, planning, and training, and in decisions relating to pay and promotion.
- Ensure that those giving appraisals have adequate training in interpersonal interaction, listening and communication skills, as well as the ability to be objective, so that both parties feel comfortable in the context of the evaluation.
- Make sure that all parties involved in an appraisal understand its purpose.
- Reduce paperwork associated with the appraisal to as little as possible, and make sure that appraisal forms are well designed and adequately piloted before use.
- Regularly review appraisal systems, based on feedback gathered from participants, so that they continue to meet the changing needs of employees.

Summary

Looking at what we have learnt so far: the economic rationalistic decisions of the 1990s have been questioned given their long-term impact on company viability. It turns out that the majority of employees that were sacked during downsizing programmes were the ones that actually did the work, and those left behind were required to do more work with fewer resources and lower morale. The increased stress associated with the combined threats of job loss and work intensification has led to higher levels of burnout, in which employees no longer feel capable of performing, and which results in even greater costs to employers. Nevertheless, one of the strongest mediators of stress and burnout is workplace support. Supervisory support, in which a supervisor or manager possesses skills in mentoring, counselling, and coaching and uses these skills to help his or her charges meet their potential, is a prime method for enhancing employee satisfaction, commitment, and performance. However, these skills are not intuitive, and require the support of the organization in order to foster and develop techniques that motivate. Specifically, when organizations attempt to engender trust, they also increase employee satisfaction, and for supervisory support to occur, it is also important that managers and supervisors feel supported.

Like empowerment, the ability to participate meaningfully at work is also a strong predictor of positive employee satisfaction and performance. Meaningful participation encompasses the need to feel needed, and is increased through greater attention to employee autonomy, accountability, and recognition, especially regarding adequate skills utilization, task clarity and significance, social interaction, and supervisory input. Another way that organizations can increase employee perception of meaning at work is through adequate feedback. Performance evaluations or job appraisals are most effective when used to determine what an employee needs to do to perform better, to provide positive critique, to enhance job satisfaction, and when based on subjective criteria. They are least effective when used to assess whether an employee has met his or her targets, or to evaluate performance based on quantitative factors. Moreover, they must be perceived as fair, just, equitable, and devoid of discrimination.

REVIEW QUESTIONS

1. Explain how the effects of economic rationalistic actions, such as layoffs, can have a negative impact on employee satisfaction and performance.

2. Describe the relationship between dissatisfaction at work, and stress and burnout.

3. Explain how supervisory and other types of support influence workplace satisfaction.

4. Is there a relationship between increased workplace participation and job satisfaction? Describe this relationship and its mechanisms.

5. What is the connection between performance evaluations and job satisfaction? How have your experiences with performance appraisals influenced your workplace satisfaction?

6. Outline why subjective variables, like job satisfaction, are important for economists, despite being largely ignored in the economic literature.

Mind-diagram summary

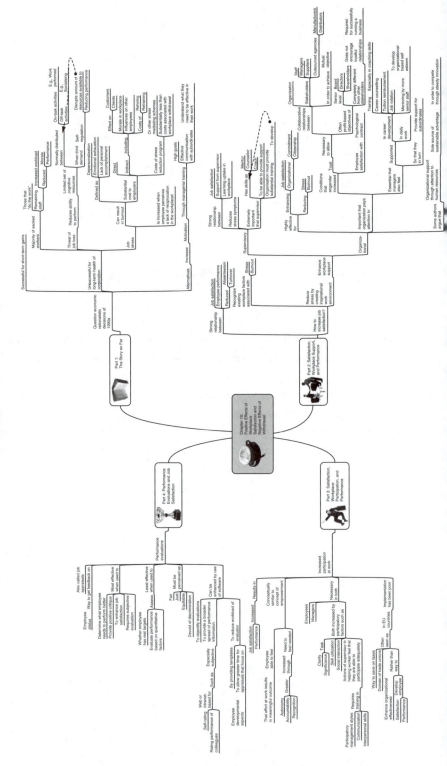

Satisfaction, Meaning, and Happiness in the Workplace

KEYWORDS Cause, behaviour, employee satisfaction, health, internal, self-esteem, workplace satisfaction.

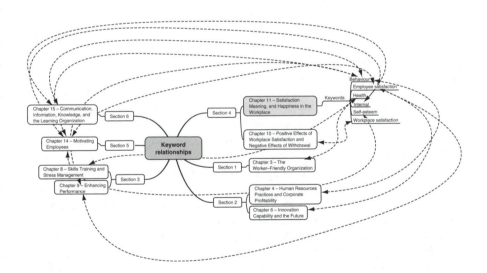

IMPORTANT CONCEPTS   Emotional support, stress and coping.

As we have discussed already, reducing the factors associated with stress and burnout can enhance both a person's workplace satisfaction and his or her performance. The benefits of stress reduction notwithstanding, in line with the suggestions of Schweitzer (1998), many workers require more than a simple lack of stress to motivate and inspire them; they desire stimulation and fun in their work role. Csikszentmihalyi (2003) has written that it is the perception of organizational support and the ability to be able to achieve meaning at work that determines a person's likelihood of long-term satisfaction. Accordingly, the following section expands on these notions, by reviewing a selection of studies and articles whose authors are concerned with methodologies and techniques for enhancing an employee's work experience and, consequently, the success of an organization.

Part 1: The importance of subjectivity

Because job satisfaction is highly related to many positive organizational outcomes, and is also highly subjective, it is often difficult for economists to understand its importance to modern business success. Recommendations to economists of the value of subjective variables such as job satisfaction in organizational performance notwithstanding, subjective variables, whilst heavily researched by psychologists and management researchers, have been largely ignored by economists who, as we have seen repeatedly, prefer to work with tangible, quantifiable variables (Sousa-Poza & Sousa-Poza, 2000). Nevertheless, this is not entirely the case. In their attempt to adequately measure job satisfaction, and the variables that predict its variation, economists Sousa-Poza and his colleague examined 1997 data from the International Social Survey Program, a part of which examined a person's self-rating of job satisfaction, finding 15,324 usable data sets representing 21 countries including the United States, the United Kingdom and other EU countries, and Japan and other Asian countries. Sousa-Poza and Sousa-Poza found that the highest levels of job satisfaction were in EU countries, followed by the United States, with Japan at a lowly 15th. Moreover, job satisfaction and subjective well-being were strongly linked to other subjective variables, such as interesting work, good relations with management, supervisory support, and the ability to work independently – factors that the authors suggested are more likely to occur in EU countries than in more-rigid social and economic climates such as Japan. Similarly, economists Levy-Garboua and Montmarquette (2004) have attempted to define the subjective variable of job satisfaction through mathematical modelling based on a literature analysis. They found that self-reported job satisfaction is really a person's experienced preference for a given job over other available opportunities, past, present and future. In other words, according to Levy-Garboua and his colleague, satisfaction represents the judgement that a given person would repeat his or her past experiences if he or she were given the choice; that is, job satisfaction is simply a person's happiness with their career decisions and actions taken in their past, their contentment with job experiences and their willingness to do them again. Thus, in the opinion of Levy-Garboua and Montmarquette, in terms of quantifying job satisfaction, managers should work on the basis that external organizational actions, designed to enhance a person's satisfaction, such as participation and support in the workplace, increased perceived control, empowerment, and work–life balance, are highly predictive of a person's contentment. More importantly for economists, the presence and quality of these activities are highly predictive of an employee's increased likelihood of remaining with the firm, higher levels of productivity, and reduced rates of absenteeism, all of which drive the firm's bottom line.

IN ACTION #10

Employee satisfaction and company profitability

If employees are, in fact, the greatest intangible assets of an organization, it stands to reason that their productivity (and, consequently, the productivity and performance of the organization as a whole) would be strongly positively related to their level of satisfaction. In fact, there is a surprisingly large body of scientific and economic literature that suggests that there is a positive and causal relationship between employee satisfaction in the workplace and company profitability. Whilst there are a vast number of variables that contribute to this relationship, analysis of their contribution towards organizational profitability (Adams, 2004) has resulted in five important factors: (i) workplace satisfaction, strong communication, high social and managerial interaction, and personal autonomy; (ii) work–life balance, health and well-being, and the recognition of individual value; (iii) reduced stress and increased perceived control; (iv) strong leadership and individual leeway; and (v) workplace happiness and support. The uptake of this research is that, if care is taken to ensure that a business functions so that employees are satisfied in each of these areas, the organization will see greater financial performance, through the increased loyalty, effectiveness and productivity of its employees.

Although these variables are intangible and, consequently, difficult to measure, they can be quantified, even in conventional accounting practices. Given that the Gallup organization has reported that employee satisfaction accounts for up to 39 per cent of the variability in financial performance in (*Fortune* 500) companies (Barrett, 1999), and given the huge number of variables that contribute to organizational performance overall, it is essential that accountants pay attention to the variables that influence employee satisfaction.

In fact, a person's subjective, emotional and internal states are the most important predictors of whether he or she will be satisfied at work (Schwartz, 2000). According to Schwartz who has reported on the results of a Gallup organization study (involving the development of a 12-item questionnaire to evaluate emotional state and professional satisfaction), companies whose employees scored more highly on ratings of emotional satisfaction (compared with low scorers) had 50 per cent less employee turnover, were 38 per cent more productive, had 50 per cent greater customer loyalty, and exceeded their profit goals by an average of 14 per cent. Specifically, these successful companies employed workers who rated the following as "above average" or "excellent": their understanding of work role expectations, their access to resources required to perform adequately, their opportunities for excellence, their recognition for good work, their perceived level of supervisor support, their perception of encouragement to develop their skills, the perceived relevance of their opinions, the alignment of the company's mission with their personal goals, their perception of the commitment of co-workers to work quality, the quality of their relationships at work, the recency of external attention to their progress, and their opportunities for learning and growth.

Part 2: Satisfaction and meaning

Each of the variables measured in the report by Schwartz (2000) was related to personal perceptions of support and meaning in the workplace and was, for the most part, a reflection of the internal states and perceptions of the employee; qualities that have received attention from other researchers. For example, Isaksen (2000), in his evaluation of meaning in the workplace, has reported that meaning is, in fact, an inherent human ability, and need not be related to the external environment, nor to any particular type of work. Rather, he has suggested that a person's state of mind can allow him or her to experience meaning in virtually any condition. According to Isaksen, who undertook a qualitative evaluation of meaning in the workplace by interviewing 28 catering employees, a sense of purpose makes life more comprehensible, and makes one's life burdens more endurable. Nevertheless, in the opinion of Isaksen, this mental state does not come without meeting certain internal and external conditions, the absence of which can lead to the typical manifestations of workplace stress,[22] including heart disease, depression, lowered self-esteem, and anhedonia (that is, inability to feel pleasure). According to Isaksen, stress symptoms in the workplace are most often observed in repetitive roles, and are often the result of a poor fit between the person, his or her job role and the surrounding environment, and between a person's interests and the opportunities inherent in his or her job. This lack of fit results in a negative evaluation of working conditions and, consequently, the loss of ability to construct meaning within the constraints of the job role. In contrast, when the conditions by which a person constructs a sense of meaning are met, by allowing a measure of control over the environment, flexibility within the job role and the encouragement of a person's creativity, many people can reach a high level of personal satisfaction in their work.

This ability to experience satisfaction in even adverse conditions is similar to the concept of "flow", a psychological state coined by Csikszentmihalyi (2003) that represents a high level of human mental functioning in which challenge and skill are equally matched. During flow, a state often experienced by athletes, a person loses his or her sense of time, concentrates absolutely, performs at an extremely high level, and feels an overwhelming sense of satisfaction and purpose. Czsitkenmihalyi has reported that when the conditions for flow are

---

[22] Refer back to Section 3 for discussions of workplace stress, and its effects on performance.

met (a supportive environment, an equal balance of challenge to existing skill, and the reinforcement of behaviours that increase challenge and skill), work can be both meaningful and enjoyable. In fact, the perception of the importance of time well spent is by no means new: Leo Tolstoy (1877) in his seminal work, *Anna Karenina*, wrote: "But time's money, you forget that, said the colonel. Time, indeed, that depends! Why, there's time one would give a month of for sixpence, and time you wouldn't give half an hour of for any money."

IN ACTION #11

Satisfaction and flow

Workplace satisfaction when taken to its endpoint can be described by "flow", an ideal mental state proposed by the famous psychologist Mihaly Csikszentmihalyi. Flow represents the perfect match between skills and challenge, and results in a state of mind in which there is pure satisfaction, in which it is not possible to make a mistake, in which perception of time disappears, and in which the activity at hand becomes totally absorbing. According to Csikszentmihalyi, it is possible to experience this state regularly at work. However, to get there, it is necessary to develop one's skills to a high degree, and be consistently challenged (but, obviously, not to the point of stress – Csikszentmihalyi suggests that challenge only becomes stress when you no longer have the resources to deal with what is being asked of you). Consequently, in your daily work life, try to take every opportunity to challenge yourself, learn new things, and hone your existing skills. You don't have to be a Buddhist monk to find meaning in everyday things, you just have to reframe what they mean to you. In other words, rather than seeing your job as "the same old thing, day in day out", seek out opportunities, try new activities, perfect your abilities, and increase the quality of your interactions with others. Remember, for many people, it is a feeling of purpose that gives them a sense of meaning in their lives; nearly everyone likes to feel that they are doing something "worthwhile". Of course, in some workplaces this is quite a challenge. In these cases, be honest with yourself; if it is not possible to find challenge or satisfaction in what you do, make change, either by seeking out a new job or by helping your employer to see the value of workers who are satisfied and purposeful.

Part 3: Happiness and health

The perception of meaning in the workplace also extends to the notion of challenge: when given the question "what motivates you?", 1563 employees responded with "being held responsible for the business results of my own work" ("Boosting work productivity", 1997). This response encapsulates the concept of autonomy and control in the workplace: that is, when people feel capable of creating their own solutions, designing their own jobs, and setting their own goals, they become more motivated and their productivity increases alongside this motivation. Thus, if one defines performance as the product of motivation and ability ("Boosting work productivity", 1997), it follows that low motivation will result in low performance. Conversely, by providing workers with the tools needed to enhance their abilities, such as training, resources, effective, communicated goals, rewards for success and high performance, and by allowing employees the autonomy to create and modify their own work roles, performance will also be increased.

The notion that motivation and productivity are linked has also been espoused by Cropanzano and Wright (2001) in their evaluation of the relationship between happiness and performance in the workplace. According to Cropanzano and his colleague, unfortunately, many Americans are unhappy: it has been estimated that in excess of 17 million regularly take antidepressants for diagnosed depression, an illness that includes behaviour that is defensive, acrimonious, and introverted, and that results in a high sensitivity to environmental stressors and the inability to recognize support, even when it is available. However, Cropanzano and Wright have reported that happy people (that is, those who regularly exhibit positive emotions that are stable over time and who seldom experience negative emotions) are more confident, outgoing, helpful and optimistic, and are less sensitive to negative events than unhappy people. Likewise, happiness at work results in motivation to work; happy people are more productive, more satisfied, and more responsive to the needs of the organization. In the light of the report of Cropanzano and his co-worker it seems surprising that so many people are unhappy. According to the investigators, because happiness is such a subjective state, it is relatively easy to engender simply by providing the precursors to happiness: a feeling of meaningfulness, the perception of support, and the belief that one is able to make a difference.

To stimulate happiness in the workplace, Howard and Gould (2000) have recommended that companies form highly placed project teams to oversee employee contentment, in which managers work as satisfaction facilitators. This process, according to Howard and her colleague, represents the real business of managers and should take priority in their everyday tasks; unfortunately, however, Howard and Gould have pointed out that few corporate strategies involve the well-being of their staff. Nevertheless, to develop happiness at work, Howard and Gould have suggested that managers attempt a thorough understanding of their workforce, both at work and outside of the workplace, to determine exactly what is important to employees. This should be followed by a strategic plan aimed at increasing employee happiness, and a consequent modification of the organizational structure to accommodate these ideals. According to Howard and Gould, although many employers see employee happiness as tangential to "real" business, this assumption serves little value and is actually counter to both company and employee interests. It follows that if employee happiness is ignored, workers will remain dispassionate to the aims of the organization and unmotivated to work positively on its behalf.

One unpleasant consequence of unhappiness is workplace incivility (Johnson & Indvik, 2001). Johnson and her colleague, who have documented increasing levels of rudeness at work since 1995, believe that employees who do not feel that their needs are being met become increasingly dissatisfied, frustrated, stressed, and angry. Unfortunately, because few people are explicitly trained in communication practices, anger management, or dealing with angry co-workers, and because even fewer managers posses the skills needed to mediate problems, or even to motivate and stimulate their subordinates, frustration is virtually inevitable: more often than not, according to Johnson and Indvik, lack of satisfaction with work boils over into workplace rudeness (such a verbal confrontations, shouting, nasty or underhanded behaviour, and selfish or thoughtless action), which, in turn, fuels conflict and greater dissatisfaction and unhappiness. Johnson and Indvik have also pointed out that the consequences of workplace incivility are not limited simply to employee frustration: 12 per cent of people exposed to regular workplace rudeness quit their jobs, 52 per cent lose work time by worrying about the conflict, and 22 per cent deliberately decrease their work productivity as a consequence of rudeness, all of which are costly to organizations. Moreover, 78 per cent report that incivility has gotten worse over the last ten years, representing an increasing problem for firms concerned with maximizing productivity and financial performance (Johnson & Indvik).

Actions counter to employee happiness also have negative health consequences for employees, some of which have been examined by Kirkcaldy, Levine, and Shephard (2000) in their study of 262 German managers. According to these investigators, job-related stress has continued to increase in the workplace, without adequate recognition by management, because of increasing work hours, driven principally by a loss of balance between work and personal life. Moreover, Kirkcaldy *et al.* have reported that when individuals take means to reduce their job stress, such as reducing their work hours or taking more regular holidays, these actions are often perceived by management as a lack of commitment to their work, with a consequent reduction in the likelihood of recognition or promotion. In a manner similar to the suggestions of other researchers, to combat this trend Kirkcaldy *et al.* have recommended that employers take extra pains to match the skills and interests of an individual to a particular job, with substantial room for job-role flexibility. Likewise, they have suggested that working hours should be flexible, customized to a person's coping skills, and his or her personality and locus of control (that is, whether a person believes that he or she is in control of events, or vice versa). In other words, people who enjoy, and who are capable of dealing with longer work hours should be given the opportunity to do so, leaving others to work to their own ability, without loss of recognition. In this way, employees are recognized for the quality, originality, and innovativeness of their work, rather than by the work hours that they keep. Lastly, Kirkcaldy and his colleagues have advised that workers be given the opportunity to improve their coping skills by undertaking regular aerobic exercise, taking breaks between projects, learning to delegate effectively and by developing efficient planning skills, whilst employers should take pains to provide diversity in the workplace (to stimulate innovation), encourage social support (especially between employees and supervisors), and match a person's circadian rhythms with his or her temporal performance (that is, to determine the timeframe in which a person works best, and then allowing him or her to work during these hours).

Other authors have recommended regular physical exercise in the workplace, in order to improve a person's satisfaction, happiness, and performance. Brophy

Marcus (2000), in her evaluation of health, sport, and workplace productivity, has reported that employees of companies that have gyms or health centres on premises are substantially more productive and work longer hours with less fatigue. Moreover, she has indicated that companies that offer perks for wellness activity, such as fitness training, see a three-to-one return on any investment made in setting up these services, realized by a substantially reduced level of absenteeism and health claims. Similarly, Rahe *et al.* (2002) have reported that companies that attend to the stress symptoms of employees before they become visible (for example, as illness or burnout), by providing stress management training and encouraging exercise in the workplace, are more successful and have happier, more-productive employees. According to Rahe and his colleagues, who assessed happiness, productivity, and employee turnover in 501 workers over a 12-month period, employers should pay particular attention to employees who are more vulnerable to the effects of stress, especially regarding those that have poor stress-coping responses, are younger, are female, have a lower occupational status, have experienced recent life change, have fewer or poorer health habits, and who exhibit low life satisfaction.

According to Wendel (1999), that physical and psychological health and happiness are strongly related is hardly coincidental. She has suggested several variables to which management should pay careful attention in order to enhance satisfaction and meaning in the workplace and, consequently, to increase the health, happiness, and productivity of employees. The first variable, meaningful work, involves the recognition of increasing role stress, and the need for a balance of time between creative and regular work. Moreover, peace of mind, personal development, a balance of life and work, flexible work options such as time, goal setting and role diversity, and health practices in and outside of the workplace should also be addressed when considering the well-being of both the individual and the organization. Wendel has also recommended that increased attention be given to productivity management, by factoring a person's positive mental and physical health into any financial output measures. Third, an investment in employees as human capital (that is, the encouragement of personal skills and professional development in employees) allows workers to become more valuable assets to an organization, resulting in a multidimensional increase in organizational performance (including financial performance measures). Lastly, health incentive programmes (for example, encouraging exercise, good nutrition, and smoking cessation) will increase a person's productivity by allowing him or her to work at a higher capacity.

Best practice: Case examples of how it's being done

Happiness and health

A large software development firm in the United States, SAS Institute, have won several awards for their commitment to employee happiness and well-being, including a regular place in the top 10 of the Fortune magazine's Annual Top 100 Companies to Work For survey, largely due to the actions and beliefs of its founder, Dr James Goodnight, regarding the importance of happy, satisfied employees for the ongoing health of the company (Reed & Clark, 2004).

To achieve the high level of workplace satisfaction among its employees, SAS have implemented a range of practices to help employees to participate in meaningful, challenging work, and be supported in that work. Moreover, SAS provide a large number of free services and facilities to their staff to address work–life balance, employee happiness, and health (including psychological well-being). Some of these include:

- fully paid comprehensive health insurance
- on-site health care with a full medical staff
- on-site recreation and fitness centre and fully paid fitness club membership for off-site employees
- on-site massage therapy, concierge, and income-tax assistance services
- counselling services for all employees
- on-site child care.

The workplace initiatives of SAS have also led to a substantial increase in the company's performance over the past ten years (Reed & Clark, 2004); as well, with one of the lowest turnover rates in the software industry SAS saves an estimated $75 million annually.

Points for action: Practical recommendations for change

Happiness and health

In order to initiate effective schemes to enhance employee health and happiness, Business Link (*Meet the Need for Work-Life Balance*, 2005) have suggested the following checklist:

- Decide what needs to be achieved through informal discussion with staff at all levels of the organization – find out what they want.
- Consult with all the employees who will be involved in the scheme and agree on selected policies, such as flextime, fitness programmes, or training goals.
- Figure out which employees will have access to the scheme, but try to make it as equitable as possible.
- Develop written procedures and policies for the implantation and evaluation of the scheme. Make sure that it is re-evaluated on a regular basis so that it continues to meet the needs of staff.
- Make sure that management support the idea: without managerial backing, the scheme is unlikely to make it off the ground.
- Try to get managers to model the underlying principles of the scheme, for example, by making sure that managers have the resources and support to be able to have an adequate work–life balance, be fit and healthy, and be happy and satisfied in their work.
- Make sure that employees are aware of, and understand, the scheme.

Summary

Happiness and meaning in the workplace go a long way towards enhancing employee satisfaction, performance, and commitment. Unfortunately, because job satisfaction is a highly subjective state, and is not readily quantifiable, it is often ignored by economists. Nevertheless, the strong correlation between job satisfaction and corporate performance suggests that qualitative variables should be highly important in modern economics. Meaning, another qualitative variable is also largely ignored in economic theory. Nevertheless, a sense of purpose in life is an inherent human need, and is strongly influenced by environmental conditions; given that most people spend a large amount of time at work, the conditions in the workplace can impact a person's sense of meaning. Internally, meaning can be stimulated by encouraging satisfaction with work, through greater participation and support. Externally, a strong sense of job "fit", job-role flexibility, and the freedom to participate in job-role determination all aid in enhancing an individual's sense of meaning at work. "Flow" – an ideal mental state in which a balance between skills development and challenge leads to feelings of intense satisfaction, loss of time perception, a sense of infallibility, and total absorption in a task – represents a pinnacle of satisfaction and meaning.

Happiness is also often overlooked by economists. After all, work is supposed to be serious, and unrelated to "fun". Despite this oversight, researchers have identified a strong relationship between happiness at work and workplace performance but, unfortunately, many people are unhappy at work, a phenomenon that often leads to incivility and rudeness in the workplace and poor performance. To enhance happiness at work, organizations should pay attention to training their managers to better understand the workforce, determining what is important to employees, supporting their interests in and outside of work, and provide opportunities for physical activity (such as on-site recreational facilities or subsidized gym memberships). These actions represent a strong investment in human capital by ensuring that employees are able to work at their best, and enhance both psychological and physical health.

REVIEW QUESTIONS

1. With regard to your own workplace experiences, explain the need for individual meaning, and how this drive is related to workplace and life satisfaction.

2. Why would employees who feel that their work is lacking in meaning not be motivated to perform?

3. If you were to attempt to increase happiness in the workplace, how would you go about it?

4. Explain how happiness at work can contribute to the health of employees.

5. Think of a time (if ever) that you felt happy at work. How did this affect the rest of your life (for example, work–life balance, relationships in and out of the workplace, overall well-being, and so on)?

Mind-diagram summary

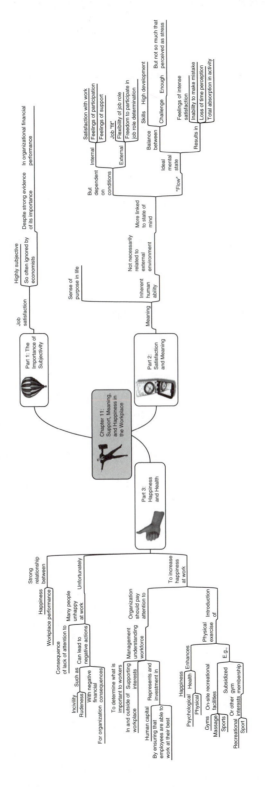

Chapter 11: Support, Meaning, and Happiness in the Workplace

Part 1: The Importance of Subjectivity

- Job satisfaction
- Highly subjective
  - So often ignored by economists
- Despite strong evidence of its importance
  - In organizational financial performance

Part 2: Satisfaction and Meaning

- Sense of purpose in life
- Meaning
  - Inherent human ability
  - Not necessarily related to external environment
  - More linked to state of mind

- But dependent on conditions
  - Internal
    - Satisfaction with work
    - Feelings of participation
    - Feelings of support
  - External
    - Job "fit"
    - Flexibility of job role
    - Freedom to participate in job role determination

- Ideal mental state "Flow"
  - Balance between
    - Skills
    - Challenge
  - High development
  - Enough
    - But not so much that perceived as stress
  - Results in
    - Feelings of intense satisfaction
    - Inability to make mistake
    - Loss of time perception
    - Total absorption in activity

Part 3: Happiness and Health

- Strong relationship between
  - Happiness
  - Workplace performance
- Consequence of lack of attention to
  - Unfortunately
    - Many people unhappy at work
  - Can lead to negative actions
    - Such as
      - Incivility
      - Rudeness
    - With negative financial consequences
    - For organization

- To determine what is important to workers
  - Supporting interests
  - In and outside of workplace
- Human capital
  - By ensuring that employees are able to work at their best

- Organization should pay attention to
  - Management understanding workforce
    - Represents and investment in

- To increase happiness at work
  - Physical exercise
    - Enhances
      - Happiness
      - Psychological Health
      - Physical
    - Introduction of
      - On-site recreational facilities
        - Gyms
        - Massage
        - Sports
      - Subsidized
        - Or other gym membership
      - E.g.,
        - Recreational Sport interests

Improving Managerial and Leadership Practices, and Motivating Employees

Introduction

Up to now we have examined the positive consequences of employee satisfaction, along with the negative outcomes of workplace stress. As well, we have reviewed recommendations for ameliorating the work environment to reduce stress, increase well-being, and to provide a sense of meaning. Some authors have proposed that organizations that follow these recommendations can be more profitable, have less staff turnover, and are publicly perceived as better places to work than non-compliant companies. Nevertheless, it remains a fact that the implementation of many of these strategies requires the effective intervention of management. Consequently, in the following section we will review the literature on effectual management and leadership, and its improvement.

Section guide

Chapter 12, "Managerial Development and Models", looks at the state of contemporary management, and how managers can improve their practice. We will also examine why so many managers have difficulty in mastering their roles, and look at how cultural influences affect managerial decisions and practices. In Chapter 13, "Transformational Leadership and the Benefits of Leadership Enhancement", we will cover the different types of leadership styles, and their advantages and flaws, especially the benefits of transformational leadership. We will also review the important area of contemporary leadership and corporate ethics, investigating both ethical theory and the ways in which corporate leaders and their organizations can increase their virtuousness by reducing their negative social and environmental impact. Lastly, in Chapter 14, "Motivating Employees", we will revisit concepts of intrinsic and extrinsic motivation and examine the most-effective ways for organizations to encourage high levels of performance from their employees by investing in mechanisms for increasing intrinsic motivation.

Reading objectives

After completing this section you will have a clearer understanding of:

- how contemporary management practices often fail to provide for the needs of employees
- why contemporary managers are often poorly prepared for their roles
- how managers can improve their practices
- how cultural differences impact the efficacy of managerial efforts
- the different theories surrounding leadership styles, their advantages and disadvantages
- current thinking in leadership and corporate ethics, and how leaders can maximize benefit whilst minimizing harm
- how intrinsic motivation can be used to enhance employee effectiveness
- why extrinsic rewards can reduce an employee's intrinsic motivation to work
- why contemporary economic theories contraindicate employee performance.

Managerial Development and Models

Accomplish, administrate, assist, beneficial, engage, standard, style.

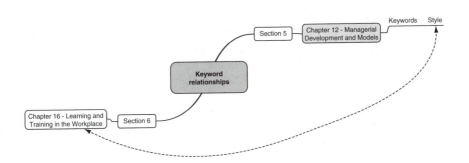

Expectancy theory, managerial learning, psychologically-based management.

Few would dispute the idea that effective managerial communication is paramount in establishing a strong executive position. In fact, notions of effective management have existed since long before modern professional models. Leo Tolstoy (1877) for example, in his work *Anna Karenina*, described an ideal manager as

> in the first place, of his extreme indulgence for others, founded on a consciousness of his own shortcomings; secondly, of his perfect liberalism – not the liberalism he read of in the papers, but the liberalism that was in his blood, in virtue of which he treated all men perfectly equally and exactly the same, whatever their fortune or calling might be; and thirdly – the most important point – his complete indifference to the business in which he was engaged, in consequence of which he was never carried away, and never made mistakes.

Management, then, could be described as the process of encouraging a person to fulfil a given role and, therefore, has more to do with older notions of leadership than more modern conceptions of facilitation. Nevertheless, this encouragement requires a level of self awareness and communicative ability that is not always available to managers. In this section we will examine the current state of management, how management can be improved, and some of the confounding factors that make management difficult.

Part 1: Contemporary managerial practices and competence

That managers are not always able to motivate has been illustrated by Cunliffe (2002) in her evaluation of dialogical practice in management. According to Cunliffe, typically management encourages dehumanization and disembodiment by focussing on non-human objectives (for example, financial targets) rather than on human relationships. Consequently, Cunliffe believes that workplace training, when initiated by management, remains focussed on these non-human goals, concentrating on theory without the buffering effects of practice or intellectual critique. Thus, in an organization, there is seldom learning for learning's sake or for the pleasure of improving one's position; learning is seen simply as a method for achieving a given financial goal. To increase humanism in the managerial process, Cunliffe has recommended that managers learn a psychological approach to supervision; that is, the encouragement of dialogical flow, the reduction of competition between departments and individuals, and the promotion of the formation of supportive relationships between the manager (in a teaching or mentoring role) and the employee (in a student role). According to Cunliffe, when these conditions are met communication becomes two-way (rather than directive), encouraging dialogue, interaction, and active participation through shared recognition of a common goal. This shared purpose can form a bridge between tacit knowledge (knowing something but not being able to communicate it) and explicit knowledge (that is, communication of ideas); the process of "talking" actually encourages creativity. Varey and White (2000) have expressed similar ideas in their evaluation of corporate communication and management. According to these authors, communication often breaks down under conditions of interdepartmental or individual rivalry, competition, or excessive independence. Moreover, Varey and White have suggested that the main cause of workplace rivalry is rooted in competition for resources, and that this is born of a lack of adequate management recognition of stakeholders. According to Varey and his colleague, typically, shareholders are perceived as the embodiment of an organization, often at the expense of other important stakeholders, such as employees, customers, and suppliers. Thus, although an organization represents a socio-economic system with multiple stakeholders, it is not managed as such. To more effectively manage an organization, Varey and White have recommended that each stakeholder be awarded his or her obligations and rights, so that managers become, in effect, social stewards (rather than "task masters") who engage in both a process of social contracting among their charges, and the drawing together of resources (including the intellectual resources inherent in the employees) to realize both social and financial wealth. Consequently, in the opinion of Varey and his colleague, a modern business can become an institution that is both economic and social, realizing a shift from profit centredness to democracy, a process that is driven by communication and transparency, and championed by people-centred managers concerned about the autonomy, satisfaction, and empowerment of their charges.

Whilst this goal of open, communicative organizations with competent managers and empowered workers is laudable, the reality of the modern workplace is often substantially removed from this ideal. Nevertheless, certain practices, mostly related to advances in HRM, illustrate the emerging state of contemporary management. For example, in her investigation of the effectiveness of modern management practices, including Total Quality Management and Self-Managed Teams, among 223 US telecommunications call-centre employees, Batt (1999) reported that when managers encouraged an increase in employee communication, interaction, participation and autonomy through the establishment and overseeing of self-managed teams, objective sales were raised by almost 10 per cent, and employees reported greater self-ratings in sales service. Conversely, TQM practices, which profess greater employee involvement, but seldom increase individual ability for influence over daily decisions, were not related to any performance gains. Paul and Anantharaman (2002) reported comparable findings. Following their examination of effective management practices among 379 Indian software company employees, Paul and his colleague described increased organizational performance in firms whose management embraced and encouraged team-based job design, comprehensive training, and development-oriented appraisal. In a similar study, Workman (2003), who looked at the responses of 151 call-centre workers on measures of teamwork and job satisfaction, found that when managers encouraged participation in high-involvement work practices (including increased decision-making autonomy, greater involvement in daily work practices, and increased participation in managerial-level decisions), job satisfaction increased significantly. Nevertheless, when management introduced autonomous work teams, satisfaction decreased. In this case, however, members of autonomous work teams were not given adequate training to deal with their new roles, and were given added responsibilities for meeting targets, without a corresponding increase in their decision-making latitude. According to Workman, this represents a managerial failure: rather than increasing employee involvement through training, communication and decision-making autonomy, managers offloaded a substantial part of their workload to employees who did not have the resources, freedom, or training to meet these new demands.

Workman's (2003) warnings about managerial failures in contemporary business have been echoed by White *et al.* (2003), who looked at the responses of 2466 United Kingdom employees on measures of "high-performance" practices, working hours, and negative work-to-home spillover. According to White and his colleagues, when managers introduce so-called high-performance work practices, such as group-working practices and performance-based pay, without paying careful attention to providing corresponding increases in employees' ability to regulate their work hours, load, and intensity, or providing resources to manage these new tasks and responsibilities, there is a strong likelihood of work intensification and a consequent reduction in employee satisfaction and performance. Moreover, White *et al.* believe that despite their popularity, these poorly thought-out management practices are a likely contributor to weak long-term organizational performance, and represent a failure of imagination and ability in senior and middle management. Similarly, Pugh, Oswald, and Jahera (2000), who assessed the effects on firm performance and employee satisfaction following the introduction of employee stock ownership programmes (ESOPs) in 180 firms, found that ESOPs only marginally increased firm performance, and only in the short term, whilst doing little for employee job satisfaction. According to Pugh and his colleagues, the failure of ESOPs to enhance individual job satisfaction or performance reflects poorly on management rather than the programme itself. They believe that ESOPs are mostly put in place, not to increase employee influence in the workplace, but rather to help organizations ward off the threat of hostile takeovers by having the majority of stock in the hands of staff and management. Consequently, because employees feel that their stock ownership is little more than an attempt by management to maintain control from outside threats, and because without direct managerial intervention ESOPs do nothing to increase employees' ability to work autonomously or exert increased control over company decision-making, neither job satisfaction nor individual performance rises, with a consequent lack of organizational performance gains.

Nevertheless, middle management is not entirely to blame for the lack of progress in contemporary managerial style. According to Koch (2004), who performed a qualitative analysis of management in consulting engineering firms, the nature of a given business has a substantial impact on the ability of management to lead effectively. For example, consulting firms, which make up an increasing proportion of modern, knowledge-based organizations, are most often driven by shifting deadlines, competition for limited resources, and variable demands from clients, all of which reduce operational effectiveness. In Koch's opinion, under these sorts of difficult circumstances the complexities of management require exceptional managerial ability to maintain organizational effectiveness, as well as individual and team creativity and innovativeness. Unfortunately, few managers are up to the task, simply because of the lack of training, support, and resources available to them.

Management and communication

As we have seen so far, management is, principally, refined communication. Excellent managers are able to pass on information to their subordinates in a way that is clear, concise, non-contradictory, timely and, above all, presented in a manner that makes people want to listen and act (that is, motivational). Why then do so many managers possess such poor communication skills? First, it's probably because very few managers are actually trained for their positions, and those that are often receive questionable guidance; very few MBA programmes, for example, stress the angle that management is a process of leadership and inspiration, rather than financial administration and book balancing. Unfortunately, in most organizations, the only avenues for advancement involve a managerial role. So, for example, if you're an excellent engineer, often the only way you're going to get a pay rise or a promotion is by taking on a managerial role. Further, chances are, to be that excellent engineer, you undertook some 5–10 years of tertiary training, combined with the expertise you acquired on the job. In your new managerial role, however, you're required to perform in a job that you have no training for, no experience in, and only a sketchy knowledge of, based on your experience with other managers (who, most likely, were in the same position as you and, consequently, were unlikely to be the best role models). Chances are that your new position is stressful, or that you feel overwhelmed. Again, unfortunately, when we find ourselves out of our depth, instead of seeking out more information, we tend to become defensive and closed off, so that our already challenged communication style degrades.

So, how can you be a better manager? First and foremost, learn to be a better communicator. Listen to your staff, seek out their opinions, and then act on them. Do the things that you say you will, quickly, and well. Learn to delegate properly so that you don't have to do everyone else's job, and don't be afraid to set challenges for your charges. To stretch an analogy, although a ship's captain does not do most of the work of running a ship, the ship doesn't run without him or her; it is his or her ability to encourage people to work towards a common purpose and to understand the overall picture that keeps the ship sailing. As well, be aware that your role is flexible. For instance, when you have more knowledge than an employee, share that knowledge by coaching him or her; but when an employee is more skilled, take a secondary role, encourage his or her progress, and learn. Remember that management should never be an ego trip: your role is to motivate others, not to make yourself look big.

Part 2: Managerial development

Despite the obvious advantages to organizations that are populated by effective managers, learning to become a manager is a difficult process, and involves skills that are seldom taught directly. Typically, people enter management because it is the only avenue for organizational advancement available to them, even when their expertise lies in a different field. This could be demonstrated in the hypothetical example of a well-trained and competent engineer who finds that her only avenue to promotion involves taking a managerial position. Although she might be highly capable in her engineering role (a combination of extensive education and experience), following the promotion she is likely to find herself in a job for which she has had little preparation or training, and no experience, her only model being those of her superiors. Ironically, had she had such poor preparation and experience in engineering, she would not have been given her original job; however, to earn more money and "progress" in her organization, she is forced to take a role for which she is largely unprepared. Nevertheless, this method of managerial promotion is commonplace, with many managers expected to learn on the job (Enos, Thamm, & Bell, 2003). Consequently, several authors have reported methods for both improving this "on the job" learning, and for better preparing managers a priori.

One such recommendation by Kleinbeck and Fuhrmann (2000) focusses on the use of psychologically based practices in management to help managers increase their effectiveness, such as self-organization, increased decision power and the development of useful performance measures. According to Kleinbeck and his colleague, who qualitatively evaluated 12 employees on measures of job-related clarity and group cohesion, managers who encouraged employees to develop and manage their own goals were seen as more effective and supportive, especially when they delegated decision power to expert groups. In this way, the manager was able to act as a feedback agent, guiding groups whilst also allowing decision latitude. Kleinbeck and Fuhrmann believe that much of this feedback can be given through the use of performance measures that question the purpose of a given team or departmental unit, its ability to produce the products it works on, and its performance based on its own interpretation of functioning. Likewise, O'Roark (2002), in her report on managerial effectiveness, has pointed out the similarity of managers and corporate leaders to psychologists, based on their abilities in listening, reshaping, and modelling. She has suggested that managers emulate psychologists, by learning how to embody a "scientist/practitioner" model; that is, by researching a given problem effectively, and then putting that research into practice with aplomb. O'Roark has also suggested that managers are substantially more effective when they are able to engender trust, can communicate vision, and have a strong understanding of motivation. To achieve these three goals, managers should, according to O'Roark, exhibit trust in themselves by developing a high level of self-efficacy, and demonstrate trust in others and in the organization. Further, they should foster their ability to visualize what is important to the well-being of both employees and the organization, whilst removing unnecessary and unproductive preconceptions, such as the necessity for managers to remain aloof.

Lastly, with regard to motivation, managers should take an ethical standpoint, be healthy in mind and body (taking time to work on their health), develop their charisma, and encourage curiosity, both in themselves and in others. According to O'Roark, this should be done whilst keeping in mind the precepts of Maslow's pyramid of self-actualization. In this model, self-actualization (that is, attaining a pinnacle of human achievement) can only be reached once base conditions are met, starting with basic needs such as food and shelter, and progressing to more complex needs, such as emotional support and security, aesthetic fulfilment, and intellectual stimulation. Thus, on the opinion of O'Roark, if an employee does not feel secure in his or her job, he or she will be unable to achieve (or aspire to) a high level of intellectual functioning or job performance.

Several commentators have also called on existing psychological theory to explain and predict managerial performance. For example, Isaac, Zerbe, and Pitt (2001) have explained effective management through the utilization of expectancy theory, which states that an individual is motivated when his or her personal experience corresponds to an acceptable level of performance, that this performance is linked to specific outcomes, and that these outcomes are personally valued. Thus, according to Isaac *et al.*, to motivate adequately, a manager needs to recognize that workers require challenges that are valued personally (because they are based on the employee's education, skills, experiences and abilities, as well as on his or her level of self-confidence) and that are not overwhelming. Moreover, in the opinion of Isaac and his co-workers, when considering a person's ability, a manager must take into account not only the worker's actual ability but also his or her perceived ability. That is, unless the worker considers himself or herself capable, he or she will be unlikely to perform on a given assignment. Corollary to this, the manager must take on a coaching role in order to give feedback to enhance and encourage a person's self-esteem and confidence: if the employee believes he or she is capable, success is more likely. Lastly, according to Isaac and his colleagues, a manager should provide clear definitions of an employee's role, goals, and projects, so that he or she can better understand the importance of his or her work to the project at hand and to the organization as a whole. In this way, employees are more likely to feel that they are not just a "cog in a machine". Thus, in the opinion of Isaac *et al.*, the traits most exhibited by effective managers can be summarized as the ability to provide effective, performance contingent reward, whilst understanding that this is done in order to enhance a person's intrinsic motivation. In doing so a manager can help to increase self-esteem, knowledge, skills and attitudes, help to establish goals that are realistic, meaningful, and achievable, and create a climate of mutual respect. Moreover, a manager should work to display sensitivity, ingenuity, and judgement, and attempt to establish working conditions that encourage the highest probability of self-motivation in his or her followers. Often this self-motivation can be encouraged through establishing meaningful discussion to determine an employee's training needs, to negotiate work assignments, and to determine pathways for development. In this way, the manager will question the employee's displayed abilities, his or her education, skills and experience, and his or her interests, goals, beliefs and motivations. In doing so, the leader assures that he or she will be perceived as credible, fair, honest, and just.

Other authors have also suggested borrowing from psychological theory in order to guide managerial practice. For instance, Bramley (1999) has indicated that managerial models, whilst useful in certain situations, are not usually able to adequately describe the needs of individual workers; consequently, managerial effectiveness represents the identification of a variety of models that are of use to different individuals and groups, and applying these models effectively. Thus, according to Bramley, when different models are applied to different people depending both on their needs and on the individual situation, management becomes the process of emphasizing understanding of the activities required for people to be effective, rather than simply demonstrating the knowledge required for action. In this vein, Bramley has recommended that managers concentrate on coaching and guiding rather than simply telling, as well as involving employees in progress reviews through joint target setting, delegating authority (allowing subordinates to make decisions and taking responsibility when required), and asking employees for their views, input and feedback before making decisions. In a similar report, the authors of the Harvard Management Update ("Nine steps towards creating a great workplace – right here, right now", 1999) have encouraged managers to look for solutions that are directly applicable to a given situation, rather than simply using company-wide templates. They have also recommended that managers take pains to understand that people stay in jobs that are intellectually stimulating and personally rewarding, and that for most people the rewards that accompany working are seldom exclusively financial. Consequently, in helping people to see the purpose of what they do, managers can help by encouraging employees to look for personal meaning in their work. Similarly, intellectual stimulation can be enhanced by challenging workers not only to succeed in their goals but also to set higher expectations of their own and their team's abilities. Nevertheless, according to the authors, this process should be accomplished without prescribing an exact methodology, rather, employees should be encouraged to use (and be rewarded for) their initiative. Job fit should also be a management consideration; managers can help to encourage meaning by tailoring a particular job to the skills and passions of the individual. Thus, for example, if a person enjoys the latitude to make decisions, and has skills in this area, a manager should engineer a position that gives the freedom to make decisions. In terms of providing employees with the resources to actually do their jobs, the authors of the Harvard report have recommended that managers keep track of employees' needs, and be available for comment, requests or assistance, getting back to people within 24 hours of a given request. Further, the report's creators have suggested that managers reward people for their performance, but that this recognition need not always be financial: simply thanking a person for a job well done can be useful. Lastly, they have indicated that it is important to remember that work does not need to be serious all the time; if fun is encouraged, people will feel less stressed, more free, more in control of their environment, and most importantly, more personally fulfilled, increasing the likelihood that they will work more productively, and reducing the chances of staff turnover.

Pollock (1998), in his report on managerial style, has expressed similar recommendations, suggesting that managers be more sensitive to the needs of employees, set and reward effective goals, and increase job satisfaction by increasing the level of fun in the workplace. Likewise, Kennedy (2001) has recommended that effective management requires managers to take the role of mentor or coach, subjugating their ego by realizing that management is about the very human process of motivating others. According to Kennedy, effective managers understand that employees require a compelling role; that is, that workers need to feel vital to the success of a team or organization by making a meaningful contribution. In order to accomplish this, Kennedy has recommended that managers be more like a personal coach than a director, encouraging people to achieve by helping them both to believe in their abilities and to understand how their actions are important to the well-being of the organization. As well, managers should recognize if or when a given person is under-stimulated and provide a means to encourage greater engagement through a change of environment, an increase in challenge (based on that person's skills and interests) or an increase in responsibility. Moreover, according to Kennedy, the effective use of incentives, financial or otherwise, is an important leadership skill; however, he has also warned that incentives become moot if the subordinate does not have sufficient faith in his or her leader, making the process of leadership the prime consideration. Lastly, Kennedy has cautioned that, although attention to management quality tends to increase when there is a perceived lag in employee motivation or productivity, management amelioration is equally overlooked when things appear to be going well (especially from a financial perspective), and it is at these times that special attention should be given to leadership. In this vein, Voros (2000) in her review of managerial style, has proposed the idea of "three-dimensional management", in which effective leadership represents a part of a spiral model that encompasses customer satisfaction, employee satisfaction, effective organizational performance, and productivity and profitability. Voros, who described several case studies of effective organizations, has reported that communication, feedback, and accountability were consistently seen by employees as the most effective leadership qualities of managers. As she has stated, "the way in which management treats its associates is the way in which its associates treats the customer" (p. 47).

Cassar (1999), in an empirical evaluation of some of the leadership and management principles discussed above, has investigated the effectiveness of non-directive management (in which the manager served in the role of facilitator, mentor or coach, rather than administrator). Following the evaluation of the leadership techniques of 108 middle managers, Cassar concluded that the majority of managers were too authoritative in their interactions with employees and, consequently, were perceived as poor leaders. As a result of this finding, Cassar has posited that managerial power to motivate comes from the stimulation of cognitive growth in subordinates: through knowledge transfer rather than by extrinsic incentives. Consequently, in order to encourage independence and self-motivation in subordinates, Cassar has recommended that managers allow workers "free working space" (p. 64); that is, the ability to work on projects that are personally interesting and that will increase existing skills and encourage new learning. Further, he has suggested that when a manager has the knowledge and expertise required for a project, he or she be more directive, but when an employee has these attributes, the manager should take a more-participative role. From a cognitive-behavioural psychological perspective, this approach, according to Cassar, can increase employee motivation through tactical leader direction, rather than by enforcement, and can result in increased employee participation by developing effective, two-way communication.

The importance of communication and trust in managerial style has been highlighted by Martins (2002) who evaluated personality traits and the trust relationship between 6528 employees and their immediate supervisors in 22 South African firms. Defining trust as "articulating and embodying a moral code that cares about people", Martins reported that trust is significantly influenced by management practices, specifically through supportive behaviour, credibility, team management, and information sharing. These behaviours are, in turn, influenced by the manager's personality traits, especially the "Big Five" traits of openness to experience, agreeableness, and conscientiousness. Consequently, in Martins's opinion, trust, an essential for adequate interactions between managers and employees, is highly dependent on behaviours that are inherent in certain personality traits, and which represent good management. From Martins's findings it might be concluded that it would be beneficial for organizations to evaluate the personality traits of managers. Nevertheless, Harland (2003), in her investigation of types of personality assessment in 255 MBA students, cautions that the act of personality assessment can have potentially negative consequences. According to Harland, if a test is to be given, it is important that respondents perceive that they have control over both the way in which they answer test items and the way in which their responses will be used. For example, forced-choice questions (that is, questions that require a yes or no answer) can make participants feel that they are being manoeuvred into an answer that does not adequately describe their personality, resulting in stress and distrust of the tester's motives. Likewise, when organizations use the outcomes of a personality assessment to make decisions about promotion or managerial competence, they potentially signal to their managers that, rather than assessing an individual's merits and providing opportunities for growth and change, the firm is more interested in pigeon-holing employees based on a test that might or might not be accurate. Consequently, according to Harland, attempts to increase managerial effectiveness by identifying persons with traits more suited to management can backfire by alienating employees through the assumption that managerial effectiveness cannot be learnt, and that only certain persons are fit for managerial positions.

Managerial effectiveness has also been related to how well managers recognize and deal with the effects of workplace stress in their subordinates. After evaluating the responses of 540 New Zealand managers on stress-management responsibility, Dewe and O'Driscoll (2002) reported that although managers appeared to understand the rhetoric associated with stress management, they seldom understood the magnitude of a given problem. According to Dewe and O'Driscoll, the majority of interviewed managers held the belief that stress management was not their responsibility; rather individual workers were responsible for dealing with their own stress. Moreover, the majority of managers understood the term "effective management" to mean only "somewhat or moderately effective" and, consequently, mistakenly overrated their ability to manage stress in their subordinates. In concurrence with several of the authors reviewed above, Dewe and his colleague indicated that when an organization takes action to reduce stress, and a manager works to increase an employee's ability to manage stress, he or she will be perceived as more competent, more effective, and more trustworthy by his or her subordinates, increasing the likelihood of increased employee productivity. Thus, in the opinion of Dewe and O'Driscoll, when managers take an approach that places responsibility, awareness and understanding of an employee's individual needs above financial indicators, they are more likely to succeed in motivating their employees.

One suggestion for better managing stress in oneself and in others has been made by Schmidt-Wilk (2000), who investigated the effects of transcendental meditation training for 30 managers in three international companies. According to Schmidt-Wilk, managers reported both personal and organizational benefits to their meditation training. Personal improvements included greater abilities to concentrate and remain awake; fewer feelings of aggression, worry, and stress; improved physical, psychological, and emotional health; improved interpersonal relations with co-workers and subordinates; and increased decision-making abilities. Managerial team developments included better communication; increased awareness of company and team needs and values; more effective, fact-based decision making; greater trust and openness; as well as increased team cohesiveness and alignment, all of which translated to more effectual performance at an organizational level. Based on their findings, Schmidt-Wilk has postulated that managers who practise transcendental meditation will develop in a more holistic way, allowing the development of both cognitive abilities and personally beneficial traits, as well as increasing their coping skills by developing a buffer against environmental stress, and enhancing team qualities, such as greater trust, openness, acceptance, coherence, and teamwork.

Despite the plethora of recommendations for managerial and leadership development, Collins and Holton (2004) believe that many organizations are simply unaware of the best managerial development processes and, consequently, are failing to provide adequate training. In their meta-analysis of 83 peer-reviewed studies of managerial development, Collins and her co-worker reported that whilst many organizations are beginning to concentrate on training that highlights managerial teams and organizational transformation, they are failing to assess the relationship between their training programmes and ongoing organizational performance. Moreover, the majority of firms do not conduct needs analyses, to determine which managerial skills are required to enhance company performance, before initiating training programmes, nor are they evaluating the effectiveness of these interventions and reporting their findings. This oversight, in the opinion of Collins and Holton, highlights the gap between academic research and organizational uptake. Put simply, firms are committing large amounts of money towards training schemes without first assessing their worth or determining their level of success, resulting in patchy, piecemeal training that does not guarantee managerial and leadership development, let alone increased employee performance or greater organizational success. Consequently, Collins and Holton believe that organizations should take a more empirical stance towards training, making sure that it is effective, will meet the organization's needs, will be of benefit, and that adequate evaluation and follow-up be conducted in order to fine-tune and improve development programmes.

In support of the findings of Collins and Holton (2004), in his large-scale evaluation of the effectiveness of managerial and leadership development programmes, Hamlin (2004) also pointed out that despite massive organizational spending on managerial training, there is little evidence to suggest that this training results in more-effective managerial behaviour or organizational performance. According to Hamlin, this disparity occurs because managers do not see the types of training that they receive as having any relevance to the real world of management: most training has a limited relationship to what managers actually do and, especially in MBA programmes, is often outmoded, is seldom influenced by findings from empirical research, and is not likely to be focussed on factors that actually contribute to increased organizational performance. Consequently, in order to determine the factors that are most effective for increasing managerial ability and that are most relevant to real-world application, Hamlin collected and analysed a large number of critical management incidents. He then sought to determine the effectiveness or ineffectiveness, as seen by managers themselves, of interventions to remedy these incidents, with a resultant series of recommendations for the shaping, content, and evaluation of managerial development training. Among his recommendations, Hamlin has highlighted six categories of managerial behaviour that were found to be the most effective for increasing both staff and organizational performance. The first, effective organization and planning and proactive management, points to behaviour in which managers are well organized, think ahead, make sure things are done in good time, make use of existing systems and resources, set and maintain high standards for themselves and others, take initiative to resolve problems, and proactively confront issues that are delicate or difficult. The second category – participative, supportive, and proactive leadership – focuses on management behaviour geared towards providing active support and guidance to subordinates, responding immediately to requests for help, providing backing and personal support for staff who are stressed or experiencing difficulties, taking time to get to know staff, creating a climate of trust, active listening, praising when due, defending staff from unfair criticism or attack, supporting teams through problems, and helping subordinates learn from their mistakes. The third factor, empowerment and delegation, requires that managers delegate effectively, and encourage their charges to take on new responsibilities, giving them the freedom to make their own decisions without close supervision and allowing idea experimentation and development. The fourth, a genuine concern for people (that includes looking after the interests and developmental needs of staff), involves behaviour that allows for quick and effective response to problems, the ability to deal with difficult issues, fair allocation of work for self and for others, support to staff wishing to develop new ideas, bringing staff achievements to the attention of senior management, ready congratulations and praise for good work, recognition, nurturing and development of latent ability, initiating and supporting career development, identifying training needs, and taking time to coach, train, and mentor subordinates. The fifth factor, open and personal management and inclusive decision-making, focusses on a management style that involves actively listening to the views and opinions of subordinates, the encouragement of staff in planning, decision-making and problem solving, and the development of trust. Lastly, Hamlin has described effective management through wide-ranging communication and consulting, in which managers consult on and discuss change plans with their team, proactively seek ideas, hold frequent, effective meetings, and gather relevant facts whilst judging ideas on their merits. On the other hand, according to Hamlin, the least effective managerial approaches included a lack of consideration or concern for staff, uncaring or self-serving management, tolerance of low performance or standards, abdication of roles and responsibilities at critical times (failing to set an example), and resistance to change or new ideas. Thus, in Hamlin's opinion, by recognizing both effective and ineffective management behaviours, organizations can identify contemporary behaviour that is unproductive, and design development programmes that encourage more effectual managerial behaviour. By doing so, firms are more able to take an active role in the development of their managers and the betterment of organizational performance, rather than simply relying on an external training method that might or might not be effective or meet the organization's needs.

In summary, although many methods have been proposed for effective management and the development of managerial ability, certain key characteristics, such as openness, communicability, inclusiveness and support, are most likely to result in strong managerial efficiency, especially regarding the development and increased productivity of staff. Moreover, with the variety of management development tools available, it is essential that organizations conduct adequate analyses of these techniques, both before their implementation to determine if they meet the needs of the firm and its employees and, afterwards, to make sure that they have been effective.

Part 3: Management and culture

The recommendations of investigators notwithstanding, with the surplus of leadership enhancement advice available to managers, it is important to note the warnings of Davison and Martinsons (2002) regarding the misapplication (despite beneficial intent) of managerial practice. These investigators, who reported on the attempted application of modern leadership practices in Hong Kong, indicated that these practices were, in fact, highly culturally sensitive and, as well, differed strongly in their effect from individual to individual; in fact, according to Davison and his colleague, in several Hong Kong companies that had implemented the change advice of managerial experts, many employees that had supposedly been given greater autonomy, encouraged in self-motivation, and rewarded contingent to their performance actually felt lost, unsupported, and at a loss as to how to realize their new roles. Consequently, Davison and his co-worker have recommended that the process of employee "empowerment" requires substantial managerial flexibility: recognizing that effective change requires a combination of skills and knowledge, presented over time, and employing a mentoring or coaching approach, so that employees can develop experience in these new processes without feeling alienated. In this way the approach becomes meaningful to, and even desired by, employees (reducing resistance), rather than representing a process of blind observance of modern trends. Most importantly, managers must recognize cultural differences: Davison and Martinsons' finding illustrate that what works well in one culture might be inappropriate in another.

Cultural differences can, therefore, have a large effect on the effectiveness of managerial ability and organizational performance. According to Kuchinke (1999), culture can be conceptualized as a complex association of norms, values, assumptions, attitudes, and beliefs that are characteristic of a particular group, and which are perpetuated through socialization, training, rewards, and sanctions; effectively, cultures represent both a group's attempts to adapt to an external environment and its strategy for survival. Kuchinke has described five dimensions that represent cultural differences, and that can be used to explain different cultural expectations and behaviours. The first, power-distance, represents the extent to which less powerful members of a group or society accept and expect that power be distributed unevenly. Bureaucratic societies, such as South American nations are typically described as high power-distance, whilst more egalitarian societies, like the Scandinavian countries, have a lower power-distance. The second factor, individualism, represents the degree to which group members expect individuals to orient action towards personal rather than group gain. Using this metric, the United States has been described as highly individualistic, whilst China is more collectivistic. The third variable, masculinity is used to describe the extent to which there is a distribution of stereotypical gender-role behaviour. For instance, in more-masculine countries like Mexico, stereotypically male roles, such as assertiveness, aggression, and toughness are held in high regard (mostly among men). On the other hand, in more-feminine countries, such as Denmark, behaviours including caring, nurturing, and other more modest behaviours are reinforced among both genders. The fourth dimension, uncertainty avoidance, is described as the degree to which group members are uncomfortable with change, ambiguity, or uncertainty. The final variable, long-term orientation, describes group action towards long-term results and the future, rather than short-term goals and immediate gratification.

Based on these cultural variations, it appears obvious that managerial and leadership approaches that are successful in one culture might have little or no effect in another. In order to investigate this assertion further, Kuchinke (1999) evaluated leadership style and its effectiveness among 3537 employees from a *Fortune* 500 company with sites in both the United States and Germany. He found that US managers employed a leadership style that was more focussed on vision, a desired future, and optimism, and were more charismatic than German managers, a finding he attributed to German resistance towards the negative charisma displayed by the Nazis during the Second World War. Consequently, according to the findings of Kuchinke, US managerial styles are substantially less effective when attempted with German employees. Extended beyond Kuchinke's study, these findings suggest that, especially in global enterprises, managerial styles and organizational expectations that work well in the firm's home country might be totally inappropriate in a regional office, requiring that the organization rethink its overseas HR and other strategies.

Another potentially variable cultural element is that of teams. Kuchinke's (1999) definition of culture can be applied not only to different countries but also to groups, potentially within the same organization or even the same department. According to Dackert, Loov, and Martensson (2004), autonomous or self-managed teams, created under the assumption that they will drive innovation and continuous improvement, require leadership that takes into account the "cultural" needs of each team. Following their investigation of 98 professional employees, divided into 14 autonomous teams, and evaluated on team climate and managerial style, Dackert and his colleagues concluded that team innovation was reduced when managerial style dictated a low level of participation and clarity of objectives. Moreover, the investigators reported a positive relationship between leadership that was high in change, development orientation and employee orientation, and team innovation. In other words, the culture of innovation in teams is largely dependent on leader behaviour oriented towards growth and change, as well as towards employee participation and support.

One cultural variable seldom acknowledged by researchers is business size: small businesses represent a substantially different workplace culture to those of large organizations, and are therefore likely to have different needs and outlooks to those of larger firms. For instance, Henderson, Sutherland, and Turley (2000), who looked at management development in 50 United Kingdom SMEs, reported that many SME owners or directors were unaware of the need for management development, saw it as a financially or time costly diversion, or were not able to find leadership or managerial development courses suited to the needs of SMEs. This last case represents a cultural bias towards larger organizations, by focussing management development exclusively on the needs, and within the means of large businesses, despite the fact that SMEs represent, in a large number of industrialized countries, the principal economic force (Henderson *et al.*). Given the mass of organizational benefits to managerial development, including increased employee well-being and productivity, and financial improvement, it is unfortunate that many SMEs are unaware of, or unable to receive, adequate training in this area.

Consequently, it appears that cultural differences, between countries, departments, and businesses, can result in biases and oversights that result in negative consequences to both organizations and their employees. Given the importance of effective management in achieving positive organizational goals, it makes sense that firms assess not only the way in which their managers lead but also the situations in which these leadership styles are the most effective.

Best practice: Case examples of how it's being done

Managerial development

Cummings (2000), in his case study of American Biodyne, a US-based health care company, has described the importance of psychologically based management. According to Cummings, in the development and ongoing practice of American Biodyne, managers were trained in, and encouraged to use, the skills regularly employed by psychologists, such as active listening, feedback, coaching, and skills development. Consequently, the relationship between managers and subordinates became strongly supportive: employees felt that managers were able to respond to and effectively deal with problems, and were dynamic in their practice, whilst managers relied on their staff to help with ideas development, provide useful upward feedback, and engage in committed, high-performance work. As well, American Biodyne was structured on a minimum bureaucracy model, allowing managers to make decisions relevant to their work and needs, without having to constantly refer to their superiors, or request extensive financial approval. In this way, management were able to deal with problems and make innovations without a bureaucratic chain of approvals and paperwork, resulting in smooth business flow. More importantly, by taking their emphasis away from regular accounting and financial-based decisions, managers and their staff were free to make creative suggestions and changes, culminating in a strong innovative base that allowed the company to become competitive and, despite the movement away from economically based decision-making, highly profitable. Consequently, following a series of corporate expansions, the firm has evolved into a highly profitable enterprise with a satisfied, committed employee base.

Points for action: Practical recommendations for change

Managerial Development

Following their investigation of 84 managers from a US *Fortune* 500 company on measures of managerial proficiency, informal learning, knowledge transfer, and learning activities, Enos *et al.* (2003) reported that a large proportion of learning and development in management was not being provided by formal training programmes, even though the organization had spent a substantial amount of money on establishing and maintaining a training process. Instead, Enos *et al.* found that, for the most part, managers learn informally, and that managerial proficiency is more likely to be the result of this informal learning than from formal training programmes. Nevertheless, on the whole management skills continue to be lacklustre, suggesting that the informal learning received by many managers is poor, most likely the result of inadequate modelling by superiors, and an inherent lack of understanding, within the organization, of effective managerial styles. Consequently, to enhance managerial effectiveness and reduce wasted outlay on ineffective formal training, Enos and his co-investigators have recommended the following:

■ That organizations redirect their funding for training from formal training programmes, to informal, on-the-job practice.

- Cultivate the metacognitive abilities of skilled managers in order to encourage managerial development in lesser-skilled managers.

- Encourage mentoring, coaching, and shadowing programmes within the organization, whereby less-experienced managers can learn in-situ from the observation and direct input of more-efficacious managers.

- Provide strong support and incentives for managers to take on more effective managerial styles, by installing systems that provide information, resources, rewards, and timely, effective feedback.

Summary

Contemporary managers are often poor motivators, the result of an overdependence on financial targets at the expense of human relationships. This is not surprising, however, in the light of poor managerial training, support, and resources, combined with inadequate understanding of human factors in motivation. Effective management is not intuitive, and requires training that is rarely offered in a way that is relevant to real-world situations. Moreover, because managerial paths are commonly the only way to advance within an organization, managers are often instated for their non-managerial abilities, independently of any ability, aptitude or desire to manage. Psychologically based managerial techniques, such as listening, reshaping, and modelling, can be utilized effectively to help motivate staff, by recognizing needs, skills and abilities, helping employees to feel needed, worthwhile, and important. These techniques can also help to identify and deal with workplace stress and its antecedents, and stimulate intellects, interest, and the desire to work and learn. Nevertheless, the most effective managerial behaviours are those in which the manager focusses on six factors: organization and planning, participative support, empowerment and delegation, a genuine concern for people, open and personal management, and wide-ranging communication and consultation.

Often overlooked in managerial training and practice are the cultural differences that preclude certain management styles. For example, western notions of empowerment can be easily misapplied in eastern cultures. Consequently, the five dimensions of cultural difference (power-distance, individualism, masculinity, uncertainty avoidance, and long-term orientation) should be examined carefully before attempting to apply particular managerial methods in different cultural groups.

REVIEW QUESTIONS

1. Explain why many contemporary managers are often unable to adequately motivate heir staff.

2. As a manager, what would you do to increase your ability to communicate with your subordinates?

3. Explain why are many newly promoted managers are often poorly prepared for their managerial roles.

4. Describe the managerial traits that are most useful for enhancing employee satisfaction, productivity, and commitment, and explain why these traits are effective.

5. As an HR manager, what could you do to increase the leadership abilities of managers within your company? Illustrate with any personal observations from your own experience.

6. Outline how cultural differences can affect managerial effectiveness.

Mind-diagram summary

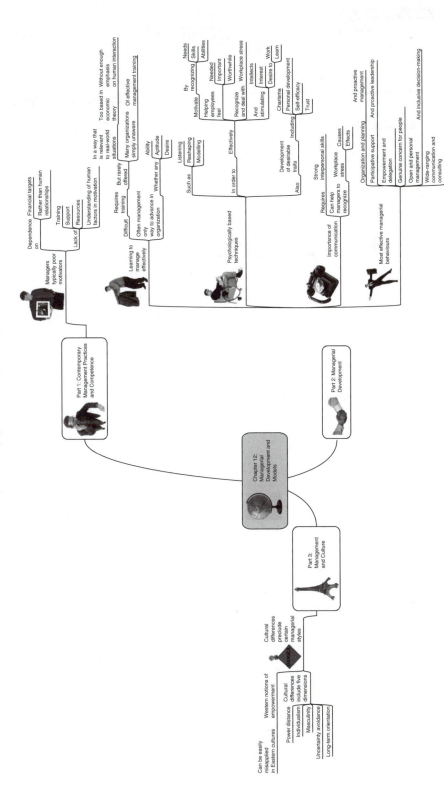

Chapter 12: Managerial Development and Models

Part 1: Contemporary Management Practices and Competence

- Managers typically poor motivators
  - Dependence on
    - Financial targets
    - Rather than human relationships
  - Lack of
    - Training
    - Support
    - Resources
    - Understanding of human factors in motivation

- Learning to manage effectively
  - Difficult
  - Requires training
  - But rarely offered
  - Often management only way to advance in organization
  - In a way that is relevant to real-world situations
  - Many organizations simply unaware
    - Whether any
      - Ability
      - Aptitude
      - Desire
    - Of effective management training
  - Too based in economic theory
  - Without enough emphasis on human interaction

- Psychologically based techniques
  - Such as
    - Listening
    - Reshaping
    - Modelling
  - In order to
  - Effectively
    - Motivate
      - By recognizing
        - Needs
        - Skills
        - Abilities
    - Helping employees feel
      - Needed
      - Important
      - Worthwhile
    - Recognize and deal with
      - Workplace stress
    - Intellects
      - And stimulating
        - Interest
        - Desire to
          - Work
          - Learn
    - Charisma
    - Personal development
      - Self-efficacy
      - Trust
  - Including
    - Development of desirable traits
  - Also
    - Strong interpersonal skills

- Importance of communication
  - Requires
  - Can help managers to recognize
    - Workplace stress
      - Causes
      - Effects

- Most effective managerial behaviours
  - Organization and planning
  - Participative support
  - Empowerment and delegation
  - Genuine concern for people
  - Open and personal management
  - Wide-ranging communication and consulting
  - And proactive leadership
  - And proactive management
  - And inclusive decision-making

Part 2: Managerial Development

Part 3: Management and Culture

- Cultural differences preclude certain managerial styles
  - Western notions of empowerment
    - Can be easily misapplied in Eastern cultures
  - Cultural differences include five dimensions
    - Power distance
    - Individualism
    - Masculinity
    - Uncertainty avoidance
    - Long-term orientation

Transformational Leadership and the Benefits of Leadership Enhancement

KEYWORDS Competitive, dimension, downsize, duty, economist, empowerment, global, inspire, leader, mentor, moral, policy, profit, risk, serve, strength.

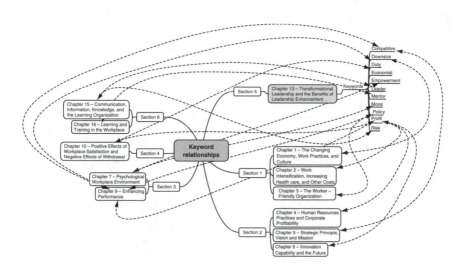

IMPORTANT CONCEPTS   Cultural awareness, transactional leadership, transformational leadership.

Part 1: Leadership styles: Adaptive, transformational, and transactional leadership

In their two-part article on adaptive leadership, Glover, Friedman, and Jones (2002) have highlighted several of the maladaptive attempts at change by sometimes well-meaning managers. For example, according to Glover and his co-workers, the obligatory training course run by an efficiency expert, or the implementation of a new, company-wide, computer-based, time management system might appear effective, but more often than not insufficient thought has been given to either the underlying issues that led to the need for changes or the potential consequences of the change process. In other words, if the management practices that led to poor time management are not dealt with, a new computer system, for example, will not repair the existing problem. Consequently, Glover *et al.* believe that management improvement is really a question of leadership amelioration through a style that they have labelled "adaptive leadership". In this model, leaders pay specific attention to their openness to change, to understanding a given context, and to remaining flexible in the way in which they deal with problems, allowing them to be able not just to think "outside the box", but to "change the box". Further, according to Glover and co-workers, adaptive leaders take pains to understand the culture of their organization, whilst simultaneously seeking an adaptive relationship between the organization and its external environment through creative problem solving. This requires a cognitive style that can be described as both highly accommodating and assimilating. "Assimilation" refers to the ability to assimilate new ideas into an existing cognitive framework, whilst "accommodation" describes the ability to take concepts outside of an existing cognitive schema and to create new schemas that are adapted to these new ideas. The combination of accommodation and assimilation is referred to as "adaptation", and allows a flexible approach to information, decisions, and leadership (Glover *et al.*).

In the second part of their article, Glover, Rainwater, Friedman, and Jones (2002) further explored the notion of maladaptive leadership as the result of an imbalance between assimilation and accommodation. According to Glover *et al.*, on the one hand, maladaptive leadership can result in one of three scenarios. First, when a leader exhibits low assimilation and low accommodation, his or her organization can fall into cultural "traps", because he or she will make decisions in a predictable way, simply because that is the way they have always been made; this approach relies too much on conservatism and linear modelling, in attempting to predict the future from the past. As a result, Glover and colleagues have suggested that these leaders seldom respond appropriately to change or challenge. The second problem, high assimilation but low accommodation, often results in "knee-jerk" reactions, such as downsizing decisions, because the leader addresses only short-term solutions without addressing the long-term consequences. Thus, leaders who use this cognitive style often find themselves successful in the short term, but their decisions seldom lead to longer-term successes. The third problem, according to Glover and his co-authors, is a cognitive set involving low assimilation but high accommodation. In this case, the leader often takes too much risk, making changes without being adequately informed. Whilst this is often well intentioned, without sufficiently evaluating the background or history of a situation, problems are likely to occur. On the other hand, the adaptive leader balances both assimilative and accommodative thinking, acquiring and exhibiting cultural knowledge through information, creativity and vision, creating synergy from diversity (being aware of the "and" rather than the "or"), and anticipating sustainability.

It would appear, in the light of the recent and highly publicized corporate scandals of Enron, WorldCom, Tyco, and Arthur Anderson, that many corporate leaders are not particularly adaptive or highly imbued with vision or notions of sustainability; or, if they are, not in a way that is ethically laudable. Whilst we will address corporate and leadership ethics later in this section,[23] it pays to look at current leadership theories beyond those of adaptive leadership, including a review of their merits, and their uses in the contemporary corporate world. In fact, two leadership styles have received substantial research focus since the early 1990s: transactional and transformational leadership (Bass, Waldman, Avolio, & Bebb, 1987). Transactional leadership involves a relationship in which the leader contracts (or transacts) with his or her subordinates to exchange a commodity that is of value to both parties; for instance, the leader obtains the work efforts and skills of the employee, whilst the employee is given a salary and possible contingent rewards based on his or her performance (Bass, 1990). However, transactional leadership does not emphasize a relationship between the leader and the follower that addresses anything more than the pursuit of this transaction; consequently, it is unlikely that a transactional leader would attempt to develop a mutual or ongoing relationship that lends itself to higher purposes, such as the mutual attainment of a shared vision. Thus, transactional leadership is more representative of management than actual leadership: managers are typically more concerned with getting the most productivity out of their charges than in helping subordinates achieve their best. Transformational leadership, on the other hand, occurs when leaders interact with their followers in such a way that a personal transformation can occur which, according to Whittington, involves an increase in both motivation and morality: effectively, transformational leadership involves a covenant relationship rather than a contractual one, which is characterized by reciprocity of interest and mutual vulnerability. Transformational leaders effect this transformation in their followers through a combination of ascribed charisma, inspirational motivation, intellectual stimulation, and individual consideration, motivating individuals to do more than they initially expected they could do, and raising their awareness of the significance of a given outcome (such as the long-term success of their organization). In other words, transformational leaders inspire a transcendence of self-interest for the good of the organization by supplying their followers with many of their fundamental psychological needs, such as support, feelings of purpose and perceived control, and timely, personalized feedback (Whittington, 2001). Consequently, transformational leaders tend to be admired, respected, and trusted by their

---

[23] See chapter on Leadership and Corporate Ethics below.

followers, who identify with and attempt to emulate them, resulting in increased employee creativity and innovation. Nevertheless, according to Whittington, to earn this credibility transformational leaders must consider the needs of others (or the organization) above their own; share risks with their followers (rather than letting subordinates take risks exclusively); demonstrate high standards of moral conduct;[24] engender faith by developing a joint sense of mission between themselves and their followers through the convincing articulation of an attractive, mutual future; communicate clear expectations and demonstrate a commitment both to their goals and the shared vision; and provide intellectual stimulation by questioning assumptions, reframing problems, and approaching existing situations with a fresh approach. In this vein, Whittington has warned of pseudo-transformational leaders, who utilize many of the elements of transformational leadership to further their own agenda: delivering bogus empowerment by promising employees greater freedom and resources to act on their own judgments, but then failing to deliver, and by attempting to increase their personal status by establishing manipulating agendas, maximizing personal outcomes at the expense of other parties, and by squelching conflicting viewpoints.

IN ACTION #13

Transformational leadership

Too often, modern managerial practice is overly concerned with administration at the expense of leadership. As an employer, or head of an organization, this oversight is equally true; your ability to lead is at least as important as your ability to administrate. Each organization requires a figurehead, someone in which trust and admiration can be placed. As a boss, managing director, or CEO, it is your responsibility to model charisma, drive, and passion in your daily interactions, both with your staff and with outside contacts; if you do not project a strong belief in the abilities and worth of your organization, it is also unlikely that your employees will believe in these values (typically, corporate leaders who are seen as strong, competent, and qualified, command a greater respect from their followers). Moreover, studies have shown that effective corporate leaders possess many of the same qualities as good psychologists. They have a strong sense of empathy, are expert communicators, listen attentively, have a high level of self-efficacy (that is, situationally specific self-confidence), and have mastered a variety of techniques for increasing their ability to cope with stress. It pays, therefore, to work on these skills, remembering that very few people possess these abilities inherently; they need to be developed, through practice, emulation, and refinement, over a period of time. Great leaders are made, not born.

One leadership style, known as adaptive or transformational leadership, is particularly effective for motivating others. In fact, transformational leaders are consistently rated as better, more effective leaders than their transactional counterparts (that is, people who manage by using situational bargaining, such as extrinsic

---

[24] See the section on Leadership and Corporate Ethics below for a discussion on the differences between morals and ethics, and the philosophy of ethical behaviour.

rewards or threats). Transformational leadership requires the ready assessment of corporate culture, and an understanding that few things remain static. Consequently, being able to respond to challenge flexibly and laterally helps. Effectively, this means keeping an open mind by being receptive to new possibilities and options, being able to harness the resources that are available to you (your staff have more to offer than you might think), and being adaptive when challenged (just because something has worked in the past doesn't mean it will continue to).

Part 2: Benefits of adaptive and transformational leadership versus transactional leadership

Although at first glance transformational leadership behaviours appear almost stereotypically ideal, when developed they are certainly effective in increasing organizational and individual performance. Walumbwa, Orwa, Wang, and Lawler (2005), for example, have cited research that demonstrates the consistent effectiveness of transformational leadership on company performance across cultures. Moreover, in their study of the responses of 158 Kenyan bank employees versus those of 189 US bank workers on measures of job satisfaction, organizational commitment, and perceptions of transactional leadership behaviours in their superiors, Walumbwa and his co-investigators reported that despite the substantial differences between Kenya and the United States, transformational leadership behaviours significantly increased both job satisfaction and organizational commitment (reducing turnover intention) in both cultures. In a similar study, Sosik, Potosky, and Jung (2002), who investigated managerial self-regulation and leadership in 64 managers and 192 subordinates, found that effective leaders were more adaptive in their behaviour, and more capable of self-monitoring their behavioural patterns and changing their behaviour when they felt they were wanting; especially with regard to their transformational leadership abilities, including interpersonal style, approachability, and communication and goal setting abilities. Sosik and his colleagues also reported that transformational leaders inspired greater motivation in subordinates than did their non-transformational counterparts. Likewise, Masi and Cooke (2000) have examined the beneficial aspects of transformational leadership by comparing transformational and transactional leaders. When Masi and his colleague contrasted the leadership styles of 2596 active duty mid-level leaders, station commanders and recruiters in the US Army with subunit performance, they found that whilst transformational leadership was met by subordinates with increased productivity and motivation, transactional leadership styles resulted in decreased subordinate commitment and a corresponding drop in productivity. Like Sosik *et al.*, Masi and Cooke ascribed the dimensions of intellectual stimulation, individual consideration, and charisma to transformational leaders. However, according to Masi and Cooke, these traits are distinctly unlike those found in transactional leadership, the more common directive style, in which leaders attempt to motivate others by monitoring their subordinates' mistakes and by engaging in behavioural bartering (for example, trading rewards for goal completion). Jaskyte (2003) has also investigated the outcomes of transformational leadership. After examining 41 US government employees on measures of job satisfaction, organizational commitment, and perceptions of change in the work environment, Jaskyte found that supervisory transformational leadership styles were the best predictors of employee job satisfaction. Specifically, when subordinates believed that their supervisors were helping with employee professional and personal problems, showing concern for individual subordinates, encouraging participation in important decisions, sought dissenting opinions to test the soundness of ideas, encouraged time management, setting high standards, and were fair, respectful and informative, employees were significantly more satisfied in their work, were more committed to the organization, and were less likely to quit.

In an article concerned with perceived leadership legitimacy and profitability in organizations, Keyes, Hysom, and Lupo (2000) have pointed out that positive organizations (that is, workplaces that employees find to be enjoyable and stimulating places to work) ensure that their leaders have legitimate authority, and that this legitimacy substantially increases employee well-being. In other words, according to Keyes *et al.*, in positive organizations leaders are encouraged to operate in such a way that their subordinates admire and respect their authority, without seeing that authority as overbearing or stressful. Because, in the opinion of Keyes and his associates, well-being is a subjective process, to encourage employee satisfaction a leader must take into account an individual's perceptions and evaluations, as well as his or her quality of life and psychological and sociological functioning; thus, subjective well-being and mental health are comprised of emotional well-being, itself a combination of happiness and life satisfaction, the coherence of a person's perceived organizational integration, acceptance, contribution and actualization, and an individual's positive functioning, including self-acceptance, opportunities for personal growth, perceived life purpose, environmental mastery (or control, see Section 4 above), autonomy, and positive relations with others. Keyes *et al.* have posited, therefore, that leadership legitimacy comes from a combination of employee endorsement, authorization, and propriety, as well as an appropriate (perceived) blend of leader's qualifications and experience, and the leader's apparent ability to actually get things done. The legitimate leader is thus imbibed with the qualities of authoritative delegation, the ability to share information equitably, and the ability to share authority with subordinates. According to Keyes and co-workers, when an organization is led by such individuals, employees show a higher level of loyalty, interest, and productivity, and the organization realizes a greater level of financial success. Thus, it is the way in which people are led, and the qualities exhibited by the leader, more than the immediate environment, that motivates; moreover, it is the leader's activities that encourage the conditions for motivation, such as autonomy, purpose, and environmental control, that are so beneficial to workplace satisfaction (see Section 3 above). Fairris's (2002) review of transformed workplaces under the auspices of transformational leaders shows similar conclusions: when workers are empowered by their leaders to be more autonomous, better able to contribute to the decision-making process, and are inspired by the practices and actions of their supervisors, they are more satisfied at work, and are more productively efficient. Nevertheless, Fairris has pointed out numerous examples of supposed transformational practices that can have negative organizational consequences. For example, according to Fairris, systems such as TQM and just-in-time (JIT) production, whilst promising greater employee empowerment, seldom actually allow increased worker participation. Rather, these systems elevate financial performance by reducing the amount that it costs a firm to employ their workers by, for instance, reducing overtime payments by requiring that teams be responsible for meeting management-set deadlines and linking pay to the achievement of these goals. Consequently, whilst certain systems, such as autonomous work teams, can lead to greater employee empowerment and participation, under the TQM and JIT versions of teams, management retains control over the type of projects assigned to these teams, as well as their available resources, the timeframe for completion, and completion standards, simultaneously reducing employee autonomy and increasing work intensity in a manner that Whittington (2001) has described as both pseudo-transformational and ineffective.

Whilst transformational leadership is important for for-profit firms, according to Jaskyte (2004), because of the non-monetary focus of transformational leadership, it can be highly valuable also to non-profit organizations. Following her comparison of 247 employees from 19 US, non-profit, human-services organizations on measures of organizational innovativeness, transformational leadership, and organizational culture, Jaskyte found that innovation, employee motivation and their performance were strongly related to transformational leadership practices, but that the majority of organizations did not benefit from transformational leaders. Rather, the traditional, transactional leadership exhibited in these firms resulted, in Jaskyte's opinion, in a lack of ability to change successfully to meet new challenges from the external environment. Given her findings of increased innovativeness in transformationally led organizations, Jaksyte believes that despite their differences in motivation, non-profit and for-profit firms alike require leadership that is people- and detail-oriented, focussed on outcomes, aggressive in its drive to achieve a vision and, above all, innovative.

Buchen (2003) has also portrayed the importance of innovative principles and the practice of transformational leadership as largely responsible for the success of both for-profit and non-profit organizations. According to Buchen, problem solving in businesses is consistently held back by a combination of the increasing complexity of the problems, combined with a lack of both innovative thinking and the leadership required to stimulate innovative thought. Most importantly, innovative thinking, or as Buchen describes it "next step thinking", requires attention to three dimensions: mission, the future, and holism. As Buchen explains it, mission represents a company's ability to define and look towards the future as well as the degree to which the organization is oriented towards innovation and knowledge seeking; in other words, to be innovative, a firm's mission must include directives that implicitly evoke innovation, learning, and kinship. Future orientation requires that the organization look towards solutions rather than simply defining problems, by looking forward and employing a leapfrogging strategy (that is, observing the innovations of competitors and moving past them rather than merely imitating). Moreover, a futuristic company will welcome rather than avoid collaboration and collaborative relationships, both within the firm and between likeminded companies with overlapping or complementary skills. Lastly, holism refers to an organization's ability to carry forward and recreate a "big picture", in which leaders avoid tunnel vision, and do not settle for early, simple solutions instead of solutions that can be self-managing in the future.

To illustrate his assertions, Buchen (2003) has provided several leadership innovation suggestions. Typically, according to Buchen, because of their reliance on accounting-based decisions, firms have lacked an innovative outlook that embraces the future, a failing that has been repeatedly illustrated by the economic rationalistic practices of the 1980s and 1990s. Under this model, when firms found that they could no longer compete with emerging industrial nations on a wage for productivity basis, they responded either by moving production offshore, or by cutting costs, downsizing, or investing in cost-cutting technologies. Ironically, however, in Buchen's opinion, these activities did result in a positive outcome: empowerment. Middle managers, traditionally the level of management responsible for translating upper-level decisions into meaningful practice and who were themselves the victims of cost-cutting and downsizing, found themselves required to meet higher productivity demands with fewer resources and, naturally, started to shift the increased managerial burden to lower-level workers. This natural empowerment, according to Buchen, has actually been beneficial for employees, because of the resultant increase in their ability to impact working practices, be more autonomous in their actions, and have greater control over their work goals and activities. Thus, Buchen believes that although capitalism is traditionally a vertical process whilst democracy is horizontal, the reduction of middle-management layers, and the increased managerial powers of lower-level employees has resulted in a form of horizontal or democratic capitalism, in which senior management take a distinctly greater leadership role, directing and inspiring more autonomous workers, rather than transmitting remote precepts through a middle-management layer.

One way to encourage a firm's transition from a vertical, hierarchical system to a more democratic, horizontal, transformationally led organization is through the directed application of training and learning. According to Buchen (2003), this is best accomplished by replacing the head of human resources with a Chief Learning Officer (CLO), responsible for the direction of learning and training throughout the firm. Buchen believes that the appointment of a CLO represents the endpoint in an adaptation in HR from simple personnel management to the coordinated development and nurturing of organizational human capital, increasing the worth, creativity, and innovative capability of the organization. Thus, a CLO fills a unique position within the firm and, ideally, is highly qualified in learning, including learning theory, communications modes, brain research, computing, and instructional design. Moreover, the CLO should have an appreciation of both the art and the difficulty of instruction and learning, the ability to evaluate learning effectiveness through methodological investigation, and be capable of managing firm-wide learning resources by streamlining and enhancing training schemes to be more effective and approachable. Lastly, a CLO needs to be able to develop linkages between human resources, middle management, the market and customer needs, pressure from stockholders, and balance the need for innovation with real returns of investment. This can be accomplished largely through strong research abilities, including consistent review and study of the contemporary academic and practice-based literature (including interdisciplinary learning), and a futuristic outlook; understanding the future of job roles within the organization, by predicting what employees will need in order to remain innovative, and establishing a strong link between employee participation, productivity and job satisfaction, managerial and leadership styles, and corporate structure and innovative missions (Buchen). In other words, the CLO guides innovation not only by providing employees with the training and resources required to succeed in their job roles, but also by teaching senior managers to lead effectively, shaping their leadership style to be transformational by encouraging corporate leaders to be less directive and more inspirational and motivational. Consequently, employees see a leader who has learned to motivate by caring about the future of the organization, including its important stakeholders, rather than simply about economic-based rationales.

Finally, whilst transformational leadership abilities can be learnt, developed, and refined, they are also strongly linked to a person's personal values and characteristics (Kim & Shim, 2003). According to Kim and his colleague, as well as transactional and transformational leadership styles, people take on leadership roles that affect the way in which they interact with their subordinates. For example, transformational leadership styles include open system roles, reflected in an open, adaptive leadership style, and human relations roles, seen in leaders who prefer facilitative or mentoring-based styles. However, transactional leaders are characterized by rational goal roles, making them more task oriented and work focussed, and internal process roles which include leadership behaviours that focus more on coordination and monitoring. Following their measurement of leadership roles, personal values, and job characteristics among 205 retail managers at a national US retail chain, Kim and Shim found that both a person's gender and his or her personal values had a significant influence over their type of leadership style. Explicitly, women were more likely to display leadership roles that were more adaptive and human relative, making them well attuned for transformational leadership behaviours. Moreover, transformational leadership roles were more likely to be demonstrated by persons whose personal values included beliefs in strong friendships, helpfulness, forgiveness, and compassion. Unfortunately, given that Kim and Shim reported a return rate to their questionnaire of only 14 per cent, putting into doubt the representativeness of their sample, their findings might not be applicable to the greater business world.

Part 3: Leadership and corporate ethics

Given that, of late, corporate scandals appear to have been relatively widespread, and widely reported by the media, it is appropriate that our discussion of leadership practices also include a section on leadership and corporate ethics, especially in the context of the spread of transformational leadership, commonly touted as an ethical leadership style. Whether a given leader's style is transformational or transactional, however, his or her legitimacy and credibility is, according to Kanungo (2001), dependent on the moral standing and legitimacy of his or her views and actions. Nevertheless, because a transactional leadership style is more likely to be rooted in self-interest, and because ethical practices require that self-interest be put behind the interest of the organization as a whole, it is difficult to equate transactional leadership with ethical practice. In other words, whilst transactional leaders use control strategies to induce compliance behaviour among their followers, such as valued resource exchanges which seldom give rise for opportunities for greater autonomy, self-development, or self-determination, transformational leaders are often seen as more ethical because they employ more empowering rather than controlling strategies (Kanungo). In fact, Kanungo, who defined "ethical leadership" as "that which is morally good or that which is considered morally right", as opposed to what is considered legally or procedurally right, believes that in order to behave ethically, leaders must pay attention to their motives, actions, and character, the outcomes of which influence the moral development of both the leader and his or her followers. However, in the opinion of Kanungo, the real test of ethical leadership is the leader's intent. Altruistic intent, manifest in transactional leaders as a combination of self-interest or egoistic intent, with altruistic concern for others, results in a follower's expectation that the leader's behaviour will lead to a mutually beneficial outcome: a combination that has been labelled "mutual altruism". However, when altruistic intent is applied tranformationally, there is a greater likelihood of moral altruism, in which the leader places his or her concern for others over personal needs, resulting in a sense of duty to others without regard for self-interest.

To understand leadership ethics in more detail, it is necessary to delve a little deeper into the philosophy of ethics, to determine how an individual's behaviour can be considered to be beneficial to others, or to himself or herself. In his review of ethical perspectives and leadership styles, Aronson (2001) has defined "ethical theory" as the study of standards for determining, simply, what is good or bad, right or wrong, whilst "morality" has been described as the effects of a person's actions on the lives of others. Ethical systems are further characterized by deontological and teleological practices. Aronson describes deontological ethics, or the study of moral obligation, as behaviour in which the ends do not justify the means, rather the characteristics of a given behaviour or action are used to determine whether it is inherently right. Deontological ethics are further classified by whether they are based on rules or actions. Deontological rules specify that under all circumstances, individuals should follow a predetermined set of ethical rules or standards so that ethical judgement is based upon a general or guiding principle. Deontological acts, on the other hand, allow for ethical actions according to individual or societal norms; that is, depending on a given situation or behaviour, exceptions to the rule can be made as long as the actor considers the rights and dignity of those affected by the behaviour or action. Thus, regardless of the consequences, deontological acts are concerned with the moral values inherent in an action itself, not with its outcomes (Aronson). Alternatively, teleological ethics are concerned with achieving the greater good, stressing the outcome rather than the intent of a given behaviour. Thus, in teleological ethics, an act is judged to be moral if it produces a greater amount of good than evil. Teleological ethics can be further subclassified by ethical egoism, act utilitarianism, or rule utilitarianism. In ethical egoism, it is the individual who evaluates the moral implications of his or her actions, so that he or she considers an act to be moral or immoral based on how well it assists in achieving personal objectives; thus, all other outcomes outside of the actor's personal agenda become irrelevant to the ethical decision (Aronson). Obviously, ethical egoism can be dangerous in leaders, especially those imbued with great power, and can be viewed as a form of despotism: when an individual gauges the ethical validity of his or her actions based on how well the outcome serves his or her personal agenda, it is unlikely that that outcome will positively affect the lives of others. Rule utilitarianism can be equally as dangerous, because it can be manifest as fanaticism. Adherents of rule utilitarianism base their actions on a set of rules that are used to determine the greatest good for the greatest number of people, and choose, uphold, and modify these rules based on their utility to a given situation. Lastly, act utilitarianism requires that behaviours be evaluated in terms of their potential to produce the greatest amount of good for the greatest number of people. Unlike rule utilitarianism, act utilitarianism uses rules as a guide, but not as a part of the ethical decision process; rather, each act is evaluated based on its utility for achieving the highest level of good. Nevertheless, according to Aronson, ethical problems are best approached from a "value ethics" approach which combines deontological and teleological approaches to find an outcome that is most suited to a given situation. Thus, a virtuous ethical act could be based not only on its potential outcome, but also on the way in which it is performed. In this way the interests of the many and the few can be balanced in a way that minimizes harm at any level.

Aronson (2001) has also posited that, in order for an organization to be ethical, it is important not only that its leader behave ethically but also that his or her leadership behaviours be ethical. According to Aronson, when evaluating ethical leadership behaviour it must be assessed based on both the leader's moral development, and his or her altruistic intent. To this purpose Aronson has proposed an ethical zone for leadership behaviours, which can encompass various leadership styles. For example, managers' or directive leaders' actions are considered ethical when they include benevolent autocratic actions (such as looking out for the needs of staff when making decisions), or consultative or participative behaviours. Nevertheless, although these behaviours can help to involve followers, they do not seek to elevate followers beyond a limited agenda and are therefore limited in their ability to do good. Likewise, the contingent rewards used by transactional leaders not only can be considered ethical, in that they encourage honesty, truth, fairness, and trust, but also fall short in terms of addressing subordinates' higher needs, or helping them to internalize the organization's vision. Consequently, according to Aronson, the highest level of ethical behaviour occurs in transformational leadership, because a transformational style is based on virtuous ethical behaviours: altruism and a genuine concern for achieving a greater good through ethical actions that do the least harm.

In his review of corporate ethics and the actions of corporate leaders, Whittington (2001) has used recent corporate scandals to highlight the power wielded by modern CEOs, a group that he identifies as the most powerful in modern society. Consequently, in assessing corporate ethics, it is necessary to examine directly both the moral foundations of the market place and the moral position of corporate leaders within that framework. According to Whittington, power is a rational construct pertaining to the amount of perceived control that a given person or organizational subunit has over others; further, the greater the dependency of a follower on a leader, the greater the power of the leader over his or her subordinates. Consequently, given that CEOs remain in control of the majority of decisions and actions taken within a firm, they possess supreme power over employees, production and distribution. Nevertheless, this absolute power is not necessarily unethical: Whittington has identified three power dimensions that he uses to determine ethical behaviour, including the motive and resources of power holders, the motives and resources of power recipients, and the relationship between power holders and recipients. Consequently, Whittington distinguishes ethically between leaders and power wielders by defining leaders as those who use power ethically, in the context of the relationship between themselves and their followers and who, through this connection, induce followers to achieve goals that represent the values, motivations, wants, needs, aspirations, and expectations of the leader, the individual and the organization as a whole. In this way, leadership becomes mutually beneficial and, indeed, transformational. Conversely, power wielders use the resources of their power bases that are relevant to the achievement of their own agendas. Thus, power wielders behave unethically by treating people as objects for personal betterment, whilst leaders include people in a mutually shared vision: "all leaders are actual or potential powerholders, but not all powerholders are leaders" (Whittington). Whittington, like Kanungo (2001), goes on to determine ethical leadership based on motive, that is, by asking why leaders actually lead. According to Whittington, on the one hand, transformational leaders lead purely for altruistic reasons, rooted in their intent to help others, and in their dominant preoccupation with the organization and its members, seceding personal interest to those of the firm. Consequently, transformational leaders draw from the resources of their personal power base, such as their own expertise and charisma, rather than using the talents of others to acquire power. Because transformational leaders are principally concerned with creating a better quality of life for those around them, Whittington sees transformational leadership as fundamentally ethical. On the other hand, power wielders and pseudo-transformational leaders are egoistic in their motives, basing their actions on the intent to serve their own ends through avoidance affiliation, using relationships to protect themselves from the consequences of their actions, establishing personal power by demanding and expecting followers' loyalty and effort and using the expertise of others to assist in their own plans, and pursuing achievement as an end to itself, confusing the needs of the organization with their own. With these descriptions in mind, Whittington has described the ideal leader as a servant of the organization: in his servant first model Whittington proposes that CEOs model their behaviour based on a servant role before that of leader, in which they take on a teaching role; develop a deep commitment to identifying and clarifying the will of others; increase their abilities in conceptualizing beyond day-to-day details to encompass a broader perspective, and use foresight, based on past and present realities to foresee the likely outcome of a course of events; act as a steward, holding the organization in trust for the greater good of the firm; and build a sense of community among various members of the organization.

Transformational leadership, therefore, extends beyond the behaviour of the leader, to affect the workings of the organization as a whole. Thus, when an organization is led ethically, it is more likely to engage in ethical actions. For example, Pillai, Scandura, and Williams' (1999) investigation of transformational leadership and organizational ethics in the form of organizational justice, determined a strong relationship between leadership style, perceived justice, and job satisfaction. Following their comparison of 765 professional employees from American, Australian, Indian, Columbian, and Middle-Eastern countries on measures of job satisfaction, leadership style and organizational justice, Pillai *et al.* reported a significant relationship between transformational leadership practices and perceptions of organizational justice: employees worldwide felt that they were being treated more fairly, and were more satisfied, when their supervisor's or manager's leadership behaviour was transformational, principally because the quality of exchanges between leaders and followers resulted in a more trusting relationship based on mutual collaboration rather than expectation.

The positive and widespread relationship between transformational leadership practices and ethical action notwithstanding, as we have already discovered, cultural differences can affect the way in which people and organizations understand ethical behaviour. In their review of ethical capability in multinational corporations, Buller and McEvoy (1999), who defined organizational ethical capability as a combination of the knowledge and skills required to understand ethical frameworks (that is, being able to respond effectively to cross-cultural ethical decisions), have described the facilitation of ongoing learning regarding international ethics as the leadership, teamwork, and effective organizational culture, and through the development of HR and other systems that acquire, sustain, and develop these practices. In other words, for a multinational firm to behave ethically, it must understand ethical diversity and ethical conflicts, and develop the infrastructure to allow managers and other leaders to work effectively within these different frameworks. Moreover, according to Buller and his colleague, when an organization behaves in an ethical manner, it develops a sustainable source of competitive advantage. However, this advantage requires that the organization pay attention to three key areas. First, by understanding the interdependence of various stakeholders within a multinational corporation, the firm can develop strong relationships between the host country head office, and the firm's international employees, customers and suppliers. When the needs of these stakeholders are met, in a manner that meets ethical scrutiny, the firm stands to increase its worldwide corporate reputation, increase employee solidarity, loyalty, commitment and productivity, and lower the costs of maintaining a complex network of suppliers, customer, agents and geographically dispersed employees. Second, by thinking ethically (that is, by maintaining a virtuous ethical policy of maximizing good whilst minimizing harm), including understanding of the various ethical frameworks inherent in global business, and by showing sensitivity to differences among ethical perspectives in varying cultures, the firm can develop a culture of ethical action. Lastly, by responding to ethical challenges through the allocation of sufficient resources to effective issues management, taking appropriate ethical actions in a timely manner and ensuring that systems, structures and procedures are in place to create and sustain ethical actions throughout the organization, organizations can further create a lasting culture of ethical behaviour. To affect such a system, Buller and McEvoy have propounded the benefits of transformational leadership, because of the propensity of transformational leaders to create and sustain an ethical framework for governance. Nevertheless, according to these authors, establishing a transformationally led system of management is not simple, requiring buy-in from the CEO, the board, and other senior managers, a process that requires three stages: awakening, in which the need for ethical change is understood; envisioning, during which a vision of the future is created and committed to by managers and employees alike; and rearchitecting, entailing the creation of the organization necessary to achieve and support this new vision. Further, to accomplish this sort of change, Buller and his coauthor have recommended three specific processes. First, enhanced organizational learning requires the creation of a shared mindset among internal and external stakeholders. To realize this unification, senior HR managers, in combination with other senior managers in the multinational corporation and its overseas affiliates, need to develop a consensus on appropriate HR practices that take into account cross-cultural ethical and other differences (rather than simply expecting that the systems used in the home country will be applicable in other cultures). Furthermore, a code of ethical practice needs to be established that is globally integrative, but locally responsive, allowing for multinational ethical practices. Second, managers throughout the organization need specific training in order to generate, reinforce, and sustain competencies relating to ethical differences, to understand ethics and ethical outcomes, to make effective decisions in the face of ethical conflicts, and to be adaptable and flexible. Ideally, this process is put into practice alongside the creation of ethical partnerships with suppliers, customers, and other organizations, by finding a common ethical ground. Finally, communication from the highest levels to lowest levels needs to be clear and transparent, so that there is a clear understanding of actual needs, requirements, and practices, allowing for realistic, useful decisions, rather than merely the interpretations of murky, top-down directives.

One example, highlighted by Buller and McEvoy (1999), of an ethical policy in action was that of a large computer manufacturer in the early 1980s. In this particular case, a senior executive was negotiating with a South American country for a very large contract and was told that for an additional "fee" (bribing being an established cultural practice in that country) the government would make the sales process very easy for the company. Despite the loss of a very large potential revenue stream, the senior executive, citing the company's ethical policy regarding bribes, refused the contract outright and declined to do future business with that country – a decision that was backed by the company's board and CEO. Other, less-specific examples of ethical practice could include the refusal to do business with countries that have consistently violated human rights, have a poor environmental record, or who are belligerent in their foreign policies. Alternatively, ethically aware multinational organizations could choose to do business with ethically corrupt countries or organizations on the proviso that positive changes are made prior to accepting a contract, and that these changes be sustained and developed during the course of the relationship under the supervision of the multinational.

Cultural differences aside, based on the increasing ability of global corporations to control world events, Squires (2002) has highlighted the importance of an ethical stance by multinational organizations. According to Squires, now and in the future, organizational ethical responsibility and social and environmental responsibility are increasingly important for financial viability. Put simply, for an organization to survive financially in an increasingly complicated world threatened by environmental and social instability, Squires believes that corporations must become ethically responsible corporate citizens, looking towards the longer-term consequences of their present actions, rather than focussing on quarterly financial statements and the short-term aspirations of their shareholders. This requires a complicated balance of pressures from stockholders and other influential stakeholders, against the future viability of the firm, and necessitates leadership that is focussed on ethical and sustainable practices. Thus, for example, for an oil company to expect to survive, given a decreasing fossil fuel supply and an increasing number of environmental problems caused by fossil fuel consumption, without developing practices that will allow it to sustain operations (albeit in different ways), is not only impractical but delusional. Thus, according to Squires, corporate citizenship versus the more common corporate psychopathy (for example, environmentally and socially destructive behaviour for short-term gain without heed of longer-term consequences) requires leadership that is focussed on the large, complicated picture that encompasses the present and the future, including the myriad problems faced by, and even caused by, the firm.

IN ACTION #14

What can leaders do?

So, what can you do in your workplace? Keeping the aforementioned principles in mind, the following tips can and will help to increase employee satisfaction and productivity, reduce employee turnover, ameliorate managerial ability, and enhance company performance and profitability. Remember though, that like any professional undertaking, you are more likely to achieve what you want with professional assistance.

1. Foster an environment in which employees have some control of their environment, their workload, pace and interaction. By allowing choice you engender participation. Reward your employees for high achievement in a timely fashion.

Praise and recognition are useful, but it's better to find out what each employee is most motivated by, and provide it.

2. Allow employees to establish a sense of meaning in the workplace. If people feel that they are listened to, and that their opinions and ideas make a difference, they can be empowered to act with passion and initiative. Employees that feel that their work (and by extension life) is meaningless will have little love for their boss.

3. Practise communicating. Become expert at stating your thoughts, feelings and wants in a concise and precise manner, and learn how to listen.

4. Establish a system to allow employees to get some form of physical activity. This is not easy to do without outside help, so get it. There are many excellent programmes to choose from, but make them accessible and easy for your employees.

5. Encourage, research in, and implement programmes for, managerial excellence. Managers should learn the principles of human motivation and become expert communicators.

6. Evaluate your ideas of professionalism and try and replace outmoded notions with the idea that professionalism is about what you do and how well you do it, rather than how you behave and how well you dress.

7. Become electic in your thinking. There is no one solution, and many ways of getting where you want to go. Take a bit of everything, be scientific and use the parts that work. Don't be afraid to throw out the aspects that don't work for you.

Best practice: Case examples of how it's being done

Benefits of adaptive and transformational leadership versus transactional leadership

In their case study of Timpson Ltd., a UK-based organization that had consistently rated in the top five of the annual *Sunday Times* 100 Best Companies to Work For survey, the UK Department of Trade and Industry (DTI, *Inspirational Leadership*, 2004) have highlighted the benefits of the transformational leadership style of John Timpson, Timpson Ltd's CEO. According to the DTI, managers at Timpson have a large amount of leeway in their decision-making, allowing them to manage their sections with a large amount of autonomy. For instance, managers of retail outlets are able to set their own prices for stock, spend up to £500 resolving a complaint without having to escalate it, and control stock levels and ordering. Moreover, individual staff are encouraged to come up with new ideas for better business practices and given the freedom and support to test them. Staff are also encouraged to take control of their own training and are rewarded for developing their human capital worth: the more training they do, the greater their bonus entitlements. As well, a series of informal bonuses and recognition schemes are coupled with a trust-centred environment; consequently, staff report feeling able to pursue their own work without undue managerial scrutiny. Lastly, staff at Timpson have a great deal of admiration and support for John Timpson and his leadership abilities, which corresponds to a low level of employee absenteeism and turnover.

Leadership and corporate ethics

In a case study of the ethical practices of Tesco, the United Kingdom's largest supermarket chain, Segal, Sobczak, and Triomphe (2003) have praised many of the organization's activities. According to Segal *et al.*, Tesco have sustained a long-running campaign of local regeneration and employment practices (such as providing training and employment for the long-term unemployed), donations (such as computers to schools), and ethical trading practices with their suppliers. Segal and his colleagues have concluded that despite the criticisms that have been levelled at many supermarket chains for their low-income employment practices, poor employee involvement, unfair buying prices, and inadequate environmental concerns, Tesco has made several important ethical gains that represent a commitment to reducing their negative societal and environmental impact.

A more-robust example of corporate restructuring to provide a powerful, ethically based modern firm is that of Interface Inc. and its CEO, Ray Anderson. In his review of contemporary corporate practices, Bakan (2004) has high-lighted the transformational and virtuous ethical practices of Anderson, who has modified the practices of his company, Interface, the largest manufacturer of office carpet worldwide, to be as environmentally and socially sound as is currently feasible. Anderson has described his vision in the following way:

> If we're successful, we'll spend the rest of our days harvesting yester year's carpets and other petrochemically derived products, and recycling them into new materials; and converting sunlight into energy; with zero scrap going to the landfill and zero emissions into the ecosystem. And we'll be doing well. . . very well. . . by doing good. That's the vision. (Achbar, Abbott, & Bakan, 2004)

As a consequence of his efforts, over the past ten years Anderson had reduced the environmental impact of Interface by over a third, by redesigning their products and manufacturing processes to incorporate renewable energy sources, and through waste reclamation and reduction, product recycling and reuse, and a substantial reduction in emissions. Moreover, Interface spends a proportionally large amount on employee training and development, relying on Interface staff to be active, through ideas, participation, and feedback, in the process of becoming a fully self-sustaining and sustainable organization that balances their resource productivity and product design concepts, resulting in a net result of zero harm, either environmentally or sociologically, the endpoint of Anderson's vision. Because of his work and the transformation of Interface, the organization and its CEO have received numerous awards for their ethical practices, including international prizes for sustainable development (Achbar *et al.*, 2004).

Points for action: Practical recommendations for change

Benefits of adaptive and transformational leadership versus transactional leadership

According to the DTI (*Inspirational Leadership*, 2004), the most effective leaders incorporate the following aspects in their leadership style:

- A strong strategic focus – making sure that the organization focusses on its strengths and does not overextend its reach.
- Lateral thinking – ability to draw on multiple ideas, and take a much broader view than usual. Encouragement of others to also approach problems laterally, remaining solution-focussed without necessarily following a traditional path to achieve results.
- Vision and communication – the strong design and communication of a clear, inspirational vision for the future of the organization, communicated to employees in a way that allows them to share the leader's enthusiasm for the organization's future, so that they are motivated to work for the firm's benefit.
- Principles – a strong ethical stance that embodies principles of commitment and courage, and an expectation of high standards in themselves and their subordinates. Most important is honesty, openness, and a respect for and commitment to their employees.
- Reflection – being able to introspect, admit to mistakes and take appropriate action to mend and learn from errors. To be learning focussed, so as to continue to increase knowledge and understanding, and encourage others to learn and grow consistently.
- Risk taking – ability to "bend the rules" and take calculated risks based on experience and ability as well as encouraging others to take, and supporting them for, measured risks.
- Accessibility – available and personable, making time to speak with and listen to their employees. Important that they be contactable, rather than hidden behind administrative staff.
- Values – belief in the importance of skills and training as well as an optimistic, motivated attitude.

Consequently, the DTI (*Inspirational Leadership*, 2004) has reported that under the influence of transformational or inspirational leaders, employees report feeling:

- Listened to – employees feel that their managers and supervisors are interested in their ideas and feedback, and that those ideas are consistently put into practice to help modify or improve work processes.
- Involved – employees feel encouraged to express their opinions and are involved in change practice. They are also given the autonomy to get on

with their jobs without excessive scrutiny, and are supported through the availability of resources, feedback, and recognition.

- Fun – employees are able to have fun at work and the importance of a light-hearted attitude is paramount. Business is seldom effective when everything is taken excessively seriously, and employees who work in a relaxed, more fun-filled environment are less stressed and more productive.

- Trusted – employees feel trusted and respected by their employer, and describe a work environment that is open and honest.

- Appreciated – employees are regularly recognized for their work. This can be as simple as a "thank you" from their employer or manager, encouraging a feeling that their work is valuable and matters to the organization.

- Valuing – not only do employees feel valued, but also value themselves, their workmates, and their clients or customers. Regular, useful, formal and informal feedback allows employees to understand how their contributions make a difference to the firm.

Summary

Leadership styles are vitally important to the health of an organization. Adaptive leadership is represented by the ability to adapt to changing ideas, problems, environments and challenges, and incorporates a balance between assimilation (taking in new ideas to an existing cognitive framework) and accommodation (the ability to take concepts from outside an existing cognitive schema). Transformational leadership is personified in a covenant relationship between a leader and his or her followers, affected through charisma, inspirational motivation, intellectual stimulation, and individual consideration. Transformational leadership inspires the transcendence of self-interest for the interests of the organization at large. Transactional leadership, on the other hand, is represented by a commodity exchange between the leader and the follower (that is, something given in exchange for something in return). Because the leader–follower relationship is based around this transaction, transactional leaders often fail to account for non-transactional aspects of leadership that inspire loyalty, such as development or vision, resulting in an outcome that is based on management by contract rather than leadership through inspiration.

Transformational leadership is strongly related to elevated company performance and employee satisfaction and commitment, largely because of the ability of transformational leaders to be adaptive and flexible, and to engineer an innovative outlook, which in turn drives company innovation and increases competitiveness.

An important aspect of leadership is the recognition of a leader's ethical responsibilities. Given the large number of recent corporate scandals, it appears that corporate leaders have largely neglected their ethical responsibilities. Ethical theory includes, on the one hand, teleological ethics in which an action is judged based on the greatest good, even if it is morally unsound. Deontological ethics, on the other hand, involves the evaluation of actions based on their inherent rightness. Virtuous ethics represents a balance of teleological and deontological ethics, so as to maximize good whilst minimizing harm, and is the preferred outcome of transformational leadership: itself rooted in ethical practice because it is based on the benefit of agents outside of the self, and therefore implies a level of benevolence. In the light of poor corporate behaviour, and with regard to the huge power that contemporary CEO's wield, it needs to be understood that the personal ethical actions of corporate leaders have a strong effect on the ethical actions of the organization. Likewise, the actions of a corporation can influence the ethical abilities of its leader.

REVIEW QUESTIONS

1. Describe the different leadership styles and their benefits and disadvantages. Illustrate with any personal experiences of the effects of these styles on your work performance.

2. What, if any, are the differences between adaptive and transformational leadership? How do they contrast with transactional leadership?

3. How does leadership style affect both individual and organizational ethics?

4. List the various ethical philosophies, analysing both their values and flaws.

5. What are virtuous ethics? Have you personally experienced the benefits of virtuous ethical practice and, if so, how has it affected your working experiences?

Mind-diagram summary

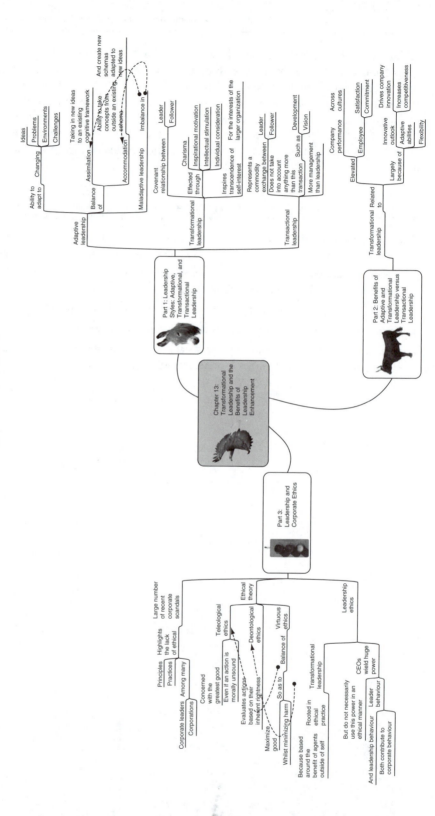

Chapter 13: Transformational Leadership and the Benefits of Leadership Enhancement

Part 1: Leadership Styles: Adaptive, Transformational, and Transactional Leadership

- Adaptive leadership
  - Ability to adapt to
    - Changing
      - Ideas
      - Problems
      - Environments
      - Challenges
  - Balance of
    - Assimilation
      - Taking in new ideas to an existing cognitive framework
    - Accommodation
      - Ability to take concepts from outside an existing schema
      - And create new schemas adapted to new ideas
  - Maladaptive leadership
    - Imbalance in
- Transformational leadership
  - Covenant relationship between
    - Leader
    - Follower
  - Effected through
    - Charisma
    - Inspirational motivation
    - Intellectual stimulation
    - Individual consideration
  - Inspires transcendence of self-interest
    - For the interests of the larger organization
- Transactional leadership
  - Represents a commodity exchange between
    - Leader
    - Follower
  - Does not take into account anything more than this transaction
  - More management than leadership
  - Such as
    - Development
    - Vision

Part 2: Benefits of Adaptive and Transformational Leadership versus Transactional Leadership

- Transformational Related leadership to
  - Elevated
    - Company performance
    - Across cultures
  - Employee
    - Satisfaction
    - Commitment
  - Largely because of
    - Innovative outlook
      - Drives company innovation
      - Increases competitiveness
    - Adaptive abilities
    - Flexibility

Part 3: Leadership and Corporate Ethics

- Ethical theory
  - Large number of recent corporate scandals
  - Highlights the lack of ethical
    - Principles
    - Practices
    - Among many
      - Corporate leaders
      - Corporations
  - Teleological ethics
    - Concerned with the greatest good
    - Even if an action is morally unsound
    - Maximize good
    - Whilst minimizing harm
    - So as to
  - Deontological ethics
    - Evaluates actions based on their inherent rightness
  - Virtuous ethics
    - Balance of
- Leadership ethics
  - Transformational leadership
    - Rooted in ethical practice
    - Because based around the benefit of agents outside of self
  - CEOs wield huge power
    - But do not necessarily use this power in an ethical manner
  - Leader behaviour
    - And leadership behaviour
    - Both contribute to corporate behaviour

Motivating Employees

KEYWORDS Accommodate, adapt, behaviour, choice, employee motivation, employee satisfaction, freedom, internal, intrinsic, self-esteem.

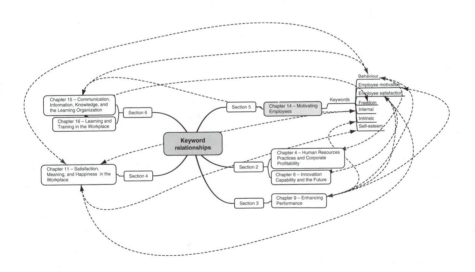

IMPORTANT CONCEPTS Perceived control, positive affectivity, role-breadth self efficacy.

Part 1: Rewards, and extrinsic and intrinsic motivation

Strong leadership abilities are paramount to organizational success, but effective leadership styles alone are not necessarily sufficient for motivating employees to perform to a high level. Likewise, whilst it is of substantial motivational benefit to provide a work environment that is highly stimulating and low in stress (see above), several authors have proposed more specific models for explaining and enhancing a person's motivation to work. Parker (2000), for instance, has argued that in modern workplaces, to maintain motivation, employees need roles that are broad, open-ended, independent, and flexible and that allow for proactive use of knowledge, interpersonal skills, cooperation, and the ability to display initiative. To encourage these qualities, she has proposed two motivational models, flexible role orientation (FRO) and role-breadth self-efficacy (RBSE). In the first, a "job" is redefined as something more akin to an exercise in cross-training. That is, rather than having a strict job description, an individual is encouraged to use his or her own judgement and initiative to contribute to the development and productivity of a team, with no particular limitations to his or her actions. The second, RBSE, involves the development of a person's confidence in carrying out roles outside the tasks prescribed to his or her job role. In this case, by encouraging a person to be comfortable in pushing his or her boundaries, and to learn new skills, he or she is likely to become more comfortable with new roles, and show less psychological and physiological response to the strain of adaptation to new responsibilities and environments. According to Parker, persons high in RBSE show higher performance and tenacity in task completion, especially when their role involves high-significance tasks, and are more satisfied in their jobs than their less-confident workmates. Thus, in Parker's opinion, workers are most motivated when they are free to expand their job roles beyond a basic job description and are able to take initiative in a creative manner. Moreover, when workers are able to learn new skills and become comfortable in a variety of roles, they are more likely to be confident, productive, and satisfied at work.

The productivity benefits of flexible job-roles and increased confidence in multiple work-based situations have been examined empirically by Richer, Blanchard, and Vallerand (2002), who assessed motivation, workplace satisfaction, emotional exhaustion and worker turnover in 490 university alumni. They found that workplace motivation was directly associated with perceived work characteristics and to a person's feelings of relatedness to his or her tasks. That is, when a person's tasks were seen as restrictive, and he or she did not feel that those tasks were related to his or her skills, there was a corresponding increase in emotional exhaustion and turnover intent. In contrast, those persons who felt free to explore multiple roles and to increase the personal relevance of their job tasks by learning new skills were more motivated, and felt that their work was more relevant.

The findings of Richer *et al.* (2002) have been echoed in sentiment by Darlington (2002) in his article on workplace motivation. According to Darlington, the majority of motivational problems at work are the result of a lack of perceived control and freedom, coupled with the seeming inability to enhance existing skills or learn new ones; under these conditions employees quickly become frustrated, lose initiative, and take on a victim role. The solution, in Darlington's opinion, is to allow employees to become directly involved in decision-making and task analysis, to encourage them to develop their own solutions to problems, and to recognize these contributions. Branham (2001), in his assessment of motivation at work, has come to a similar conclusion, suggesting that the recognition of performance, in the form of formal and informal rewards, is a primary factor in job satisfaction and motivation. According to Branham, informal rewards, which can take the form of recognition or praise, should, in line with behavioural theory, be prompt so that the reward is paired with the action to be reinforced. Moreover, informal rewards should be accompanied by an explanation of why the reward is being given, include equal recognition of individual and team contributions, and should be matched to a person's personal preferences, the significance of the achievement and, most importantly, customized to a person's values (because each person has a different idea of what is rewarding). As well, formal rewards which, traditionally, have included advancements or promotion, or stock ownership, can also take the form of incentives customized to a person's preferences, such as education or that best fit a person's needs, including access to health or fitness programmes.

Other authors have also reported on the value of non-traditional motivational models. For example, Norgaard (2001) has indicated that traditional incentives, such as pay rises and recognition through advancement, do not stimulate creativity, talent, or responsibility. According to Norgaard, because a person has no control over the method or timing of these types of incentives, he or she can be resistant to the changes that they imply. In other words, rather than perceive a promotion as a reward, an employee might resent being taken away from the job and people he or she enjoys, to take on a role (such as a managerial position) in which he or she has little training or experience. In this case, even a rise in pay cannot compensate for a loss of contentment or enjoyment. Thus, in Norgaard's opinion, the best form of incentive is that which encourages a person's intrinsic motivation or his or her desire to work for its own inherent reward. As Branham (2001) has suggested, these can include customized formal or informal rewards, delivered in a timely manner.

Catlette and Hadden (1999) have also highlighted the importance of intrinsic motivation in the workplace. They have reported that employees are most motivated by challenging, meaningful work of which they can feel proud, combined with a clear sense of purpose and direction, backed up by information that is timely, accurate, and relevant. They have also recommended that employees be encouraged in feelings of competence, a belief in the fairness, justice, and reciprocal caring of the organization and, lastly, the feeling that their work is "worth it" (that is, that it embodies a balance of interest and investment, and that it is adequately supported by the employee's superiors). These situations, according to Catlette and his colleague, set up a state in which the job becomes its own reward, independent of financial compensation.

The notion that it is intrinsic rather than extrinsic factors that are most motivating in the workplace has also been investigated empirically. In their evaluation of 435 students and 348 employees on measures of intrinsic motivation, reward expectancy, and performance, Eisenberger, Rhoades, and Cameron (1999) reported that expectation of reward actually decreased intrinsic motivation, because of a corresponding reduction in perception of control. Thus, according to Eisenberger *et al.*, for a reward to be effective it must be contingent on high performance, allowing the perception of freedom of action. In other words, when a person, team or organization as a whole is free to choose whether or not to make the effort to attain a high level of performance, the choice itself becomes the source of intrinsic motivation, whilst the actual recognition of performance (that is, extrinsic reward) takes a secondary role.

Similar to the findings of Eisenberger *et al.* (1999), in a study of 500 managers in Hong Kong (Chiu, 1999), pay equity was not found to be significantly related to employee motivation or happiness. Rather, it was intrinsic motivators, such as a person's sense of positive affectivity and self-efficacy, that predicted his or her motivation to work. Likewise, in their study of 335 French employees' motivation to participate in training, Guerrero and Sire (2001) reported that it was intrinsic motivators, such as increases in work satisfaction and enhanced organizational effectiveness consequent to training, rather than external incentives (such as pay) that influenced participation. All the same, according to Guerrero and her colleague, in France, training programmes (which are government mandated) are often associated with job insecurity (that is, a training programme is perceived as a managerial statement of mistrust in a worker's abilities); thus, Guerrero and Sire believe that it is the responsibility of management to encourage self-efficacy in workers so that training, and its potentially positive results, becomes rewarding in its own right.

Despite the number of psychologically based studies of intrinsic motivation in the workplace, there has been a corresponding reluctance by many economists to accept the reality of intrinsic motivational factors. Nevertheless, economists Benabou and Tirole (2003) have developed an economic model of intrinsic and extrinsic motivation to address the lack of economic contributions to an area dominated by psychological and sociological research. Not surprisingly, their conclusions are similar in many respects to the findings of psychological researchers, suggesting that economic models can readily include subjective indicators, like intrinsic motivation and employee satisfaction. Specifically, Benabou and his colleague found that (as we saw in Section 3 in the section on incentives and reward) when extrinsic rewards increase, intrinsic motivation can suffer, especially when an employee doubts his or her ability or is unsure of his or her commitment to a given project. In other words, when a person is offered a reward for successful completion of a project, he or she is less likely to perceive the project as intrinsically attractive because the reward is interpreted as a sign that the task is aversive or dull, and that an extra "carrot" is required to encourage participation. Contingent rewards and rewards offered in advance of a project's completion can also reduce employees' perceptions of control, because the presence of a reward contingent on a certain action reduces the ability to feel a sense of choice in the level or type of participation on a given project. Likewise, Benabou and Tirole reported that although extrinsic rewards might serve as positive reinforcers in the short term, over the long term intrinsic motivation will drop, because, eventually, the reward becomes the only incentive to perform, replacing any intrinsic desire to participate. Lastly, Benabou and Tirole's model showed that one of the most successful ways to increase intrinsic motivation towards a task is to raise an employee's level of empowerment at work, by increasing his or her level of discretion in choosing how and when he or she will work, and by elevating the ability to participate in decision-making surrounding a project or task.

Other economists have also reached similar conclusions. For example, Arocena and Villanueva (2003), in their economic model of motivation in the workplace, have made some interesting propositions which also parallel existing psychological theories. Like Benabou and Tirole (2003), they have suggested that high monetary (extrinsic) incentives can "crowd out" an employee's intrinsic motivation by representing a potentially intrinsically attractive task as dull or unpleasant. Moreover, they have proposed that individuals high in intrinsic motivation, labelled as persons with "high positive achievement attitudes", are most strongly motivated by their access to what they perceive as high-value jobs. That is, when employees with high positive achievement attitudes are given positions in which they have a high level of autonomy, flexibility, responsibility, perceived control over working conditions, and are able to identify with their roles and tasks, they perform substantially better than they would in lower value positions. Consequently, according to Arocena and his colleague, in the interests of increased productivity, performance, and human capital development, organizations should take pains to identify individuals higher in positive achievement attitudes, and increase their access by redesigning their work to include greater flexibility, control, and empowerment. Needless to say, it would make sense that organizations also look at ways to increase a person's achievement attitudes. In this way, not only could they increase performance, loyalty, and efficiency by encouraging those who are already intrinsically motivated, but they could also raise the intrinsic motivation levels and performance of the remaining workers.

In an interesting evaluation of 215 MBAs, Heath (1999) has indicated that, despite the reported need for intrinsic motivators inherent in most workers, managers invariably misattribute and oversimplify the motivations of others. According to Heath, most people use lay motivation theories when ascribing motivations to others, believing themselves to be intrinsically motivated, but supposing others to be motivated more by external events, especially by tangible rewards. Heath found that, in his sample, this motivational attributional error was dominant in the majority of decisions regarding others, labelling it "extrinsic motivational bias". Given that most people understand that they are intrinsically motivated but mistakenly assume that others are not, Heath has recommended that managers be trained to understand that, in fact, the motivations of others are similar to their own. Heath has also suggested that, in all likelihood, this attributional error represents the reason that most managers believe that they can motivate their subordinates exclusively through extrinsic means.

Nevertheless, extrinsic motivators, according to Hannan (2005), can be interpreted in a way that does increase intrinsic motivation. Following her investigation of 64 professionally employed MBA students on wage changes and worker effort, Hannan found that it was the individual's perception of generosity behind the wage change that influenced his or her output, rather than the wage change itself. Specifically, if firm profit had decreased and workers were still given a wage rise, worker productivity increased, but this effect was not observed following a wage rise based on increased company profits. Likewise, when wages stayed constant worker output was reduced following increased profit, but was increased when company profits decreased. In other words, when the organization was doing well, wage raises were interpreted as a meaningless gesture, reducing employees' intrinsic motivation to work effectively, however, when wages were increased or remained steady despite profit declines, the act was seen as more generous, increasing employees' feelings of loyalty and commitment to the firm, with a corresponding increase in their intrinsic motivation to perform.

It would appear from our review of motivation at work that motivating employees is not as hard as employers seem to think it is. Rather, it is the conditions at work, including the lack of empowerment, inability to make change, and dearth of autonomy, that often result in conditions of low workplace morale. In fact, several investigators have come to similar conclusions. For instance, Minkler (2004), who surveyed 1905 randomly selected US workers on both their intrinsic motivation to work and their propensity to shirk, reported that shirking is not the problem that economists assume it to be. Instead, Minkler found that the majority of workers do not shirk, even when they are not being monitored. In other words, despite the opportunity to slacken their work output, most workers feel a sense of "moral duty" or intrinsic motivation to work, especially when they feel committed to their employer – feelings that are substantially increased when the job involves high levels of flexibility and autonomy, and is perceived to be both interesting and fair. Consequently, Minkler has proposed that agency theory, on which many economists base their projections about employee motivation (that is, employees can only be motivated to work by extrinsic means, and will shirk whenever possible), needs to be fundamentally altered in order to take intrinsic and other intangible motivational factors into account. People, Minkler asserts, are not machines, and behave in complicated, often intangible, ways that cannot be modelled by existing, overly simplistic economic models. Jalajas and Bommer (1999) have reached similar conclusions. Following their examination of motivation, performance, commitment, and downsizing among 150 engineers from 15 high-tech US firms, Jalajas and his co-investigator found that, in organizations that had downsized their staff, it was not the actual downsizing that led to the consequent reduction in performance, but rather feelings of loss of control, breaches of the psychological contract, and the inability to continue to contribute effectively to the organization, each of which reduced employees' intrinsic motivations to perform. Nevertheless, it was still possible for downsizing to occur without severely damaging the morale of remaining workers, as long as the process was framed in such a way that it was not seen as an assault on the psychological contract. However, according to Jalajas and Bommer, because most managers do not properly understand the importance of intrinsic motivation, and because decisions to downsize are often made based on economic theories and recommendations (which most often fail to take into account human factors), downsizing is often carried out in a way that damages employees' motivation and commitment. Keeping in mind the findings of Hannan (2005), in which employees only saw pay rises as motivators when they were perceived as genuine (that is, when the firm had lowered profit but gave raises anyway), we can interpret Jalajas and Bommer's findings to mean that although motivation is fragile, it is also relatively easy to cultivate; if downsizing can be carried out without seriously affecting motivation and performance, most organizations should have little difficulty in increasing employee motivation, as long as they invest in the training and resources necessary for employee well-being (such as the factors we discussed at length in Sections 3 and 4). Unfortunately, firms continue to be driven by misguided or ill-informed leaders who rely on outmoded motivational techniques, a problem that, as we have seen, has now even begun to attract the criticism of economists. In fact, in his model of workplace incentives, Oyer (2004), like many of the other authors reviewed in this section, has proposed that the compensation and reward models used by many firms are antagonistic to the encouragement of intrinsic motivation in employees, simply because they disallow any measure of employee control in achieving them.

IN ACTION #15

Understanding the physiology of motivation

Motivation has, in recent times, become a maligned and misused word. Many of us want "it", few understand "it" and, of late, "it" has become the centre of a large industry aimed and improving "it". Nevertheless, to become motivated, to stay motivated and to motivate and maintain change in the self and in others, it is necessary both to understand motivation as a process, and to comprehend the ways in which it can be encouraged. By defining and practising motivation and motivational change, we can harness and use them in our daily lives to change behaviour and thought. This helps us to achieve our desired goals in business, to find and maintain positive relationships with the people around us, and to assist us in living our lives in a healthy and constructive manner.

Motivation: what is it?

Let's begin with a definition of motivation, from which we can build a framework of understanding. Motivation can be understood as a complex interplay of the neurological pathways dedicated to reinforcing behaviours, and the psychological interpretation of the events surrounding that reinforcement (Adams & Kirkby, 2001). Further, motivation can be seen as the impetus to perform a given action, whether that action is a positive event, such as a constructive behaviour change, or a negative one, such as repeating a behaviour that is detrimental to our psychological or physical health. The psychological aspects to motivation are dependent on a wide variety of variables, including the intensity of the experience, the emotions felt at the time, the location and the people, as well as one's history of reaction to similar experiences. Because they are so complex, it helps to understand (as best we can) the workings of the neurological pathways that deal with motivational processes, in order to better understand the psychological aspects.

Neurology basics

The brain consists of over a trillion tiny electrical and chemical transmission cells called *neurons*. Neurons are the computing components of the brain, and connect to one another in massively complex ways to create neural pathways that process information. When considered as a whole, the brain is divided into three main levels (the brain stem, the mid-brain, and the cerebral cortex), each of which governs a different aspect of human functioning (ranging from simple, regulatory processes to higher thought and creativity). Within each of these levels, there are multiple structures, responsible for governing different human faculties. One such structure, the mesolimbic-dopamine system, found in the mid-brain, is responsible for a large proportion of human motivational processes through the reinforcement of behaviour. However, to better understand its function, we first need to examine the workings of the brain at a neuronal level.

Neurons

Each neuron is a complex cell made up of several interacting parts. The neuron can be thought of as a sort of computer, with multiple inputs (called *dendrites*) and the ability to connect to other neurons (effectively the network output) through a structure known as a *synapse*. The neuron is electro-chemical in its function. This means that although it transmits internal information electrically, it connects to other neurons chemically, using compounds called *neurotransmitters*. The process works something like this: a neuron is stimulated by some sort of influence (another neuron, or an external event, for example) via one of its dendrites (inputs). An electrical signal is sent to the cell body via an electrically shielded pathway (the axon). Depending on the strength of the signal, the cell body releases neurotransmitters (a specific type for a specific type of neuron) into the space between the neuron and its neighbour (the synaptic gap). Each of these neurotransmitters has a specific chemical shape (imagine a key) that can only "fit" into the equivalently shaped receptor (imagine a lock) of its neighbour (the neuroreceptor on the dendrite of the abutting neuron). When the neurotransmitter (or, more accurately, enough neurotransmitters) reaches the appropriate receptor (the key fitting the lock), the second neuron either fires a new electrical signal through its axon to its cell body (an excitatory neuron) continuing the process or stops the signal (an inhibitory neuron). Leftover neurotransmitters are "reuptaken" to the original neuron and recycled. Thus, although much more complex, a neuron is a little like a transistor, that is, it either passes information on or does not. Of course, the process is substantially more complex, and also involves a second phase of processing (postsynaptic neurotransmission). However, this is beyond the scope of our present discussion.

We can illustrate the neurotransmission process, in a basic way, by describing how psychotropic medications can work in the brain. Modern antidepressants, known as selective serotonin reuptake inhibitors (SSRIs), are used to counter diagnosed clinical depression. Research has shown that persons with clinical depression are often low in a particular neurotransmitter, serotonin.

The lack of this neurotransmitter reduces the ability of the serotogenic neurons to communicate effectively leading, eventually, to the psychological experience of depression. SSRIs effectively shut down the ability of the neuron to reuptake leftover synaptic serotonin for recycling (it shuts down the reuptake "pump"), leaving more serotonin in the synapse to bind to the receptors of the next neuron.

This, in turn, increases the strength of the ongoing electrical signal and reduces the psychological experience of depression.

Although it might seem that chemical transmission would be slow, in reality, this process takes only millionths of a second, mostly because of amazing reaction speeds, coupled with very small distances (synaptic gaps measure in fractions of micrometres). Although speeds vary depending on the type of cell (neuron) and the type of neurotransmitter (of which there are many, including serotonin, dopamine, beta-endorphin, glutamate, GABA, and anandamide), they are still very fast, hence our ability to think quickly!

Why we are motivated – the mesolimbic dopamine system

As previously noted, the mesolimbic dopamine system (MDS) is located in the mid-brain, which, among other things, contains systems responsible for emotion, memory, and motivation. The MDS is the principal motivational structure in the brain and works by rewarding us for engaging in certain behaviours.

The MDS evolved in an earlier stage of human development, in fact, long before we became remotely human. Its chief purpose is to make sure that we engage in behaviours and activities that could increase the likelihood of our survival. Originally, this meant things like eating when we're hungry, drinking when we're thirsty, sexual behaviours, and maternal and paternal behaviours. Because these actions help us to survive (one of the principle goals of evolution) we were (and still are) rewarded for these behaviours in the form of a neurotransmitter called *dopamine*. The effects of dopamine in this part of the brain are profound and highly desirable. In fact, you've experienced this sensation many times – each time you feel satisfaction or pleasure, when you, for instance, eat chocolate, see a beautiful sunset, or make love, you are experiencing activation of the MDS.

To complicate things, the MDS has powerful connections to the emotion, learning, and higher processing centres of the brain. These connections also make evolutionary sense. If an experience is pleasurable and worth repeating (from a survival perspective), it is worth remembering, and so strong links are created to the memory centres of the brain. Moreover, because strong emotions evoke vivid memories, to enhance the strength of the memory, activation of the MDS often invokes an emotional response, which is tied to the eventual memory. Finally, the higher processing centres (the bits we think with) are also connected to the experience, so that we can interpret and reason about the behaviour, and so that it can influence our conscious (as well as unconscious) actions (such as our decision to repeat the behaviour in the future).

This brings us to the fascinating bit! Because of its powerful influence in the brain, activation of the MDS evokes strong behavioural change. Unfortunately, the system evolved a long time ago, and has not yet modified itself to distinguish between survival behaviour and other types of behaviours that can also stimulate MDS activity. This means that many modern behaviours (we'll go into examples in a minute) can activate the MDS (it does not differentiate) and, consequently, often behaviours that can actually be counterproductive are strongly reinforced. The example of addition will help to illustrate. Addition can have either chemical or behavioural origins. For instance, it is possible to become addicted to behaviours like gambling, exercise, sex, and eating (to name a few), as well as the more well-known chemicals (for example, heroin, amphetamines, alcohol, nicotine, caffeine), because of their excessive MDS stimulation and the consequent dopaminergic reward. As a result, the MDS can be "hijacked" by contraindicative behaviours, reducing our chances of survival! Depending on the degree of this "hijacking", the MDS can virtually take over our behaviour, activating the memory centres to lay down very powerful memories, and strongly influencing conscious and unconscious thought processes regarding our present and future actions. Thus, as far as the brain is aware, the activity of gambling, for example, can be interpreted as being as important as eating, and reinforced in the same way. Similarly, cocaine directly stimulates the MDS by mimicking dopamine. The brain thinks that the consequent dopamine elevations were the result of an important (survival) event, and lays down strong emotive memories and higher brain centre pathways to make sure we continue to repeat the behaviour.

So, how we are motivated?
By understanding better the actions of the MDS on memory, emotion, and higher processing, we can begin to understand how many of the things that we think we have full conscious control over are actually manipulated at a deeper level, by an ancient but powerful brain mechanism. That is not to say that we cannot have conscious control over our actions but without being aware of these processes, we cannot be in control of their influence! Simply, when you don't feel motivated to start a project, or when you drop out half way through "lack of steam", your MDS is influencing your thoughts, because the activity you're trying to start or complete is not of "interest" to it. Consequently, you are not being rewarded for the action: you get no pleasure from it (and dopamine is pleasurable).

So, is it all about the MDS? Not completely, it's just one part of a complex system. But at a fundamental brain level, the MDS has immense influence over our behaviour by modifying the system. In learning how to manage this scheme (remember, it is connected to the higher function centres, and this relationship is two-way), we can learn how to motivate ourselves and others in a very powerful manner. Consequently, psychological techniques and systems that have been designed both to change behaviour can be highly effective in stimulating motivation.

Part 2: Relationships, environment, and goal setting

Whilst commentators have stressed the importance of intrinsic motivators, like satisfaction, meaning, and balance, in enhancing a person's willingness to work, others have emphasized the necessity for motivators that are extrinsic but that are intangible or without financial indicators. One such motivator is a person's relationships with others in the workplace. Haslam, Powell, and Turner (2000), for example, in an investigation of 191 scientific research staff, reported that when they were evaluated on measures of motivation, satisfaction, and relationships, workers with the highest levels of workplace motivation and satisfaction showed a significantly stronger sense of organizational identification. According to Haslam *et al.*, organizational identification is, in itself, a product of the quality of relationships within the organization, so that a person gauges his or her self-image by the depth and fulfilment of interaction with those around him or her. Thus, when a person perceives his or her interactions with others as meaningful, purposeful, and directed towards a common goal, he or she feels more accepted by, and motivated to work for, the organization. Lee and Koh (2001) expressed a similar idiom when describing empowerment. According to these authors, empowerment in the workplace is representative of the sum of a person's positive interpersonal relationships at work (especially with his or her supervisor), his or her psychological state, and his or her level of self-efficacy. Likewise, Beaubien (2001), in her review of employee motivation, reported that although intrinsic motivators, such as understanding, personal satisfaction, and feelings of empowerment, were highly necessary for workplace satisfaction, the relationships in the workplace were also paramount to effective motivation. Moreover, in Beaubien's opinion, the relationship between an employee and his or her supervisor is the most important, especially because it is the supervisor's actions that help the employee to increase his or her intrinsic motivation by understanding the value of his or her own behaviours. Nonetheless, according to Beaubien, this relationship is seldom effective when the supervisor takes a power-differentiated role; rather, when the supervisor takes the role of teacher, mentor, or coach, sharing his or her knowledge or expertise, becoming invested in the employee's well-being and fostering a mutual relationship, intrinsic motivation to work can be heightened substantially.

According to Adler, Milne, and Stablein (2001), who defined motivation as an "individual's activation and degree of persistence in undertaking goal-directed behaviour", both the motivational environment (labelled situational motivation) and an individual's desire to learn contribute to employee motivation. In their investigation of 143 undergraduates on measures of learning motivation and work interest, Adler and his colleagues found that individual motivation can be enhanced in several ways. First, individuals with high growth need strength (GNS), a rating of curiosity and learning drive, are more motivated when presented with a stimulating environment or project, or when their supervisor or manager is more animated and passionate in their interpersonal interactions. Consequently, by increasing the level of stimulation in the work environment by inspiring a person's curiosity, intellect, or interests, high GNS workers will respond with greater output, creativity, initiative, and productivity. Moreover, according to the findings of Adler *et al.*, the majority of people are more motivated when their work environment or job structure is modified to include four important aspects: identity, variety, autonomy, and feedback. Specifically, motivation is increased when a person is able to identify with his or her work by, for example, being able to see a project through to its completion; participating in projects that allow the exercising and development of multiple skills and talents; feeling that a given task is significant to the accomplishment of larger roles, such as the organization's goals and needs; and participating in projects that are considered interesting and worthwhile. Likewise, motivation, and consequential involvement and performance, increases when a task or project is varied, allowing the worker to learn, participate, and develop in a variety of ways, and avoiding boring, repetitive work. In fact, Adler *et al.* believe that even traditionally dull work can be made variable, so that a person's time is distributed between new, challenging, and familiar tasks. Moreover, the findings of Adler and his colleagues indicate that autonomy at work is extremely important for ongoing motivation. Thus, an employee should have some control over choosing the types of work and projects he or she engages in, how the work is scheduled (work flexibility), how it is assigned (ability to delegate responsibilities), as well as greater involvement, where available, in decision-making, strategic thinking and feedback for improving the work environment and systems.

Another lauded intangible motivator is the ability to set, manage, and achieve goals autonomously and in cooperation with others. Van Eerde (2000), in her review of procrastination versus motivation to complete aversive tasks, has indicated that procrastination (that is, the avoidance of the implementation of an action) is an emotion-oriented coping mechanism, aimed at escaping a given problem through the short-term avoidance of an immediate stressor. In the workplace, stressors are varied, and can include time pressures, personal distraction or impulsiveness, or organizational situations, such as task performance expectations, and either excessive or insufficient challenge. Unfortunately, according to Van Eerde, procrastination as a strategy for dealing with workplace stress is seldom successful. However, in Van Eerde's opinion, the key to overcoming procrastination is effective goal management: learning to prioritize tasks, using time and resources effectively, understanding the expectations of others, realizing the necessity of challenge, and increasing the belief in one's ability to achieve a given goal. Regrettably, because these skills are seldom taught or recognized before, during, or following entry to the workforce, few people are competent in goal management for themselves or for others. Consequently, according to Van Eerde, procrastination is endemic in most organizations, and will remain so until employees are given the tools necessary to understand how to avoid it.

Some of the conditions necessary for teaching goal management in the workplace have been addressed by Peters and Steinauer (1997). According to these authors, it is the organization's responsibility to understand clearly the mechanisms of goal management, and up to supervisors to communicate these procedures to their subordinates in an erudite manner. Primarily, this communication can be realized by managerial role modelling of effective goal management practices. However, in addition, managers should be able to explain that a goal is a specific, realistic, and challenging outcome that is describable, achievable within a given timeframe and, most importantly, flexible (that is, that it should be able to be changed readily on the basis of new information). Consequently, supervisors should assist employees in setting and achieving goals, and provide feedback in the form of positive critique that is both timely and fair. In the opinion of Peters and his colleague, once the employee is comfortable in this process and has demonstrated understanding, he or she should be encouraged to, and given personal responsibility for, setting, managing and achieving his or her own goals. Ongoing support, performance contingent reward, and follow-up by management can also help to reinforce these new skills. According to Peters and his co-worker, follow-up should be focussed on performance targets that track progress towards goal achievement, and involve discussion with employees of both progression and problems.

In a less practical but more far reaching article to that of Peters and Steinauer (1997), Kaipa (2000) has suggested that goal setting be valued and developed within an organization to such an extent that individuals are able to set, and work towards, long-term goals that will also become the goals of the organization as a whole. According to Kaipa, these goals will be directed towards generational sustainability, allowing an organization to look beyond daily management towards its place in society and its influence on future generations. In this way, goal management becomes a powerful tool for propelling an organization from a culture of individual opportunity, to one of common good. In his transtheoretical model, Kaipa has envisioned that goal setting and achievement, when directed beyond the individual, can allow for an increased spiritual quality of life which, in turn, engenders emotional freedom and wisdom, both for individuals and for the organizations with which they work.

Best practice: Case examples of how it's being done

Rewards, and extrinsic and intrinsic motivation

In their 15-year longitudinal investigation of CIGGC, an Australian gas cylinder manufacturer, Chenhall and Langfield-Smith (2003) chartered the effects of a series of management-led initiatives in order to increase worker motivation. Initially, to counter very poor employee performance and morale, the organization initiated a series of mechanistic control systems, based on financial rewards. These included gain sharing, and contingent bonus schemes, but although worker productivity increased somewhat, along with elevated employee satisfaction scores, the gains were relatively short term, a failure that Chenhall and his colleague attribute to the extrinsic nature of the reward system. A second round of initiatives proved more successful; driven by the need to boost both productivity and competitive innovation, management instigated the development of self-managed teams, in which shop-floor employees were encouraged to contribute their skills and tacit knowledge to both the construction processes and the development of new products. For the most part, this change was highly successful. However, team members objected to the more "managerial style" duties their new role entailed. Employees resented being asked to participate in decision-making processes, such as marketing schemes and strategic decisions, for which they felt they were poorly qualified and which they believed were the domain of management. Given that pay rises did not accompany the new team-based expectations, employees felt that managers were simply piling their work onto shop-floor workers. To correct this situation, team responsibilities were restructured to reduce managerial-like decisions whilst retaining the ability to contribute to day-to-day operations, and a series of HR practices were implemented to increase intrinsic motivation in the workforce, and reduce the dependency on overtime and contingent bonuses. This included training in intra- and inter-team cooperation, self-leadership, and social bonding. Following a small amount of resistance, employees reported feeling greater satisfaction in their work (their ideas were being used to create new products and ways of improving existing products), higher self-esteem, greater workplace satisfaction, increased identification with their work, and a greater sense of self-worth. Moreover, although explicit extrinsic financial rewards were reduced, employees reported feeling more motivated to work, based on their increasing attachment to and intrinsic reward from their everyday work. Simultaneously, absenteeism and missed work time from striking and other disputes dropped sharply, increasing CIGGC's financial performance and allowing them to become one of the most successful gas cylinder manufacturers in Australia.

Points for action: Practical recommendations for change

Leadership and corporate ethics

In their report on corporate social responsibility in Europe, Segal *et al.* (2003) have cited several defining criteria chosen by the European Parliament for a green paper on European social practice by corporations. Segal *et al.* recommend that the following criteria should be taken into account by organizations wishing to incorporate an ethical component to their practice:

- the voluntary nature of corporate practices – voluntarily going beyond mandatory obligations and providing a higher standard of practice than the industry average;
- the sustainability of the practices – representing both the long-term viability of the project, and the long-term commitment by the organization to these practices. This helps to distinguish between marketing strategies and real corporate social initiatives;
- partnership – between the organization and those outside of the organization, such as communities, charities, and the beneficiaries of their activities;
- transparency – willingness of the organization to make their actions and practices available to open public scrutiny. This, again, helps to avoid publicity stunts by which an organization can claim ethical action without backing up their claims with readily available data, open to critique.

Furthermore, Segal and his colleagues (2003) have provided three extra standards by which to rate these criteria:

1. the level of consideration given by the organization towards the impact of its activities on both the physical and natural environment
2. the amount of commitment by the organization to serving local or global communities, especially with regard to voluntary contributions that support cultural, humanitarian, or environmental practices
3. the implications, both financial and otherwise for the organization, based on its fiscal decisions, especially regarding implications for its working practices, employment conditions, and the equability of its working environment.

Another similar rating system was developed by the Canadian magazine Corporate Knights ("Our Methodology: How We Find the Best 50 Corporate Citizens in Canada", 2005), which focusses on ethically based practices among national and international corporations. To rank Canadian organizations on ethical practice, Corporate Knights employs a 13-point rating system that addresses the following:

- disclosure of company affiliations, political funding, and policy positions on key ethical, sociological and environmental issues
- publication of membership and sponsorship of external organizations which advocate ethically based practice
- identification of opportunities for raising their regulatory and ethical standards
- development of strong and defensible definitions of legitimate activities under differing political cultures
- public policy relating to sustainable development
- implications of various dealings with stakeholders
- consistency of practice and rhetoric
- open discussion of public policy with stakeholders beyond the company's shareholders
- development of joint statements with external stakeholders
- published responses to government consultations and mandates
- development of long-term company sustainability transition plans
- determining public policy barriers to ethical practice
- sharing of sustainability vision with both policymakers and the public and taking an active stance on the development of public policy in support of sustainable development.

Summary

Intrinsic motivation can be defined as the internal motivation to participate in a given activity without the need for external motivators. When employees are intrinsically motivated to work, they are more likely to take initiative, be more productive, and enjoy their work. However, the majority of workplace reward schemes focus on extrinsic rewards, such as wage rises or other financial rewards, which can actually signal to employees that their tasks are dull or uninteresting, and remove any sense of control over task involvement, participation level or sense of achievement. In fact, agency theory, an influential economic theory that governs the way many organizations attempt to reward their staff, assumes that motivation is purely extrinsic and that without external motivation workers will shirk their responsibilities. Nevertheless, many modern commentators, including economists, sociologists, and psychologists dispute the validity of agency theory, based on its inability to address or account for intrinsic motivational factors. Consequently, whilst workplace motivation is not particularly complicated, it is often poorly understood, especially by many managers, resulting in misapplied motivational strategies.

One way to enhance intrinsic motivation at work is through the encouragement of workplace relationships that are strong, positive, and supportive. Moreover, a stimulating work environment that encompasses the options of flexibility, autonomy, the ability to participate in decision-making, and the capacity to set and accomplish goals has also been implicated in the development of high levels of intrinsic workplace motivation.

REVIEW QUESTIONS

1. Explain how and why an individual's perception of control can influence his or her motivation.

2. Describe the differences between intrinsic and extrinsic motivation.

3. Give an explanation of how extrinsic rewards can damage an employee's intrinsic motivation to work.

4. As a manager, how would you motivate your staff to perform at a high level for a sustained period?

5. Explain agency theory, and how it can get in the way of effective employee motivation.

6. Think back to a time in your work history in which you were highly motivated. List the factors, both internal and external, that contributed to your level of motivation.

Mind-diagram summary

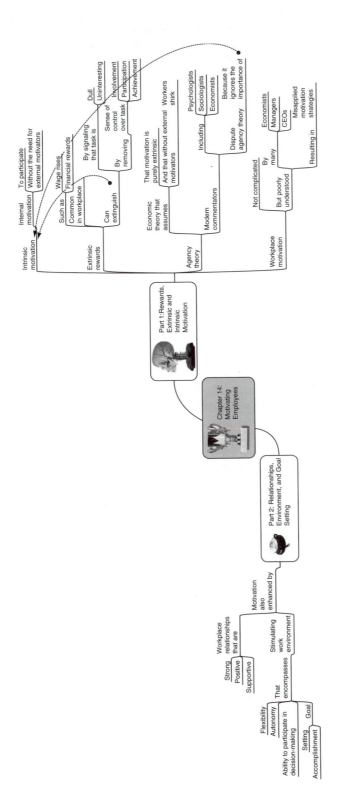

Chapter 14: Motivating Employees

Part 1: Rewards, Extrinsic and Intrinsic Motivation

- Intrinsic motivation
  - Internal motivation
  - To participate
  - Without the need for external motivators
- Extrinsic rewards
  - Such as
    - Wage rises
    - Financial rewards
  - Common in workplace
  - Can extinguish
  - By signaling that task is
    - Dull
    - Uninteresting
  - By removing
    - Sense of control over task
      - Involvement
      - Participation
      - Achievement
    - Workers shirk
- Agency theory
  - Economic theory that assumes
    - That motivation is purely extrinsic
    - And that without external motivators
  - Modern commentators
    - Including
      - Psychologists
      - Sociologists
      - Economists
    - Dispute agency theory
      - Because it ignores the importance of
- Workplace motivation
  - Not complicated
  - But poorly understood
    - By many
      - Economists
      - Managers
      - CEOs
    - Resulting in
      - Misapplied motivation strategies

Part 2: Relationships, Environment, and Goal Setting

- Motivation also enhanced by
  - Workplace relationships that are
    - Strong
    - Positive
    - Supportive
  - Stimulating work environment
    - That encompasses
      - Flexibility
      - Autonomy
      - Ability to participate in decision-making
  - Goal
    - Setting
    - Accomplishment

Enhancing Organizational Communication, Knowledge, and Learning

Introduction

A large proportion of the research and articles reviewed so far have referred to interpersonal processes in the workplace, whether between co-workers or between supervisors and subordinates. Nonetheless, many of the methods and techniques that have been recommended for enhancing and improving employee satisfaction and productivity (and consequently organizational effectiveness and financial performance) also require strong communication skills. As well, most of the techniques and recommendations we have seen require a strong ability to be able to learn effectively, and apply that learning in a practical, everyday work environment. Accordingly, this final section reviews the literature on communication and knowledge uptake and transfer in the workplace, as well as organizational and individual learning processes, practices, and models.

Section guide

In Chapter 15, "Communication, Information, Knowledge, and the Learning Organization", we will look at ways that organizations can enhance their ability to communicate, both internally and externally. As well, we will evaluate the concept of knowledge transfer, define both organizational learning and the "learning organization", and discover why both of these ideas are paramount to the success of the modern firm. In Chapter 16, "Learning and Training in the Workplace", we will examine learning at work, understand why workplace learning occurs best when people are motivated, and determine the most-effective means of increasing a person's motivation to learn, including practices such as mentoring. We will also look at the problems with formal workplace training, and examine practical means for increasing the transfer of formal learning to practical, workplace applications. Ways to enhance the effectiveness of training and the importance of informal learning practices will also be reviewed.

Reading objectives

By the end of this section you will have a better comprehension of:

- why communications practices need to be improved in most organizations
- the benefits of strong company-wide communications
- how knowledge accumulation and distribution aids organizational performance
- the concept of the "learning organization" and its relationship to individual and organizational learning
- the benefits of organizational learning practices
- learning at work, learning enhancement, and the importance of motivation to learn
- how to increase motivation to learn at work
- the importance of informal learning and the encouragement of informal communication of tacit knowledge in the workplace
- why formal training is often ineffective, despite the large amounts spent annually, and how training can be improved by encouraging learning transfer
- how workplace support and environment affect the transfer of learning.

Communication, Information, Knowledge, and the Learning Organization

Behaviour, company-wide, engagement, facilitate, hierarchical, internal, knowledge, leader, mediate, member, risk, teamwork.

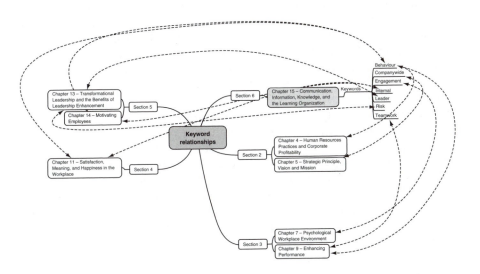

Organizational and change communication.

The majority of the information we have seen so far refers to positive organizational and individual change to enhance workplace effectiveness and productivity, and individual satisfaction and performance. However, we have also seen that, in many cases, one of the largest barriers to effective change is a lack of adequate communication skills or understanding. Consequently, this chapter is centred on communication and knowledge processes within organizations.

Part 1: Communication and knowledge

Many of the investigations and articles reviewed in this book have been concerned with the implementation of workplace change; however, according to Barrett (2002), change cannot be enacted effectively without adequate communication practices. Barrett has defined meaningful organizational communication as an interaction that is both informational and educational, and that motivates and positions people to support the strategies and goals of their organization. Consequently, according to Barrett, organizational communication must limit misunderstandings, ensuring that messages are clear and consistent, be assessed for its efficacy in an ongoing fashion, and, most importantly, encourage increased performance. Moreover, in Barrett's opinion, whenever possible, information should be communicated face-to-face, rather than through print or electronic means that are open to ready misinterpretation. According to Barrett, if management desires change both in its subordinates and within the organization, it is their responsibility to model the behaviour that they expect of employees, by providing information that is actually meaningful and relevant to the target audience and that is tailored specifically (for example, technical language for technicians, lay terms for salespeople).

The observations and recommendations of Barrett (2002) notwithstanding, unfortunately, organizational information flow is seldom clear and, therefore, often not readily understandable. In reality, communication is a complex concept that when practised effectively, embodies the mutual exchange of information between individuals, between individuals and organizations, and between and within organizations. Although, at an organizational level, communication can take many forms, it is a clear, understandable flow of information that leads to mutual understanding. Nevertheless, as Clutterbuck (2001) has pointed out, in many organizations, information often only flows one way (that is, top down) and is often confounded by conflicting communications (for example, contradictions from different departments within the same company). In Clutterbuck's opinion, without clear, concise information which flows from both the top down and the bottom up, it is very difficult for an organization to function effectively. Consequently, Clutterbuck has recommended that efforts be made to enhance common understanding throughout an organization, so that everyone has access to the same information (rather than to distorted or complicated versions), and that each person understands how his or her actions can affect the rest of the company. To achieve this state Clutterbuck has proposed six communication enhancing processes. First, leaders need to be credible by role-modelling effective communication flow. Second, it is necessary that pains be taken to raise the communication quality of an organization, both internally and externally. Third, this effectiveness needs to be assessed regularly through internal and external feedbacks. Fourth, information should not be overwhelming, and should be limited internally to only those items that are necessary; it is highly dysfunctional, for example, for workers to read upward of two-hundred e-mails daily, many of which contain versions (often conflicting or confusing) of the same information. Fifth, the benefits of effective communication need to be marketed within the organization, to individuals, and to teams, and be combined with training in communication style, efficiency and clarity; thus, for example, employees should be encouraged to filter the information they pass on to others, making sure that it is consistent and non-contradictory to the message that they are trying to send (for example, not just hitting the forward button on their e-mail client). Lastly, goals communicated to any level of the organization need to be clear and precise, so that they cannot be easily misunderstood.

Dirks and Ferrin (2001), despite agreeing with the principles of Clutterbuck (2001), have suggested that for these assumptions to be implemented, it is also necessary for employees to trust both the organization's ability to provide information effectively and one another. According to Dirks and his colleague, trust is a psychological state that represents an individual's understanding of relationships which involve risk and vulnerability. Consequently, trust becomes a moderator between how a person interprets another party's past and present actions and how he or she assesses that party's likelihood of a future behaviour. Trust, therefore, can have a substantial effect on performance, positive attitudes and perceptions, and can have a distinctly compromising effect on communication. Thus, issues of trust are of particular relevance during or following organizational actions that can affect or compromise trust, such as downsizing: if a person evaluates future organizational behaviour based on negative past or present actions, it will be difficult for that person to regain his or her trust in the organization. Based on this premise, Dirks and Ferrin have concluded that for communication to be effective, the development of trust must be a high priority in an organization, as its absence can result in increased employee anxiety, lowered performance, and a consequent reduced likelihood of clear communication.

Another method for increasing communication flow is to reduce the amount of interpersonal conflict in the workplace. Friedman, Tidd, Currall, and Tsai (2000) have pointed out that because each person in an organization has a different personality and interpersonal style, it is necessary to recognize that most people differ in their ideas regarding effective communication. According to Friedman *et al.*, this is especially relevant for those who have poor existing interpersonal styles. To improve communication, therefore, Friedman and his colleagues have suggested that the interpersonal styles necessary for successful communication, such as prosocial attitudes, high self-efficacy, and a belief in interactions in which both parties benefit (that is, win-win), be modelled by management and other influential organizational members. Further, by recognizing ineffective communicational styles, such as the avoidance of conflict, the domination of interactions, obliging, ingratiating or passive behaviour, and attributional errors in task disagreement (that is, mistaking task disagreement for personal animosity), leaders can reshape dysfunctional behaviour towards functional interaction.

IN ACTION #16

Communication practices

It takes years to learn a truly effective interpersonal communication style, but the basics are easy. Nevertheless (and not very surprisingly), most of us get them wrong consistently and, consequently, often take offence at trivial things. Moreover, we are seldom able to say what we want to, or even what we mean. At an organizational level, this problem is endemic and responsible for many day-to-day problems (Avtgis, 2000). Given these problems, there are three distinct issues to be aware of when attempting to communicate with another person. First, most people cannot distinguish between critique and criticism. This is because, in general, we have a tendency to take things personally. As soon as we hear "you" or "should", most of us feel the need to defend ourselves. This causes the first party to respond in kind, and the communication is doomed. To overcome this, try replacing the word "I", with "you", using carefully phrased statements. Generally, information can be exchanged using "I think", "I feel", and "I want" statements, without giving offence. For example: "I think that your work in general is excellent" (the person is likely to listen to this), "however, I feel a little disappointed with your participation in recent team meetings" (clear, specific and time-oriented message), "and I would like an opportunity to talk about how we can improve the discussion process; are you free at 3 pm?" (this provides a specific time to deal with the problem and potential solution), "what do you think?" (feedback). Although this type of communication feels awkward at first, with practice, it can be spontaneous and natural. Contrast it with the more typical "Your performance in the last team meeting was terrible, pull your socks up!"

A related problem in communication involves specificity: we seldom say what we mean. Consequently, rather than communicating our wants or needs in a manner that can be understood, we confuse the listener with jargon, ramble, or just plain gibberish! Try recording your next frustrating conversation (with permission from the other party of course). Listen to what you said and to how the other party responded. Try practising how the conversation could have gone had you stated your thoughts, feelings and desires in a concise and listenable manner. More importantly, make your statements precise, specific, and time related (rather than imprecise, non-specific and global). Practise with others (in a non-critical environment) and keep practising until you walk away from the majority of encounters feeling that both people got what they wanted.

The final aspect of communication is perhaps the most important: listening. Again, most of us are poor listeners, in fact, often we use the time whist the other person is talking to figure out what we're going to say next. Consequently, most people end up having two separate conversations, and both leave frustrated because they feel the other didn't listen (it's valid because they didn't). To become a better listener, take a leaf out of psychotherapy practice, and learn verbal and non-verbal listening skills. Verbal skills include the acknowledgment of what the other has said. The easiest way to do this is to paraphrase statements back to your co-worker.

This is also a great way to confirm whether you have understood or not, and encourages the other to be more precise in his or her communication. If there isn't enough specificity in the statement ask for more. For example: "You're not satisfied with my performance, and you would like me to change. Can you please tell me what, specifically, you would like to see?" Again, with practice, this can sound natural and spontaneous. As well, non-verbal listening skills make the other person feel that they are being listened to and are pretty simple. They can be summed up with the acronym SOLVER: Sit squarely; Open posture (don't cross your arms or legs); Lean forward; Verbal modulation (pay attention to the tone of what you say); Eye contact; and Reflection (try and reflect the body positioning and language of the other).

Communication entails the ability to be able to transfer information effectively. However, useful information transfer involves both the delivery and uptake of information. Ideally, within an organization, the effective transfer of knowledge (or applied information) results in a group of people who share information about a common goal: the well-being and future of the organization. Thus, organizational knowledge is the product of the transfer of knowledge between individuals, teams, and departments within an organization, and is representative of that organization's intellectual assets. Csikszentmihalyi (2003) has reported that, often, the most successful companies (in terms of both financial performance and staff satisfaction) have invested heavily in developing their intellectual assets.[25] In fact, according to McDougall and Beattie (1998), organizational learning is nothing more than the development of intellectual assets, and is, therefore, enhanced by the encouragement of individual learning; in other words, the more the employees know, the more a company knows, especially when employees are encouraged to share that knowledge.

One way in which to enhance the production and distribution of knowledge is through the development of strong relationships within the organization, between firms, and with consumers or clients. For instance, according to Lagerstrom and Andersson (2003), most firms, from SMEs to multinational organizations, have difficulty in communicating information effectively – the consequence of a complex array of issues, including geographical dispersion, hierarchical organizational levels, interdepartment rivalry, poor management, lack of communication channels, and a lack of understanding of the importance of knowledge sharing. Following their investigation of knowledge creation and sharing in a multinational organization, Lagerstrom and her colleague have emphasized the need for the creation of diverse teams, in order to overcome communications difficulties. Because the aim of these teams is to effectively distribute important information throughout the organization, Lagerstrom and Andersson have recommended that they be comprised of representatives from various parts of the organization: for example, from different countries, departments, sites, or even teams within the same site or

---

[25] Otherwise known as human capital, which we investigated in some depth in Section 2.

department. Regular meetings of these teams can help to inform members of organizational practices throughout the firm, allowing them to share qualitative information of successful and unsuccessful practices, make and receive recommendations, develop company-wide suggestions and strategies and, most importantly, to distribute this information back to their own areas, allowing information to spread throughout the firm. Cohendet, Creplet, Diani, Dupouet, and Schenk (2004) have made similar recommendations. Based on four qualitative case studies of US-based organizations, Cohendet and his colleagues have proposed that organizations encourage the formation of "knowledge-intensive communities" in order to enhance the accumulation, generalization, and distribution of organizational knowledge. Effectively, these communities represent flexible groups of like-minded individuals, who meet informally to discuss and develop ideas and share their understanding of procedures (tacit knowledge). Nonetheless, because they have no clear boundaries and no viable or explicit hierarchy, when they exist, these communities are seldom acknowledged or supported within organizations, despite, according to Cohendet *et al.*, representing powerful repositories of useful knowledge and, based on members' passion and commitment to what they do and how they do it, being able to substantially reduce an organization's costs regarding the generation and accumulation of knowledge. For instance, Cohendet *et al.* have described the example of Xerox technicians who developed an information repository for copy machine repair, based on their combined tacit knowledge. Although this repository bore virtually no resemblance to the company's official repair manuals, the knowledge gathered by experienced technicians allowed them to perform better work in less time, simply through the application of acquired understanding of best practice. Despite having no official status or support this knowledge community directly benefited the company through more effective, quicker, and less costly repairs. Consequently, knowledge-intensive communities can allow firms to access and even codify the tacit knowledge of their experienced workers, merely by allowing and encouraging their regular interaction. However, because there are no formal rules governing the development of knowledge-intensive communities, they tend to be held together based on their members' passion, commitment, and shared trust, all of which can be easily damaged through organizational interference. Accordingly, Cohendet and his coinvestigators believe that management should encourage both the frequency of interactions and the intensity of communications of these informal groups, to better enhance knowledge expansion and distribution within the organization.

Benavides Espinosa, Urquidi Martin, and Roig Dobon (2003) have expanded on the recommendations of Lagerstrom and Andersson (2003), and Cohendet *et al.* (2004), by espousing the creation of knowledge-sharing communities not just within but also between organizations. According to Benavides Espinosa *et al.*, in organizations, knowledge represents the accumulation of know-how, reasoning and understanding, and is more effectively obtained and transferred when organizations collaborate, not only with other like-minded firms but also with universities and other research organizations. Effectively, this allows for the creation of knowledge networks through strategic alliances; by sharing information with compatible organizations, a firm gains access to knowledge not readily available in the public domain. Following their investigation of work practices, job training, organizational networking, and outside collaboration practices among 977 Californian employees (representing employees from 1 per cent of all Californian firms that employ over 20 people), Erickson and Jacoby (2003) have reached a similar conclusion. Based on their findings, Erickson and his coauthor believe that because modern firms rely largely on knowledge accumulation, transfer and application to remain innovative in a knowledge-based economy, the most effective method for obtaining and distributing knowledge is through the development of social, inter-organizational, and professional networks. According to Erickson and Jacoby, these networks represent the voluntary collaboration and exchange of information among individuals, groups and organizations, enhance access to knowledge, and promote trust, norms of reciprocity or social capital, and incentives for further knowledge sharing. Moreover, professional networking allows for the creation of skills vital to trading knowledge necessary to increase innovation, implementation and results, especially when this information is not readily available to most organizations. Thus, based on their findings that managerial participation in multiple social and professional networks resulted in greater and more intense adoption of high-performance work practices, more effective employee-training programmes, and better company reorganization (resulting in better innovative and financial performance in the firm), Erickson and his coinvestigator have recommend that managers be encouraged to and rewarded for their participation in professional networks outside of the organization.

Another way of enhancing effective knowledge transfer is by utilizing the resources of a firm's clients or customers. Jeppesen and Molin (2003), citing the examples of consumer-led development in software gaming companies, have pointed out that especially in technological or information-based organizations, the end-users (particularly expert users) of a given product or service are likely to possess a great deal of knowledge about how it might be improved. Moreover, because many of these users are often involved in the enhancement or ongoing development of a product or service, and because the results of this development can be obtained by the organization at little or no cost, this population represents a massive organizational asset. Consequently, in Jeppesen and Molin's opinions, firms that have a client base that includes expert users should invest in tools and mechanisms (such as setting up online communities, development tools, and feedback channels) for accessing and utilizing this knowledge base.

Part 2: The learning organization

Although there are several systems for acquiring and distributing knowledge in firms, in recent years researchers and practitioners have popularized the notion of the "learning organization", in which the firm itself is designed around methods for enhancing the uptake and flow of knowledge. Yang, Watkins, and Marsick (2004), for instance, following their investigation of the experiences of 836 employees from multiple US firms have defined the "learning organization" as a firm or other collective that espouses systems thinking and a learning, strategic and integrative perspective. More specifically, they have described the learning organization as one in which there is a predisposition towards collaboration, adaptive capacity, and an orientation towards future sustainability. Consequently, the learning organization incorporates team learning, emphasizing the learning activities of groups rather than focussing on the rules that define team functioning; shared visions of the future, encouraging employee commitment and programme enrolment rather than just compliance; and the ability to see interrelationships, rather than simply linear, cause–effect chains of association. Moreover, Yang *et al.* have suggested that, to enhance firm-wide learning, organizations must focus on facilitating the continuous learning of all its members, and on understanding the mechanisms for encouraging this learning. This can be achieved through a learning approach to strategy (that is, examining past approaches, and the efforts of competitors, and learning from their successes and failures), participative policymaking, rewarding flexibility, encouraging experimentation and self-development, teamwork and cooperation, and developing the ability to transfer knowledge across organizational boundaries.

Following the development of their model of organizational learning, Mulholland, Zdrahal, Domnigue, and Hatala (2001) have highlighted the aspects most likely to enhance an organization's ability to encourage company-wide learning. According to these authors, unlike the traditional, regimented team structures found in most hierarchical firms, the majority of organizational learning is social in nature and occurs primarily within informal communities of practice (cf. knowledge-intensive communities), which, as Cohendet *et al.* (2004) pointed out, do not necessarily have a formal team structure. Consequently, because social, informal engagement between employees is collaborative by nature, to encourage organizational learning the organization must first promote an open, collaborative environment. Further, because it is valuable for a firm to have highly knowledgeable and proficient employees, it makes sense that an organization would advance the development of this expertise through a commitment to the effective dissemination of knowledge between employees, groups and, potentially, other organizations. In this vein, Mulholland and his coauthors have described three levels of organizational learning. The first, individual learning, encompasses the increasing development of professional workers so as to encourage the growth of tacit knowledge and skills that increase employees' abilities to perform in their work roles. By encouraging the expansion and use of implicit knowledge, organizations can develop what Mulholland *et al.* describe as "reflection in action", or the ability to codify tacit knowledge by generating and modifying templates from the observation of actions guided by tacit knowledge, in order to make this knowledge explicitly available throughout the organization. This, is turn, guides group learning, in which the organization encourages the formation of knowledge communities, independent of formal, structured teams, in which members meet to discuss, disseminate, and develop group tacit knowledge, and which can then be imported into conventional teams to help guide practice, strategy, and action. Lastly, organizational learning describes the process of the transmission of knowledge across departments or regional offices, and even between collaborating organizations. Again, the informal development of tacit knowledge, and its use as a conduit for developing explicit, easily transmissible information, serves as a guide for organizational-level strategy and action, using expert knowledge to generate direction and innovation. In other words, by harnessing the tacit knowledge (or human capital) of its expert employees, an organization can learn how to approach complex situations, innovate, compete, and become sustainable, and allow this learning to guide more-effective action.

The use of tacit knowledge to guide organizational learning has also been highlighted by Jorgensen (2004). According to Jorgensen, the emerging global knowledge economy has placed increasing emphasis on the need for individuals to work collaboratively, and the creation of synergistic partnerships within and between organizations in order to facilitate a coordinated, competitive effort. This human-centred attitude suggests that the development of human and social capital is vital for organizational success, so approaches that encourage employee learning, collaboration and participation become prerequisites to effective business practice. Unfortunately, as Jorgensen has pointed out, and as we will see below in our discussion of workplace training, most contemporary firms are only focussed on employee development through formal training programmes that address short-term needs and functional responsibilities, with a distinct preference for codified, explicit knowledge that can be written down and measured. Besides the difficulty of transferring training to the workplace,[26] this approach also limits the development of employee expertise and proficiency, because it fails to recognize the value, or encourage the development of tacit knowledge. In fact, based on his review of the literature, Jorgensen has shown that tacit knowledge is best developed through the real-world application of explicit knowledge (such as manuals or formal training), resulting in expert knowledge: the fusion of knowing, know-how, and reflection, and constructed through application and social interactions in order to evaluate, share, and improve on one's experiences by attempting to apply knowledge in the real world. Moreover, because tacit knowledge cannot be readily codified, expertise, the result of tacit knowledge development, is not easily transmitted through formal training, instead, requiring both cooperation and interaction in a real-world setting. Consequently, to develop tacit knowledge, collaboration becomes substantially more important than conventional training, and requires that managers shift their focus from the management of people to the management of ideas, information, and innovation, encouraging expert collaboration between their subordinates by taking on coaching, mentoring, and counselling roles. With these factors in mind, Jorgensen has proposed a model of effective organizational learning and effective work that stimulates tacit knowledge development through the accumulation of social and human capital, leadership that encourages learning, a commitment to life-long learning, an organic organization based around knowledge communities, substantial employee participation and engagement, coupled with autonomy, and a tolerant culture that recognizes

---

[26] See the section entitled "Workplace Training and Transfer of Learning" below.

diversity and individual needs. In contrast, barriers to organizational learning include managerial styles that lack trust; low levels of workforce participation, including little room for worker discretion, innovation, or learning; just-in-time training geared towards short-term needs without focussing on the long-term requirements of individuals and the organization; and time scarcity, eschewing individual learning because of managerial and organizational demands, a tight work schedule, and the competing pressures of work and home life.

In a more-focussed article, Cho (2002) has reported on the strong relationship between organizational behaviour that encourages self-directed learning (that is, learning that is undertaken and completed informally and under the auspices and direction of the individual) and the creation of organizational learning activity. According to Cho, most self-directed learning opportunities at work take place in a social context through interaction with others (much like Jorgensen's (2004) transmission of tacit knowledge). Moreover, Cho has reported that employees with a greater propensity towards self-directed learning are more likely to recognize the importance of interaction with others in order to guide learning, and so naturally collaborate with their colleagues to enhance learning outcomes. Consequently, the act of informal, collaborative interaction encourages the dissemination of knowledge through the organization. Thus, interestingly, although self-directed learning is normally undertaken for reasons of personal growth or interest, rather than for the development of the organization, the behaviour of self-directed learners is directly in line with the requirements for a learning organization: the creation of learning strategies based on interaction with others and the environment through inquiry, dialogue, collaboration, and team learning, and the encouragement of an environment in which these learning strategies are openly promoted. In other words, according to Cho, when an organization encourages individuals to direct their own learning experiences and to collaborate informally during their learning, it also increases the learning behaviour of the organization as a whole, by encouraging the transmission and accumulation of tacit knowledge and its use as a guide for organizational action.

The benefits of informal and self-directed learning notwithstanding, as we have seen, most workplaces are not particularly geared towards integrating learning with the everyday practices at work. Ellstrom (2001) has addressed this issue in his review of the integration of work and learning, in which he has defined organizational learning as "changes in organizational practices (including routines and procedures, structures, technologies, systems, and so on) that are mediated through individual learning or problem solving processes". In other words, like Cho (2002), Ellstrom believes that organizational learning is dependent on accumulated individual learning. Consequently, according to Ellstrom, to successfully integrate learning and work, five critical factors need to be addressed. First, the learning potential of each task should be increased by raising task complexity and variety. However, giving employees the opportunity to engage in greater task variety must be mediated by also increasing an individual's perception of his or her ability to complete a task through the development of knowledge levels and self-efficacy; once a person believes that he or she is capable, he or she can identify and take advantage of objective working conditions (like increased project variety). One way to achieve broader, task-integrated roles with greater learning potential is by redesigning jobs so that they incorporate a wider range of activities and access (Ellstrom); however, this also requires organizational restructuring, reducing the verticality of hierarchical work structures, so that positions are more horizontal and wide ranging. The second critical factor in achieving integration between learning and work is the development of opportunities for feedback, evaluation, and reflection on the outcomes of one's work activities. In Ellstrom's opinion, learning only occurs when people are supplied with information about the results of their actions, so the provision of useful, timely, and action-oriented feedback can help employees understand how to improve their work. Third, it is important that a balance be found between formalization of work processes and flexibility in work roles, actions and discretionary abilities. For instance, bureaucratic rules can limit the latitude or scope of employees to carry out tasks, find solutions, or innovate; however, standardization can help in efforts to codify and distribute tacit knowledge. Consequently, it is necessary to find equilibrium between regulated processes that help learning and knowledge distribution, and flexible systems that allow employees a greater scope of action. Fourth, it is crucial that employees be allowed and encouraged to participate both in handling problems and developing work processes. As most workplace learning is experiential,[27] dealing with errors, disturbances, and problems at work is vital for learning to occur. Likewise, allowing employees to contribute their expertise towards developing innovative systems is more likely to increase interest, motivation, and engagement, and to encourage rapid learning through collaborative interaction with others. Finally, integrating learning and work requires a set of working conditions that encourage learning. For example, thought needs to be given to increasing employee access to adequate learning resources, including objective factors (like enough time to participate in formal education, and time to reflect, observe, think, and exchange knowledge informally with others), and subjective factors, such as a readiness to learn, and sufficient knowledge of a task to warrant curiosity about improving knowledge in that area. In other words, if employees do not have the conceptual tools or satisfactory explicit knowledge regarding a given task, it will be hard for them to identify or interpret their experiences on that task in a way that increases their tacit knowledge (that is, in a way that allows them to learn, and increase their ability to perform). Consequently, Ellstrom has concluded that the learning potential of a given job is a function of these five factors, noting the different motivations, confidences and abilities of individual employees and, equally importantly, the organizational design in which they have to work; strictly hierarchical organizations leave little flexibility for job and task diversity, or for the creativity and free thinking that leads to ongoing innovation.

In their empirical investigation of organizational learning, Kontoghiorghes, Awbrey, and Feurig (2005) have distinguished between organizational learning (with its focus on individual learning, viewing knowledge as individually based)

---

[27] See the section below on "Learning and Motivation to Learn" for a more in-depth discussion of why most workplace learning happens on the job rather than in the classroom.

and the notion of the learning organization (in which organizational focus is shifted to learning at individual, group, and organizational levels, and in which the firm facilitates the learning of all its members, continuously transforming itself). Consequently, according to Kontoghiorghes *et al.*, a learning organization is defined by its ability to allow and inspire open communication, risk taking, support and recognition for learning, resources to perform, teamwork, rewards for learning, a learning environment, and ongoing management of knowledge. To further investigate the dimensions most important for successful integration of learning in the organization, Kontoghiorghes and his coinvestigators examined the responses of 579 employees in a US automotive firm on measures of learning transfer and learning behaviour within the organization. They found that learning organizations were better able to adapt to change, quickly introduce new products and services, and perform better financially than more-traditional firms, especially when they devoted substantial resources to developing a culture of trust, experimentation, flexibility and teamwork, and employee participation; encouraged open communication, sharing of information, risk taking and the promotion of new ideas; and made resources to affect these actions readily available.

IN ACTION #17

Developing organization learning

Organizational learning happens when conditions are put in place to encourage both individual learning and company-wide communication. Basically, because organizations are the sum of their constituent members, the more that each individual knows, the more knowledge is held by the organization. Moreover, corporations that make it easy for employees to share this knowledge without limitations tend to find themselves with a vast pool of readily accessible intellectual resources. It's very important, therefore, to understand that one of the most important roles for organizational leaders is to develop system that allow people to master their skills and to learn new ones, and then to pass these abilities on to others.

The instinctive solution to problems of organizational learning is to implement training programmes. However, if employees aren't motivated to learn, all the training programmes in the world won't help. There are two main problems with most workplace training. First, workers seldom have a say in the type of training that they get. Decisions regarding training needs are usually made by upper management, often on "expert" advice. Unfortunately, when employees aren't asked what they need and, instead, are given what management think they need, there's little chance of learning actually occurring. In the employee's eyes, the training will represent another attempt at managerial influence over what he or she does, and could be perceived as a slight on his or her abilities. However, if the training is of interest to employees (because they have chosen it based on what they need) they will be much more motivated to learn. Second, many workplace training initiatives take the form of workshops or seminars, outside of the regular workspace (that is, not where the employee actually does his or her job). Whilst this saves money, both in terms of the trainer's and employees' time, it does not take place in a real environment and is, by definition, generalized. Therefore, for an employee to put his or her new ideas into practice, he or she needs to extrapolate from a hypothetical situation to an everyday environment. Unless this process is backed up by a sympathetic coach (for example, his or her supervisor) who has expert knowledge in its implementation, it's highly unlikely that the skills presented during training will actually be put into practice. Further, the employee might not have access to the time, tools, resources or information needed to apply new behaviours. Consequently, many companies spend large amounts of money on training that makes little or no difference, simply because there is no way for the new knowledge to be realized, let alone passed on.

A solution lies in making it possible for people to learn in-situ, in real time, and with adequate resources, support and follow-up information. This is more expensive in the short term, but much more efficacious in the longer term because it actually allows employees to learn new things. Once a person feels competent in a new skill, he or she will also feel more confident to teach it to others, spreading knowledge throughout the organization. As well, by finding out what employees actually need before imposing mandatory training, organizations find that workers will be more motiated to participate in their training, will take more away, and will try harder to implement the suggested changes.

In a similar investigation, Ellinger, Ellinger, Yang, and Howton (2002), who compared financial indicators against the learning-based responses of 400 mid-level managers in several US manufacturing firms, reported a strong, positive relationship between organizational learning and organizational performance. Specifically, they found that when firms promoted continuous learning opportunities, inquiry and dialogue, and collaboration and team learning; developed systems to capture and share tacit knowledge; empowered employees to work towards a collective company vision; and supported leadership that modelled support and learning at an individual and team level, there was a significantly greater likelihood of positive financial performance than in comparable, non-learning organizations. Ellinger and her colleagues have cited their findings as strong evidence for the business case of the learning organization, but warn against attempts to apply learning practices without adequate research into, or understanding of, effective practice. To do so, they caution, is to undermine the legitimacy of learning-organizational benefits by encouraging snake-oil interventions, pushed by poorly qualified consultants and other "experts", and that will have, in all likelihood, little lasting benefit.

With Ellinger *et al.*'s (2002) counsel in mind and given a lack of information on precisely what to look for when attempting to make organizational changes that affect greater learning, Ortenblad (2004) has outlined four types of learning organizations, each of which has benefits for certain types of firms. The first, labelled the "learning-at-work organization", is a relatively simple process in which learning is encouraged in the workplace through both formal and informal programmes. However, because learning and knowledge are context dependent and because it is difficult to transfer knowledge from formal training to actual practice,[28] Ortenblad has suggested that this type of system, whilst better than nothing, is lacking because there is no integration between formal and informal learning. The second type, the "organizational-learning organization", in which knowledge created by structured processes for continuous improvement of existing routines and the evaluation and questioning of work processes, is considered ideal from a management perspective, because managers control the way in which employees are encouraged to learn and apply that learning. Nevertheless, what is ideal from a management perspective is not necessarily best for the organization, especially when managerial practices limit the expansion or development of organizational learning and knowledge. A better system, according to Ortenblad, is a "learning climate" in which there are no set rules for how systems are questioned or developed or for how people should learn. Rather, the organization sets a climate that facilitates individual learning and the sharing of knowledge by providing resources, time, and space for employees to interact and collaborate informally. Put another way, much like the suggestions of Cho (2002) and Ellstrom (2001), Ortenblad's learning climate allows organizational learning to occur because the organization actively encourages individuals to take time to enhance their expertise and to share this knowledge with co-workers, resulting in greater proficiency, an accumulation of human capital, and greater organizational performance. Lastly, Ortenblad has outlined a "learning structure" in which an organization's hierarchy is replaced with a more organic, flexible structure, based around the precept that learning is a precondition for flexibility. In this scenario, the organization is decentralized, employees work in flexible teams, and decision-making is based on interaction between these teams. Nevertheless, this flexibility can, according to Ortenblad, result in a certain level of organizational chaos or anarchy and, to be effective, requires that the firm be small and well integrated, with excellent communication abilities. Nevertheless, in an already turbulent environment, such as those in which many consulting firms operate, a flexible learning structure can allow an organization to be highly innovative, reflexive, and responsive to changing market needs and, consequently, remain highly competitive under challenging economic conditions.

In summary, for organizations to become places in which learning is both encouraged and developed so that the employees' experience, proficiencies, and tacit knowledge can be used to enhance organizational performance, an environment conducive to informal collaboration is essential. Because workplace learning is predominantly informal and given the social nature of effective knowledge sharing, a learning organization requires active support for learning in the objective form of time, support, and resources, and in the subjective form represented by individuals who feel confident to learn, and apply their learning to their work roles. Consequently, managers who encourage flexibility, autonomy, and delegation and who behave in a coaching or mentoring role can

---

[28] Again, see the section below entitled "Workplace Training and the Transfer of Learning" for more information on why formal training is seldom effective in actual work conditions.

increase the likelihood of a successful learning environment and the lucrative application of organizational knowledge substantially.

Best practice: Case examples of how it's being done

Communication and knowledge

In his case study of effective communications and knowledge transfer practices, Pollitt (2000) has highlighted the recent actions of AT&T, Microsoft, and IBM. According to Pollitt, given their increasing need for highly skilled knowledge workers and faced with a shortage of young, qualified candidates, these organizations have started investing in the US education system in order to provide a potential future stream of employees. For example, AT&T, a large telecommunications firm, provide free Internet access and web-based training to schools, as well as grants to help teachers better understand and communicate new technology. Similarly, Microsoft has trialled a system to allow students and teachers free and continuous access to the Internet, especially with regard to online interaction between students, educators, parents, and the larger community. Moreover, IBM's "Wired for Learning" programme allows parents to communicate directly with their children's teachers, examine completed and evaluated assignments, and compare their child's progress against others in his or her class, school, and state. Pollitt believes that these attempts, although motivated by the need for new talent in the workplaces, are an excellent representation of organizations collaborating positively with the community at large. In the same vein, Pollitt has also described the case of Maytag, a large US appliance manufacturer who, for some time, have had trouble attracting qualified knowledge workers to their central offices in Iowa. As a consequence, Maytag set up a collaborative programme with Iowa State University, providing funding, buildings, and other resources to offer a local four-year engineering degree, with a large proportion of graduates from this programme recruited directly to Maytag. This community investment by Maytag has not only increased the knowledge infrastructure of the firm, but also encouraged local community development, increasing Maytag's organizational profile. In fact, according to Pollitt, the development of, or collaboration with, universities is an increasingly large part of corporate practice in the United States, with estimates that by 2010, corporate universities could outnumber traditional US universities. Pollitt believes that by investing heavily in ties with educational institutions, corporations not only provide themselves with ready access to well-trained knowledge workers, but also remain innovative by obtaining access to the latest research produced at the university. Given that, in information technology, there is an enormous amount of knowledge turnover, it is absolutely necessary for an innovative organization to be at the forefront of R&D; moreover, the academic freedoms associated with universities tend to allow a broader, more lateral research scope than traditional R&D departments. As Pollitt has pointed out, Sun Microsystems typically generate over 75 per cent of their revenue from products that are less than two years old, requiring an enormous amount of R&D spending to develop effective new products. Nevertheless, following the development of their own corporate university, they were able to increase their innovative ability dramatically, allowing them to compete more effectively whilst simultaneously reducing R&D costs.

The learning organization

Griggs and Hyland (2003) have pointed out that in countries with a high wage market and a lack of governmental support for specific industries, there is an increasing demand on organizations to provide better products and services but at an increasingly lowered cost. Because they cannot compete directly with organizations in low-wage countries, high-wage firms must learn how to continue to provide high-quality products and services without alienating their workforce. Consequently, given the increasing need for highly educated, skilled employees, any action that increases the likelihood of employee turnover is likely to reduce company survivability. This is especially true in smaller countries with a highly educated workforce who suffer from "brain drain", in which the most knowledgeable and desirable employees are enticed overseas by the promise of better pay and conditions. According to Griggs and his coinvestigator, the learning organization, which encourages increased individual development alongside enhanced communication and the accumulation and utilization of valuable human capital, represents an effective way to encourage employees to remain with the firm. Because the notion of a learning organization requires that employees be nurtured in order to increase their value to the firm, practices such as downsizing become anathema, because of the possibility of an irreversible loss of human capital. With these principles in mind, Griggs and Hyland have described the learning practices of an Australian aerospace manufacturing firm, which competes directly with overseas organizations, many of which have actively attempted to recruit the firm's key employees. According to Griggs and Hyland, following a downsizing programme in the mid-1990s, the organization lost a substantial portion of its knowledge base, a problem that was highlighted by increased production demands several years later, during which the organization realized that many of its key workers had either been let go or had been headhunted by competing firms. Realizing its vulnerability, the firm has since been making efforts to increase its attractiveness to its existing employees by recognizing the value of their knowledge and skills. Unable to attract the necessary number of replacement staff, the company attempted the introduction of flexible work teams, in which multi-skilled employees were moved from low- to high-demand projects, which was extended in order to multi-skill both technical and managerial staff. Consequently, through collaboration with a local university, the company began to offer in-house postgraduate training in management and technical skills specifically geared to the employees' and company's needs. A focus of this training was the encouragement of intra-organizational teamwork and the creation of organizational enthusiasm for learning, and the critical questioning and innovation that stemmed from the application of that learning. Simultaneously, attempts were made to capture and formalize the informal and tacit knowledge inherent in the practices of skilled employees: a direct attempt by senior management to understand and apply the firm's accumulated human capital. According to Griggs and Harvey, the main consequences of the company's actions included the increased ability to maintain and utilize human capital, the consistent accumulation and codification of new human capital, and the increased ability for employees both to understand the firm's needs and to communicate problems to management in a way that could be acted upon. As a consequence the firm has reportedly been able to increase its innovative abilities, allowing it to compete successfully with its foreign opposition.

Points for action: Practical recommendations for change

The learning organization

Wenger (1996) has made the following recommendations for optimizing organizational learning through informal knowledge communities, in which like-minded employees meet informally to discuss and apply ideas, and enhance and share their tacit knowledge:

- View learning as work and working as learning. Learning appears in many contexts, resulting in many opportunities to learn that might not be recognized in a traditional context. When everyday work situations can be viewed as learning opportunities, the organization and its employees can increase learning dramatically.

- Informal learning is more likely to result in benefits than formal learning. Because of the large number of potential informal learning opportunities, and because informal learning occurs alongside actual work, it is extremely important that an organization encourage situations that enhance informal learning, such as informal collaboration.

- Because informal learning often takes place in informal communities, it is important that all employees have access to these communities. For instance, if a female manager is excluded from networks because of her gender, she will not be able to learn from community interaction in the workplace. Consequently, it is necessary to identify any blocks to workplace participation in these communities.

- Learning should match practice as much as possible. Because informal learning communities are often concerned with the sharing and development of tacit knowledge and its real-life application, it is important that any formalized learning follow a similar pattern: the application of theory in everyday, work-based situations.

- Communities of practice should be treated as assets. Because informal learning communities are often based on mutual interest and the desire to improve performance, they are extremely important for the development of innovative ideas and practices that are of direct benefit to the organization. Encouraging their formation and collaboration should be a priority.

- Because participation in knowledge communities is usually voluntary, it is important to reward members for their involvement above and beyond their regular work remuneration.

- Generate mechanisms for ideas and innovations developed in communities of practice to be utilized. If the fruits of informal learning need to be formalized before they can be accepted or used in everyday work situations, it is unlikely that they will be developed, and the community will reduce its organizational input. Consequently, by making it easy for knowledge communities to apply their ideas, managers are harvesting valuable human capital.

- Recognize that the informal learning within knowledge communities does not always look like work. Despite the value of ideas and innovations developed in informal gatherings, managers often see these interactions as time away from "real work". When managers encourage constructive, informal collaboration, they are enhancing organizational learning by allowing the dissemination and development of tacit knowledge within the firm.

- Recognize that new practices emerging from knowledge communities might, at first, appear to be unrelated or incompatible with current practices. However, given time, these new ideas could dramatically alter the effectiveness of a given system or method. Consequently, it is important that managers allow time for new ideas to show their merit.

- Encourage interaction between separate knowledge communities. Although knowledge communities are informal and flexible, they are often limited to the interests of their members. By encouraging interaction between groups, when ideas that were of little value in isolation are exposed to different ways of thinking, they can grow to become valuable organizational contributions.

- Allow informal learning communities to direct their own learning. If groups of employees are interested in learning new skills, make sure they have the resources to access the information they require, and the time to learn and apply their learning to everyday work.

- Let employees know that their learning efforts are appreciated, and that they are enhancing the organization through their learning efforts.

Similarly, Smith (1999) has highlighted the importance of collaborative learning among individuals for successful organizational learning. In the model developed by Smith, collaborative learning occurs in the context of regular work through the evaluation of one's efforts. Simply put, an employee carries out his or her everyday role as usual, but is then encouraged to observe the results and effectiveness of their performance. The key to learning more about a role and developing ways to improve it comes from thinking about the results of a given action, especially through informal collaboration with co-workers, a supervisor, a mentor, or outside agents; and through developing "enablers" or, simply, anything that can help to improve performance. According to Smith, enablers can include a particular understanding, new knowledge, activities, attributes or capabilities that enhance an employee's ability to carry out his or her work roles. For example, through informal interaction with others, an employee might learn a new skill or simply utilize another person's knowledge or expertise to help simplify or clarify his or her own work. Once these enablers have been developed, Smith has suggested that employees be given the opportunity to apply them in a real-life situation, and then modify them in order to optimize their effectiveness.

Put concisely, Smith's (1999) model suggests that:

- Employees be able to see the direct and ongoing results of their efforts, with access to useful and meaningful critique.

- Employees be given time to evaluate and think about these results, especially with regard to how their actions could be improved to better their performance.

- Employees be encouraged to interact informally with other workers or other agents within or outside of the organization, to discuss their actions (and feedback from those actions) and to develop strategies for improving performance.

- Lastly, employees be given the opportunity to apply their ideas, strategies, skills or knowledge in an attempt to improve the outcomes of their everyday work roles. It is important that they be supported during this process, and encouraged to expand on and modify this application so that it can be optimized. By improving their performance, they effectively increase the performance of the organization.

Based on his literature review, Goh (2003) has drawn attention to five characteristics and management practices that are vital for effective organizational learning. These include:

- *The clarity of organizational mission and vision.* Both the firm and each of its units must have a clear and well-described mission. Moreover, employees need to understand this mission and how what they do in their work roles contributes towards its realization. By building a shared vision, in which employees are encouraged to help the organization reach its future goals, Goh believes that employees are stimulated to learn in order to enhance their ability to actuate the firm's mission. This occurs because employees are able to comprehend the gap between the vision and the organization's current state, and are therefore better able to attempt to narrow this gap.

- *Leadership commitment and empowerment.* Like the concepts we reviewed in Section 5, Goh suggests that leaders must be committed to organizational learning in order for it to occur. Moreover, through accessibility and accountability, leaders must be a part of this learning climate, and help to use mistakes and failures as part of an ongoing programme of learning. In effect, the organization becomes an active field experiment, in which variables are assessed and modifications made, based on experiences with these variables. Consequently, the organization becomes dynamic, learning continuously by interacting with its environment. Within this framework, employees are empowered to make decisions and take measured risks.

- *Experimentation and rewards.* Again, using the analogy of a field experiment, an organization can encourage its members to be experimental in their thinking and actions: by trying new things based on previous performance, and refining actions so that they become more effective, a company is able to continue to compete. Reward systems that recognize innovation and risk taking further encourage this behaviour, as does the freedom to experiment with new techniques and ideas, and the support and resources to apply them in an everyday context.

- *Effective transfer of knowledge.* Knowledge is only transferred when communication is clear, concise, and focussed. It is also important that commutation crosses internal boundaries, such as departments and teams, so that the entire organization is aware of the firm's requirements, and that the organization be able to take note of and act on external demands, such as customer or client feedback, or the actions of competitors.

- *Teamwork and group problem solving.* Collaboration between individuals, especially in an informal context must be encouraged and supported. Moreover, the organization needs to put into place structures that allow individuals to collaborate and communicate easily and effectively, so that employees are better able to solve problems and improve effectiveness without relying on senior management. Teamwork and collaboration help knowledge transfer, and allow for better understanding of the organization as a whole.

Finally, and perhaps most importantly, Harris (2002) has pointed out that whilst the ideas behind the learning organization are important and necessary for continued organizational development, it is also necessary that firms actually learn from their mistakes. Citing her investigation of organizational learning in financial institutions, Harris has shown that in many institutions, the organization was unable to learn from errors, but instead encountered the same problems time and time again. One reason for this oversight is the inappropriate use of resources. For example, Harris reported that in one company, whilst considerable resources were given over to IT projects, there were little or no resources allocated to the measurement of the effectiveness of the new programmes or for analysis of why problems had occurred and how they could be corrected in the future. Moreover, in several organizations, project leaders were regularly changed, so that their successors were placed in their new position without prior experience or coaching, leading to them making the same mistakes as their predecessors. As well, according to Harris, organizations are often prone to introducing innovations in one area of the firm, especially those areas that are performing poorly, but failing to extend the lessons learnt through this application to other areas or departments until they also fail to perform. This "band-aid" approach does little to encourage organizational learning or the spread of communication between departments. Consequently, Harris has recommended that organizations take pains to carefully analyse the consequences of changes or innovations, and then apply the lessons learnt from these interventions to future situations, or apply lateral solutions to other parts of the organization.

Summary

Organizational communication represents the mutual exchange of information between individuals. Clear, effective communication is extremely important to the successful functioning of any organization, consequently, every effort should be made to minimize misunderstandings, ensure that messages are clear and consistent, and make sure that communication is (where possible) face to face and two way. Nevertheless, in many organizations, communication is seldom clear or understandable, and often only flows one way (that is, top down). As a result, one way to enhance organizational communication is to provide training in order to reduce interpersonal conflict, especially between workers and supervisors, and among colleagues.

Organizational knowledge can be described as the accumulation of intellectual assets and human capital, and the effective transfer of that knowledge between groups of people who share a common goal. Organizational knowledge development is increased through the development of strong relationships: within organizations through the development of diverse teams to spread information throughout the organization and through the encouragement of knowledge communities, in which like-minded employees interact informally to develop repositories of tacit knowledge; between firms, by encouraging relationships with other like-minded organizations, and with universities and other research institutions; and with clients, who can represent a very useful expert user group with specific knowledge of a firm's products or services.

"Learning organization" is a term applied to firms that are designed around methods for enhancing knowledge uptake and flow. Learning organizations have a predisposition towards collaboration, adaptive capability, and an orientation towards future sustainability. Three levels of organizational learning have been described. The first, individual learning, represents the encouragement of individual skills and the development of tacit knowledge. Second, group learning, is the interaction of individuals, often informally, to discuss, disseminate, and develop their abilities in order to utilize group tacit knowledge and guide practice, strategy, and action. Third is organizational learning, defined as the transmission of group and individual knowledge across departments, regional offices, and between collaborating organizations.

Organizational learning is enhanced by informal and social interaction between individuals with a focus on tacit knowledge and through self-directed learning, in which informal learning is directed by the individual and takes place in a social context (encouraging the transmission of tacit knowledge and creating an environment for knowledge sharing). Moreover, the integration of learning and work can greatly enhance an organization's ability to develop knowledge. Actions that enhance organizational learning include the redesign of jobs to incorporate a wider range of activities and information access; development of regular opportunities for feedback, evaluation, and reflection on the outcomes of work activities; a balance between work formalization and flexibility in work roles; encouraging employees to participate in handling work problems and developing workplace practices; the development of conditions that support learning, such as recognition of learning achievements, access to adequate resources, and time to think, reflect, observe and exchange knowledge with others; and support for continuous, on-the-job learning opportunities.

REVIEW QUESTIONS

1. List three ways in which you could improve communication in the workplace, explaining why they would be effective.

2. Describe the process of interdepartmental and interorganizational collaboration and examine how it can enhance knowledge uptake and distribution.

3. Explain "knowledge-intensive communities" and highlight how they are valuable for the transmission of tacit knowledge.

4. Describe the "learning organization" and investigate how organizational learning contributes to the functioning of a learning organization.

5. Outline the concept of tacit knowledge, and explain how you would harness its effective use to guide organizational learning.

6. Explain why organizational learning is often dependent on individual learning.

Mind-diagram summary

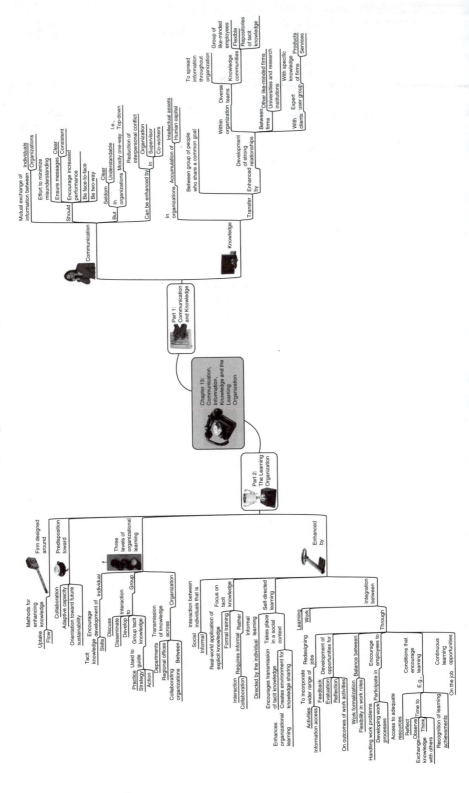

Chapter 15: Communication, Information, Knowledge and the Learning Organization

Part 1: Communication and Knowledge

Communication

Mutual exchange of information between

- Individuals
- Organizations

Should
- Effort to minimize misunderstanding
  - Clear
  - Consistent
- Ensure messages
- Encourage increased performance
  - Be face-to-face
  - Be two-way

But
- Seldom
- Clear
- Understandable
- In organizations
- Mostly one-way
- Top-down

Can be enhanced by
- Reduction of interpersonal conflict
- In Organization
  - Supervisor
  - Co-workers

Knowledge

In organizations
- Accumulation of Intellectual assets
  - Human capital

- Development of strong relationships
  - Between group of people who share a common goal

Transfer
Enhanced of by
- To spread information throughout organization
  - Group of like-minded employees
  - Knowledge communities
    - Flexible
    - Repositories of tacit knowledge

- Within
- Diverse organization teams

- Between
  - Other like-minded firms
  - Universities and research institutions
  - With specific knowledge of firms

- With
  - Expert clients
  - user group of firms
    - Products
    - Services

Part 2: The Learning Organization

- Firm designed around
- Predisposition toward

Methods for enhancing knowledge
- Uptake
- Flow

- Collaboration
- Adaptive capacity
- Orientation toward future sustainability

Three levels of organizational learning
- Encourage development of
  - Individual
  - Group
  - Organization

- Tacit knowledge Skills
  - Discuss
  - Disseminate
  - Develop
  - Interaction to
  - Group tacit knowledge

- Strategy
- Practice
- Action
- Used to guide

- Transmission of knowledge across
  - Departments
  - Regional offices

- Collaborating organizations
- Between

Enhanced by

- Social
- Informal
- Interaction between individuals that is

- Focus on tacit knowledge

- Real-world application of explicit knowledge
  - Requires informal
  - Formal training
  - Rather Informal learning
  - Directed by the individual learning
  - Takes place in a social context

- Interaction
- Collaboration
- Encourages transmission of tacit knowledge
- Creates environment for knowledge sharing

- Self-directed learning

- Learning
- Work
- Integration between

Through

- Enhances organizational learning
- Information access
- On outcomes of work activities
- Handling work problems
- Developing work processes

- Activities wider range of
  - To incorporate
  - Redesigning jobs
  - Development of opportunities for
    - Feedback
    - Evaluation
    - Reflection

- Work formalization
- Flexibility in work roles
- Balance between

- Participate in
- Encourage employees to

- Access to adequate resources
- Time to
  - Reflect
  - Observe
  - Think
- Exchange knowledge with others

- Recognition of learning achievements

- Conditions that encourage learning
  - E.g.
- Continuous learning opportunities
- On the job

Learning and Training in the Workplace

KEYWORDS Context, course, creation, experience, freedom, mentor, self-manage, style, voluntary.

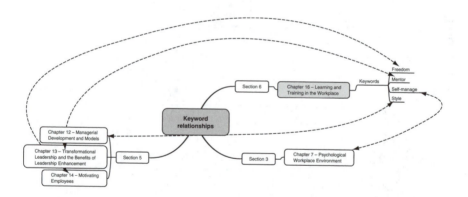

IMPORTANT CONCEPTS Knowledge architecture, knowledge management, knowledge sharing.

Part 1: Learning and motivation to learn

If organizational learning is dependent on the learning efforts of individuals, it makes sense that organizations wishing to increase their learning capacity should pay close attention to the learning behaviour of their employees. In his review of individual learning within organizations, Elkins (2003) has suggested that companies focus on transformational learning in order to increase the likelihood of individual learning practices. According to Elkins, transformational learning occurs when individuals, either gradually or suddenly, begin to reflect critically, recognizing that previously held attitudes and beliefs had constrained their ability to understand their current contextual experiences. As a consequence, they begin to modify their behaviours and attitudes to better reflect the dynamics of their present experiences. Put simply, transformational learning is the outcome of some form of realization that the ways in which one thinks, acts, or works are no longer adequate to operate effectively in one's current work role, and represents the changes made in order to be able to function more efficiently. This process, in Elkins' opinion, is entirely cognitive (that is, it is a mental experience), occurring through critical reflection on thoughts, actions, and behaviours and, as such, requires a series of mental steps. First, some form of trigger occurs, involving an experience, event or crisis that cannot be resolved through the application of previous problem-solving strategies. Second, the individual (or group – Elkins states that transformational learning can also be applied beyond the individual) appraises the situation to come to grips with inabilities in the context of the new experience. Third, new or different ways of explaining or accommodating the new experience are explored. Fourth, alternative roles, ways of behaving, or ways of dealing with the problem are experimented with. Finally, on finding a successful solution, this alternative is integrated into a person's or group's set of coping behaviours, and practised in daily life. To better apply the principles of transformational learning in an organizational setting, Elkins has suggested that managers search for variables that are good predictors of job performance (such as factors that stimulate curiosity to learn) and then encourage development in these areas by supporting employees through the stages of transformational learning. According to Elkins, a recent example of transformational learning occurred when Ford automotive attempted to raise organizational learning based on the belief that if its employees could learn faster and more effectively than Ford's competitors, the firm would be more productive. Given that this required that individual learning be enhanced, senior management realized that a greater emphasiz on soft skills that encouraged learning was required, such as the development throughout the company of personal, interpersonal, and professional skills. With the emphasis on communication, individuals were encouraged to collaborate and share information informally, and in teams. Ford's managers found that the consequent increase in communication skills allowed teams to be more successful, and better able to take in, process, and share new information more effectively. In effect, the realization that the organization's abilities were not adequate to a given task (in this case, performance through learning), followed by adaptation and integration, resulted in an organizationally led programme that prompted transformational learning at an individual level, but that resulted in company-wide change. Consequently, according to Elkins, it is important that firms identify the measurable human capabilities required for effective work (especially in areas like interpersonal skills, planning, and strategic organizing), which represent employees' key competencies, and encourage individuals to enhance and develop their knowledge and proficiency in these areas.

In their empirical investigation of increasing learning at work, Martocchio and Hertensein (2003) recommended that individual learning can be increased when firms attempt to boost employees' orientation towards learning. Following their evaluation of 96 US university employees on measures of cognitive ability, declarative knowledge, and self-efficacy subsequent to technical training, Martocchio and his colleague reported that when employees were more learning oriented, they had significantly higher post-training self-efficacy, and were more likely both to have learnt effectively and to have used this new knowledge in the workplace. Moreover, when the focus of training programmes was taken away from performance outcomes and oriented towards simple participation and enjoyment of the training session, participants showed higher self-efficacy and more effective learning. Consequently, Martocchio and Hertensein have recommended that even if the firm's goal is to increase performance through increased individual learning, employees be encouraged to learn simply for the sake of learning, rather than for performance goals. In this way they will be more confident about learning and more likely to learn and pass on their new knowledge, resulting in the intended outcome of greater performance, but without the limitations imposed by pressure to perform.

Another way of increasing the likelihood of effective learning is to encourage the institution of mentoring within an organization (Swap, Leonard, Shields, & Abrams, 2001). According to Swap and his colleagues, mentoring embodies the recognition that expertise (defined as the ability, by dint of practical experience, to recognize patterns that are not visible to less-experienced practitioners) in any given area takes up to ten years of practical experience to develop. Thus, those persons within an organization who have genuine expertise represent a highly valuable, intangible asset. Moreover, because, as we will see below, learning by experience rather than by theory has stronger practical applications, those with expertise are ideally suited to pass on their knowledge in a practical manner. According to Swap *et al.*, the institution of mentoring, whereby an expert is paired with someone younger and less experienced, can allow such a passage; the informal nature of such a relationship, embodying informal teaching, inspiration, storytelling, learning through observation and practice, and the development of metacognition within an expert framework, represents an ideal mechanism for learning. Similarly, Roth (2000) has suggested that mentoring can be highly effective in aiding a person's understanding of the complexity of real-life situations, especially around complex affairs that require expert knowledge. According to Roth, the actual state of affairs at work, or "first-order reality", is too often misinterpreted through a person's limited ability to perceive what is actually going on ("second-order reality"). Consequently, by helping an employee to link everyday expertise to his or her expectations and interpretations, mentors can increase the complexity with which that person interprets his or her world, and the way in which he or she deals with daily problems.

IN ACTION #18

Managers as mentors

Like employers, a large part of a manager's job should, theoretically, be about facilitating learning. One excellent way of doing this is to institute mentoring programmes in the workplace. Effectively, mentoring involves pairing an employee with expertise in a given area, with someone who wants (or needs) to learn more about that field. The mentor then takes on a certain amount of responsibility for guiding, training, and coaching his or her protégé, especially with regard to experiential learning (that is, learning on the job). Further, because a mentor does more than just provide instruction, the ensuing relationship can help provide a junior employee with the skills and confidence to do his or her job in a way that is much better than simply learning "on the job" through trial and error. Because of his or her expertise, a mentor is better able to determine, in advance, the shortfalls in his or her pupil's approach and, consequently, can correct issues before they become problems. As a manager, it is quite appropriate to take on mentoring roles, but it is important to be wary of perceived favouritism. It is better, therefore, to supervise the mentoring process, and to determine that the mentoring relationships be set up to run smoothly: making sure that subordinates know that if something goes wrong he or she can count on a supervisor to help sort it out.

In action #17 we focussed on the necessity of determining what employees actually want and need before offering training. However, not everyone is capable of clearly understanding or defining their needs, especially when they are confused about their job roles. A technique known as "motivational interviewing" can be extremely useful in helping people to understand what they really need. This method, originally developed to help initiate behaviour change in drug addicts, is a powerful way of helping someone to self-determine how and why they need to change, without actually telling them. Basically, when most people are told what they should do, they are naturally resistant; this is normal human behaviour (so social psychologists tell us). As well, people are much more likely to listen to what they say to themselves, than to what other people tell them. Consequently, motivational interviewing is, simply, a method for getting people to talk about the things that they like and dislike in their daily lives, and then to have them focus on how they could change the things they are dissatisfied with. See Appendix I below for an overview of motivational interviewing.

In their literature review and economic model of mentoring in organizations, Arai, Billot, and Lanfranchi (2001) have reported that mentored workers have greater career success than their non-mentored colleagues. More importantly for organizations, mentored workers are more productive and proficient, by dint of their informal training. In fact, according to Arai *et al.*, through their actions in coaching, sponsoring and training, mentors help their charges to increase their skills and abilities, and prepare them for advancement within the firm, a process that represents the accumulation and transfer of organizational human capital. Arai *et al.*'s findings have been backed up empirically by Hegstad and Wentling (2004), based on their in-depth interviews of employees in 17 *Fortune* 500 companies. Like Arai *et al.*, they found that mentored employees performed better; however Hegstad and Wentling also discovered that mentored workers were more committed to the organization, were more likely to be retained, had lower turnover intention, were more motivated, and possessed a greater self-confidence and stronger self-image than their non-mentored counterparts. Moreover, Hegstad and her co-worker identified several forms of mentoring: traditional one-on-one relationships and group mentoring, in which several employees work together to share expertise, effectively forming a mentoring team. Either way, so long as the person or persons in the mentoring role are experienced, knowledgeable, and committed to providing personal and professional developmental support to the protégé, it is likely that the mentoring relationship will enhance individual performance, increase learning, and help to raise organizational knowledge. This is especially true when the protégé takes on his or her own role as mentor for junior employees, passing on accumulated knowledge, and encouraging the informal transfer of information. The benefits of mentoring notwithstanding, Hegstad and Wentling have also suggested that, for mentoring to be more effective, the firm pay careful attention to several factors that can help both the mentor and the protégé. For example, the mentoring programme should be developed in such a way that employee and organizational needs are aligned, so that mentors are encouraging the right skills. As well, the design, development, implementation, and evaluation of the mentoring programme should be overseen by a person or persons with a strong understanding of the theory and application of mentoring. For instance, a substantial amount of research should go into the programme's design, so that it incorporates expert theory and practices recommended in the professional literature, and encompasses some clear guidelines for measuring successful outcomes. Moreover, there should be substantial development of supporting materials, such as guides, growth plans, and supportive information, to help steer the mentoring relationship. In terms of implementation, Hegstad and Wentling believe that any mentoring programme should be piloted prior to company-wide execution, be completely voluntary, have stringent selection criteria and a systematic matching process, involve training for mentors (covering process and participant issues), and establish a coordinator and mentor team to oversee the whole process. Lastly, the mentoring programme should be regularly evaluated through written and verbal evaluations, and the results used to modify and improve the experience.

The importance of a strong system for putting an effective, assessable mentoring programme in place has also been highlighted by Williams (2001). In her review of the training abilities of technical experts, Williams has pointed out that just that a person has technical expertise and proficiency in a given area does not mean that he or she will have the ability or the inclination to pass that knowledge on effectively. Consequently, Williams has recommended that all potential candidates for mentoring roles undergo some training in delivering adult training and education, as well as evaluation and training in interpersonal, coaching, and communication skills. Without these abilities, neither the protégé nor the mentor is likely to benefit from the mentoring relationship.

Whilst certain methods for enhancing individual and, consequently, organizational learning can be very effective, the most important aspect for enhancing learning involves increasing an individual's desire or motivation to learn. According to Wiethoff (2004), learning motivation is the result of a person's attitude towards behaviours required in order to learn: he or she will evaluate the possible outcomes of the learning process and come to the belief that this behaviour will lead to one of several conclusions. If this outcome is perceived as desirable, motivation to participate in learning behaviour will increase. Perceived control over the behaviour also affects motivation. Weithoff has predicted that the more the control a person believes that he or she has over learning behaviour, the greater the motivation to participate. Likewise, subjective norms influence motivation; if a person believes that significant others approve of the learning behaviour, there is a greater likelihood that he or she will want to participate.

The perception of control in motivation to learn has also been highlighted by Van der Sluis and Poell (2003). After following the career paths of 63 alumni from a European business school's MBA course, Van der Sluis and his coinvestigator found that when people felt in charge of their own career development and, in particular, their ability to learn, they took greater pains to seek out learning opportunities on the job and to further their tacit knowledge. This effect was increased when employees felt that they had adequate supervisory support for learning, especially when their supervisor aided them in setting and achieving learning goals and targets. Egan, Yang, and Bartlett (2004) reported similar findings following their study of motivation to learn, job satisfaction, turnover intention, and organizational learning culture in 245 professional employees from 13 US firms. According to Egan *et al.*, in firms with a stronger learning culture, including organizational and supervisory learning support, opportunities for advancement based on learning initiatives, rewards for teamwork, motivational job design, growth opportunities, and encouragement to use learnt skills on the job, employees were substantially more satisfied and less likely to consider quitting. Moreover, in learning-based firms, employees were more motivated to transfer learnt skills to the workplace, apply those skills, and pass them on to others.

Effective learning can also affect the bottom line of company survivability. Rowden (2002), based on his study of learning behaviour and satisfaction in 794 employees of 12 mid-sized US companies, has pointed out that 99.7 per cent of businesses in the United States are small to mid-size, providing 80 per cent of US employment, and more than 51 per cent of the gross domestic product. Nevertheless, 85 per cent of all small businesses in the United States fail within the first five years largely, Rowden believes, because of an inability to adapt, a consequence of poor organizational learning stemming, in part, from the belief that learning requires a commitment to expensive formal training programmes. According to Rowden, workplace learning, which, in fact, is mostly comprised of informal or incidental on-the-job experiences, should be focussed both on organizational goals, such as encouraging greater employee participation in decision-making and job responsibilities, and on individual goals, including personal needs for advancement, development, recognition, and acceptance; however, in small and mid-sized businesses, these factors are often ignored. Nevertheless, Rowden has reported that, in small and mid-sized firms, when learning behaviour is actively encouraged there is a significant increase in employee job satisfaction and feelings of recognition resulting, for the most part, in stronger organizational performance, and a greater likelihood of company survival and growth. These results were equally valid for both informal, on-the-job learning, and formal training programmes, a finding that shows that small firms do not necessarily have to spend large amounts on external training in order to enhance organizational and individual learning.

Another investigation of workplace learning and job performance, this time focussed on the role of adult curiosity in learning, has been carried out by Reio and Wiswell (2000). In their literature review, Reio and his colleague highlighted the importance of curiosity in adult learning, arguing that, like children, adults require intrinsic motivation to learn, and that curiosity, which does not lessen noticeably as people age, provides one of the strongest motivations to engage in a new behaviour (however, unlike children, adults are more passive in their curiosity, but still require that a new activity peak their curiosity through its novelty and intrinsic interest). According to Reio and Wiswell, curiosity in adults, especially regarding learning behaviours, is heightened by the ability to self-direct learning opportunities, in which learning is both the responsibility and under the control of the learner. As well, Reio and Wiswell have shown that, in an organizational setting, curiosity-inspired learning is more likely to occur under the guidance of mentors, or supportive supervisors and co-workers, because this strong behavioural modelling sets up conditions in which curiosity will be peaked, and behaviours repeated and maintained. Consequently, when curiosity is modelled and rewarded, individuals are more likely to place themselves in situations that foster learning, choose to obtain information, apply that knowledge in a work setting, and transfer the knowledge to others. To validate their hypotheses, Reio and Wiswell assessed 233 service industry employees on measures of curiosity, learning and job performance, finding that curiosity is, in fact, one of the strongest internal motivators for workplace learning. Consequently, Reio and his coinvestigator have recommended that, because thinking and learning are mediated by the context in which they are situated, such as factors that stimulate an employee's curiosity instead of focussing purely on explicit knowledge acquisition (a process that can result in lowered motivation), employers should concentrate on learning approaches, including mentoring, modelling, coaching and on-the-job practice, that actually increase motivation to learn.

A consistent theme in many of the studies reviewed so far has been the importance of freedom for employees to regulate their own learning behaviour, so that they are more motivated to expose themselves to learning opportunities, and to transfer their acquired knowledge to everyday work tasks. In this vein, Clardy (2000) believes that self-directed learning motivation is actually a function of contextual factors, rather than the result of some inherent personality trait that directs learning behaviour. Following his investigation of 56 employees from five US firms, Clardy described three levels of motivation to learn. In the first condition, "induced learning", specific events at work require that employees engage in limited learning to redress a specific imbalance between their skills and their duties. Given that this type of learning involves neither self-direction by the learner nor the ability to control the type of learning, induced learning was not found to be highly motivating. "Voluntary learning", in which employees were free to undertake learning programmes that they found interesting but that were not linked to precipitated job changes were substantially more motivating. However, when employees were free to align their learning interests with programmes that could enhance their job performance, a process labelled "synergistic learning", motivation was increased even further. In this last condition, employees were able to act and learn of their own accord, but could immediately utilize this new knowledge to improve their on the job abilities, increasing both their intrinsic motivation to learn and to their desire to transfer this learning to their work.

Unlike Clardy's (2000) suggestion that contextual factors influence a person's desire to learn, Naquin and Holton (2002) believe that inherent personality traits are important in both a person's motivation to learn and the desire to transfer this learning to the workplace. Following their evaluation of 229 US employees on measures of personality, affectivity and motivation to learn, Naquin and Holton proposed the construct of "Motivation to Improve Work through Learning" (MTIWTL) which incorporated motivation to learn, desire to transfer that learning to the workplace, and performance outcomes. According to their findings, Naquin and his co-worker showed that the principle predictors of a high MTIWTL score were extraversion, or an individual's preference for interpersonal interaction, and positive affectivity, or a person's tendency to interpret situations positively. Moreover, MTIWTL scores were indirectly related to employees' affective commitment to their work, which in turn was mediated by their conscientiousness (that is, their preference towards conscientious behaviours such as punctuality and trustworthiness) and their agreeableness (for example, their ability to interact with others in a pleasant and open manner). Because of their findings that certain personality traits are influential in employees' desire to learn and to apply their learnt knowledge, and because of the importance of the accumulation of human capital in organizational success, Naquin and Holton have recommended that HR departments pay careful attention not only to employees' personality traits but also to the contextual factors that help to motivate learning. That is, because not everyone is likely to be high in MTIWTL propensity (and therefore less likely to voluntarily engage in learning and transfer behaviours), unless they wish to recruit only employees with strong MTIWTL personality profiles, it is important that employers focus on factors that encourage individuals to learn independently of their inherent personality traits, such as control over learning practices and strong supervisory support.

Despite the repeatedly demonstrated benefits of individual and, by extension, organizational learning towards organizational success, employers often take a laissez-faire attitude towards learning. In fact, given that a $1 investment in individual learning in the workplace can produce $3 worth of economic activity

(Westbrook & Veale, 2001), it is surprising that company leaders are not more focussed on learning enhancement. However, according to Westbrook and Veale's study of 1031 full-time employees from 60 US firms, despite the fact that most people, managers and CEOs included, are aware of employees' desires for ongoing learning in order to stay competitive, work-related learning is not made a priority because organizational learning is not seen as an essential characteristic of a successful business. Consequently, although lip-service is paid to the "learning organization", Westbrook and Veale believe that because self-directed learning is not often actively encouraged or supported, few employees feel confident about using work time to engage in self-directed learning and, when they do, devote minimal time to learning and seldom complete what they have started. In other words, because of a lack of belief by senior management in the importance of organizational learning, there is a substantial disconnect between the need for continual learning often promoted by HR departments as part of their "learning organization" strategy, and the actual learning behaviours of employees.

We have seen that the perceived costs associated with organizational learning represent a barrier for many firms: they expect that learning can only be achieved through investment in expensive training programmes. However, one way of encouraging self-directed learning without the necessity of spending large amounts on training, is by recognizing that the majority of workplace learning is informal, or "learning that is predominantly unstructured, experimental, and noninstitutionalised" (Ellinger, 2005). In fact, according to Ellinger, with as much as 70 per cent of workplace learning occurring informally (and because informal learning is mostly tacit and pre-integrated with workplace activities), it takes ready precedence over formal training programmes, allowing learning to occur without excessive spending. Nevertheless, Ellinger has warned that informal, self-directed learning does not just happen spontaneously. Following her qualitative investigation of 3500 employees in the eastern United States, Ellinger found that informal learning only occurs when leaders and managers are strongly committed to providing a supported learning environment. According to Ellinger, this can only occur when employers seek to create informal learning opportunities, such as mentoring programmes and on-the-job training, act in a mentoring or coaching role themselves, visibly support and make space for learning, encourage risk taking, demonstrate the importance of knowledge sharing, give positive feedback and recognition, and act as effective learning role models – behaviours and actions that are not financially expensive. Even so, Ellinger has shown that, when they lack commitment to learning, leaders and managers actually inhibit and suppress self-directed, informal learning and, by extension, organizational learning. Lack of time and resources for learning represent a typical example of this suppression: whilst they might think that encouraging employees to meet deadlines represents effective management, by not giving employees time to learn, managers can cripple an organization's ability to accumulate human capital, and use this capital to compete successfully. Nonetheless, to expect leaders and managers to understand the value of workplace learning intuitively is a stretch. Ellinger has pointed out that managers need training in the importance and encouragement of informal learning. In fact, when given adequate training (preferably in an informal, on-the-job manner), managers can readily learn the effective mentoring, coaching and feedback skills required for creating an informal learning environment. Moreover, when they learn that informal employee interaction is the most effective way to stimulate informal learning and tacit knowledge transfer, managers are more likely to encourage and make provisions for this type of behaviour.

Other researchers have also highlighted the importance of informal learning in the workplace, especially with regard to managerial development and proficiency. In their investigation of 84 managers on measures of proficiency, informal learning, and transfer of learning measures, Enos *et al.* (2003) reported that not only do managers learn the majority of their skills informally, but also managerial proficiency is almost completely dependent on the quality of this informal learning. Effectively, managers learn to manage through the social process of interacting with others and imitating modelled behaviour. When this interaction involves a continuous cycle of challenging experiences, action and reflection, under the guidance of a knowledgeable mentor, a manager is substantially more likely to successfully transfer his or her newly gained, useful knowledge to the workplace. However, without this guidance, there is a greater likelihood of significant gaps in a manager's abilities. According to Enos *et al.*, effective learning takes place when conditions are met, usually through effective social interaction, that help to combine a person's metacognitive knowledge with their ability to self-regulate: metacognitive knowledge provides internal information about a specific task, its demands, and what it will take to accomplish that task, whilst effective self-regulation controls the correct application of metacognitive knowledge in order to reduce the gap between current and desired abilities. In other words, under useful guidance, managers learn both the skills required to deal with everyday work situations and the ability to use this knowledge to continue to learn and behave in a helpful, effective manner. Consequently, managerial proficiency becomes the product of informal learning and the successful transfer and evolution of this learning in new situations and environments. Obviously, effective, proficient managers are a boon to any organization, nevertheless, Enos and his colleagues have shown that whilst effective managerial skills are most likely learnt on the job, most organizations are still focussed on formal training programmes which, as we will see below, are not very effective for teaching applied skills. Accordingly, they have recommended that managerial training be deformalized, instead placing the emphasis on recognizing informal learning opportunities in the workplace, such as interpersonal interactions, observation of effective techniques, and challenging job assignments under the supervision of an expert mentor. Moreover, rather than focussing on completion of managerial training, firms should direct their attention towards developing managerial expertise and proficiency by actively developing managers' metacognitive skills, allowing managers to control their own learning paths, opportunities, content, sequence, and pace, and shifting the focus from training performance to workplace proficiency. As Enos *et al.* have pointed out, when managers possess a strong set of metacognitive abilities, they are more likely to actively seek out ongoing, informal learning opportunities and transfer the knowledge gained through these interactions into everyday practice. What is more, proficient managers who understand learning will encourage it in their subordinates, creating a low-cost chain of organizational learning opportunities.

In summary, organizational learning is a function of contextual factors that encourage individuals to engage in self-directed learning, to apply this knowledge towards their everyday work and to transfer it to others, a process that enhances the accumulation of organizational human capital. Motivation to learn is increased by the freedom to control and direct one's own learning, the ability to be able to apply it in a way that enhances both one's own work and the success of the organization, and through active support from mentors, supervisors, or co-workers. Nevertheless, despite the financial and other performance benefits associated with organizational learning, a lack of belief in the necessity of ongoing learning in order to be successful hampers individual attempts to increase tacit knowledge. Lack of faith in the effectiveness of learning could be a by-product of fears of high costs associated with training; however, because the majority of workplace learning occurs informally, on the job, managers can easily enhance learning by modelling effective learning behaviour, without needing to invest heavily in formal training programmes.

Part 2: Workplace training and transfer of learning

Despite the principles of self-directed and organizational learning, and ignoring the fact that most workplace learning occurs informally, on the job, organizations spend and continue to spend enormous amounts of money on formal training programmes: Carter (2002) has estimated that 90 per cent of US corporations use formal training programmes, costing over US$55 billion annually. Accordingly, it is important that training be used effectively; otherwise it represents little more than an enormous waste of money. No return on investment on training also means a reduction of funding for training programmes, and a loss of belief in its effectiveness. Consequently, this section is focussed on the effective use of training and factors that help to transfer knowledge gained in a training environment to real-world applications.

According to Tracey, Hinkin, Tannenbaum, and Mathieu (2001), a large variety of variables influence training success, including instructional design, the programme's educational literature, its sequencing, opportunities for workplace practice of training and, most importantly, participants' motivation pretraining, which influences preparation for, performance during, and learning transfer after a training programme. As we have already seen, motivation to participate is largely predicted by a person's self-efficacy: if there is belief that learning is possible, motivation to participate increases. Accordingly, in their literature review, Tracey *et al.* have indicated that self-efficacy can be readily increased by developing internal or individual factors, such as a person's organizational commitment or job involvement, and external factors, including the extent to which an organization, managers, and job conditions allow for learning and development to occur. Thus, in effect, learning is only likely to occur when individuals have the belief in their ability ("can do"), and the desire to participate ("will do"): participants must believe that they are capable, but without active support for learning (in the form of managerial encouragement, organizational conditions, and job flexibility), there is little likelihood of pretraining motivation or, consequently, training success. In support of these assertions, based on their examination of 420 managers from 10 hotels participating in a skills training programme, Tracey and his coinvestigators concluded that learning motivation is, in fact, the product of self-efficacy and the work environment. That is, by increasing employee confidence through careful encouragement of the successful completion of tasks and responsibilities, and by modifying the work environment to support learning behaviours, staff will be more willing to undertake training and more likely to learn from, and apply their training in the workplace. Moreover, when employees show a positive reaction to their training, they are more likely to attempt to apply their newfound skills to their work and be motivated to attend future training sessions. Thus, if the workplace is not geared towards learning processes, in terms of support, resources, and culture, no matter how enlightening the content, formal training is unlikely to be successful, by dint of employees' lack of motivation to learn or apply the subject matter.

IN ACTION #19

Employee control over learning

Because you have probably been required to attend training sessions that you felt were of little relevance to you, you are probably frustrated with the lack of opportunities to learn things that actually help you in your work (rather than what you are told you should learn). As well, you might have experienced the frustration that comes from being told that a particular type of training is necessary for workplace improvement, without being offered any support or follow-up. So that, no matter how stimulated you were by what you learnt, you were unable to implement any change in your everyday tasks. Nonetheless, to make sure that you have both opportunities to learn and to apply the things you have learnt, it is important that you understand what you want and need to make your work more pleasant and productive. To do this, you can start by evaluating what it is that helps you to be productive and that you feel works, and to then list the things that don't work, or that hinder your performance. These can be either (or both) issues external to you, such as poor workplace design, management or workplace procedures, or skills that you would like to improve in yourself, such as time management, goal setting, stress coping or communication. Once you know what you want to be improved, negotiate with your supervisor to determine how these changes can be made. Push for training or action that will actually help you in your work life, and that takes place in-situ, so that you can make real change. Also, make sure that you will have the resources and support to allow these changes to continue. For example, make sure that your supervisor is able to coach you through the process, and that you have enough time and other resources to make it happen (for example, if you are expected to finish an important project whilst relearning your communication skills, it's unlikely that the training will stick). Finally, stay with it: the changes you make will help you to enjoy what you do more, because you will be better at it and have more personal resources available to you.

Interestingly, contrary to the reaction findings of Tracey *et al.* (2001), following their study of training programmes for 283 automotive technicians from a large US company, Tan, Hall, and Boyce (2003) have reported that how employees felt about their training which had little impact on its effectiveness. Rather, similar to the suggestions of Tracey and his coauthors, Tan *et al.* reported that learning and training transfer were more likely to occur when participants were given the opportunity to practise their new skills in the actual workplace, and received adequate time, support and resources to allow this to occur. As a result, given that training effectiveness is most often evaluated based on employee feedback questionnaires (for example, quality of instructor, relevance of materials, depth of coverage, and so on), Tan *et al.*'s results suggest that internal measures of training success are largely irrelevant. Instead, Tan and his colleagues believe that longitudinal observation of the use of trained skills on the job, and the assessment of organizational results consequent to employee training attendance are substantially better techniques for evaluating training effectiveness. Of course, this assumes that there are mechanisms in place to encourage employees to use their skills on the job. Likewise, Morgan and Casper (2000), who statistically analysed the training perception responses of 9128 US government agency employees, indicated that the efficacy of most training programme evaluations is highly flawed, simply because they tend to assess only participants' training feedback, rather than their ability to apply the training to their work. Nonetheless, whilst Morgan and his co-worker acknowledge that managerial support for skills application is extremely important, they have also pointed out that training transfer is also dependent on the ability of the instructor, and how applicable the training is to actual, everyday job usage. Consequently, Morgan and Casper have suggested (like Tan *et al.*) that rather than simply getting trainees to fill out satisfaction questionnaires, a practice that they believe is driven mostly by its low required effort and low cost, training effectiveness should be evaluated by assessing both the extent to which it is applied in the workplace and the level of organizational change (such as increased performance) that occurs as a result of the training.

Similar to Tracey *et al.* (2001), Morgan and Casper (2000), and Tan *et al.* (2003), Hertenstein (2001) has shown that employee motivation has a lot to do with training success. However, he has also proposed that a person's beliefs about training interact directly with the design of a training programme, making it possible to predict the likelihood of successful learning. After randomly assigning 100 university undergraduates to one of two groups, a spaced practice (that is, a typical class in which participants meet once or twice a week for 12–20 weeks) and a massed practice group (that is, an intensive all-day learning environment that presents the same amount of information as the spaced practice, but over several days), Hertenstein found that participants who believed that their ability could be increased through learning (that is, goal orientation or self-efficacy regarding learning abilities) responded significantly better to massed practice training, whilst those who had a lower self-efficacy regarding their ability to learn did better in the spaced practice scenario. Accordingly, Hertenstein has recommended that training programmes be geared towards a person's level of pretraining self-efficacy or, more effectively, that pains should be taken to increase self-efficacy in trainees prior to their training.

Carter (2002) has extended the findings of Hertenstein (2001), by proposing that training can be improved by specifically matching training styles to individual cognitive ability. Based on her evaluation of 93 undergraduates following two training conditions, on measures of cognitive ability and learning, Carter reported that participants with a higher verbal comprehension ability did better in a traditional lecture-based training programme; whilst those with stronger general reasoning ability performed better in simulation activities, which used role playing, case studies, and mock-ups to imitate the work environment and develop skills through hands-on practice. As a consequence, Carter has suggested that before employees participate in training programmes, their cognitive styles should be measured in order to determine what type of training best suits them.

We have discussed at some length the motivational factors behind learning and training; however, as we have also seen, a person's intentions to utilize their newfound knowledge can be easily confounded by factors such as low motivation, lack of support, or inadequate or poorly matched training that interfere with the transfer of learnt knowledge to the workplace. Learning transfer refers to an individual's ability to find a practical application for the skills (or explicit knowledge) learnt in a training session, and to practise these skills sufficiently in an applied environment so that they can be internalized as tacit knowledge. Unfortunately, learning and training are often confused, with many managers assuming that if workers are attending training sessions, they must also be learning. In their assessment of this poor correlation between most workplace training and increased productivity, Wright and Geroy (2001) have highlighted the problem of organizational resistance to learning. According to Wright and his co-worker, up to 70 per cent of workplace training is simply "wasted time", because management does not encourage the implementation of the ideas presented during training or because the training addresses the wrong issues. For example, stress management training can be highly effective, but unless the underlying causes of stress are evaluated and acted upon and trainees are encouraged to utilize their training in their everyday work, the training becomes an exercise in symptom rather than problem management. Consequently, Wright and Geroy have suggested that for training to be effective and, therefore, for the organization to develop from the increase in shared employee knowledge, that management pay attention to two key issues. First, that motivation for worker participation need be increased by making the trainer a "human competence engineer". That is, the trainer should be aware that actual workplace change is more important than the training itself, and that the purpose of training is, in fact, to enable change. To realize this goal, the trainer works with employees to help them actually change the way in which they work, addressing (in-situ and in real time) the problems that limit their ability to be effective. Wright and Geroy's second recommendation requires that managers become champions of learning, both as facilitators and coaches. In this way, and by keeping in mind that workplace learning builds organizational value (through more-highly trained, satisfied, committed employees), they can encourage increased organizational trust, and greater workplace participation. Consequently, if leadership can be defined as the ability to motivate others to perform a (potentially undesirable) task, and being able to coach a person through that task, managers who follow this model can become better leaders rather than simply administrators.

In their review of the literature pertaining to learning transfer following training, Yamnill and MacLean (2001), like other authors we have reviewed, have identified worker motivation and the workplace climate as key variables in success of the training. Specifically, they have recommended that to increase employee motivation to transfer training to the workplace, the employee needs to interpret the training as having fulfilled his or her training expectations and desires, and perceive it as useful for his or her job or career advancement. Moreover, if the employee does well during training, he or she is more likely to be motivated to apply that training in the workplace, a finding that suggests that training should be participatory rather than performance based (that is, in performance-based training those who do not do well immediately are less likely to learn effectively or use their trained skills at work). Lastly, workers with higher organizational commitment and job satisfaction will also be more motivated to transfer learning. With regard to the transfer climate, Yamnill and his coauthor have suggested that an organizational "learning culture" is largely a construct of the relationship between employees' attitudes and behaviour and the organizational context. In other words, whether a person transfers his or her learnt skills form a training programme to his or her job is the product of whether he or she perceives that this transfer is both possible and supported. This, in turn, is encouraged by a combination of situation and consequence cues following training (Yamnill & MacLean). On the one hand, situation cues serve to remind trainees of opportunities to apply what they have learnt during a training course, when they return to work, and includes goal cues (for example, managers set goals that encourage the application of new skills on the job); social cues, in which cues arise from behaviours exhibited by co-workers (for example, managers returning from a training course are seen to be managing better than their non-trained colleagues); task cues, which refer to the nature of the job itself (for example, having access at work to the software that the training course focussed on); and self-control cues (for example, being able to use a newly learnt skill to handle a job-related problem). Consequence cues, on the other hand, refer to the feedback that trainees receive after they have successfully applied their newly learnt skills, knowledge, or attitudes. According to Yamnill and MacLean, if this feedback is positive, trainees are more likely to continue to apply their learnt skills, integrating them into their everyday abilities. However, negative or non-existent feedback, or open punishment (for example, a supervisor derides an employee for late work after the employee attempted to apply course-taught skills) are all likely to reduce or remove any present or future motivation to transfer learnt content to the workplace.

The importance of environmental perceptions, transfer motivation, and situational and consequence cues notwithstanding, Yamnill and MacLean (2001) have pointed out that the actual training is also of key importance in determining whether information is learnt and transferred to the work environment.

For example, training transfer can be greatly improved by increasing the degree of correspondence between training setting stimuli, conditions and responses, and the actual workplace. That is, if the training task is extremely similar to the actual processes required at work, trainees should have little difficulty when it comes to utilizing their training in the work setting. Yamnill and his colleague have labelled this process "near learning", because the training is as near as possible to actual work conditions, and believe that it is most applicable in technical training, when the desired outcome is for trainees to be able to mimic specific behaviours and procedures. However, for situations in which employees are expected to be more creative in their problem solving, such as managerial development training, Yamnill and MacLean have proposed the idea of "far learning". In far learning, training is focussed on the underlying principles, concepts, and assumptions of the skills or behaviours being learnt, and on practising them in different contexts and in novel situations. Moreover, during training there is a greater emphasiz on discussion and application of learnt materials in situations deliberately chosen by the trainee and, ideally, following training, employees are encouraged to use their skills in situations outside of those covered by the course. In this way, trainees become adept at generalizing their knowledge to a wide variety of contexts, being able to transfer knowledge from one sphere to another by understanding the fundamental concepts that are applicable across different environments. As a result, given that training programmes are expensive, and of little use if their content is not transferred to the workplace, Yamnill and his co-worker have proposed that HR departments encourage transfer of training by collaborating with management and trainers to develop strategic goals for training programmes (aligning the training with organizational, departmental, and individual needs); by encouraging managers to provide clear performance objectives so that employees know exactly what is expected of them pre- and post-training; to provide the necessary support for post-training transfer, and give prompt, useful feedback; and to ensure that training meets individual and organizational needs, to utilize the feedback and ideas of trainees in designing future training programmes. Montesino (2002) has reached similar conclusions based on his examination of the perceptions of training support among 183 field managers and trainees. He reported that when trainees felt that the content of their training was aligned with the goals of the organization, there was a significantly greater usage of training on the job, and greater training-transfer behaviours (for example, support) by managers, a finding that has prompted his suggestion that HR departments need to work to build partnerships between trainees, trainers, and managers in order to support training-transfer behaviours. Given that Montesino has indicated that less that 10 per cent of training expenditure is transferred to the job, but that many HR departments have emphasized state-of-the-art, formal training programmes above behaviours and environmental conditions that enhance training transfer, it makes sense that, simply by encouraging a learning environment and training managers to support learning in their subordinates, learning transfer would increase.

In this vein, following their assessment of the responses to measures of learning transfer, self-efficacy, learner motivation and supervisory support by

4562 employees from 15 firms in 3 different countries, Holton, Chen, and Naquin (2003) have concluded that organizational differences are largely responsible for the amount of learning transfer following training. Specifically, they found low training transfer across all examined firms, and reported that in public sector organizations training transfer was particularly poor, because trainees were more likely to perceive that their supervisor would oppose use of any new skills or techniques presented during training and present considerable resistance to any attempts at change. Moreover, public sector employees felt that attempts to change would be met with negative personal and career consequences, including negative critique and direct and indirect punishment from their supervisor. Holton *et al.* went on to point out that whilst private sector employees were more inclined to transfer training to the workplace, employees of non-profit organizations were the most likely to experience learning transfer, based largely on strong levels of supervisor support for learning. Consequently, Holton and his coinvestigators concluded that, despite the large amounts spent by organizations on workplace training, the actual transfer of skills from training to the job can be severely hampered by the substantial disconnect between job expectations and training content, coupled with poor organizational and supervisory support, which actively discourages trainees from applying learnt skills to their work.

A danger of this lack of support for learning transfer is the likelihood of a loss of employee motivation for future learning, as well as reduced loyalty, organizational commitment, and productivity (Marks & Lockyer, 2004). According to Marks and her colleague, who investigated learning transfer behaviours in five companies over a four-month period, employees, in particular knowledge workers, feel heavily pressured to acquire new skills but are seldom able to obtain the training they require to stay "current". Nevertheless, to ensure consistent innovation over competitors, many modern firms are concerned with having an "expert" workforce and expect their employees to maintain expertise in dynamic fields, alongside consistent pressure to remain productive and innovative. Consequently, when organizations either lack the ability to provide adequate ongoing training, or do not support workers in transferring trained skills into their ongoing work, they risk alienating their key employees. In contrast, based on their findings, Marks and Lockyer have shown that if an organization takes pains to meet the skill acquisition and transfer needs of its employees, there will be a corresponding increase in employee commitment and effort, and a likely increase in job satisfaction and productivity.

In an empirical investigation of training transfer, Richman-Hirsch (2001), who looked at the work environment, training performance and training transfer of 360 US university employees, reported that brief post-training initiatives can significantly increase training transfer. According to Richman-Hirsch, the two main conditions of learning transfer are maintenance (or the length of time that trained skills continue to be used on the job) and generalization (the application of trained skills to tasks or settings beyond the original training context). Richman-Hirsch has shown that when short goal setting and self-management training session are given on top of regular training, trainees maintain and generalize trained skills to a much greater degree. In Richman-Hirsch's study, goal setting training consisted of a brief session explaining that, in order to enhance task persistence and mobilize effort, goals should be specific and challenging. Likewise, self-management training vignettes taught people to avoid relapsing to pre-training states by assessing potential obstacles to their performance, monitoring ways in which the environment hinders or aids performance, planning coping responses for facing obstacles, and self-administering rewards for successfully overcoming or avoiding these obstacles. As a result of her findings, Richman-Hirsch has recommended that HR personnel should consider developing an environment that aids trainees to set goals and self-manage through the encouragement of environmental and supervisory support mechanisms for skill acquisition and transfer, especially with regard to employees' perceptions of learning supportiveness in the work environment. Moreover, they should direct supervisors to reward all behaviours that reflect skills acquisition and job-related personal development (for example, through programmes such as pay for knowledge and skill-based pay). If trainees fail to transfer training to their work, supervisors should be encouraged to identify barriers that are blocking the trainee's ability or motivation to transfer, through interviews or informal conversations, and take pains to address problems or perceived faults.

The effectiveness of goal setting on training transfer has also been examined empirically by Brown (2005), who assessed 72 Canadian government employees on their self-efficacy and transfer of learning following a one-day training programme. According to Brown, the average US employee receives 28 hours of training a year at a cost of $800, but, typically, very little is transferred to the workplace. Nevertheless, based on his findings, Brown has shown that transfer can be significantly enhanced by increasing pre-training self-efficacy, and encouraging appropriate goal setting (that is specific and challenging). Specifically, Brown reported that setting proximal goals, or goals that refer to shorter-term events, encouraged trainees to transfer learning, because they were focussed on specific and challenging behaviours.

From a slightly different perspective, Lorenzet, Salas, and Tannenbaum (2005) have shown that training transfer can be enhanced through the deliberate use of errors during training. Based on their investigation of 90 US undergraduates, Lorenzet et al. found that when training included deliberate errors, and when participants were informed beforehand that these errors would occur and were aided both in correcting these errors, and selecting appropriate correction strategies, there was a greater level of accuracy and performance, as well as more successful training transfer. Moreover, those participants who had experienced deliberate errors (and been instructed in how to deal with them) showed greater self-efficacy when they were able to apply their new skills independently of the trainer, greatly increasing their chances of successful learning transfer to the workplace. Lorenzet and his co-workers explained this result as the consequence of richer feedback both on the errors made by trainees and on the best ways to respond to the error so that it did not reoccur. In other words, when people get to see what can go wrong and learn how to deal with it in a safe environment, they are much more likely to want to apply their new skills to their daily work tasks.

Independent of learning transfer following training, one major problem with workplace training is the propensity for employees to forget what they have learnt, resulting in the need for retraining that is expensive, both in terms of the cost of the trainer, and lost time and productivity whilst workers are in retraining. In an attempt to address this problem, Jaber, Kher, and Davis (2003) have developed a mathematical model to describe and predict both workplace learning and forgetting, which suggests that forgetting can be reduced by applying three principles to both the original training and the application of that training on the job. First, the amount of practical experience in applying training negatively predicts the amount of forgetting. Consequently, by allowing and encouraging employees to apply learnt skills in the workplace, the chances of forgetting are reduced. Second, the longer an employee is unable to practice learnt skills, the greater the likelihood that he or she will forget them. As a result, employees should regularly be given the opportunity to practise learnt skills, even when they are not being used for the task or project at hand. Lastly, level of forgetting is dependent on the rate at which a skill or behaviour is learnt: more rapid learning tends to result in faster forgetting, so it is important to allow employees time to master the application of their new skills.

So, as we have seen, although a large amount of money is spent on organizational learning and training, unless systems are put in place to encourage effective learning transfer, the training is, for the most part, useless. Nevertheless, when training is effectively transferred there are highly positive outcomes, both for employees and the firm. For example, according to Bartlett (2001), who investigated 337 professional US employees on measures of organizational commitment and training transfer, when employees perceive strong access to training and the supported ability to apply that training in the workplace, there is a substantially greater level of organizational commitment and individual productivity. This finding has prompted Bartlett to recommend that HR professionals adopt a broader perspective towards training, especially with regard to the importance of managerial support for learning transfer, so that employees can boost their tacit knowledge through the real-life application of trained skills. Similarly, van Leeuwen and van Praag (2002) have listed benefits to employees, employers, and even governments from the successful institution of effective training and learning transfer. For instance, employees tend to benefit from higher wages, an extended working lifetime, greater status within the firm, increased job security and employability, as well as better enjoyment of their work. Likewise, following successful training programmes, employers gain increased employee productivity, stronger worker commitment, and less deterioration of their human capital. Lastly, governments benefit from a better educated and more productive population, and a likely reduction in payouts based on sickness and unemployment benefit claims.

Best practice: Case examples of how it's being done

Learning and motivation to learn

Dymock (1999) has described the case example of a large Australian company that introduced a formalized mentoring programme in an attempt to enhance the leadership abilities of its management. Dymock found that, following the careful matching of mentors and protégés, the majority of protégés reported a substantial benefit to their work as a result of their regular mentoring sessions. Specifically, protégés reported increased self-confidence and organizational abilities, as well as a greater perceived ability to manage more effectively. Moreover, protégés believed that they had a greater understanding of the organization and its internal processes, were more motivated to learn and expose themselves to learning opportunities and, most importantly, under the guidance of their mentors, were better able to apply theoretical (explicit) knowledge to practical workplace applications.

Likewise, in his case example of improved workplace learning, Goh (2003) has highlighted the actions of a *Fortune* 500 firm, following an organizational needs assessment, to increase effective knowledge transfer. To enhance employee motivation to learn new skills and to apply these skills to their work, the company instigated employee-led training programmes, in which workers were able to identify learning gaps which were documented and distributed across the organization through an internal database. Specific training programmes were then developed based on the items that were most obviously lacking. Moreover, the firm instigated a mentoring programme to help junior employees understand and apply trained material in the work environment. Lastly, employees were encouraged to take control over their own learning, through organizational provision of greater access to requested materials, including time away from projects in order to enhance learning, and informal interaction with co-workers to help the divestment of tacit knowledge gained through these self-directed learning programmes. On follow-up, Goh reported a significant increase in the learning capabilities of the organization, due largely to an increased motivation to learn among individual employees. According to Goh, the firm has since reported a stronger ability to innovate, greater goal achievement, and increased employee and company performance.

Workplace training and transfer of learning

In his case example of workplace training transfer in a large US manufacturing firm, Mallinger (2000) has emphasized the importance of self-managed training, in which an employee is responsible for their own learning and training development, controlling the pace and content of training programmes. According to Mallinger, having been disappointed with previous consultant-based training enhancement programmes that had failed to demonstrate training transfer to the work environment, the firm decided to invest in a self-managed training programme. During these sessions, managers with different task responsibilities were placed in teams of four or five, and collaborated on training objectives during their formal training. Following training, team members were encouraged to continue with their collaboration and were actively rewarded with enhanced training budgets for their departments if their mutually developed ideas led to demonstrated project progress. Moreover, the increasing collaboration between team members, both formally and informally, led to increased knowledge sharing and a greater propensity to apply formal training to the workplace, to discuss this application and to collaboratively develop improvements that enhanced the training content in real-world applications. Mallinger has described a practical application of this process: the organization had been experiencing problems with parts shortage, slowing down production. Following their training, the cross-functional teams were able to identify problems with parts storage and retrieval as the consequence of poor interdepartmental cooperation. Accordingly, by encouraging a greater level of communication between departments, and developing better solutions for storage and retrieval (especially at times of peak demand), it became substantially easier for the manufacturing arm of the firm to access parts from storage and supply when needed.

Points for action: Practical recommendations for change

Learning and motivation to learn

Because learning is unlikely to occur without a desire to learn, Cunningham and Iles (2002) have recommended a series of actions that organizations can take to enhance employee learning motivation. Effectively, they have suggested that learning be promoted as an underlying aspect of all employee actions, so that everyday work is seen as a learning opportunity. To achieve this, Cunningham and his coauthor have proposed the following:

- The pay framework should include measures that are related directly to learning and that are quantifiable.
- Terms such as "training" and "development" be replaced with "learning" so that a greater emphasiz is placed on the action of learning rather than simple participation.
- Job competency profiles be rewritten so that they weight behavioural skills over technical skills.
- Achievement of objectives, such as the promotion of learning and the active application of learned skills to the workplace be rewarded.
- To train managers in understanding the importance of learning and its encouragement, especially with regard to the development and utilization of company-wide human capital.
- Staff be encouraged to keep some sort of personal learning log in order to self-measure their own learning.
- Managers understand current learning theory and individual learning styles, in order to encourage learning behaviours in their subordinates.
- For managers and team leaders to model learning behaviour by sharing their own learning with staff, both formally and informally.
- For managers and team leaders to receive training in leadership, teamwork, and change-management skills.
- For individual employees to be empowered to manage their own learning, and be supported in enhancing their own knowledge.

In a similar set of recommendations, Hill, Bullard, Capper, Hawes, and Wilson (1996) have suggested that management pay particular attention to the following aspects of learning:

- *Multi-skilling and cross-training.* "Multi-skilling" refers to the ability for individuals to undertake various job roles, even though it might be outside of their immediate job description. "Cross-training", on the other hand, allows employees to experience the occupational and professional roles of other workers, giving them a greater breadth of experience and knowledge about the way in which an organization is run and, consequently, the ability to better contribute to a team environment.

- *Information storage, retrieval, and access.* Whilst, traditionally, many managers are loathe to make information easily available, preferring instead to guard it within their team or department, Hill *et al.* believe that wide distribution of relevant information is vital for learning to occur, because employees are better able to access the information they require, without advanced, specific or expert knowledge.

- *Congruency in reward systems.* It is important that reward systems back up the idea that learning is of value to the organization and that employee learning is appreciated. However, according to Hill *et al.*, it is also important that, culturally, reward systems be perceived as equitable.

- *Continuous learning.* Hill *et al.* suggest that the concept of learning implies a cognitive process that involves reaching beyond what is familiar and attempting to develop knowledge further. Consequently, employees should be encouraged to attempt to improve their knowledge base continuously, rather than remaining satisfied with having achieved a particular qualification.

- *Flexible learning.* It is important that flexibility be available within the organization for learning to actually occur, especially in knowledge workers who might attempt to apply an innovative process in response to an on-the-job problem. Without the flexibility and support to experiment, it is very unlikely that employees will view learning as a priority, no matter what the rhetoric from the HR department.

- *Skills formation and self-respect.* If employees do not have a strong self-belief in their ability to learn, they are unlikely to be willing to expose themselves to learning opportunities or to excel in training programmes. This is an especial problem among low-skilled workers, who often feel defensive and resistant to new learning programmes. Consequently, managers need to develop a more open learning culture, in which learning is seen as a positive and worthwhile action, and in which the participation in learning, rather than specific performance during training, is rewarded.

- *Teams as learning units.* Whilst people learn better in a like-minded, dynamic and compatible group, teams do not become effective learning units simply through their inception. Consequently, appropriate team design, in which individuals are selected for their ability to interrelate and bring useful, diverse knowledge and skills to the group, is paramount.

Summary

Organizational learning is enhanced through the development of individual motivation to learn. Transformational learning, in which individuals reflect on critical perspectives, resulting in a transformational change in their attitudes, beliefs, and practices, is a particularly powerful method of learning motivation. One way to enhance transformation learning is through the encouragement of mentoring: the use of expertise within an organization to support learning in junior employees. When properly applied, mentoring can increase the success, performance, proficiency and self-efficacy of employees, whilst simultaneously increasing their affective commitment towards the organization. Moreover, individuals can be encouraged to learn when their feelings of control over the learning experience are raised by allowing them to self-direct their own learning behaviour; by providing strong supervisory support for learning and the application of learnt skills; by encouraging adult curiosity through attention to intrinsic interest in participation, especially under the guidance of a mentor or supportive supervisor; through informal learning, in which individuals are able to model the effective behaviour of other employees in a social context; and by increasing learning self-efficacy, by raising a person's perception of his or her ability to learn. These recommendations notwithstanding, whilst the development of learning and motivation to learn is undoubtedly implicated in increased job performance, managers and supervisors are often reluctant to encourage learning because of their lack of understanding of the learning process or of its importance in organizational success.

Workplace learning practices, such as training, have little effect if the skills and techniques covered in a training programme are not transferred to the workplace. Four factors must be considered in order to encourage learning transfer: effective training, in which the training style is matched to the cognitive abilities of participants; support for learning application from the organization, and from supervisors and peers; the ability to practise new skills in the actual workplace, including room to make mistakes and to learn from those errors (allowing learning to occur through the conversion of explicit knowledge to tacit knowledge); and the motivation to learn and apply that learning in the workplace.

REVIEW QUESTIONS

1. What would you do to enhance individual learning in the workplace? Why?

2. Describe three benefits of mentoring in organizations.

3. Outline how mentoring can enhance an individual's motivation to learn.

4. Explain informal learning and why it is important for on-the-job ability.

5. Why is a majority of formal training ineffective? Illustrate with a personal example.

6. If it were up to you, how would you enhance learning transfer between formal training and on-the-job application?

7. Examine the relationship between the workplace environment, learning, and learning transfer.

8. What is the role of supervisor, organization, and peer support in effective learning transfer?

Mind-diagram summary

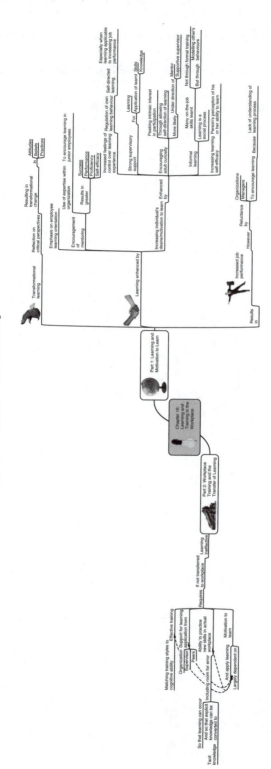

Transformational learning

Reflection on critical perspectives

Resulting in transformational change — in Attitudes, Beliefs, Practices

Emphasis on employee learning orientation

Use of expertise within organization

Encouragement of mentoring — Results in greater — Success, Performance, Proficiency, Self-efficacy

Increased feelings of control over learning experience

Regulation of own learning behaviour — To encourage learning in junior employees

Self-directed learning — Especially when learning applicable to increasing job performance

Learning enhanced by

Increasing individual's desire/motivation to learn — Enhanced by

Strong supervisory support

Encouraging adult curiosity — Peaking intrinsic interest in participation — Through allowing self-direction of learning — More likely

Learning — For — Application of learnt — Skills, Knowledge

Informal — Learning is a social process — Many on-the-job skills learnt — Under direction of — Mentor, Supportive supervisor

Not through formal training — But through — Modelling other's behaviours

Results in — Increased job performance — However — Reluctance by — Organizations, Managers — To encourage learning — Because — Lack of understanding of learning process

Increasing learning — Person's perception of his or her self-efficacy — Increasing learning — Person's perception of his or her ability to learn

Part 1: Learning and Motivation to Learn

Chapter 16: Learning and Training in the Workplace

Part 2: Workplace Training and the Transfer of Learning

Learning ineffective — If not transferred to workplace — Requires

Matching training styles to cognitive ability — Effective training

Organization, Supervision, Peers — Support for learning application from

Ability to practice new skills in actual workplace — Including room for error

Motivation to learn — And apply learning — Largely dependent on

Tacit knowledge — So that learning can occur — And so that explicit knowledge can be converted to

Conclusions

In this book we have covered a very wide range of articles and studies on workplace improvement for increased organizational performance. Despite the variety of opinions, models, and techniques put forward by the authors of these works, two main themes have stood out. First, the changes to workplace functioning since around the mid-1980s, in terms of reduced employment security, organizational streamlining through downsizing and layoffs, and the increasing use of temporary employment contracts, have resulted in a substantial increase in workplace stress and its consequences: reduced physical and psychological well-being, decreased workplace satisfaction, increased employee turnover, and reduced productivity. Second, these dissatisfactions and productivity reductions have resulted in a workforce that is, for the most part, no longer motivated to perform well. As we have seen, without effective employee functioning, organizational performance has also suffered, often, in terms of the loss of intangible resources, far beyond the shorter-term financial gains that were expected as the result of economically driven corporate change.

Given the direct relationship between employee satisfaction, well-being and happiness, and organizational financial performance, many companies have instituted programmes intended to reverse the harm that has resulted from economically-driven change management. These efforts have included the recognition of the need for effective HR management, a strong corporate vision, and the understanding that the intangible assets inherent in the skills, knowledge, and expertise of employees, are necessary for organizational innovation. Further, companies that have taken pains to enhance their employees' feelings of personal control over their work environment (and their use of time, reward structures, and goal setting and management) and that have recognized the need to provide work environments that stimulate health, reduce stress, and develop skills through supported learning practices have been rated as more financially successful; they have also been rated as better places to work and, as such, have encouraged greater employee loyalty and performance. Lastly, by acknowledging the value of effective management as a motivational tool, and the need for clear communication flow, these organizations have set an example for modern business practice. Thus, the 21st-century organization can be both profitable and equitable, blurring the distinction between work and everyday life by taking care of its employees, and by allowing individuals to feel a sense of purpose and meaning in their work lives.

Glossary

Absenteeism: being absent from work for reasons of actual or supposed illness or injury.

Affective commitment: an employee's emotional commitment to his or her employer. High affective commitment increases the chances that an employee will remain with an organization.

"Big Five" personality: the five stable personality traits of neuroticism, extraversion, openness to experience, agreeableness, conscientiousness.

Burnout: emotional or physical breakdown resulting from stress.

CEO: Chief Executive Officer.

CFO: Chief Financial Officer.

CLO: Chief Learning Officer.

Downsizing: reduction in organizational spending, often by laying off workers.

Economic rationalism: economic theory popular in the 1980s and 1990s; advocates the reduction of organizational costs, often through *downsizing*.

Empowerment: employees' perception of their ability to make change in the workplace (for example, being able to participate in workplace decisions).

Ergonomics: science of modifying the environment to increase human performance.

***Fortune* 500**: a listing, prepared annually by Fortune magazine, of the 500 largest US industrial corporations, and ranked by sales.

HPWP: High-performance Work Practices – practices designed to enhance employee satisfaction and empowerment through greater workplace participation and collaboration.

HPWS: High-Performance Work Systems. See *HPWP*.

HRM: Human Resources Management.

Human capital: the intellectual resources of an organization's employees.

Humanism: philosophy of human-centred practice that places human values above other priorities.

Intrinsic motivation: desire to perform an action for its own reward, rather than for an external incentive.

JIT: Just-in-time production – a system designed to reduce organizational costs by producing or manufacturing on demand.

MBA: Master of Business Administration.

Mentor: individual with particular expertise who takes on a supportive teaching role with a less-experienced colleague.

Mission: an organization's commitment to a type of business and to a distinctive role in the marketplace. Mission is reflected in the firm's attitudes to consumers, employees, suppliers, competitors, government, and others.

Perceived control: an individual's perception of control over his or her immediate environment. Higher perceived control is likely to result in lowered stress.

Presenteeism: reluctance to perform based on a lack of motivation; or appearance at work, despite illness or other ailment that reduces performance.

Psychological contract: implied (but often not stated and unwritten) contract between an employee and his or her employer that includes the employee's expectations regarding the employer's duty of care.

Self-actualization: the theorized intrinsic need to reach a state of perfection; requires the prior fulfilment of more basic conditions, such as food and shelter, emotional stability, and intellectual and aesthetic stimulation.

Self-efficacy: situationally specific self-confidence.

SME: Small-medium enterprise – usually an organization that employs 50 or less workers.

Stakeholders: persons who have some stake in an organization; can include shareholders, employees, management, clients, customers, and even the extended community.

Tacit knowledge: knowledge of an action or process that has been gained through practical experience and that is not easily transmitted through explicit means (such as conventional training).

Telecommuting: flexible working practice that allows employees to work from a remote location through the use of telecommunication (for example, web access, telephone).

TQM: Total Quality Management – a system the purports to increase employee empowerment through better access to information.

Vision: organizational strategy that encompasses future goals, and how the organization will achieve those goals.

Appendix

Motivational interviewing

Think back to the last time someone told you that you should do something (for example, start something, finish something, make some health change, and so on). Was your initial reaction one of instant capitulation and compliance? Did you welcome the suggestion and take pains to follow the advice? Chances are you didn't; in fact, it's more likely that you came up with excellent reasons why you didn't need or want to change, and why the other person was wrong! Moreover (and somewhat strangely), we often react in the same way to our internal dialogue; we actually argue against our own advice! So, why are we perverse in our responses to change suggestions, even when those suggestions are from legitimate professionals, and could save our life, our relationship, or our job? Mostly, because we resent being told what to do and strive to assert our own position, even when (often) we know that that position is not tenable. This is sometimes referred to as pride, and sometimes as pigheadedness!

Given the natural, human tendency to resist suggestion to change, how can we initiate change in ourselves and others, without meeting immediate resistance? What if we were encouraged to provide our own reasons for change? After all, we are much more likely to listen to ourselves than to someone else. This line of reasoning forms the basis of the practice of Motivational Interviewing (MI).

In fact it has been established, through clinical research, that the more we are confronted to change, the less likely that we will make that change or maintain it in the future (Miller & Rollnick, 2002). Traditional, "therapies" like those used in Alcoholics Anonymous (AA), often do more harm than good. In fact, a natural recovery rate from alcoholism is some six times more likely than recovery through AA! Consequently, William Miller and Stephen Rollnick, the developers of motivational interviewing, reasoned that if conventional, confronting styles of therapy and change agency were ineffective, then a smarter technique that works with a client's own ambivalence was needed.

In effect, MI is a method for encouraging someone to focus on his or her own reasons for change, and to develop those reasons to a point at which the ambivalence towards change see-saws towards change behaviour. Anyone who engages in a behaviour that they are not completely convinced is correct, healthy, or productive (for example, smoking, procrastination, over-eating, and so on) will feel ambivalence; that is, they will experience the typical misgivings we all feel when engaging in such behaviours. Chances are, even at a subconscious or subvocal level, they have already expressed some doubts about the behaviour. Using MI techniques, a "therapist" (that is, anyone seeking to facilitate change in another) can help a person vocalize their ambivalence. Because we are more likely to listen to ourselves than to another, the internal voice of doubt can be extremely effective in helping us decide to change. Once the decision to change has been made, the therapist's role is to guide that change in a constructive and maintainable way. Although the advanced application of MI is beyond the scope of this article (anyone wanting to learn more about MI and how to apply it should read Miller and Rollnick's excellent book *Motivational Interviewing: Preparing People for Change*), we will summarize the basic methods of MI, and learn how to apply them in everyday business and personal life.

Basic MI Methodology

As we have discussed, MI is about harnessing pre-existing ambivalence towards a behaviour. The fact that MI uses two or more people to aid change illustrates that effective change is, in fact, an interpersonal process rather than an internal one. That is, motivation to change is often found in the interplay between persons. Consequently, the person acting in the role of change agent is the one who needs to develop the skills needed to encourage change, and is, therefore, the one we'll focus on (interestingly, in cases of self-change, the change agent and subject can be the same person).

In order to encourage change, the change agent needs to develop several skills, both for understanding and to react. These fall into two main categories: listening and responding. Most of us aren't very good at listening. In fact, often, when we are supposed to be conversing (that is, listening) we use the time when the other person speaks to figure out what we're going to say next! Obviously, it's hard to respond accurately and usefully to someone else if you have little or no idea of what they actually said. The easiest way to train yourself to listen to others (and these skills are equally applicable in just about any situation where listening is required) is to pay attention to what the other person is saying, and then reflect it back to them by paraphrasing them. This technique has been employed by psychologists for years, to good effect. By listening well enough to be able to paraphrase, you are forcing yourself to pay attention, and the act of rephrasing allows you to clarify with the other person whether what you think you heard was actually what they meant. Moreover, the other person is satisfied, because they've heard you repeating back a version of his or her words. A simple example could go like this:

Person A: "I don't feel good at work; it seems that no one listens to me"
Person B (*normal*): "I can't stand my boss; he's always asking me to work late"
    or
Person B (*actually listening*): "You're not satisfied because it feels like no one hears what you're saying"

This simple distinction makes all the difference, and is known as "active listening". In the first response, we have a typical reaction, the responder has sort of heard Person A, and has used what he or she heard to start complaining about his or her favourite topic, his or her own problems! The second response, however, is focussed on Person A's statement, and is neutral (neither agreeing nor disagreeing). Notice that the second response is not phrased as a question, but a statement; it affirms what Person A said. If it's wrong in content or interpretation, Person A now has an opportunity to correct the interpretation. Most importantly, it allows Person A to continue, rather than being cut off by a thoughtless response. This way, Person A has the opportunity to actually communicate the problem, so that something can be done about it. Of course, active listening is not just a method for allowing someone to whine. It has its place in encouraging someone to talk about his or her problems, in order to enact some sort of change.

Despite the simplicity of active listening, it takes quite a bit of practice before it becomes natural (you don't want to sound like the stereotype of a movie psychologist!). Moreover, by itself, it doesn't do that much. Rather, it provides the backdrop for the second aspect of MI, appropriate response.

At the heart of any change is ambivalence which, simply, is the internal disparity between a desire to maintain the status quo and the desire to make change. Ambivalence is, in effect, the engine of change, because without the confusion of ambivalence, there is no need to question the status quo and, consequently, no need to change. It is, therefore, the job of the motivational interviewer to work with ambivalence, by encouraging an individual to build on his or her doubts about the current behaviour, whilst simultaneously increasing his or her desire for change. As was mentioned before, when we are told what we should do, we more often than not take the opposite stance. However, when we are encouraged to develop our own arguments for change, we are much more likely to listen. In MI, this is called "change talk", and can be encouraged in several ways.

In fact, the more the change talk, both internal and external, the more likely that change will occur, and be maintained (Miller & Rollnick, 2002). Broadly speaking, change talk can be categorized by discussion of the disadvantages of the status quo, the advantages of change, optimism for change, and talk about intention to change. Every time a person engages in change talk, the ambivalence shifts in favour of the change and away from the status quo. Moreover, by encouraging change talk we can enhance a person's belief in his or her ability to change. This belief is known as "self-efficacy" (self-confidence applied to specific situations), and is an extremely powerful motivator for change.

The following exchange illustrates the development of change talk by using active listening and acting on ambivalence (in all examples take the "interviewer" to mean the person attempting to encourage change, and the "client" as the person attempting to change – also, for the purpose of illustration, the session has been sped up somewhat):

Client: I can't get anything done, I feel like such a failure. Whenever I have a deadline, I put things off until too late. I think I'm going to get fired.

Interviewer: You can't get anything finished, even though you've tried many times. *(Active listening)*

Client: That's right, and I think my boss is starting to get fed up.

Interviewer: It seems to me that having tried so many times, you must actually be quite a good self-starter, but it's the finishing you're having trouble with. *(Reflection and boosting self-efficacy)*

Client: I don't know about that, but you're right, I don't ever seem to be able to finish something once I've started it.

Interviewer: So you're telling me that you've never, not even once in your life, been able to finish something, no matter how small? *(Active listening, questions status quo)*

Client: Well, I wouldn't say that exactly, sure, I've finished things, just not most of the time.

Interviewer: Tell me about one of the times that you did finish something, something that you're proud of. *(Boosting self-efficacy, encouraging change talk)*

Client: You're trying to trick me.

Interviewer: Not at all, you told me that you never finish anything, but I think that might be an exaggeration, only because just about everyone, no matter how unmotivated, has been able to finish something at some stage. In fact many people are probably quite proud of one or two things that they've accomplished. *(Active listening, reframing)*

Client: Well . . . OK, there was this time not too long after I started in my job, maybe two months in. I was really excited to have got the job, and really felt like I'd be able to make a change. I was asked to head up a research project, coordinating a team, and reporting back to management. We did really well, and I was actually given a promotion a few months later.

Interviewer: That sounds great, but I'm confused. What happened between then and now to change you from such a confident worker to someone who says they can't finish anything? *(Open-ended questioning, clarification)*

Client: I don't know . . .

Interviewer: You have no idea what changed you from an ideal worker, to someone with no confidence to complete a project. *(Active listening, reflection, encouraging change talk)*

Client: Well, not no idea. I suppose I lost my confidence over time because my new boss started tightening up the deadlines, and I felt pressured to perform. I wanted to do a good job, but there wasn't enough time. In the end I just started making excuses, trying to get more time, but I found that I wasn't doing anything with the time, just getting more and more stressed.

Interviewer: The increasing pressure to perform reduced your feeling of control. You felt pressured to perform, but the pressure wasn't motivating, in fact it reduced your enthusiasm. *(Active listening, reflection, encouraging change talk)*

Client: That's exactly it! It's not like I'm lazy, I want to do a good job, and I hate feeling unmotivated. I used to love my job, now each morning I feel stressed. It would be great if I could get my old enthusiasm back.

Interviewer: I believe you; you don't strike me as unmotivated, just at the end of your tether. *(Boosting self-efficacy, encouraging change talk)*

Client: Absolutely, if only I could do something about it.

Interviewer: Well, there are many things that we could do, including several techniques that my other clients have had a lot of success with. With your permission, I'd like to work with you to generate some solutions. What do you think? *(Encouraging change, asking permission)*

Client: OK, let's give it a go.

Although it would most likely take several sessions and more advanced MI techniques to achieve this change commitment, this example illustrates some of the basic processes of MI (up to the point of initiating change strategies). At this point the client has gone from despairing about his or her lack of ability to do things, to a point of readiness to make change. Try it out on yourself and, when you feel confident, start using active listening and change talk (in yourself, and encouragement in others) in your daily home and work life. To assist with your development as a motivational expert, the following section includes several more examples of MI processes.

Practical application of motivational interviewing to work and life

The following scenarios provide further illustration of MI processes. As in the above examples, the timeframe has been sped up. It is very rare for change talk to appear as rapidly as in these exchanges. It should be noted, therefore, that these scenarios are illustrative only, and are not intended as templates or therapies.

Application of MI at work

Motivating a colleague to be more punctual (n.b., this could be an interchange between any two workers, including a supervisor and supervisee).

Worker 1: I really liked the presentation you gave the other day, but it would probably have been a lot better if you'd gotten to the meeting on time. What do you think?

Worker 2: Yeah, well I was running late because my computer wasn't working properly and I had to make last minute changes to the presentation.

Worker 1: What about the time before that, you know, when you had to co-present and you got there 10 minutes late.

Worker 2: Is this an inquisition? So what if I was late a couple of times.

Worker 1: A couple of times?

Worker 2: OK, so I'm late a lot. I can't help it if I have to work with people and equipment that holds me up. I can't ever get things done around here.

Worker 1: I'm not making judgement on your actions, it just seems to me that excuses are one thing and action another.

Worker 2: What's that supposed to mean? Are you telling me that I make things up?

Worker 1: Hey, relax. I don't think this needs to be an argument, I just feel that there are lots of ways of making change to be more time efficient, and I'd like to help if I can.

Worker 2: So you're telling me that you're the king of time management.

Worker 1: Not at all. But there are some things that I've learnt that I find very helpful for getting things done.

Worker 2: Well, I think I'm fine.

Worker 1: You're fine; there are no problems with your time management.

Worker 2: Now, you're being sarcastic.

Worker 1: What makes you think that?

Worker 2: Well, first you imply that I'm late all the time, and then you tell me I'm fine . . .

Worker 1: Well, you tell me . . . How do you feel about your time management?

Worker 2: Like I said, it's not me; it's the people around me and the lousy computer.

Worker 1: There are absolutely *no problems* with your time management abilities, your computer and co-workers are the problem *every single time*.

Worker 2: Well, that's not what I said exactly. Not every single time. I suppose that sometimes I find it hard to get started.

Worker 1: Occasionally, you have difficulties motivating yourself.

Worker 2: Yeah, it's hard you know? The people I work with don't make it easy for me, and you know about the deadlines. No wonder I'm late for the meetings.

Worker 1: The pressure here at work gets to you and the people aren't supportive.

Worker 2: Yeah, I really don't feel supported. I'd like to feel more motivated, I'd even like to be on time to those stupid meetings . . .

Worker 1: You'd like to change, but you don't feel like you have the resources to do it.

Worker 2: That's right . . .

Worker 1: Well, like I said, I know a few techniques for time management that were taught to me by that performance psychologist who came to the office a while ago. They work really well for me, and I know some other people who've had some great results using them. If you'd like, I could arrange for him to work with you next week? He's doing another series of sessions.

Worker 2: Well, OK, I suppose it couldn't do any harm. As long as it doesn't take too much of my time!

Note that this exchange went a lot less like a counselling session, and more like a standard exchange in the workplace. Nevertheless, with some subtle manipulation, Worker 1 has managed to get Worker 2 to start talking about his or her time management issues, and evoked some change talk. Notice also that Worker 1 used mostly active listening skills and restatement (but not much questioning) to achieve this goal.

Application of MI at home

Motivating a friend to quit smoking

Friend 1: How did your doctor's appointment go?

Friend 2: It was fine.

Friend 1: Really, no problems? That's great.

Friend 2: Well, mostly it was good, but she told me that she's worried about my cough.

Friend 1: How so?

Friend 2: Well, she said that it's probably because of my smoking, which I think is rubbish, and that I should cut down or quit.

Friend 1: I'd noticed that it was getting worse . . .

Friend 2: Now you sound like her, next you'll be telling me I should quit.

Friend 1: I wouldn't dream of telling you what you should do. Anyway, I doubt I could influence you; you have to make up your own mind.

Friend 2: That's right, anyway I like smoking.

Friend 1: You like smoking, but you don't like the coughing.

Friend 2: Well yeah, the coughing sucks . . .

Friend 1: But the rest is fine – everything else about smoking is great.

Friend 2: Well, maybe not great. I don't like having to have a cigarette first thing after I wake up, and it costs a lot.

Friend 1: So the coughing, the cost and the need aren't so good, but the rest is.

Friend 2: Well, plus I wanted to start exercising, but I can't really do that with the smoking, can I? I mean it's hard to climb stairs! Can you imagine me jogging?

Friend 1: Actually, I can. I've been looking for an exercise partner for a while...

Friend 2: And you think that I'd be able to do that? You're dreaming!

Friend 1: Perhaps you'd forgotten that I started exercising 6 months ago, after I quit...

Friend 2: Oh yeah... How's that going?

Friend 1: To tell the truth, the first 2 weeks were awful. But after that I really started to feel better. After 3 weeks I actually found that I could climb stairs again without wheezing so much. It wasn't so hard to start exercising after that and I feel a lot better now.

Friend 2: So it wasn't as hard to quit as you thought?

Friend 1: No it was hard, but there are lots of ways to make it easier. It doesn't have to be all willpower, like those nicotine patch ads make you think. I didn't even use a patch or gum, just some techniques that a psychologist friend of mine showed me.

Friend 2: What sort of techniques?

Friend 1: Oh nothing hard, just some relaxation stuff, how to distract when I was craving, and how to break the mental associations between cigarettes and smoking situations. Also, some information about what the nicotine was doing in my brain. It really helped though.

Friend 2: Do you think I could learn those things?

Friend 1: Sure...

In this scenario, Friend 1 has not tried to persuade, shame, cajole, or trick Friend 2. He or she just used MI techniques to elicit change talk. Remember, the more change talk, the more likely that change will happen. Also, once a person starts talking about change, he or she is more likely to listen to alternatives, and to consult someone with expertise in achieving the desired change.

References

ABS. (1998). *Participation in Sport and Physical Activities*. Canberra: Department of the Arts, Sport, the Environment, Tourism and Territories.

Accounting for People. (2003). London: Task Force on Human Capital Management.

Achbar, M., Abbott, J., & Bakan, J. (2004). The Corporation. Retrieved 27th October, 2005, from http://www.thecorporation.com.

Adams, J. (1999). *Exercise Dependence: A Multidimensional Phenomenon*. Unpublished PhD, La Trobe University, Melbourne, Australia.

Adams, J. (2004). Organisational Amelioration through the Development of Positive Workplace Practices. 2004, from www.eclectic-consulting-ltd.com.

Adams, J., & Kirkby, R. J. (2001). A review of the physiological, neurological and behavioural aspects of addiction. *Australian Journal of Primary Health, 7*, 25–33.

Adler, R. W., Milne, M. J., & Stablein, R. (2001). Situated motivation: An empirical test in an accounting course. *Revue Canadienne des Sciences de l'Administration/Canadian Journal of Administrative Sciences, 18*(2), 101–115.

Ageing and Work in Europe. (2004). Dublin: European Foundation for the Improvement of Living and Working Conditions.

Agesa, J., & Monaco, K. (2004). Industry racial employment by skill level: The effects of market structure and racial wage gaps. *Journal of Labor Research, 25*(2), 315–328.

Allan, C., Brosnan, P., Horwitz, F., & Walsh, P. (2001). From standard to non-standard employment: Labour force change in Australia, New Zealand and South Africa. *International Journal of Manpower, 22*(7–8), 748–763.

Allen, N. J., & Meyer, J. P. (1990). The measurement and antecedents of affective, continuance and normative commitment to the organization. *Journal of Occupational Psychology, 63*(1), 1–18.

Almer, E. D., & Kaplan, S. E. (2002). The Effects of flexible work arrangements on stressors, burnout, and behavioral job outcomes in public accounting. *Behavioral Research in Accounting, 14*(0), 1–34.

Amoore, L. (2004). Risk, reward and discipline at work. *Economy and Society, 33*(2), 174–196.

Andrikopoulos, A. A., & Prodromidis, K. P. (2001). The qualitative element in organization behavior. *Journal of Socio-Economics, 30*(4), 353–362.

Arai, M., Billot, A., & Lanfranchi, J. (2001). Learning by helping: A bounded rationality model of mentoring. *Journal of Economic Behavior and Organization, 45*(2), 113–131.

Arocena, P., & Villanueva, M. (2003). Access as a motivational device: Implications for human resource management. *Kyklos, 56*(2), 199–221.

Aronson, E. (2001). Integrating leadership styles and ethical perspectives. *Revue Canadienne des Sciences de l'Administration/Canadian Journal of Administrative Sciences, 18*(4), 244–256.

Avtgis, T. A. (2000). Unwillingness to communicate and satisfaction in organizational relationships. *Psychological Reports, 87*(1), 82–84.

Bacon, N., Wright, M., & Demina, N. (2004). Management buyouts and human resource management. *British Journal of Industrial Relations, 42*(2), 325–347.

Bakan, J. (2004). *The Corporation: The Pathological Pursuit of Profit and Power*. New York: Free Press.

Barnett, R. C. (1999). A new work-life model for the twenty-first century. *Annals of the American Academy of Political and Social Science, 562*(0), 143–158.

Barrett, D. J. (2002). Change communication: Using strategic employee communication to facilitate major change. *Corporate Communications, 7*(4), 219–231.

Barrett, R. (1999). Why the future belongs to values added companies. *Journal for Quality & Participation, 22*(1), 30–36.

Bartel, A. P. (2004). Human resource management and organizational performance: Evidence from retail banking. *Industrial & Labor Relations Review, 57*(2), 181–203.

Bartlett, K. R. (2001). The relationship between training and organizational commitment: A study in the health care field. *Human Resource Development Quarterly, 12*(4), 335–352.

Baruch-Feldman, C., Brondolo, E., Ben-Dayan, D., & Schwartz, J. (2002). Sources of social support and burnout, job satisfaction, and productivity. *Journal of Occupational Health Psychology, 7*(1), 84–93.

Bass, B. M. (1990). From transactional to transformational leadership: Learning to share the vision. *Organizational Dynamics, 18*(3), 19–31.

Bass, B. M., Waldman, D. A., Avolio, B. J., & Bebb, M. (1987). Transformational leadership and the falling dominoes effect. *Group & Organization Studies*, Vol 12(1) March 1987, 73–87.

Batt, R. (1999). Work organization, technology, and performance in customer service and sales. *Industrial and Labor Relations Review, 52*(4), 539–564.

Batt, R. (2004). Who benefits from teams? Comparing workers, supervisors, and managers. *Industrial Relations, 43*(1), 183–212.

Batt, R., Colvin, A. J. S., & Keefe, J. (2002). Employee voice, human resource practices, and quit rates: Evidence from the telecommunications industry. *Industrial and Labor Relations Review, 55*(4), 573–594.

Batt, R., & Valcour, P. M. (2003). Human resources practices as predictors of work-family outcomes and employee turnover. *Industrial Relations, 42*(2), 189–220.

Baughan-Young, K. (2001). The color of success. *Journal of Property Management, 66*(5), 68–70.

Beaubien, E. (2001). Motivation 101. *Executive Excellence, 18,* 12–14.

Beers, T. M. (2000). Flexible schedules and shift work: Replacing the "9-to-5" workday? *Monthly Labor Review, 123*(6), 33–40.

Beishon, M. (2000). Getting better by design. *Director, 54,* 85.

Bekker, M. H. J., Nijssen, A., & Hens, G. (2001). Stress prevention training: Sex differences in types of stressors, coping, and training effects. *Stress & Health, 17*(4), 207–218.

Belout, A., Dolan, S. L., & Saba, T. (2001). Trends and emerging practices in human resource management: The Canadian scene. *International Journal of Manpower, 22*(3), 207–215.

Benabou, R., & Tirole, J. (2003). Intrinsic and extrinsic motivation. *Review of Economic Studies, 70*(3), 489–520.

Benavides Espinosa, M. D. M., Urquidi Martin, A. C., & Roig Dobon, S. (2003). The transmission of knowledge by means of strategic alliances: An application in the hotel industry. *Journal of Transnational Management Development, 8*(3), 19–34.

Benavides, F. G., Benach, J., Diez-Roux, A. V., & Roman, C. (2000). How do types of employment relate to health indicators? Findings from the Second European Survey on working conditions. *Journal of Epidemiology & Community Health, 54*(7), 494–501.

Berg, P., Appelbaum, E., Bailey, T., & Kalleberg, A. L. (2004). Contesting time: International comparisons of employee control of working time. *Industrial & Labor Relations Review, 57*(3), 331–349.

Berg, P., Kalleberg, A. L., & Appelbaum, E. (2003). Balancing work and family: The role of high-commitment environments. *Industrial Relations, 42*(2), 168–188.

Bergmann, T. J., Lester, S. W., De Meuse, K. P., & Grahn, J. L. (2000). Integrating the three domains of employee commitment: An exploratory study. *Journal of Applied Business Research, 16*(4), 15–26.

Best Companies: Best Practice. (2004). London: Department of Trade and Industry.

Bhanthumnavin, D. (2003). Perceived social support from supervisor and group members' psychological and situational characteristics as predictors of subordinate performance in Thai work units. *Human Resource Development Quarterly, 14*(1), 79–97.

Black, S. E., & Lynch, L. M. (2001). How to compete: The impact of workplace practices and information technology on productivity. *Review of Economics and Statistics, 83*(3), 434–435.

Black, S. E., & Lynch, L. M. (2004). What's driving the new economy? The benefits of workplace innovation. *Economic Journal, 114*(493), F97–116.

Bolin, K., Jacobson, L., & Lindgren, B. (2002). Employer investments in employee health: Implications for the family as health producer. *Journal of Health Economics, 21*(4), 563–583.

Bond, F. W., & Bunce, D. (2001). Job control mediates change in a work reorganization intervention for stress reduction. *Journal of Occupational Health Psychology, 6*(4), 290–302.

Boosting work productivity. (1997). *Research Technology Management, 40*, 58.

Bosma, N., van Praag, M., Thurik, R., & de Wit, G. (2004). The value of human and social capital investments for the business performance of startups. *Small Business Economics, 23*(3), 227–236.

Boswell, W. R., & Boudreau, J. W. (2000). Employee satisfaction with performance appraisals and appraisers: The role of perceived appraisal use. *Human Resource Development Quarterly, 11*(3), 283–299.

Bowles, S., Gintis, H., & Osborne, M. (2001). Incentive-enhancing preferences: Personality, behavior, and earnings. *American Economic Review, 91*(2), 155–158.

Bramley, P. (1999). Evaluating effective management learning. *Journal of European Industrial Training, 23*(3), 145–154.

Branham, L. (2001). Recognize results. *Executive Excellence, 18*, 17–19.

Brophy Marcus, M. (2000). Workouts at work can sweeten long days, but don't cut loose on the boss. *U.S. News & World Report, 128*, 57.

Brown, T. C. (2005). Effectiveness of distal and proximal goals as transfer-of-training interventions: A field experiment. *Human Resource Development Quarterly, 16*(3), 369–387.

Brown, W. A., & Yoshioka, C. F. (2003). Mission attachment and satisfaction as factors in employee retention. *Nonprofit Management & Leadership, 14*(1), 5–18.

Brutus, S., Ruderman, M. N., Ohlott, P. J., & McCauley, C. D. (2000). Developing from job experiences: The role of organization-based self-esteem. *Human Resource Development Quarterly, 11*(4), 367–380.

Buchen, I. H. (2003). Future-imbedded innovation methodologies. *Foresight, 5*(3), 3–9.

Buller, P. F., & McEvoy, G. M. (1999). Creating and sustaining ethical capability in the multi-national corporation. *Journal of World Business, 34*(4), 326–343.

Butler, M. P. (2003). Corporate ergonomics programme at Scottish & Newcastle. *Applied Ergonomics, 34*(1), 35–38.

Buzan, T. (1989). *Use Your Head* (3rd ed.). London: BBC Books.

Carter, S. D. (2002). Matching training methods and factors of cognitive ability: A means to improve training outcomes. *Human Resource Development Quarterly, 13*(1), 71–87.

Cassar, V. (1999). Can leader direction and employee participation co-exist? Investigating interaction effects between participation and favourable work-related attitudes among Maltese middle-managers. *Journal of Managerial Psychology, 14*(1–2), 57–68.

Catlette, B., & Hadden, R. (1999). Contented cows. *Executive Excellence, 16*(8), 18–21.

Chami, R., & Fullenkamp, C. (2002). Trust and efficiency. *Journal of Banking and Finance, 26*(9), 1785–1809.

Chan, K. C., Gee, M. V., & Steiner, T. L. (2000). Employee happiness and corporate financial performance. *Financial Practice and Education, 10*(2), 47–52.

Chatterji, M., & Tilley, C. J. (2002). Sickness, absenteeism, presenteeism, and sick pay. *Oxford Economic Papers, 54*(4), 669–687.

Che, Y.-K., & Yoo, S.-W. (2001). Optimal incentives for teams. *American Economic Review, 91*(3), 525–541.

Chenhall, R. H., & Langfield-Smith, K. (2003). Performance measurement and reward systems, trust, and strategic change. *Journal of Management Accounting Research, 15,* 117–143.

Cherry, M. (2004). Are salaried workers compensated for overtime hours? *Journal of Labor Research, 25*(3), 485–502.

Chiu, R. (1999). Does perception of pay equity, pay satisfaction, and job satisfaction mediate the effect of positive affectivity on work motivation? *Social Behavior & Personality, 28*(2), 177–184.

Cho, D. (2002). The connection between self-directed learning and the learning organization. *Human Resource Development Quarterly, 13*(4), 467–470.

Clardy, A. (2000). Learning on their own: Vocationally oriented self-directed learning projects. *Human Resource Development Quarterly, 11*(2), 105–125.

Clarke, R. (2005). *Flexible Working: Impact and Implementation an Employer Survey.* London: Chartered Institute of Personnel and Development.

Clemmer, J. (2002). That EMPOWER word again! *Canadian Manager, 27,* 23.

Clutterbuck, D. (2001). The communicating company. *Journal of Communication Management, 6*(1), 70–76.

Cogan, M. (2000). Human capital: An investment whose time has come. *Employee Benefit News, 14,* 48–52.

Cohendet, P., Creplet, F., Diani, M., Dupouet, O., & Schenk, E. (2004). Matching communities and hierarchies within the firm. *Journal of Management and Governance, 8*(1), 27–48.

Collins, A., & Harris, R. I. D. (1999). Downsizing and productivity: The case of UK motor vehicle manufacturing 1974–1994. *Managerial and Decision Economics, 20*(5), 281–290.

Collins, D. B., & Holton, E. F. (2004). The effectiveness of managerial leadership development programmes: A meta-analysis of studies from 1982 to 2001. *Human Resource Development Quarterly, 15*(2), 217–248.

Competing in the Global Economy: The Innovation Challenge. (2003). London: Department of Trade and Industry.

Conlin, M. (2002). The war against excess worker waistage. from http://search.epnet.com/direct.asp?an=8693761&db=bsh.

Cooke, F. L. (2002). Harnessing the firm-specific knowledge of the maintenance workforce for organizational competitiveness. *Technology Analysis and Strategic Management, 14*(1), 123–140.

Cowling, M. (2005). *Still at Work? An Empirical Test of Competing Theories of the Long Hours Culture.* London: The Work Foundation.

Cromwell, S. E., & Kolb, J. A. (2004). An examination of work-environment support factors affecting transfer of supervisory skills training to the workplace. *Human Resource Development Quarterly, 15*(4), 449–471.

Cropanzano, R., & Wright, T. A. (2001). When a "happy" worker is really a "productive" worker: A review and further refinement of the happy-productive worker thesis. *Consulting Psychology Journal: Practice & Research, 53*(3), 182–199.

Crossman, A., & Lee-Kelley, L. (2004). Trust, commitment and team working: The paradox of virtual organizations. *Global Networks, 4*(4), 375–390.

Csikszentmihalyi, M. (2003). *Good Business: Leadership, Flow and the Making of Meaning.* London: Hodder and Stoughton.

Cummings, N. A. (2000). Psychology and the new entrepreneurship: Possibilities and opportunities. *Psychologist Manager Journal, 4*(1), 27–43.

Cunliffe, A. L. (2002). Reflexive dialogical practice in management learning. *Management Learning, 33*(1), 35–61.

Cunningham, P., & Iles, P. (2002). Managing learning climates in a financial services organisation. *Journal of Management Development, 21*(6), 477–492.

Dackert, I., Loov, L.-A., & Martensson, M. (2004). Leadership and climate for innovation in teams. *Economic and Industrial Democracy, 25*(2), 301–318.

Darlington, H. (2002). People – your most important asset Part 4 – motivating the best. *Supply House Times, 45,* 68–70.

Davison, R., & Martinsons, M. G. (2002). Empowerment or enslavement?: A case of process-based organisational change in Hong Kong. *Information Technology & People, 15*(1), 42–59.

de Jonge, J., Bosma, H., Peter, R., & Siegrist, J. (2000). Job strain, effort-reward imbalance and employee well-being: A large-scale cross-sectional study. *Social Science & Medicine, 50*(9), 1317–1327.

de Kok, J., & Uhlaner, L. M. (2001). Organization context and human resource management in the small firm. *Small Business Economics, 17*(4), 273–291.

Delbridge, R., & Whitfield, K. (2001). Employee perceptions of job influence and organizational participation. *Industrial Relations, 40*(3), 472–489.

Demerouti, E., Bakker, A. B., de Jonge, J., Janssen, P. P. M., & Schaufeli, W. B. (2001). Burnout and engagement at work as a function of demands and control. *Scandinavian Journal of Work, Environment & Health, 28*(4), 279–286.

Dewe, P., & O'Driscoll, M. (2002). Stress management interventions: What do managers actually do? *Personnel Review, 31*(2), 143–165.

Dex, S., & Scheibel, F. (2001). Flexible and family-friendly working arrangements in UK-based SMEs: Business cases. *British Journal of Industrial Relations, 39*(3), 411–431.

Dirks, K. T., & Ferrin, D. L. (2001). The role of trust in organizational settings. *Organization Science, 12*(4), 450–467.

Dolan, S., Belout, A., & Balkin, D. B. (2000). Downsizing without downgrading: Learning how firms manage their survivors. *International Journal of Manpower, 21*(1–2), 34–46.

Drago, R., & Garvey, G. T. (1998). Incentives for helping on the job: Theory and evidence. *Journal of Labor Economics, 16*(1), 1–25.

Duffy, V. G., & Salvendy, G. (1999). The impact of organizational ergonomics on work effectiveness: With special reference to concurrent engineering in manufacturing industries. *Ergonomics, 42*(4), 614–637.

Dunn, G. (2001). Cultivating performance. *Journal of Property Management, 66*(5), 48–50.

Durkalski, E. (2001). Staying on top-strategies for success. *Paperboard Packaging, 86,* 34–38.

Dymock, D. (1999). Blind date: A case study of mentoring as workplace learning. *Journal of Workplace Learning: Employee Counselling Today, 11*(8), 312–317.

Eaton, S. C. (2003). If you can use them: Flexibility policies, organizational commitment, and perceived performance. *Industrial Relations, 42*(2), 145–167.

Egan, T. M., Yang, B., & Bartlett, K. R. (2004). The effects of organizational learning culture and job satisfaction on motivation to transfer learning and turnover intention. *Human Resource Development Quarterly, 15*(3), 279–301.

Eisenberger, R., & Rhoades, L. (2001). Incremental effects of reward on creativity. *Journal of Personality & Social Psychology, 81*(4), 728–741.

Eisenberger, R., Rhoades, L., & Cameron, J. (1999). Does pay for performance increase or decrease perceived self-determination and intrinsic motivation? *Journal of Personality and Social Psychology, 77*(5), 1026–1040.

Elkins, S. L. (2003). Transformational learning in leadership and management positions. *Human Resource Development Quarterly, 14*(3), 351–358.

Ellen, I. G., & Hempstead, K. (2002). Telecommuting and the demand for urban living: A preliminary look at white-collar workers. *Urban Studies, 39*(4), 749–766.

Ellinger, A. D. (2005). Contextual factors influencing informal learning in a workplace setting: The case of "reinventing itself company". *Human Resource Development Quarterly, 16*(3), 389–415.

Ellinger, A. D., Ellinger, A. E., & Keller, S. B. (2003). Supervisory coaching behavior, employee satisfaction, and warehouse employee performance: A dyadic perspective in the distribution industry. *Human Resource Development Quarterly, 14*(4), 435–458.

Ellinger, A. D., Ellinger, A. E., Yang, B., & Howton, S. W. (2002). The relationship between the learning organization concept and firms' financial performance: An empirical assessment. *Human Resource Development Quarterly, 13*(1), 5–21.

Ellstrom, P.-E. (2001). Integrating learning and work: Problems and prospects. *Human Resource Development Quarterly, 12*(4), 421–435.

Elovainio, M., Kivimaeki, M., & Helkama, K. (2001). Organizational justice evaluations, job control, and occupational strain. *Journal of Applied Psychology, 86*(3), 418–424.

Elovainio, M., Kivimaeki, M., & Vahtera, J. (2002). Organizational justice: Evidence of a new psychosocial predictor of health. *American Journal of Public Health, 92*(1), 105–108.

Elvira, M., & Town, R. (2001). The effects of race and worker productivity on performance evaluations. *Industrial Relations, 40*(4), 571–590.

Elvira, M. M., & Zatzick, C. D. (2002). Who's displaced first? The role of race in layoff decisions. *Industrial Relations, 41*(2), 329–361.

Employee Appraisal. (2005). London: ACAS.

Employee Appraisals. (2005). London: Business Link.

Employing People Guidebook. (2005). London: Business Link.

Enos, M. D., Thamm, M. K., & Bell, A. (2003). Informal learning and the transfer of learning: How managers develop proficiency. *Human Resource Development Quarterly, 14*(4), 369–387.

Ensher, E. A., Grant-Vallone, E. J., & Donaldson, S. I. (2001). Effects of perceived discrimation on job satisfaction, organizational commitment, organizational citizenship behavior, and grievances. *Human Resource Development Quarterly, 12*(1), 53–72.

Erickson, C. L., & Jacoby, S. M. (2003). The effect of employer networks on workplace innovation and training. *Industrial and Labor Relations Review, 56*(2), 203–223.

Fairbrother, K., & Warn, J. (2003). Workplace dimensions, stress and job satisfaction. *Journal of Managerial Psychology, 18*(1), 8–21.

Fairris, D. (2002). Are transformed workplaces more productively efficient? *Journal of Economic Issues, 36*(3), 659–670.

Fessler, N. J. (2003). Experimental evidence on the links among monetary incentives, task attractiveness, and task performance. *Journal of Management Accounting Research, 15*, 161–176.

Fitzenberger, B., & Wunderlich, G. (2004). The changing life cycle pattern in female employment: A comparison of Germany and the UK. *Scottish Journal of Political Economy, 51*(3), 302–328.

Flannery, R. B. (2002). The psychological contract: Enhancing productivity and its implications for long-term care. *American Journal of Alzheimer's Disease & Other Dementias, 17*(3), 165–168.

Flexible Working. (2004). London: Department of Trade and Industry.

Friedman, R. A., Tidd, S. T., Currall, S. C., & Tsai, J. C. (2000). What goes around comes around: The impact of personal conflict style on work conflict and stress. *International Journal of Conflict Management, 11*(1), 32–55.

Gadiesh, O. (2001). Transforming corner-office strategy into frontline ACTION. *Harvard Business Review, 79*, 72–80.

Gallinsky, E., Bond, J. T., Kim, S. S., Backon, L., Brownfield, E., & Sakai, K. (2004). *Overwork in America: When the Way We Work Becomes Too Much.* Families and Work Institute.

Ganster, D. C., Fox, M. L., & Dwyer, D. J. (2001). Explaining employees' health care costs: A prospective examination of stressful job demands, personal control, and physiological reactivity. *Journal of Applied Psychology, 86*(5), 954–964.

Gibbs, M., Merchant, K. A., van der Stede, W. A., & Vargus, M. E. (2004). Determinants and effects of subjectivity in incentives. *Accounting Review, 79*(2), 409–436.

Glover, J., Friedman, H., & Jones, G. (2002). Adaptive leadership: When change is not enough (Part one). *Organization Development Journal, 20*(2), 15–32.

Glover, J., Rainwater, K., Friedman, H., & Jones, G. (2002). Adaptive leadership: Four principles for being adaptive (Part two). *Organization Development Journal, 20*(4), 18–38.

Godard, J. (2001). High performance and the transformation of work? The Implications of alternative work practices for the experience and outcomes of work. *Industrial and Labor Relations Review, 54*(4), 776–805.

Goh, S. C. (2003). Improving organizational learning capability: Lessons from two case studies. *Learning Organization, 10*(4), 216–227.

Gollan, P. J. (2003). All talk but no voice: Employee voice at the Eurotunnel call centre. *Economic and Industrial Democracy, 24*(4), 509–541.

Green, F. (2004). Why has work effort become more intense? *Industrial Relations, 43*(4), 709–741.

Griggs, H. E., & Hyland, P. (2003). Strategic downsizing and learning organisations. *Journal of European Industrial Training, 27*(2–4), 177–187.

Guastello, S. J., & Johnson, E. A. (1999). The effect of downsizing on hierarchical work flow dynamics in organizations. *Nonlinear Dynamics, Psychology, and Life Sciences, 3*(4), 347–377.

Guerrero, S., & Sire, B. (2001). Motivation to train from the workers' perspective: Example of French companies. *The International Journal of Human Resource Management, 12*(6), 988–1004.

Guest, D. E., & Peccei, R. (2001). Partnership at work: Mutuality and the balance of advantage. *British Journal of Industrial Relations, 39*(2), 207–236.

Guest, D. E., Michie, J., Conway, N., & Sheehan, M. (2003). Human resource management and corporate performance in the UK. *British Journal of Industrial Relations, 41*(2), 291–314.

Hadjimanolis, A. (2000). A resource-based view of innovativeness in small firms. *Technology Analysis & Strategic Management, 12*(2), 263–281.

Hamlin, R. G. (2004). In support of universalistic models of managerial and leadership effectiveness: Implications for HRD research and practice. *Human Resource Development Quarterly, 15*(2), 189–215.

Hannan, R. L. (2005). The combined effect of wages and firm profit on employee effort. *Accounting Review, 80*(1), 167–188.

Harland, L. K. (2003). Using personality tests in leadership development: Test format effects and the mitigating impact of explanations and feedback. *Human Resource Development Quarterly, 14*(3), 285–301.

Harris, L. (2002). The learning organisation: Myth or reality? Examples from the UK retail banking industry. *Learning Organization, 9*(2), 78–88.

Harrison, R., & Kessels, J. (2004). *Human Resource Development in a Knowledge Economy: An Organisational View.* New York: Palgrave MacMillan.

Haslam, S. A., Powell, C., & Turner, J. C. (2000). Social identity, self-categorization, and work motivation: Rethinking the contribution of the group to positive and sustainable organisational outcomes. *Applied Psychology, 49*(3), 319–339.

Hayward, C. (2001). Wish you weren't here. *Financial Management (CIMA), July/August,* 42–45.

Heath, C. (1999). On the social psychology of agency relationships: Lay theories of motivation overemphasize extrinsic incentives. *Organizational Behavior & Human Decision Processes, 78*(1), 25–62.

Hedge, A. (2000). Where are we in understanding the effects of where we are? *Ergonomics, 43*(7), 1019–1029.

Hegstad, C. D., & Wentling, R. M. (2004). The development and maintenance of exemplary formal mentoring programmes in fortune 500 companies. *Human Resource Development Quarterly, 15*(4), 421–448.

Henderson, R., Sutherland, J., & Turley, S. (2000). Management development in small business: A sub-regional examination of practice, expectation and experience. *Regional Studies, 34*(1), 81–86.

Heron, P., & Thompson, M. (2001). *Innovation and the Psychological Contract in the Knowledge Business*. Oxford: Templeton College.

Hertenstein, E. J. (2001). Goal orientation and practice condition as predictors of training results. *Human Resource Development Quarterly, 12*(4), 403–419.

The high cost of "presenteeism". (2002). *Worklife Report, 14,* 11.

High Performance Through People. (2005). London: Department of Trade and Industry.

High Performance Workplaces. (2004). London: Department of Trade and Industry.

Hill, R., Bullard, T., Capper, P., Hawes, K., & Wilson, K. (1996). Learning about learning organisations: Case studies of skill formation in five New Zealand organisations. *The Learning Organization, 5*(4), 184–192.

Hodson, R. (2001). Disorganized, unilateral, and participative organizations: New insights from the ethnographic literature. *Industrial Relations, 40*(2), 204–230.

Hodson, R. (2002). Worker participation and teams: New evidence from analyzing organizational ethnographies. *Economic and Industrial Democracy, 23*(4), 491–528.

Holton, E. F., Chen, H.-C., & Naquin, S. S. (2003). An examination of learning transfer system characteristics across organizational settings. *Human Resource Development Quarterly, 14*(4), 459–482.

Hoppe, M.-T. (1999). The owner of time has the power. *Foresight, 1*(4), 362–367.

Howard, B., & Gould, K. E. (2000). Strategic planning for employee happiness: A business goal for human service organizations. *American Journal on Mental Retardation, 105*(5), 377–386.

HP Guide to Avoiding Info-Mania. (2005). Helwett Packard.

Hsieh, Y.-M., & Hsieh, A.-T. (2003). Does job standardization increase job burnout? *International Journal of Manpower, 24*(5), 590–614.

Hui, M. K., Au, K., & Fock, H. (2004). Empowerment effects across cultures. *Journal of International Business Studies, 35*(1), 46–60.

Hull, R., & Kaghan, W. (2000). Innovation: But for whose benefit, for what purpose? *Technology Analysis & Strategic Management, 12*(3), 317–325.

Hundley, G. (2001). Why and when are the self-employed more satisfied with their work? *Industrial Relations, 40*(2), 293–316.

Inspirational Leadership. (2004). London: Department of Trade and Industry.

Isaac, R. G., Zerbe, W. J., & Pitt, D. C. (2001). Leadership and motivation: The effective application of expectancy theory. *Journal of Managerial Issues, 13*(2), 212–226.

Isaksen, J. (2000). Constructing meaning despite the drudgery of repetitive work. *Journal of Humanistic Psychology, 40*(3), 84–107.

Jaber, M. Y., Kher, H. V., & Davis, D. J. (2003). Countering forgetting through training and deployment. *International Journal of Production Economics, 85*(1), 33–46.

Jalajas, D. S., & Bommer, M. (1999). The influence of job motivation versus downsizing on individual behavior. *Human Resource Development Quarterly, 10*(4), 329–341.

Jaskyte, K. (2003). Assessing changes in employees' perceptions of leadership behavior, job design, and organizational arrangements and their job satisfaction and commitment. *Administration in Social Work, 27*(4), 25–39.

Jaskyte, K. (2004). Transformational leadership, organizational culture, and innovativeness in nonprofit organizations. *Nonprofit Management and Leadership, 15*(2), 153–168.

Jeppesen, L. B. O., & Molin, M. J. (2003). Consumers as co-developers: Learning and innovation outside the firm. *Technology Analysis & Strategic Management, 15*(3), 363.

Jimmieson, N. L. (2000). Employee reactions to behavioural control under conditions of stress: The moderating role of self-efficacy. *Work & Stress, 14*(3), 262–280.

Johnson, R. (2004). Economic policy implications of world demographic change. *Economic Review (Federal Reserve Bank of Kansas City), 89*(1), 39–64.

Johnson, P., & Indvik, J. (2001). Slings and arrows of rudeness: Incivility in the workplace. *Journal of Management Development, 20*(8), 705–714.

Jorgensen, B. (2004). Individual and organisational learning: A model for reform for public organisations. *Foresight, 6*(2), 91–103.

Jusko, J. (2002). The price tag of poor health. *Industry Week/IW, 251,* 16–19.

Kaipa, P. (2000). Knowledge architecture for the twenty-first century. *Behaviour & Information Technology, 19*(3), 153–161.

Kandel, E., & Pearson, N. D. (2001). Flexibility versus commitment in personnel management. *Journal of the Japanese and International Economies, 15*(4), 515–556.

Kantor, J., & Weisberg, J. (2002). Ethical attitudes and ethical behavior: Are managers role models? *International Journal of Manpower, 23*(8), 687–703.

Kanungo, R. N. (2001). Ethical values of transactional and transformational leaders. *Revue Canadienne des Sciences de l'Administration/Canadian Journal of Administrative Sciences, 18*(4), 257–265.

Karp, T. (2003). Is intellectual capitalism the future wealth of organisations? *Foresight, 5*(4), 20–27.

Kennedy, K. (2001). Manager as motivator. *Executive Excellence, 18,* 13–15.

Kerr, S. (2003). The best-laid incentive plans. *Harvard Business Review, 81,* 27–38.

Kerrin, M., & Oliver, N. (2002). Collective and individual improvement activities: The role of reward systems. *Personnel Review, 31*(3), 320–337.

Keyes, C. L. M., Hysom, S. J., & Lupo, K. L. (2000). The positive organization: Leadership legitimacy, employee well-being, and the bottom line. *Psychologist Manager Journal, 4*(2), 143–153.

Kickul, J. (2001). Promises made, promises broken: An exploration of employee attraction and retention practices in small business. *Journal of Small Business Management, 39*(4), 320–336.

Kilbourne, W., & Weeks, S. (1997). A socio-economic perspective on gender bias in technology. *Journal of Socio-Economics, 26*(3), 243–260.

Kim, H.-S., & Shim, S. (2003). Gender-based approach to the understanding of leadership roles among retail managers. *Human Resource Development Quarterly, 14*(3), 321–342.

Kim, S. (2002). Participative management and job satisfaction: Lessons for management leadership. *Public Administration Review, 62*(2), 231–241.

Kirkcaldy, B. D., Levine, R., & Shephard, R. J. (2000). The impact of working hours on physical and psychological health of German managers. *European Review of Applied Psychology/Revue Europeenne de Psychologie Appliquee, 50*(4), 443–449.

Kirkman, B. L., & Shapiro, D. L. (2001). The impact of team members' cultural values on productivity, cooperation, and empowerment in self-managing work teams. *Journal of Cross Cultural Psychology, 32*(5), 597–617.

Kleinbeck, U., & Fuhrmann, H. (2000). Effects of a psychologically based management system on work motivation and productivity. *Applied Psychology, 49*(3), 596–610.

Knez, M., & Simester, D. (2001). Firm-wide incentives and mutual monitoring at Continental Airlines. *Journal of Labor Economics, 19*(4), 743–772.

Koch, C. (2004). The tyranny of projects: Teamworking, knowledge production and management in consulting engineering. *Economic and Industrial Democracy, 25*(2), 277–300.

Kontoghiorghes, C., Awbrey, S. M., & Feurig, P. L. (2005). Examining the relationship between learning organization characteristics and change adaptation, innovation, and organizational performance. *Human Resource Development Quarterly, 16*(2), 185–211.

Kort, P. M., Verheyen, P. A., & De Waegenaere, A. (2003). The theory of the new economy firm: A dynamic analysis of human capital investment. *Central European Journal of Operations Research, 11*(2), 103–114.

Koys, D. J. (2001). The effects of employee satisfaction, organizational citizenship behavior, and turnover on organizational effectiveness: A unit-level, longitudinal study. *Personnel Psychology, 54*(1), 101–114.

Kuchinke, K. P. (1999). Leadership and culture: Work-related values and leadership styles among one company's U.S. and German telecommunication employees. *Human Resource Development Quarterly, 10*(2), 135–154.

Lagerstrom, K., & Andersson, M. (2003). Creating and sharing knowledge within a transnational team: The development of a global business system. *Journal of World Business, 38*(2), 84–95.

Landauer, J. (1997). Bottom-line benifits of Work/Life programmes. *HR Focus, 74,* 3–5.

Larson, J. A., & Sasser, W. E. (2000). Building trust through committed employees. *Marketing Management, 9,* 40–46.

Laursen, K., & Foss, N. J. (2003). New human resource management practices, complementarities and the impact on innovation performance. *Cambridge Journal of Economics, 27*(2), 243–263.

Lavoie, M., Roy, R., & Therrien, P. (2003). A growing trend toward knowledge work in Canada. *Research Policy, 32*(5), 827–844.

Lawson, B., & Samson, D. (2001). Developing innovation capability in organisations: A dynamic capabilities approach. *International Journal of Innovation Management, 5*(3), 377–401.

Lazonick, W. (2003). The theory of the market economy and the social foundations of innovative enterprise. *Economic and Industrial Democracy, 24*(1), 9–44.

Lee, D. R. (1996). Why is flexible employment increasing? *Journal of Labor Research, 17*(4), 543–553.

Lee, M., & Koh, J. (2001). Is empowerment really a new concept? *The International Journal of Human Resource Management, 12*(4), 684–695.

Levin, J. (2002). Multilateral contracting and the employment relationship. *Quarterly Journal of Economics, 117*(3), 1075–1103.

Levy-Garboua, L., & Montmarquette, C. (2004). Reported job satisfaction: What does it mean? *Journal of Socio-Economics, 33*(2), 135–151.

Liao-Troth, M. A. (2001). Attitude differences between paid workers and volunteers. *Nonprofit Management and Leadership, 11*(4), 423–442.

Lloyd, P. J., & Atella, M. D. (2000). Positive leadership that inspires: Theoretical and empirical perspectives from positive psychology, existential theory, and hardiness research. *Psychologist Manager Journal, 4*(2), 155–165.

Loehr, J. (2001). The making of a corporate athlete. *Harvard Business Review, 79*(1), 120–129.

Lorenzet, S. J., Salas, E., & Tannenbaum, S. I. (2005). Benefiting from mistakes: The impact of guided errors on learning, performance, and self-efficacy. *Human Resource Development Quarterly, 16*(3), 301–322.

Madsen, S. R. (2003). The effects of home-based teleworking on work-family conflict. *Human Resource Development Quarterly, 14*(1), 35–58.

Mallinger, M. (2000). *The Learning Organization in Practice.* Culver City, CA: The Graziado School of Business and Management.

Manders, A. J. C., & Brenner, Y. S. (1999). Globalization, new production concepts and income distribution. *International Journal of Social Economics, 26*(4), 559–569.

Mandeville, T. (1998). An informative economics perspective on innovation. *International Journal of Social Economics, 25*(2–4), 357–364.

Mani, B. G. (2002). Performance appraisal systems, productivity, and motivation: A case study. *Public Personnel Management, 31*(2), 141–160.

Marks, A., & Lockyer, C. (2004). Producing knowledge: The use of the project team as a vehicle for knowledge and skill acquisition for software employees. *Economic and Industrial Democracy, 25*(2), 219–245.

Martin, J. J., & Gill, D. L. (1991). The relationship among competitive orientation, sport confidence, self efficacy, anxiety, and performance. *Journal of Sport and Exercise Psychology, 13*(2), 149–159.

Martins, N. (2002). A model for managing trust. *International Journal of Manpower, 23*(8), 754–769.

Martocchio, J. J., & Hertensein, E. J. (2003). Learning orientation and goal orientation context: Relationships with cognitive and affective learning outcomes. *Human Resource Development Quarterly, 14*(4), 413–434.

Masi, R. J., & Cooke, R. A. (2000). Effects of transformational leadership on subordinate motivation, empowering norms, and organizational productivity. *The International Journal of Organizational Analysis, 8*(1), 16–47.

Mayo, A. (2000). The role of employee development in the growth of intellectual capital. *Personnel Review, 29*(4), 521–533.

McDougall, M., & Beattie, R. S. (1998). The missing link? Understanding the relationship between individual and organisational learning. *International Journal of Training & Development, 2*(4), 288–300.

McGrattan, E. R., & Rogerson, R. (2004). Changes in hours worked, 1950–2000. *Quarterly Review (Federal Reserve Bank of Minneapolis), 28*(1), 14–33.

McKnight, D. H., Ahmad, S., & Schroeder, R. G. (2001). When do feedback, incentive control, and autonomy improve morale? The importance of employee-management relationship closeness. *Journal of Managerial Issues, 13*(4), 466–482.

McMurray, A. J., Scott, D. R., & Pace, R. W. (2004). The relationship between organizational commitment and organizational climate in manufacturing. *Human Resource Development Quarterly, 15*(4), 473–488.

Meet the Need for Work-Life Balance. (2005). London: Business Link.

Meyer, J. P., & Smith, C. A. (2000). HRM practices and organizational commitment: Test of a mediation model. *Revue Canadienne des Sciences de l'Administration/Canadian Journal of Administrative Sciences, 17*(4), 319–331.

Miller, J. S. (2003). High tech and high performance: Managing appraisal in the information age. *Journal of Labor Research, 24*(3), 409–424.

Miller, W. R., & Rollnick, S. (2002). *Motivational interviewing: Preparing People for Change* (2nd ed.). New York: Guildford Press.

Minkler, L. (2004). Shirking and motivations in firms: Survey evidence on worker attitudes. *International Journal of Industrial Organization, 22*(6), 863–884.

Montesino, M. U. (2002). Strategic alignment of training, transfer-enhancing behaviors, and training usage: A posttraining study. *Human Resource Development Quarterly, 13*(1), 89–108.

Morgan, R. B., & Casper, W. J. (2000). Examining the factor structure of participant reactions to training: A multidimensional approach. *Human Resource Development Quarterly, 11*(3), 301–317.

Muhlau, P., & Lindenberg, S. (2003). Efficiency wages: Signals or incentives? An empirical study of the relationship between wage and commitment. *Journal of Management and Governance, 7*(4), 385–400.

Mulholland, P., Zdrahal, Z., Domingue, J., & Hatala, M. (2001). A methodological approach to supporting organizational learning. *International Journal of Human-Computer Studies, 55*, 337–367.

Nachbagauer, A. G. M., & Riedl, G. (2002). Effects of concepts of career plateaus on performance, work satisfaction and commitment. *International Journal of Manpower, 23*(8), 716–733.

Naegele, G., Barkholdt, C., Vroom, B. D., Andersen, J. G., & Krämer, K. (2003). *A New Organisation of Time Over Working Life*. Luxembourg: European Foundation for the Improvement of Living and Working Conditions.

Naquin, S. S., & Holton, E. F. (2002). The effects of personality, affectivity, and work commitment on motivation to improve work through learning. *Human Resource Development Quarterly, 13*(4), 357–376.

Nine steps towards creating a great workplace – right here, right now. (1999). *Harvard Management Update, 4,* 1–4.

Nollen, S. D. (1996). Negative aspects of temporary employment. *Journal of Labor Research, 17*(4), 567–582.

Norgaard, M. (2001). Motivating people. *Executive Excellence, 18,* 19.

O'Neill, P. (2001). Financial narratives of the modern corporation. *Journal of Economic Geography, 1*(2), 181–199.

O'Roark, A. M. (2002). The quest for executive effectiveness: Consultants bridge the gap between psychological research and organizational application. *Consulting Psychology Journal: Practice & Research, 54*(1), 44–54.

Ortenblad, A. (2004). Toward a contingency model of how to choose the right type of learning organization. *Human Resource Development Quarterly, 15*(3), 347–350.

Ory, D. T., Mokhtarian, P. L., Redmond, L. S., Salomon, I., Collantes, G. O., & Choo, S. (2004). When is commuting desirable to the individual? *Growth and Change, 35*(3), 334–359.

Our Methodology: How We Find the Best 50 Corporate Citizens in Canada. (2005). Retrieved 27th October, 2005, from http://www.corporateknights.ca/.

Oyer, P. (2004). Why do firms use incentives that have no incentive effects? *Journal of Finance, 59*(4), 1619–1649.

Pancheri, P., de Martino, V., Spiombi, G., Biondi, M., & Mosticoni, S. (1985). Life stress events and state-trait anxiety in psychiatric and psychosomatic patients. *Issues in Mental Health Nursing, 7*(1–4), 367–395.

Parker, S. K. (2000). From passive to proactive motivation: The importance of flexible role orientations and role breadth self-efficacy. *Applied Psychology, 49*(3), 447–469.

Part-Time Is No Crime: So Why the Penalty? Interim Report of the EOC's Investigation into Flexible and Part-Time Working, and Questions for Consultation. (2005). Manchester: Equal Opportunities Commission.

Part-Time Work in Europe. (2005). Dublin: European Foundation for the Improvement of Living and Working Conditions.

Partnership Working and Involving Employees. (2005). London: Department of Trade and Industry.

Paul, A. K., & Anantharaman, R. N. (2002). Business strategy, HRM practices and organizational performance: A study of the Indian software industry. *Journal of Transnational Management Development, 7*(3), 27–51.

Paul, A. K., & Anantharaman, R. N. (2004). Influence of HRM practices on organizational commitment: A study among software professionals in India. *Human Resource Development Quarterly, 15*(1), 77–88.

Paul, R. J., Niehoff, B. P., & Turnley, W. H. (2000). Empowerment, expectations, and the psychological contract—managing the dilemmas and gaining the advantages. *Journal of Socio-Economics, 29*(5), 471–485.

Pauly, M. V., Nicholson, S., Xu, J., Polsky, D., Danzon, P. M., Murray, J. F., *et al.* (2002). A general model of the impact of absenteeism on employers and employees. *Health Economics, 11*(3), 221–231.

Pendleton, A., Wilson, N., & Wright, M. (1998). The perception and effects of share ownership: Empirical evidence from employee buy-outs. *British Journal of Industrial Relations, 36*(1), 99–123.

Performance Evaluations. (2005). London: Business Link.

Peters, T., & Steinauer, J. (1997). Setting goals for employees. *Incentive, 171*(5), 61–63.

Pettijohn, C. E., Pettijohn, L. S., & d'Amico, M. (2001). Characteristics of performance appraisals and their impact on sales force satisfaction. *Human Resource Development Quarterly, 12*(2), 127–146.

Physical Activity and Health: A Report of the Surgeon General. (1996). Atlanta: U.S. Department of Health and Human Services, National Center for Chronic Disease Prevention and Health Promotion.

Pillai, R., Scandura, T. A., & Williams, E. A. (1999). Leadership and organizational justice: Similarities and differences across cultures. *Journal of International Business Studies, 30*(4), 763–779.

Poelmans, S. A. Y., Chinchilla, N., & Cardona, P. (2003). The adoption of family-friendly HRM policies: Competing for scarce resources in the labour market. *International Journal of Manpower, 24*(2), 128–147.

Pollitt, D. E. (2000). Making education and training work: Case studies of good practice. *Education + Training, 42*(7), 397–426.

Pollock, T. (1998). A personal file of stimulating ideas, little-known facts and daily problem solvers. *Supervision, 58,* 24–27.

Porter, A. L., & Bostrom, A. (1996). Less labor, longer lives: Time to share. *Technology Analysis & Strategic Management, 8*(3), 315–329.

Potter, E. E. (2003). Telecommuting: The future of work, corporate culture, and American society. *Journal of Labor Research, 24*(1), 73–84.

Pousette, A., & Hanse, J. J. (2002). Job characteristics as predictors of ill-health and sickness absenteeism in different occupational types – a multigroup structural equation modelling approach. *Work & Stress, 16*(3), 229–250.

Poutsma, E., Hendrickx, J., & Huijgen, F. (2003). Employee participation in Europe: In search of the participative workplace. *Economic and Industrial Democracy, 24*(1), 45–76.

Preston, A., & Burgess, J. (2003). Women's work in Australia: Trends, issues and prospects. *Australian Journal of Labour Economics, 6*(4), 497–518.

Preuss, G. A. (2003). High perfromance work systems and organziational outcomes: The mediating role of infromation quality. *Industrial & Labor Relations Review, 56*(4), 590–605.

Price, J. L. (2001). Reflections on the determinants of voluntary turnover. *International Journal of Manpower, 22*(7–8), 600–624.

Probst, T. M. (2002). Layoffs and tradeoffs: Production, quality, and safety demands under the threat of job loss. *Journal of Occupational Health Psychology, 7*(3), 211–220.

Pugh, W. N., Oswald, S. L., & Jahera, J. S., Jr (2000). The effect of ESOP adoptions on corporate performance: Are there really performance changes? *Managerial and Decision Economics, 21*(5), 167–180.

Purcell, P. J. (2000). Older workers: Employment and retirement trends. *Monthly Labor Review, 123*(10), 19–30.

Rahe, R. H., Taylor, C. B., Tolles, R. L., Newhall, L. M., Veach, T. L., & Bryson, S. (2002). A novel stress and coping workplace programme reduces illness and healthcare utilization. *Psychosomatic Medicine, 64*(2), 278–286.

Raines, J. P., & Leathers, C. G. (2001). Telecommuting: The new wave of workplace technology will create a flood of change in social institutions. *Journal of Economic Issues, 35*(2), 307–313.

Reed, P. S., & Clark, S. M. (2004). *Win-Win Workplace Practices: Improved Organizational Results and Improved Quality of Life.* Washington DC: U.S. Department of Labor – Women's Division.

Reio, T. G. J., & Wiswell, A. (2000). Field investigation of the relationship among adult curiosity, workplace learning, and job performance. *Human Resource Development Quarterly, 11*(1), 5–30.

Rhoades, L., Eisenberger, R., & Armeli, S. (2001). Affective commitment to the organization: The contribution of perceived organizational support. *Journal of Applied Psychology, 86*(5), 825–836.

Richard, O. C., & Johnson, N. B. (2001). Strategic human resource management effectiveness and firm performance. *The International Journal of Human Resource Management, 12*(2), 299–310.

Richbell, S. (2001). Trends and emerging values in human resource management. *International Journal of Manpower, 22*(3), 261–268.

Richer, S. F., Blanchard, C., & Vallerand, R. J. (2002). A motivational model of work turnover. *Journal of Applied Social Psychology, 32*(10), 2089–2113.

Richman-Hirsch, W. L. (2001). Posttraining interventions to enhance transfer: The moderating effects of work environments. *Human Resource Development Quarterly, 12*(2), 105–120.

Rickard, S. (1999). Future employment and ageism in Britain. *Foresight, 1*(5), 427–440.

Riedel, J. E., Lynch, W., Baase, C., Hymel, P., & Peterson, K. W. (2001). The effect of disease prevention and health promotion on workplace productivity: A literature review. *American Journal of Health Promotion, 15*(3), 167–191.

Roberts, G. E. (2002). Employee performance appraisal system participation: A technique that works. *Public Personnel Management, 31*(3), 333–342.

Roehling, P. V., Roehling, M. V., & Moen, P. (2001). The relationship between work-life policies and practices and employee loyalty: A life course perspective. *Journal of Family and Economic Issues, 22*(2), 141–170.

Rogier, S. A., & Padget, M. Y. (2004). The impact of utilizing a flexible work schedule on the perceived career advancement potential of women. *Human Resource Development Quarterly, 15*(1), 89–106.

Ronen, S. (2001). Self-actualization versus collectualization Implications for motivation theories. In M. Erez & U. Kleinbeck (Eds), *Work motivation in the context of a globalizing economy* (pp. 341–368).

Roth, G. L. (2000). Constructing conversations: Lessons for learning from experience. *Organization Development Journal, 18*(4), 69–78.

Rowden, R. W. (2002). The relationship between workplace learning and job satisfaction in U.S. small to midsize businesses. *Human Resource Development Quarterly, 13*(4), 407–425.

Rowe, M. M. (2000). Skills training in the long-term management of stress and occupational burnout. *Current Psychology: Developmental, Learning, Personality, Social, 19*(3), 215–228.

Rubery, J., & Grimshaw, D. (2001). ICTs and employment: The problem of job quality. *International Labour Review, 140*(2), 165–192.

Sagie, A., Birati, A., & Tziner, A. (2002). Assessing the costs of behavioral and psychological withdrawal: A new model and an empirical illustration. *Applied Psychology, 51*(1), 67–89.

Said, A. A., HassabElnaby, H. R., & Wier, B. (2003). An empirical investigation of the performance consequences of nonfinancial measures. *Journal of Management Accounting Research, 15*, 193–223.

Sakellariou, C. (2004). Gender-earnings differentials using quantile regressions. *Journal of Labor Research, 25*(3), 458–484.

Sandberg, K. D. (2001). The case for slack: Building "Incubation Time" into your week. *Harvard Management Update, 6*, 6–8.

Sandburg, K. W., & Vinberg, S. (2000). Information technology and learning strategies in small enterprises. *Behaviour & Information Technology, 19*(3), 221–227.

Schmidt-Wilk, J. (2000). Consciousness-based management development: Case studies of international top management teams. *Journal of Transnational Management Development, 5*(3), 61–85.

Schmidt, D. E., & Duenas, G. (2002). Incentives to encourage worker-friendly organizations. *Public Personnel Management, 31*(3), 293–308.

Schroeder, D. H., & Costa, P. T. (1984). Influence of life event stress on physical illness: Substantive effects or methodological flaws? *Journal of Personality and Social Psychology, 46*(4), 853–863.

Schwartz, T. (2000). The greatest sources of satisfaction in the workplace are internal and emotional. *Fast Company, 40*, 398–402.

Schweitzer, C. (1998). Creating an inspiring workplace. *Association Management, 50*, 33–37.

Segal, J.-P., Sobczak, A., & Triomphe, C.-E. (2003). *Corporate Social Responsibility and Working Conditions.* Dublin: European Foundation for the Improvement of Living and Working Conditions.

Shatte, A. J., Reivich, K., & Seligman, M. E. P. (2000). Promoting human strengths and corporate competencies: A cognitive training model. *Psychologist Manager Journal, 4*(2), 183–196.

Singh, J. (2000). Performance productivity and quality of frontline employees in service organizations. *Journal of Marketing, 64*(2), 15–34.

Smith, A., Ockowski, E., Noble, C., & Macklin, R. (2003). New management practices and enterprise training in Australia. *International Journal of Manpower, 24*(1), 31–47.

Smith, P. A. C. (1999). The learning organization ten years on: A case study. *Learning Organization, 6*(5), 217–223.

Sosik, J. J., Potosky, D., & Jung, D. I. (2002). Adaptive self-regulation: Meeting others' expectations of leadership and performance. *Journal of Social Psychology, 142*(2), 211–232.

Sousa-Poza, A., & Sousa-Poza, A. A. (2000). Well-being at work: A cross-national analysis of the levels and determinants of job satisfaction. *Journal of Socio-Economics, 29*(6), 517–538.

Spector, P. E. (2002). Employee control and occupational stress. *Current Directions in Psychological Science, 11*(4), 133–136.

Spiezia, V. (2002). The greying population: A wasted human capital or just a social liability? *International Labour Review, 141*(1/2), 71–113.

Squires, J. (2002). Values and the social responsibility of global business. *Journal of Transnational Management Development, 7*(4), 27–43.

Stein, F. (2001). Occupational stress, relaxation therapies, exercise and biofeedback. *Work, 17*(3), 235–246.

Steiner, C. J. (2001). How important is professionalism to corporate communication? *Corporate Communications, 6*(3), 150–156.

Stevens, J., Brown, J., & Lee, C. (2004). *The Second Work-Life Balance Study: Results from the Employees' Survey*. London: Department of Trade and Industry.

Storey, J., Quintas, P., Taylor, P., & Fowle, W. (2002). Flexible employment contracts and their implications for product and process innovation. *The International Journal of Human Resource Management, 13*(1), 1–18.

Sue, D. W., Parmam, T. A., & Santiago, G. B. (1998). The changing face of work in the United States: Implications for individual, institutional, and societal survival. *Cultural Diversity and Mental Health, 4*(3), 153–164.

Sull, D. N. (1999). Why good companies go bad. *Harvard Business Review, July/August,* 1–9.

Sverke, M., & Hellgren, J. (2002). The nature of job insecurity: Understanding employment uncertainty on the brink of a new millennium. *Applied Psychology, 51*(1), 23–42.

Swan, J., & Cooper, C. L. (2005). *Time, Health and the Family: What Working Families Want*: Working Families.

Swap, W., Leonard, D., Shields, M., & Abrams, L. (2001). Using mentoring and storytelling to transfer knowledge in the workplace. *Journal of Management Information Systems, 18*(1), 95–115.

Szulanski, G., & Amin, K. (2001). Learning to make strategy: Balancing discipline and imagination. *Long Range Planning, 34*(5), 537–556.

Tan, J. A., Hall, R. J., & Boyce, C. (2003). The role of employee reactions in predicting training effectiveness. *Human Resource Development Quarterly, 14*(4), 397–411.

Tansky, J. W., & Cohen, D. J. (2001). The relationship between organizational support, employee development, and organizational commitment: An empirical study. *Human Resource Development Quarterly, 12*(3), 285–300.

Taris, T. W., Peeters, M. C. W., Le Blanc, P. M., Schreurs, P. J. G., & Schaufeli, W. B. (2001). From inequity to burnout: The role of job stress. *Journal of Occupational Health Psychology, 6*(4), 303–323.

Temporary Agency Work in the European Union. (2003). Dublin: European Foundation for the Improvement of Living and Working Conditions.

Thompson, M. (2002). High performance work organisations in UK aerospace. *Templeton Executive Briefing.*

Thoms, P., Dose, J. J., & Scott, K. S. (2002). Relationships between accountability, job satisfaction, and trust. *Human Resource Development Quarterly, 13*(3), 307–323.

Tolstoy, L. (1877). *Anna Karenina* (R. Pevear & L. Volokhonsky, Trans.). London: Penguin Books Ltd.

Tomer, J. F. (2001). Understanding high performance work systems: The joint contribution of economics and human resource management. *Journal of Socio-Economics, 30*(1), 63–73.

Tracey, J. B., Hinkin, T. R., Tannenbaum, S., & Mathieu, J. E. (2001). The influence of individual characteristics and the work environment on varying levels of training outcomes. *Human Resource Development Quarterly, 12*(1), 5–23.

Tranfield, D., Parry, I., Wilson, S., Smith, S., & Foster, M. (1999). Teamworking: Redesigning the organization for manufacturing improvements. *Technology Analysis and Strategic Management, 11*(2), 143–158.

Triantafillou, P. (2003). Psychological technologies at work: A history of employee development in Denmark. *Economic and Industrial Democracy, 24*(3), 411–436.

Tuffrey, M. (2003). *Good Companies, Better Employees: How Community Involvement and Good Corporate Citizenship Can Enhance Employee Morale, Motivation, Commitment and Performance.* London: The Corporate Citizenship Company.

Tziner, A. (2002). *Human Resource Management and Organization Behavior: Selected Perspectives.* Burlington: Ashcroft Publishing Company.

van den Broek, D., Callaghan, G., & Thompson, P. (2004). Teams without teamwork? Explaining the call centre paradox. *Economic and Industrial Democracy, 25*(2), 197–219.

Van der Sluis, L. E. C., & Poell, R. F. (2003). The impact on career development of learning opportunities and learning behavior at work. *Human Resource Development Quarterly, 14*(2), 159–179.

Van Eerde, W. (2000). Procrastination: Self-regulation in initiating aversive goals. *Applied Psychology, 49*(3), 372–389.

van Knippenberg, D. (2000). Work motivation and performance: A social identity perspective. *Applied Psychology, 49*(3), 357–371.

van Leeuwen, M. J., & van Praag, B. M. S. (2002). The costs and benefits of lifelong learning: The case of the Netherlands. *Human Resource Development Quarterly, 13*(2), 151–168.

Varey, R. J., & White, J. (2000). The corporate communication system of managing. *Corporate Communications, 5*(1), 5–11.

Voros, S. (2000). 3D management. *Management Review, 89,* 44–48.

Waclawski, J. (2002). Large-scale organizational change and performance: An empirical examination. *Human Resource Development Quarterly, 13*(3), 289–305.

Wagar, T. H. (1998). Exploring the Consequences of Workforce Reduction. *Revue Canadienne des Sciences de l'Administration/Canadian Journal of Administrative Sciences, 15*(4), 300–309.

Walumbwa, F. O., Orwa, B., Wang, P., & Lawler, J. J. (2005). Transformational leadership, organizational commitment, and job satisfaction: A comparative study of Kenyan and U.S. financial firms. *Human Resource Development Quarterly, 16*(2), 235–256.

Wang, G. G., Dou, Z., & Li, N. (2002). A systems approach to measuring return on investment for HRD interventions. *Human Resource Development Quarterly, 13*(2), 203–224.

Wax, A. L. (2004). Family-friendly workplace reform: Prospects for change. *Annals of the American Academy of Political and Social Science, 596*(0), 36–61.

Wayne, S. J., Shore, L. M., Bommer, W. H., & Tetrick, L. E. (2002). The role of fair treatment and rewards in perceptions of organizational support and leader-member exchange. *Journal of Applied Psychology, 87*(3), 590–598.

Webster, E. (2001). The rise of intangible capital and labour market segmentation. *Australian Bulletin of Labour, 27*(4), 258–271.

Wendel, S. (1999). Live long, work healthy. *Employee Benefit News, 13,* 31–36.

Wenger, E. (1996). How to optimize organizational learning. *Healthcare Forum Journal, 9,* 22–23.

West, M., & Patterson, M. (1998). Profitable personnel. *People Management, 4,* 28–32.

Westbrook, T. S., & Veale, J. R. (2001). Work-related learning as a core value: An Iowa perspective. *Human Resource Development Quarterly, 12*(3), 301–318.

Westman, M., & Etzion, D. (2001). The impact of vacation and job stress on burnout and absenteeism. *Psychology & Health, 16*(5), 595–606.

White, M., Hill, S., McGovern, P., Mills, C., & Smeaton, D. (2003). 'High-performance' management practices, working hours and work-life balance. *British Journal of Industrial Relations, 41*(2), 175–195.

Whittington, J. L. (2001). Corporate executives as beleaguered rulers: The leader's motive matters. *Problems and Perspectives in Management,* (3), 163–169.

Wiethoff, C. (2004). Motivation to learn and diversity training: Application of the theory of planned behavior. *Human Resource Development Quarterly, 15*(3), 263–278.

Williams, S. W. (2001). The effectiveness of subject matter experts as technical trainers. *Human Resource Development Quarterly, 12*(1), 91–97.

Windsor, D. (2001). The future of corporate social responsibility. *The International Journal of Organizational Analysis, 9*(3), 225–256.

Woodland, S., Simmonds, N., Thornby, M., Fitzgerald, R., & McGee, A. (2003). *The Second Work-Life Balance Study: Results from the Employer Survey.* London: Department of Trade and Industry.

Work-Life Balance and Flexible Working: The Business Case. (2004). London: Department of Trade and Industry.

Work-Related Stress. (2004). Sudbury, Suffolk: Health and Safety Executive.

Work-Related Stress. (2005). Dublin: European Foundation for the Improvement of Living and Working Conditions.

Workman, M. (2003). Results from organizational development interventions in a technology call center. *Human Resource Development Quarterly, 14*(2), 215–230.

Wright, P. C., & Geroy, G. D. (2001). Changing the mindset: The training myth and the need for world-class performance. *The International Journal of Human Resource Management, 12*(4), 586–600.

Yamnill, S., & McLean, G. N. (2001). Theories supporting transfer of training. *Human Resource Development Quarterly, 12*(2), 195–208.

Yang, B., Watkins, K. E., & Marsick, V. J. (2004). The construct of the learning organization: Dimensions, measurement, and validation. *Human Resource Development Quarterly, 15*(1), 31–55.

Yates, C., Lewchuk, W., & Stewart, P. (2001). Empowerment as a trojan horse: New systems of work organization in the North American automobile industry. *Economic and Industrial Democracy, 22*(4), 517–541.

Zivnuska, S., Kiewitz, C., Hochwarter, W. A., Perrewe, P. L., & Zellars, K. L. (2002). What is too much or too little? The curvilinear effects of job tension on turnover intent, value attainment and job satisfaction. *Journal of Applied Social Psychology, 32*(7), 1344–1360.

Zwick, T. (2004). Employee participation and productivity. *Labour Economics, 11* (6), 715–740.

Index